Making International Institutions Work

International institutions are essential for tackling many of the most urgent challenges facing the world, from pandemics to humanitarian crises, yet we know little about when they succeed, when they fail, and why. This book proposes a new theory of institutional performance and tests it using a diverse array of sources, including the most comprehensive dataset on the topic. Challenging popular characterizations of international institutions as "runaway bureaucracies," Ranjit Lall argues that the most serious threat to performance comes from the pursuit of narrow political interests by states – paradoxically, the same actors who create and give purpose to institutions. The discreet operational processes through which international bureaucrats cultivate and sustain autonomy vis-à-vis governments, he contends, are critical to making institutions "work." The findings enhance our understanding of international cooperation, public goods, and organizational behavior while offering practical lessons to policymakers, NGOs, businesses, and citizens interested in improving institutional effectiveness.

RANJIT LALL is an Associate Professor of International Political Economy and a Fellow of St. John's College, University of Oxford. His research has received the American Political Science Association's Merze Tate Award and the Center for Effective Global Action's Leamer-Rosenthal Prize for Open Social Sciences. He previously worked as an economist at the Bank of England and an editorial writer at the *Financial Times*.

Making International Institutions Work

The Politics of Performance

Ranjit Lall

University of Oxford

CAMBRIDGE
UNIVERSITY PRESS

Shaftesbury Road, Cambridge CB2 8EA, United Kingdom

One Liberty Plaza, 20th Floor, New York, NY 10006, USA

477 Williamstown Road, Port Melbourne, VIC 3207, Australia

314–321, 3rd Floor, Plot 3, Splendor Forum, Jasola District Centre,
New Delhi – 110025, India

103 Penang Road, #05–06/07, Visioncrest Commercial, Singapore 238467

Cambridge University Press is part of Cambridge University Press &
Assessment, a department of the University of Cambridge.

We share the University's mission to contribute to society through the pursuit of
education, learning and research at the highest international levels of excellence.

www.cambridge.org
Information on this title: www.cambridge.org/9781009216289

DOI: 10.1017/9781009216265

First published 2023

A catalogue record for this publication is available from the British Library.

Library of Congress Cataloging-in-Publication Data
Names: Lall, Ranjit, author.
Title: Making international institutions work : the politics of performance / Ranjit Lall.
Description: Cambridge ; New York : Cambridge University Press, 2023. |
Includes bibliographical references and index.
Identifiers: LCCN 2022048456 (print) | LCCN 2022048457 (ebook) |
ISBN 9781009216289 (hardback) | ISBN 9781009216241 (paperback) | ISBN
9781009216265 (epub)
Subjects: LCSH: International agencies–Evaluation. | Organizational
behavior. | International organization.
Classification: LCC JZ4839 .L35 2023 (print) | LCC JZ4839 (ebook) |
DDC 658.1/8–dc23/eng/20221230
LC record available at https://lccn.loc.gov/2022048456
LC ebook record available at https://lccn.loc.gov/2022048457

ISBN 978-1-009-21628-9 Hardback

In memory of Sanjaya Lall

Contents

Figures

Tables

Acknowledgments

I first became interested in the performance of international institutions during lengthy elementary school vacations in Geneva. My father, an economist who frequently worked with United Nations (UN) development agencies based in the city, would return home at the end of each day with casual but penetrating assessments of his collaborators. Some of these institutions, his comments suggested, were making impressive progress in alleviating poverty, raising living standards, and promoting industrialization in the developing world; others were falling hopelessly short, squandering resources, authority, and credibility as they failed to make any tangible difference on the ground. Over the years, I became increasingly interested in whether my father's anecdotal appraisals of the UN were accurate – and, if so, what explained their strikingly varied nature. Why, I wondered, might some international institutions perform better than others?

It was not until my doctoral studies at Harvard University that I began to explore this question seriously. I was fortunate to be guided by a wise, generous, and dedicated group of advisers. Jeffry Frieden urged me to ask "big" questions and offered incisive analytical comments at every step of the journey. Beth Simmons showed me unexpected connections between different schools of thought and levels of analysis, and taught me how to marry theory with systematic empirical evidence. Walter Mattli has been an inspirational mentor, teacher, and friend since my undergraduate days, shaping my approach to this and other research in myriad ways. Gary King, a de facto member of my dissertation committee, ignited my interest in quantitative research methods and imparted pieces of astute scholarly and professional advice throughout graduate school.

At various stages of the research process, I have benefited from conversations with and feedback from many other scholars, including Kenneth Abbott, James Alt, Ben Ansell, Anthony Atkinson, Tim Büthe, Allison Carnegie, Austin Carson, Bejamin Cohen, Christina Davis, Daniela Donno, Andrew Eggers, Luca Enriques, Adam Glynn, Julia

Gray, Alexandru Grigorescu, Peter Hall, Dan Honig, John Ikenberry, Torben Iversen, Melissa Lee, Helen Milner, Soledad Artiz Prillaman, Robert Putnam, Sebastian Rosato, Peter Rosendorff, David Rueda, Jacob Shapiro, Alistair Smith, Jack Snyder, Anton Strezhnev, Jonas Tallberg, Yeling Tan, Dustin Tingley, Oliver Westerwinter, and George Yin. I am particularly grateful to Robert Keohane for his enthusiastic encouragement of the project at an early, uncertain stage of graduate school. In addition, I have received valuable suggestions from audiences at Columbia University, Harvard University, the London School of Economics, Notre Dame University, Princeton University, the University of California – Santa Barbara, the University of Oxford (Nuffield College and the Department of Law), Yale University, and annual meetings of the American Political Science Association and the International Studies Association.

I wrote most of this book as a faculty member at the London School of Economics. I am obliged to the Department of International Relations, chaired by Peter Trubowitz and Karen Smith during my time there, for providing me with research support, leave time, and an intellectually stimulating environment, and to Daniel Berliner, Jeffrey Chwieroth, Ben Cormier, Florence Dafe, Robert Falkner, Anna Getmansky, Milli Lake, James Morrison, Natalya Naqvi, Theresa Squatrito, and Zoe Williams for their intellectual insights and collegiality. Before coming to London, I received generous financial and institutional assistance from the Global Economic Governance Programme at the University of Oxford, the Institute for Quantitative Social Science and the Weatherhead Center for International Affairs at Harvard University, and the Niehaus Center for Globalization and Governance at Princeton University.

I completed the book on sabbatical at the University of California – San Diego. I would like to thank the Department of Political Science, in particular Thad Kousser, for arranging my visit and kindly hosting me. I am especially indebted to Lawrence Broz, Peter Gourevitch, David Lake, and Christina Schneider for participating in a stimulating manuscript workshop in November 2021, which strengthened and refined my ideas considerably. They were joined from the Midwest by Tana Johnson, Duncan Snidal, and Alexander Thompson, who have followed and graciously cheered on this research over the years. Stephan Haggard and Jason Sanwalka Davis also offered thoughtful and perceptive comments on the manuscript during my time in San Diego.

Several talented students at the London School of Economics and elsewhere have assisted this research. Jaewoo Shin, Saloni Srivastava, Celine Tseng, and David Vilalta carefully collected, verified, and cleaned data. William O'Connell perused the entire manuscript, made excellent recommendations for improving the text, and provided helpful assistance constructing the index.

At Cambridge University Press, I would like to express my gratitude to John Haslam for seeing promise in the project and for expertly guiding the manuscript through the various stages of production, to Toby Ginsberg, David Mainwaring, Chloe Quinn, and Shaheer Husanne (Straive) for their assistance in the publication process, and to two anonymous reviewers for insightful, constructive, and detailed feedback.

Finally, on a more personal note, my sincere thanks to Chris, Colin, and the rest of the McArdle family for their kindness and hospitality during my time in graduate school, and to Rita Khanna and Amar Bhattacharya for warmly accommodating me during spells of fieldwork in Washington, DC. Zeynep Pamuk has provided companionship, moral support, and affection since the first year of graduate school, and has molded and given me confidence in many of the book's core ideas. My mother, Rani Lall, and my sisters, Maya Lall and Priya Lall, have always been my greatest source of strength, support, and inspiration. I dedicate this book to the memory of my father, Sanjaya Lall. Although published long after his passing, it is inspired by his lifelong commitment to addressing important real-world problems, challenging conventional wisdoms, and following the evidence wherever it leads.

1 International Institutions and the Performance Puzzle

> Evidence from the earliest known reflections on politics in Greece down to the last few decades show that practically every serious student of politics who attempted conscientiously to understand and to describe the operation of different political regimes, orders, constitutions, or systems also accepted the obligation, not to say the opportunity, to assess the relative merits of these different systems ... [A] serious examination of politics has generally involved appraising as well as describing the performance of political systems.
>
> – Robert A. Dahl, 1967[1]

Today's international institutions seem to present a paradox. We live in an era of growing skepticism – even outright cynicism – about the benefits of rules-based cooperation between states. The stubborn persistence of old transnational problems, compounded by an apparently never-ending stream of new ones, has led many observers to conclude that the contemporary system of global governance is not fit for purpose. Meanwhile, a rising tide of populism and nationalism around the world has swept in a generation of political leaders with defiantly domestic priorities, who are less hesitant than their predecessors to call out international institutions they see as inimical to national interests.[2]

There is no dearth of institutions that have fallen short of expectations. The Food and Agriculture Organization (FAO) has struggled to fulfil its mandate of ending hunger and ensuring food security for all, making little dent in global undernourishment over the past half-century even as broader development outcomes have markedly improved. The weak leadership shown by the United Nations Environment Programme (UNEP) in the fight against climate change has been ruthlessly exposed by the international community's "utterly inadequate" efforts to curb greenhouse gas emissions, to quote United Nations (UN) Secretary-General António Guterres.[3] The World Health Organization (WHO) has failed to develop and implement the public health programs, monitoring systems, and structural reforms necessary to tackle the most

---

[1] Dahl (1967, 167).   [2] Copelovitch and Pevehouse (2019).   [3] Ahuja (2019).

deadly infectious diseases – shortcomings brought into stark relief by the coronavirus (COVID-19) pandemic. The United Nations Educational, Scientific and Cultural Organization (UNESCO) has long been a byword for dysfunction and inefficiency, blighted by near-continuous scandals and crises, the withdrawal of major member states, and the loss of core functions to rival institutions.

At the same time, international institutions are widely recognized as supplying critical public goods that improve the lives of millions of people across the globe. Even the staunchest critics of global governance readily acknowledge its instrumental role in advancing core objectives and priorities of the international community in recent decades.[4]

Examples of welfare-enhancing accomplishments by international institutions are, again, not hard to come by. The World Food Programme (WFP) has delivered life-saving food assistance to more than 70 million people each year since 1998, a feat for which it was awarded the 2020 Nobel Peace Prize.[5] Between 2011 and 2019, the World Bank financed and helped to enact vital health interventions for 769 million people; improvements in water services for 96.5 million people; the recruitment of 14 million new teachers; and the construction or rehabilitation of almost 150,000 kilometers of roads.[6] Since its establishment in 2000, Gavi, the Vaccine Alliance, has enabled more than 820 million children in 77 countries to be immunized against vaccine-preventable diseases, averting an estimated 14 million deaths.[7] There is good evidence that the UN, for all its imperfections, has reduced the incidence of armed conflict both within and between states through diplomatic and peacekeeping activities.[8]

These contrasting examples reflect more than mere anecdote or difference in interpretation. Over the past 15 years, major donor governments have begun conducting systematic comparative evaluations of international institutions, which have come to be seen as the "gold standard" of performance measurement in global governance.[9] Informed by diverse perspectives and data sources, these assessments point to a reality more nuanced than suggested by caricatures of such institutions as cumbersome bureaucracies or efficient problem-solvers: There is sub-

---

[4] Goldin (2013); Hale, Held, and Young (2013); Hale and Held (2017).
[5] WFP annual performance reports 1998–2018, available at www.wfp.org/publications [Last accessed March 4, 2020].
[6] http://ida.worldbank.org/results [Last accessed March 4, 2020].
[7] www.Gavi.org/programmes-impact/our-impact/facts-and-figures [Last accessed November 4, 2021].
[8] Fortna (2008); Goldstein (2012); Hultman, Kathman, and Shannon (2013); Pauls and Cranmer (2017).
[9] Lall (2017, 246).

stantial *variation* in performance. That is, a multiplicity of performance outcomes exists; some institutions succeed, others fail, and most lie somewhere in between. The coexistence of harsh criticism and glowing praise of global governance – of dire failures and inspiring achievements – is, the best evidence suggests, no paradox at all.

This book seeks to explain differences in the performance of international institutions. It is motivated by a conviction that there is a common logic to effectiveness and ineffectiveness. To paraphrase Milton Friedman, there is a way of analyzing performance that reveals ostensibly unconnected and disparate outcomes to be manifestations of a common causal structure or process.[10] To make this claim is not to deny the complexity or contingency of the phenomenon under study; how institutions perform is undoubtedly shaped by an array of forces acting alone and in concert, many of which are not captured by my theoretical approach. The book's goal is simply to bring a measure of analytical order to the study of institutional performance by drawing attention to a set of variables, relationships, and causal mechanisms that, holding all else constant, account for some of its striking variation across institutions and over time.

Challenging popular characterizations of international institutions as "runaway bureaucracies," this book argues that the primary obstacle to effective performance is not rogue behavior by bureaucrats but opportunistic interference by states seeking to advance particularistic interests. Counterintuitively, *the same actors who create and give purpose to institutions are often responsible for failures to realize this ambition.* The upshot is that a high degree of policy autonomy vis-à-vis states is essential for averting the most dangerous threats to performance. In contrast to another common view, I warn that such independence cannot be guaranteed by institutional design: Formal rules offer limited protection against particularistic interventions in the policy process, particularly by powerful states. Rather, discretion emerges through two bureaucracy-driven processes rooted in institutions' operational activities. First, institutions forge deep and extensive networks of operational collaboration with actors above and below the state, which give rise to broad-based, enduring coalitions for autonomy. Second, institutions exercise governance tasks that are costly to monitor, generating information asymmetries that curtail state control at key junctures of the policy process. Not unlike a resourceful military strategist confronting a more powerful foe, institutions can leverage a combination of *alliances* and *stealth* to escape subjugation.

---

[10] Friedman (1953, 33).

In addition to developing a general framework for understanding institutional performance that can be applied to diverse issue areas and time periods, this book presents rich, multimethod evidence for its conjectures from a broad canvas of global governance. My empirical investigation draws on the Performance of International Institutions Project (PIIP), a new dataset encompassing 54 institutions included in the comparative donor assessments mentioned earlier, which I compiled over the past decade.[11] Statistical tests are complemented by in-depth case studies informed by an array of primary and secondary sources, including archival materials and key informant interviews.

By shining a light on when and why international institutions succeed in meeting the challenges that motivate their creation, the book reveals a common thread running through heterogeneous performance outcomes, institutional characteristics, and patterns of bureaucratic and governmental behavior. In doing so, it enhances our theoretical grasp of issues such as interstate cooperation, global public goods, and organizational behavior – topics of wide interest to social scientists – while challenging conventional wisdoms about the creation, design, and operation of international institutions. From a more practical perspective, the findings suggest actionable lessons for policymakers and nongovernmental stakeholders seeking to improve the effectiveness – and thus viability – of global governance. *Making International Institutions Work* lays the foundation not only for a deeper and more nuanced understanding of what makes international institutions "work" but also for viable real-world measures to achieve this outcome.

Why Institutional Performance Matters

From a theoretical as well as a practical perspective, institutional performance has long been considered one of the most salient topics in the social sciences. When functioning properly, institutions reduce transaction costs and information asymmetries between parties to an exchange relationship, facilitating forms of mutually beneficial cooperation that are critical to efficient economic, political, and social outcomes. As Douglass North puts it, "Effective institutions raise the benefits of cooperative solutions or the costs of defection."[12] A considerable body of social science scholarship has analyzed the performance of domestic public institutions, such as governments, parliaments, and regulatory agencies.[13] A recent review of the public administration literature

[11] The dataset can be accessed on the author's website: https://ranjitlall.github.io/data.
[12] North (1991, 98).
[13] Public administration scholars have studied all of these institutions – though local governments have been of particular interest – attributing variation in performance to

identifies institutional performance as "possibly the most important concept" in the discipline.[14] According to a popular textbook, "virtually all of management and organization theory concerns performance and effectiveness, at least implicitly."[15] Robert Putnam, the noted political scientist, and colleagues have described institutional performance as "arguably the central dependent variable of political science."[16] In the epigraph to this chapter, Robert Dahl, the equally distinguished political theorist, highlights the long-standing centrality of performance appraisal to the study of politics. Later in the quoted piece, he refers to it as "an ancient obligation of our craft."[17]

The importance of understanding how *international* institutions perform has also been recognized by scholars. Cooperation between states has been central to the modern study of international relations (IR) and international political economy (IPE), and identifying when and how it is successfully institutionalized has been singled out as a priority for these fields.[18] Much of the earliest professional IR scholarship took the form of detailed appraisals of the policies, governance arrangements, and impact of postwar institutions such as the UN,[19] the General Agreement on Tariffs and Trade (GATT),[20] and the International Monetary Fund (IMF).[21] The principal outlet for the publication of such research was *International Organization*, a leading IR journal to this day, which was founded in 1946 with the explicit aim of promoting "a comparative study of international organizations and why they have or have not worked in

factors ranging from regulation, market structure, and management strategy to institutional resources, size, and competition. For representative collections of scholarship, see Ashworth, Boyne, and Entwistle (2010); Boyne et al. (2006); Walker, Boyne, and Brewer (2010). Sociologists have considered a similarly broad range of institutions and explanatory factors, formulating many of the concepts and hypotheses that have informed the public administration literature. For overviews, see Cameron (1986); Cameron and Whetten (1996). Political scientists have primarily focused on the impact of social capital on local and regional government performance (Cusack 1999; Knack 2002; Putnam et al. 1983; Putnam 1993) and of electoral and decision-making rules on national government effectiveness (Arter 2006; Lijphart 1999; Roller 2005; Schmidt 2002). Economists have mainly been interested in the effects of ethnic heterogeneity on local and national governance outcomes. See Alesina, Baqir, and Easterly (1999); La Porta et al. (1999); Miguel and Gugerty (2005).

[14] Andersen, Boesen, and Pedersen (2016, 852). Public administration has by far the largest literature on domestic institutional performance. Indeed, the review identifies almost 800 articles on the topic published in 10 leading disciplinary journals before April 2014.

[15] Rainey (1997, 125).

[16] Putnam et al. (1983, 58). Elsewhere, Putnam (1993, 63) calls "Who governs?" and "How well?" "the two most basic questions of political science."

[17] Dahl (1967, 167).   [18] Martin and Simmons (1998).

[19] Fox (1951); Goodrich (1947); Malin (1947).   [20] Gorter (1954).

[21] Knorr (1948).

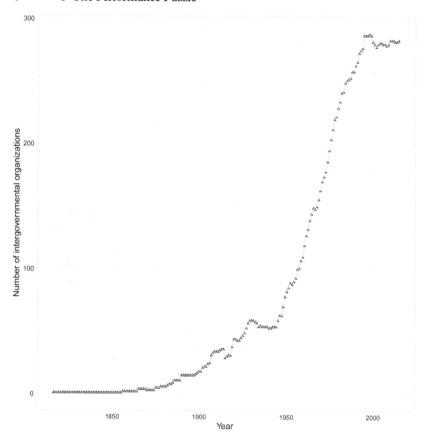

Figure 1.1 Number of intergovernmental organizations, 1816–2014

Source: Correlates of War Intergovernmental Organizations Version 3.0 datasets (Pevehouse et al. 2019).

varying circumstances."[22] For intellectual as well as practical reasons discussed subsequently, however, IR scholars have largely shied away from this undertaking in recent decades.

With the dramatic expansion in the number, resources, and scope of international institutions over the postwar era, comprehending their performance has become even more urgent. As illustrated in Figure 1.1, the number of intergovernmental organizations (IGOs) – the most studied of these institutions – rose from 59 in 1945 to 283 in 2014.[23] Other

---

[22] Katzenstein, Keohane, and Krasner (1998, 650).

[23] IGOs are usually defined as formal entities with member states and a permanent secretariat or other sign of institutionalization (Pevehouse et al. 2019, 3).

types have proliferated even faster: The population of international nongovernmental organizations (INGOs) grew from 1,993 to 8,626 over the same period,[24] while that of transnational public–private governance initiatives soared from 23 to 559.[25]

As they have multiplied, international institutions have amassed more members, resources, and staff than ever before. Figure 1.2 shows that the combined state membership of the 54 institutions in the PIIP, which are listed in Appendix B.1, has expanded more than 50-fold since 1945 (left panel). The institutions' combined annual income (middle panel) and expenditures (right panel) have approximately doubled since just the turn of the century.[26] In 2018, they collectively comprised 8,349 member states, recorded revenues of $96 billion, spent $85 billion, owned assets worth $2 trillion, and employed 140,000 staff. As the accomplishments cited earlier suggest, this geographical reach, resource base, and manpower gives them the potential to shape the fortunes of large swathes of humanity.

What is more, international institutions have branched out into issue areas far beyond those envisaged by the architects of the postwar multilateral order. Sundry problems arising from deepening interdependence between nations – "problems without passports," in former UN Secretary-General Kofi Annan's memorable expression – are now the subject of institutionalized cooperation, from climate change and financial contagion to human trafficking and disease outbreaks.[27] Remarkably, this is also true of many governance functions traditionally exercised by states and considered central to national sovereignty, such as deploying military forces, controlling migration, setting macroeconomic policy, regulating trade, and defining legal rights. The result of these developments is that it is today hard to find a policy domain in which political authority has not shifted, partially or fully, to the international level.

In his classic study *Making Democracy Work*, from which this book derives its title, Putnam sought to answer the question: "Why do some democratic governments succeed and others fail?"[28] Writing in the latter stages of the third wave of democratization, Putnam saw understanding how "strong, responsive, effective representative institutions" emerge and flourish as a vital endeavor for social scientists.[29] As the spread of democracy has stalled across much of the world and domestic governance functions continue to migrate to the regional and global levels, the time seems ripe to extend Putnam's line of inquiry to the

[24] Union of International Associations (2020).   [25] Westerwinter (2021).
[26] It is difficult to obtain reliable financial data for every institution before 2000.
[27] Annan (2002).   [28] Putnam (1993, 3).   [29] Putnam (1993, 6).

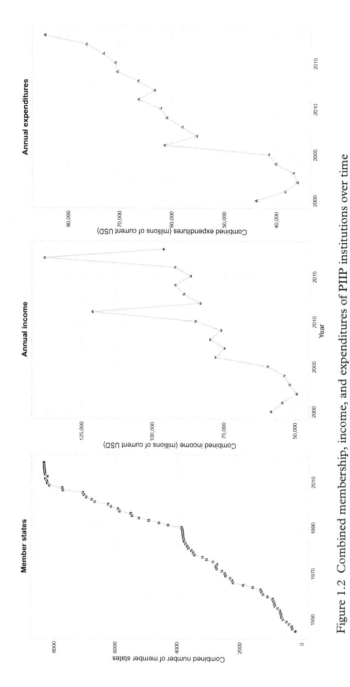

Figure 1.2 Combined membership, income, and expenditures of PIIP institutions over time

Sources: Membership data come from institutional websites and annual reports and the Correlates of War Intergovernmental Organizations Version 3.0 datasets (Pevehouse et al. 2019). For institutions that lack a formal membership structure, "partner" states are used as a substitute. Financial data are extracted from annual reports and audited accounts, acquired online and through personal communications with institutions. For financial institutions, the data reflect cash flows as well as regular operating activities.

international realm. Two decades into the twenty-first century, it seems equally – if not more – fitting to ask: Why do some *international institutions* succeed and others fail?

One Puzzle, Many Pieces

Differences in the performance of international institutions are puzzling. Consider Figure 1.3, which plots PIIP institutions' standardized average score on all indicators in the six comparative donor evaluations published by the end of 2018, which were conducted by the Australian, British, Danish, Dutch, and Swedish aid agencies and the Multilateral Organisation Performance Assessment Network (MOPAN), a group of 18 large donor nations. Scores exhibit considerable variation even among institutions with similar memberships, mandates, governance structures, and other characteristics. The FAO, the International Fund for Agricultural Development (IFAD), and the WFP are cases in point. All three institutions focus on food security issues; include almost all sovereign states as members; are governed by an executive body comprising a subset of members elected for three-year terms; are part of the UN System; and are headquartered in Rome. However, whereas IFAD and the WFP have among the highest ratings in the sample (ranking 9th and 11th out of 54, respectively), the FAO has one of the lowest (ranking 44th).

No less mystifying is the sheer diversity of both low- and high-rated institutions. The FAO, for instance, shares the bottom end of the spectrum with institutions as varied as the Commonwealth Secretariat, a 54-member diplomatic agency that seeks to strengthen ties within the Commonwealth of Nations and has no separate executive organ; and the International Labour Organization (ILO), a standard-setting body with 187 member states and a unique tripartite governance structure in which workers and employers are formally represented alongside governments. Beside IFAD and the WFP at the top end of the spectrum are institutions including the European Bank for Reconstruction and Development (EBRD), a regional development finance provider whose executive body reserves seats for major donors and makes decisions by weighted voting; and the Private Infrastructure Development Group (PIDG), an infrastructure investor with just nine member states and a governing board in which no governments are represented. What does each set of institutions have in common?

Variation in performance is also puzzling for influential theoretical perspectives on international institutions. Although not directly addressing the topic, these approaches suggest that institutions will

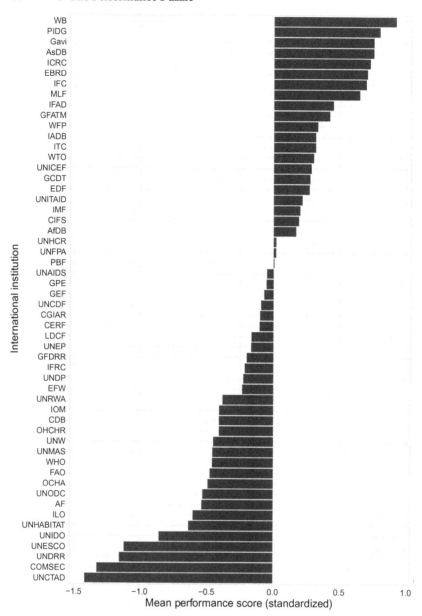

Figure 1.3 Donor ratings of institutional performance

Note: The bars show institutions' standardized mean score on all performance indicators in every wave of six comparative donor evaluations (conducted by MOPAN and the aid agencies of Australia, Denmark, the Netherlands, Sweden, and the United Kingdom).

invariably fail or succeed in meeting their designated objectives. Realism, traditionally the preeminent analytical paradigm of IR, views institutions as "epiphenomenal" to state power and interests, unable to bring about deep and lasting cooperation or to independently influence behavior.[30] In Susan Strange's wry phase, they are "a big yawn" compared with the rough and tumble of power politics.[31] John Mearsheimer, a prominent realist, elaborates: "[Institutions] reflect state calculations of self-interest based primarily on the international distribution of power. The most powerful states in the system create and shape institutions so that they can maintain their share of world power, or even increase it."[32] To the extent that institutions further the interests of powerful states, as realists confidently predict, they should always perform either effectively (if we see the promotion of such interests as their "true" goal) or ineffectively (if we take their stated objectives at face value).

Neoliberal institutionalism, which has emerged as the dominant theoretical lens for understanding the existence and role of international institutions, takes a more optimistic view of their ability to shape state behavior – yet has equally simplistic implications for their performance. Neoliberals analyze institutions as Pareto-efficient solutions to collective action problems among states stemming from uncertainty, transaction costs, legal liability, and other sources.[33] By facilitating mutually beneficial cooperation between states, neoliberal logic suggests, institutions will succeed in delivering the benefits desired by their creators; indeed, if they failed to do so, there would be little reason to establish them in the first place. It is perhaps no coincidence, then, that the growing currency of neoliberal institutionalism has been accompanied by a turn away from careful assessments of institutions' inner workings and toward the study of more abstract questions such as why states delegate authority to institutions, why institutions are designed in different ways, and whether and how institutions "matter."[34] Embracing the paradigm's functionalist spirit, many of the most influential attempts to answer these questions also view institutions as functional responses to problems of international

[30] Carr (1964); Grieco (1988); Mearsheimer (1994); Morgenthau (1948).
[31] Strange (1998, 215). [32] Mearsheimer (1994, 13). [33] Keohane (1984).
[34] Martin and Simmons (1998, 737) note that the research program on international regimes, a key intellectual precursor to neoliberal institutionalism, "demoted the study of international organizations as actors: prior to the study of international regimes an inquiry into the effects of international institutions meant inquiring into how effectively a particular agency performed its job, for example, the efficiency with which the World Health Organization vaccinated the world's needy children. When regimes analysts looked for effects, these were understood to be outcomes influenced by a constellation of rules rather than tasks performed by a collective international agency."

cooperation, again implying that they will in fact fulfil their creators' hopes.[35]

As indicated by both anecdotal and systematic evidence, however, some institutions *do* fail to meet expectations, others *do* succeed, and still others enjoy mixed fortunes. Consequently, neither realism nor neoliberal institutionalism – nor, indeed, any purely functionalist theory of institutions – offers a satisfactory account of their performance. Where these paradigms see black or white, reality is a subtle palette of grays. Herein lies the theoretical gap this book seeks to fill.

Definitions and Scope

Any serious attempt to explain the performance of international institutions must begin with a clear definition of the two concepts making up the explanandum: international institutions and institutional performance. In the process of elucidating these concepts, this section clarifies the book's substantive scope.

International Institutions

Perhaps unsurprisingly, given their central place in the study of IR, international institutions are the subject of numerous definitions. As Thomas Risse quips, "There are at least as many definitions of (international) institutions as there are theoretical perspectives."[36] At the most general level, an international institution can be understood as a set of enduring (formal or informal) norms that governs the behavior of actors in the international system.[37] In line with much of the IR literature, though, this book uses the term to refer more specifically to *a collection of explicit, coherent rules that define a formal entity with members and a permanent secretariat.* It is these kinds of centralized and bureaucratized institutions, which typically take the form of organizations, that exercise agency in their own right and can thus be meaningfully described as "performing" functions.[38] Institutions that lack members and staff – such as treaties, conventions, protocols, and resolutions – do not formulate policies, provide information, execute operational activities, or

---

[35] Abbott and Snidal (2000); Hawkins et al. (2006); Koremenos, Lipson, and Snidal (2001).

[36] Risse (2000, 605). For an overview of different conceptual traditions, see Duffield (2007).

[37] Variants of this definition have been articulated by Keohane (1988, 1989); Koremenos, Lipson, and Snidal (2001); Simmons and Martin (2003).

[38] IR scholars have tended to use the terms "international institution" and "international organization" interchangeably. See Duffield (2007).

conduct any other task; they prescribe or proscribe actions that may be taken by signatories. It is for this reason that international organizations are generally thought of as embodying a qualitatively different – deeper and more far-reaching – form of institutionalized cooperation.[39]

This book also follows most IR scholarship in focusing primarily on IGOs, the type of international institution that has traditionally enjoyed the greatest formal authority and supplied the most consequential public goods. Yet its theoretical and empirical scope is not limited to such organizations. In recent decades, complex policy challenges and capacity limitations have triggered shifts in authority from IGOs to institutions with nongovernmental members, most notably public–private partnerships (PPPs) and INGOs.[40] In many of these institutions, states continue to play an active role, whether as members (in the case of PPPs), donors, operational partners, or agents of informal influence. Despite giving analytical primacy to the relationship between states and international bureaucrats, therefore, the book's theoretical framework can still shed useful light on their performance. For this reason, as discussed in Chapter 3, the PIIP includes a small number of PPPs and INGOs that have featured in donor performance assessments.

Institutional Performance

Defining the performance of international institutions is more challenging. The conceptual literature on institutional performance is intimidatingly large and varied, straddling several social science disciplines. The difficulty of distilling this semantic ocean into a cogent definition that can be operationalized, measured, and compared across institutions may have contributed as much to the dearth of IR research on performance issues as the field's theoretical orientations.[41]

Nevertheless, it is possible to delineate four approaches to defining institutional performance in previous scholarship, the roots of which lie in foundational work in the field of organizational theory in the 1950s and 1960s. The oldest and most influential approach understands performance as the *efficient accomplishment of goals*, whether those expressed in an institution's founding document (stated goals), those reflecting what it actually seeks to do (operative goals), or those concerning the narrower administrative and operational functions it exercises (process

---

[39] Abbott and Snidal (1998); Hawkins et al. (2006).

[40] Abbott and Snidal (2009a); Büthe and Mattli (2011); Cutler, Haufler, and Porter (1999); Hall and Biersteker (2002).

[41] Lall (2017).

goals).[42] Adherents of this perspective measure performance as a function of institutional results, outcomes, and costs. A second approach, which originated as a critique of the first, focuses on institutions' capacity to *adapt to their environment*, for example, by cultivating the resources and relationships they need to survive and grow.[43] On this view, inputs are a more appropriate measure of performance than outputs. A third perspective, which emphasizes the contested and subjective nature of evaluation, sees the ability to *satisfy the demands of key constituencies* as central to performance.[44] According to this approach, performance cannot be measured without reference to the perceptions and judgments of those with a stake in institutional activities. The final approach conceptualizes performance in terms of the *procedures* by which institutions operate and engage with stakeholders, in particular the extent to which they are open, inclusive, participatory, and harmonious.[45]

How helpful are these perspectives for conceptualizing institutional performance in the international context? It is hard to deny that, in its most basic sense, performance is about completing designated tasks. The *Oxford English Dictionary* defines the term as "[t]he accomplishment or carrying out of something commanded or undertaken." Efficiency also seems an integral, albeit analytically distinct, dimension of performance: An institution that produces a higher quantity and quality of output than another with the same or fewer resources – that "does more with less," as it were – must surely be considered a better performer.

At the same time, it is difficult to avoid some element of subjectivity when evaluating the goal attainment and efficiency of international institutions. Unlike many of their domestic counterparts, these institutions often have "lofty" and "broad" goals that cannot be plausibly achieved given the resources available to them and the external constraints they confront.[46] Although process goals tend to be more concrete and tractable than stated ones, both may vary widely in difficulty across institutions. The same problem arises with efficiency: Some tasks require more resources than others, rendering simple comparisons of institutional costs misleading. Conceptualizing performance with reference to stakeholder appraisals offers an attractive way of reconciling such differences, establishing a realistic, context-specific baseline against which to

---

[42] Etzioni (1964); Georgopoulos and Tannenbaum (1957); Price (1968).
[43] Pfeffer and Salancik (2003); Thompson (1967); Yuchtman and Seashore (1967).
[44] Connolly, Conlon, and Deutsch (1980); Pickle and Friedlander (1967); Tsui (1990).
[45] Bennis (1966); Likert (1967); Nadler and Tushman (1980). For more recent variants, see Boyne (2002); Moynihan et al. (2011); Walker, Boyne, and Brewer (2010).
[46] Gutner and Thompson (2010, 232).

assess goal attainment and efficiency that reflects the expectations and shared understandings of institutions' intended beneficiaries.

The utility of the procedural and environmental approaches to conceptualization, which have fewer advocates, is less clear. To be sure, adaptability, inclusiveness, and due process are practically and normatively significant characteristics of international institutions. Treating them as dimensions of performance, however, risks stretching the concept so far as to obscure its core meaning and dilute its coherence. The literature on domestic institutional performance generally treats procedure and external context as potential *determinants* – not components – of this variable, with some studies arguing that they negatively affect it.[47] Nor do these possibilities jar with intuition; there seems nothing contradictory or paradoxical, for instance, about procedural constraints impeding progress in attaining institutional goals.[48] Indeed, as discussed later, one of this book's contributions is to explore the relationship between accountability – an important aspect of procedure – and performance in global governance.

In light of these considerations, I define the performance of international institutions as *the extent to which they are judged by (public and private) stakeholders to have made sustained and cost-effective progress toward their stated, operative, and process objectives.* This hybrid definition builds on and bridges the central insights of the goal and constituency approaches to conceptualization, placing goal attainment and efficiency at the heart of performance while acknowledging that meaningful evaluation of these dimensions must be anchored in the experience of diverse institutional constituencies. It thereby aims to preserve the essential meaning and integrity of the concept while allowing for feasible operationalization and measurement.

Note, finally, the definition's reference to process as well as stated and operative objectives. This feature stems from a recognition that steps toward these three types of goals may not go hand in hand, and that effective performance requires progress on *all* fronts.[49] An institution that meets process but not stated and operative goals may not be delivering the results ultimately desired by stakeholders. Conversely, if

---

[47] According to the "ossification thesis," for example, procedural constraints on American bureaucratic agencies hinder efficient policy development through notice-and-comment rulemaking. See Yackee and Yackee (2010).

[48] As Kanter and Brinkerhoff (1981, 333) noted four decades ago, "Indeed, some structure/process considerations involved in effectiveness research seem purely normative rather than descriptive of what generates appropriate output levels ... There is no necessary relationship between the degree of centralization of decision-making and effectiveness measures."

[49] Perrow (1961).

only stated and operative aims are realized – a less likely scenario – we cannot be confident that this outcome is attributable to the institution's own efforts (as opposed to some set of favorable exogenous forces).[50]

Tales of Deviant Bureaucrats

Although the most influential theoretical perspective on international institutions suggests little reason to expect underperformance, not all scholars share this optimism. A growing number of single-case examinations, qualitative and quantitative, document clear failures as well as successes – findings that chime with the anecdotal and evaluative evidence discussed earlier.[51] Furthermore, the few general theoretical treatments of performance issues have focused on the sources of ineffectiveness rather than effectiveness, drawing particular attention to deviant behavior on the part of international bureaucrats.[52] While built on different epistemological and ontological foundations, these "rogue-agency" theories share a key implication: Institutions that enjoy higher levels of autonomy from states are more likely to suffer from performance problems.

Rogue-agency theorists have told two types of stories about bureaucratic deviance. The first is a rationalist tale rooted in well-established models of political economy, which highlights the incentives for self-interested, utility-maximizing bureaucrats to opportunistically advance their *own* goals – such as maximizing their budget, policy authority, and perquisites – at the expense of *institutional* ones. According to a common metaphor, institutions are "Frankensteins" that have slipped the restraints of their state creators and run amok.[53] There are two subtly distinct variants of the rationalist story, both of which attribute deviant behavior to autonomy arising from information asymmetries between bureaucrats and states. One variant takes inspiration from public choice theory, viewing bureaucrats as monopolistic suppliers of goods and services desired by states.[54] The other draws on contract theory, analyzing bureaucrats as "agents" of a collective state "principal"

[50] Gutner and Thompson (2010).
[51] Barnett (2002); Bosco (2009); Gutner (2005); Hardt (2014); Howard (2008); Weaver (2008). Similar findings are reported in the small literature on the effectiveness of international environmental regimes. See Breitmeier, Underdal, and Young (2011); Helm and Sprinz (2000); Haas, Keohane, and Levy (1993); Miles et al. (2002); Young (1999, 2011).
[52] For an exception, see Gutner and Thompson's (2010) symposium on the politics of IGO performance.
[53] Guzman (2008).
[54] Dreher and Vaubel (2004); Przeworski and Vreeland (2000); Vaubel (1986); Vreeland (2003).

that, owing to monitoring and contracting costs, cannot perfectly control their actions.[55] Both imply that bureaucrats are characterized by a form of moral hazard: They have incentives to behave in ways that jeopardize institutional performance because they do not bear the full cost of this risk.

The second story, which is associated with the influential work of Michael Barnett and Martha Finnemore, has constructivist rather than rationalist underpinnings.[56] In this yarn, bureaucrats are not rational utility-maximizers but fundamentally *social* actors capable of "self-defeating and inefficient" actions that "defy rational logic" and are "at odds with their stated mission."[57] These problems emerge, Barnett and Finnemore contend, when bureaucrats exploit their rational-legal authority and control over information and technical expertise to carve out autonomy from states, enabling them to structure social knowledge and regulate state behavior. The bureaucratic cultures – conventions, rituals, and beliefs – that arise out of these practices foster pathological tendencies that ultimately undermine institutional performance, such as treating rules as ends in themselves, failing to tailor knowledge and practice to local context, and forming incoherent worldviews that lead to contradictory policies and mission creep.

By offering reasoned, theoretically grounded accounts of how performance problems manifest themselves, rogue-agency analyses help us move beyond the unhelpful assumption of uniform effectiveness. When it comes to explaining differences in performance, however, they suffer from both theoretical and empirical limitations. On the theoretical front, despite acknowledging the possibility of such variation, they offer little insight into why only *some* bureaucracies acquire enough autonomy to develop habits and practices that damage performance. In principle, their causal logic applies to all institutions – they do not explicitly demarcate scope conditions – making it hard to see how suboptimal outcomes are ever avoided. This issue points to an even broader puzzle for the rogue-agency perspective: If bureaucratic deviance and poor performance are inevitable, why do states delegate authority to institutions in the first place?[58]

With respect to empirics, rogue-agency theories are not accompanied by systematic cross-institutional evidence that autonomy is negatively

---

[55] Hawkins et al. (2006); Nielson and Tierney (2003); Pollack and Hafner-Burton (2010). Gutner and Thompson (2010, 238) summarize: "Applications of principal-agent theory to IOs [international organizations] typically assume that if institutions are not achieving the desired policy outcomes delegated by state principals, it is because the agents are pursuing self-interested behavior that deviates from expectations."

[56] Barnett and Finnemore (1999, 2004).   [57] Barnett and Finnemore (1999, 715).

[58] Stone (2008).

related to performance. Proponents of the rationalist story have by and large restricted their attention to a single institution, namely, the IMF (reflecting their political economy orientation). Barnett and Finnemore illustrate their argument with three case studies – of the IMF, UN peacekeeping, and the United Nations High Commissioner for Refugees (UNHCR) – that, while rich and suggestive, exhibit minimal variation in autonomy or performance and consider few dimensions of the latter concept. Indeed, more comprehensive evaluations of these institutions indicate that their performance has been not only markedly better than suggested by Barnett and Finnemore but also *enhanced* by bureaucratic discretion.[59] Nor are these cases the exception: A positive relationship between performance and autonomy is suggested by similar examinations across a multitude of issue areas, from trade to environmental protection to economic development.[60] What explains these "anomalous" findings?

The Argument in Brief

International institutions are the expression of a commitment by states to delegate authority to a distinct entity – an entity administered by actors with their own desires and ambitions – as a means of furthering common interests. Rogue-agency theories view this act of separation as a source of control problems that lead institutions astray from their original aims. I argue, in contrast, that bureaucratic preferences are often closely aligned with institutional purpose, and that a far more potent threat to such goals is the propensity of *states* to capture institutions in pursuit of parochial national interests. The rogue-agency perspective must be not merely tweaked but turned on its head: It is the principal, not the agent, whose opportunistic behavior endangers performance. Incentives for capture arise from an intractable time-inconsistency problem: States stand to benefit from pursuing collective interests before they engage in institutionalized cooperation but individual interests subsequently. To adapt the supernatural metaphor invoked by rogue-agency theorists, effectiveness is threatened not by "institutional Frankensteins" but by "Jekyll and Hyde states."

While sharing the realist paradigm's keen sensitivity to the role of power and interests in shaping institutions, I stress that states do not

---

[59] See, for example, Howard (2008) on UN peacekeeping, Loescher (2001) on the UNHCR, and Stone (2011) on the IMF.

[60] Abbott and Snidal (2010); Elsig (2010); Honig (2018, 2019); Schneider and Tobin (2013); Stone (2011).

always have their way. Institutions are more than collections of rules, structures, and procedures devoid of agency: They *can* and often *do* insulate themselves against particularistic governmental interventions in the policy process. Against another influential perspective, however, I reject the notion that institutional design can furnish the basis for policy autonomy. Not only are the architects of institutionalized cooperation unable to foresee how much independence will be required in the future, but formal policymaking rules lack robust and reliable enforcement mechanisms at the international level. On its own, therefore, de jure policy autonomy is unlikely to spare institutions from the ravages of state capture. The pertinent question is: Where does *de facto* policy autonomy come from?

I trace de facto policy autonomy to the discreet, frequently overlooked processes by which institutions pursue the operational demands of their mandate. Two such processes, which give rise to what I call *alliances* and *stealth* – or, more metaphorically, the "hand" and the "cloak" – are especially important. The first is the formation of a strong and wide-ranging constellation of operational partnerships with actors above and below the state, including nongovernmental organizations (NGOs), businesses, transgovernmental networks, and other international institutions. By establishing reputational linkages and advancing mutual interests through the shared exercise of authority, such relationships gives partners a direct stake in institutional effectiveness, creating a powerful and durable constituency for policy autonomy. The second process is the exercise of governance tasks that are costly for states to monitor, such as implementing substantive operations on the ground and designing complex policy interventions. High monitoring costs confer on bureaucrats a decisive informational advantage throughout the policy process, limiting states' capacity to set the agenda, block unwanted proposals, and shape governance outcomes through implementation and enforcement interventions.

While de facto policy autonomy provides a critical foundation for the efficient pursuit of institutional objectives, the direction of causation does not flow one way only. Autonomy-induced improvements in performance, in turn, gradually reinforce such discretion by raising both the opportunity costs and the domestic political costs of capture for states. Conversely, performance problems stemming from the absence of de facto policy autonomy tend to reduce these costs, entrenching state domination of the policy apparatus. In the long run, feedback processes between de facto policy autonomy and performance exhaust themselves, giving rise to multiple – and widely varying – autonomy–performance equilibria.

At the most general level, this line of reasoning suggests two hypotheses. First, institutional performance is positively associated with de facto policy autonomy but unrelated to de jure policy autonomy. Second, de facto policy autonomy is itself a positive function of (1) the quantity, depth, and breadth of operational alliances with non-state actors; and (2) the exercise of governance tasks with sizable monitoring costs for states. In addition, the argument yields an array of micro-level observable implications, including that states routinely attempt to intervene in key stages of the policy process to advance narrow interests – even if this requires circumventing formal rules and procedures; that bureaucrats take steps to shield themselves against interference and to steer policy outcomes toward stated and operative goals; that operational partners can assist in this endeavor by assembling encompassing coalitions for policy autonomy; and that hard-to-monitor governance tasks engender information asymmetries that facilitate hidden bureaucratic action and thus present an additional bulwark against capture.

Perhaps worryingly, these propositions appear to imply a tension between the performance and accountability of international institutions, often regarded as their two most significant attributes. If averting the thorniest obstacle to performance requires placing constraints on governmental policy influence, one might reason, institutions cannot be simultaneously effective and accountable. I posit, however, that if we embrace a more expansive understanding of how accountability is institutionalized in the international context, no such trade-off arises. This is because the same factors that nurture de facto policy autonomy make institutions more likely to adopt a variety of modern accountability structures – what I call *second-wave* accountability (SWA) mechanisms – that principally benefit and empower non-state actors. Notable examples include access-to-information policies, independent evaluation offices, and grievance redress systems. Once in place, moreover, SWA mechanisms can themselves deliver performance gains by bringing to light operational problems, improving the quality of decision-making, and boosting policy compliance. Importantly, these benefits are distinct from those yielded by de facto policy autonomy, implying that the latter and accountability can be complements rather than substitutes. In sum, the relationship between performance and accountability is more nuanced than first meets the eye, depending on the specific means by which institutions are held to account by internal and external stakeholders. When the conditions for genuine autonomy are in place, international institutions *can* be both effective and accountable.

Research Design

This book also contributes to *how* we study the performance of inter-national institutions. Whereas most previous scholarship has relied on case studies, I integrate multiple forms of quantitative and qualitative evidence into a unified methodological strategy that leverages their complementary strengths.[61] In pursuing this approach, I heed a growing scholarly consensus that diverse research methods are needed to fully grasp a subject as complex and multifaceted as global institutional performance.[62] My empirical investigation proceeds in three stages (summarized in Table 1.1), each of which makes use of a different technique or combination of techniques. Taken together, they offer a comprehensive and rigorous assessment of the argument's macro- and micro-level implications.

In the first stage of the inquiry, I subject my macro-level propositions to statistical tests based on the PIIP. As noted earlier, challenges of operationalization and measurement have proved a major deterrent to research on the performance of international institutions. Draw-ing on methodological insights from assessments of domestic public institutions, I seek to overcome this hurdle by constructing multidimen-sional performance indices from numerical and categorical indicators in the donor evaluations discussed previously. These measures are supplemented with data on the main explanatory variables – de facto and de jure policy autonomy, operational alliances, and governance tasks – from a host of original sources, including a multiyear survey of senior officials from all 54 PIIP institutions.

I assess my hypotheses with descriptive statistics, pooled cross-sectional regressions, and a simultaneous equations strategy that incorporates the possibility of feedback effects between performance and de facto policy autonomy. These analyses serve three methodological purposes. First, they provide systematic information on the variables of interest, revealing their range of variation in a substantively significant slice of global governance. Second, they facilitate the selection of cases for more close-range examination subsequently. Third, and perhaps most importantly, they yield empirical findings with high levels

---

[61] On the advantages of mixed-methods research designs, see Axinn and Pearce (2006); Gerring (2011); Lieberman (2005).

[62] As Gutner and Thompson (2010, 244–245) counsel, "Because they both add value to the study of IO [international organization] performance, qualitative and quantitative studies should work in tandem according to their comparative advantages and the specific empirical puzzles of interest." Similarly, Young (2011, 19858), the doyen of regime effectiveness scholars, emphasizes that "finding ways to combine quantitative and qualitative methods is a priority in studies of effectiveness."

Table 1.1 *Summary of research design*

Stage	Method	Purpose	Coverage	Issue area
1	Statistical analysis (linear regression, simultaneous equations); descriptive statistics	Providing information on variables of interest; facilitating case selection; testing macro-level propositions	PIIP (54 major international institutions); 2008–2018	All (sample substantively representative of wider institutional population)
2a	Matched case comparison (process tracing, narratives)	Testing causal mechanisms; examining direction and sequence of causal relationships	FAO, IFAD, WFP; 1945–present	Food security
2b	Second case comparison	Broadening qualitative evidence base; probing scope conditions	WHO, UNAIDS, Gavi, GFATM; 1948–present	Public health
3	Combination of statistical analysis and qualitative plausibility probe	Investigating relationship between performance and accountability	PIIP (qualitative evidence on subset); 1960–2018	All (qualitative focus on economic development)

of *external validity*, that is, generalizability to the wider universe of international institutions. This characteristic is difficult to achieve solely by means of "small-N" analysis.

Nevertheless, small-N methods are helpful for probing hypothesized causal mechanisms linking the dependent and explanatory variables, which are often difficult to capture statistically. Evidence for these micro-level implications bolsters *internal validity*, that is, the extent to which findings represent the truth in the sample of institutions under study.[63] In addition, small-N analysis throws useful light on the direction and sequence of causation between performance and de facto policy autonomy, which – given the multidetermined nature of these variables and the PIIP's fairly short temporal scope – the quantitative tests cannot establish with certainty.

With these complementarities in mind, the second stage of the investigation presents two comparative case studies of PIIP institutions, which apply process-tracing and narrative techniques to a range of sources, including policy documents, archival records, independent assessments, academic literature, and more than 140 interviews with international

[63] Gerring (2006).

bureaucrats, government representatives, and nongovernmental stake-holders (see Appendix C for further information). Two methodolog-ical features of the case studies merit mention. First, they employ a "most similar systems" design that involves comparing institutions as alike as possible *except* with respect to the dependent and explanatory variables.[64] This allows us to eliminate numerous possible alternative explanations for differences in performance (in a manner akin to the statistical technique of matching), helping us isolate the causal impact of de facto policy autonomy.[65] It thus seeks to marry the depth and rich-ness of qualitative analysis with inferential advantages usually associated with quantitative methods. Second, unlike the statistical analysis, the case studies encompass the full institutional life cycle, which is essential for assessing my claims about the sequence in which de facto policy autonomy and performance influence one another.

The first case study examines the FAO, the WFP, and IFAD, the three central pillars of global food security governance. As well as their similarity, I select these institutions because of the practical significance and timeliness of the issues they address. Food production and distribution have lagged behind improvements in general living standards around the world, impaired by wars, natural disasters, and more recently the COVID-19 pandemic. As a consequence, they continue to present one of the most exigent challenges confronting the international community today.

Lifting the veil on the puzzling discrepancy in performance noted earlier, the case study shows how, despite sharing many characteristics, the three institutions have starkly different levels of de facto policy autonomy – variation *not* reflected in their formal rules. Lacking the protection afforded by robust operational ties with non-state actors or easily concealable governance tasks, the FAO has failed to preserve the ample bureaucratic independence written into its constitution. Limited discretion has stunted staff initiatives to expand and more efficiently allocate global food supplies, with major industrialized producers – most notably the United States – preferring to use the organization as a shield for domestic agricultural interests. The WFP and IFAD have blazed the opposite trajectory, overcoming stringent formal constraints on their autonomy by assembling an expansive network of operational alliances with stakeholders, in particular civil society groups, and by undertaking specialized, technically demanding governance functions

---

[64] On most similar systems designs, see Gerring (2006); King, Keohane, and Verba (1994); Lijphart (1971). The roots of this approach stretch back to John Stuart Mill's method of difference.

[65] Nielsen (2016); Weller and Barnes (2014).

that are difficult for states to oversee. This room for maneuver has enabled the WFP to develop fast and cost-effective systems for delivering food aid in humanitarian emergencies – systems that prioritize recipient country need over political connections to donor countries – and IFAD to design and implement innovative, high-impact projects for stimulating agricultural production across the developing world.

The second case study compares four major global health institutions: the WHO, the Joint United Nations Programme on HIV/AIDS (UNAIDS), Gavi, and the Global Fund to Fight AIDS, Tuberculosis and Malaria (GFATM). Once again, these institutions were chosen on account of their affinities as well as their substantive importance – not least in light of COVID-19. A notable difference from the first case study is that two PPPs – Gavi and GFATM – are included, providing an opportunity to probe the argument's institutional scope conditions. More generally, the addition of a second issue area broadens the base of qualitative evidence for the theory, preempting potential concerns that food security constitutes a uniquely favorable domain in which to assess its micro-level implications.

In the final phase of the investigation, I turn to the relationship between performance and accountability, bringing to bear a combination of quantitative and qualitative methods. I use statistical analysis to evaluate my claim that the strength of SWA mechanisms is positively associated with the two posited sources of de facto policy autonomy. To this end, I supplement the PIIP with new data on five distinct categories of SWA mechanisms – transparency, evaluation, inspection, investigation, and participation mechanisms – stretching back to 1960. The qualitative component of the examination probes the microdynamics of the SWA–performance relationship in the issue area of economic development, further expanding the empirical lens. This exploration, which draws again on interviews, archival work, and other primary sources, illustrates the plausibility of the hypothesized causal processes linking SWA reforms with performance, operational alliances, and governance tasks, in addition to illuminating some puzzling differences in accountability structures among similar institutions.

Plan of the Book

Six chapters follow this introduction. Chapter 2 sets out the book's theoretical framework. It proceeds in three stages. First, based on a microfoundational analysis of the incentives facing states and international bureaucrats, I make the case that the former are more liable than the latter to engage in opportunistic behavior that imperils institutional performance. Second, I flesh out the concept of policy autonomy, explaining how its different components address political obstacles to performance and why it cannot be reliably established and maintained through institutional design. Third, I explore the true origins of policy autonomy, elaborating the causal mechanisms by which (certain types of) operational alliances and governance tasks insulate bureaucrats against state capture. The chapter concludes by summarizing the framework's observable implications at the macro and micro levels.

The next three chapters place these implications under empirical scrutiny. Chapter 3 tests the theory's macro-level implications by running a series of descriptive and multivariate regression analyses on the PIIP dataset. It begins by describing the dataset's scope, contents, and sources. The statistical examination is divided into four parts. The first examines the relationship between performance and policy autonomy. I find a positive association when policy autonomy is measured using a survey of international bureaucrats, a proxy for de facto policy autonomy, but no relationship when it is measured using formal rules, a proxy for de jure policy autonomy. The second part turns to the determinants of de facto policy autonomy, showing that the survey-based measure is positively predicted both by the quantity, depth, and breadth of operational alliances and by the exercise of governance tasks with substantial monitoring costs for states. In the third part, I pursue a simultaneous equations strategy to isolate the effect of performance and de facto policy autonomy on one another. The fourth part summarizes a battery of robustness checks.

Chapter 4 begins the qualitative portion of the empirical examination with the case comparison of the FAO, the WFP, and IFAD. It begins by detailing the matching strategy used to identify these institutions, documenting their similar levels of several possible determinants of performance and policy autonomy. The bulk of the chapter traces how differences in de facto – but not de jure – policy autonomy have set the institutions on divergent performance trajectories: The WFP and IFAD are autonomous and widely recognized as effective, whereas the FAO is state-dominated and notorious for performance problems. Rather than formal design features, I locate the origins of this variation in the institutions' distinct governance functions and patterns of operational collaboration with non-state actors. Interviews and archival data gathered during fieldwork at the institutions' Rome headquarters adduce key pieces of evidence in this process-tracing exercise.

Chapter 5 presents the second case study, in which the WHO, UNAIDS, Gavi, and GFATM are the objects of comparison. The structure is analogous to Chapter 4's. After enumerating the characteristics on which the four institutions are matched, I chronicle how differences in their de facto policy autonomy have given rise to disparate performance outcomes: The WHO and UNAIDS have been characterized by relentlessly declining autonomy and performance over their life cycles, Gavi and GFATM by the opposite trends. I then delve into the operational origins of these differences, which, once more, defy a purely design-based explanation. The case study draws on a similar assortment of primary sources to Chapter 4.

In Chapter 6, I consider the theory's implications for the imperative issue of accountability in global governance. I begin by expounding my argument that any apparent accountability–performance trade-off ceases to hold when we consider a broader gamut of accountability mechanisms, many of which are both more likely to be adopted by autonomous institutions and independently advantageous for performance. I provide two forms of empirical support for these conjectures: (1) statistical evidence on the relationship between SWA reforms and performance, operational alliances, and governance tasks in the PIIP sample; and (2) qualitative illustrations of process-level plausibility from the issue area of economic development, in which many SWA mechanisms were pioneered.

Chapter 7 concludes the book. It opens with a brief review of the main findings and the role of each stage of the empirical investigation in establishing them. I then discuss the book's contributions to IR, IPE, and political science as well as other fields of social science. The third section draws out lessons for policy and practice. I identify a variety of stakeholder-specific strategies for safeguarding policy autonomy and encouraging SWA reforms, contributing to a lively ongoing debate among academics and practitioners over how to achieve an effective and accountable global institutional architecture. Finally, I reflect on the book's implications for some notable emerging issues in global governance, such as institutional performance during international crises and challenges to the modern liberal order, outlining promising avenues for further research.

2   A Theory of Institutional Performance

> The performance of international institutions will be symptomatic of the domestic political priorities of influential member states. International institutions don't really have a life and a mind of their own.
>   – Samantha Power, United States Ambassador to the United Nations, 2008[1]

> Like Frankenstein's monster, IOs [international organizations] created by states may behave differently from the way they are expected to. There is always a risk that an IO will impact the system in ways that harm, rather than help, the interests of states. An IO can become a monster.
>   – Andrew Guzman, 2013[2]

On April 14, 2020, at the height of the coronavirus (COVID-19) pandemic, President Donald Trump made an announcement that stunned the international community: The United States had halted its funding of the World Health Organization (WHO) pending an investigation into the agency's "role in severely mismanaging and covering up the spread of the coronavirus."[3] The ramifications of this decision, which was widely viewed as an attempt to deflect criticism of the Trump administration's own handling of the pandemic, were grave. Almost 90,000 lives had been lost to COVID-19 around the world over the previous two weeks alone, and the United States was by far the WHO's largest donor. As dismayed public health experts were quick to point out, losing American resources would severely hamper the Organization's ability to monitor and coordinate national responses to the pandemic, potentially contributing to "widespread death and suffering."[4] Just days earlier, Tedros Adhanom Ghebreyesus, the WHO's director-general, had stressed the dangers of "politicizing COVID," sending an ominous warning to world leaders: "We will have many body bags in front of us if we don't behave."[5] On July 6, 2020, shortly after claiming to have

---

[1] Quoted in Jacobs (2013).   [2] Guzman (2013, 1000).   [3] White House (2020).
[4] Physicians for Human Rights (2020).   [5] Cohen (2020).

concluded an internal review of the WHO's response to the pandemic, the Trump administration notified the United Nations (UN) of its intention to withdraw from the Organization.

The United States' disengagement from the WHO ultimately proved short-lived: Trump's successor, President Joe Biden, halted the withdrawal and resumed financial contributions shortly after taking office in January 2021. Nevertheless, the episode had damaging consequences for the global response to COVID-19. In addition to tens of millions of dollars, the WHO lost credibility and legitimacy at a critical phase of the pandemic. As one WHO official acknowledged at the time: "When an organization's largest donor and most influential member abandons it at the height of a crisis, that severely undermines confidence and trust in its work precisely when they are needed most. Even if the United States eventually reverses course, permanent damage to the WHO – and the international fight against COVID-19 – has been done."[6]

The Trump administration's politically motivated intervention in the WHO sent shock waves around the world, with commentators labeling it "extraordinary,"[7] "astonishing,"[8] and "stunning."[9] According to the theoretical framework I elaborate in this chapter, however, it is far from an unusual occurrence in global governance. International institutions of widely varying sizes, resources, memberships, mandates, and governance structures routinely suffer from opportunistic interference by states seeking to defend and advance particularistic interests – even if this comes at the expense of agreed-upon objectives. Where many worry about "runaway bureaucracies" recklessly pursuing their own ends, I highlight state capture as a far more serious threat to institutional effectiveness. The upshot something of a paradox: Institutions are often prevented from realizing their objectives by the same actors who brought them into existence and set them such goals.

What explains this enigma? And what are the implications for understanding differences in institutional performance, the aim of this book? My framework draws attention to a key strategic dilemma, which I call the *Jekyll and Hyde problem*, that lies at the heart of rules-based international cooperation: States possess incentives to pursue collective interests before they establish institutions but particularistic interests thereafter. As a result, institutions are best placed to evade performance problems when they carve out and maintain a high degree of policy autonomy vis-à-vis states – a possibility essentially assumed away by the major theoretical paradigms of international relations (IR).

---

[6] Author interview #117 with WHO governance officer, June 9, 2020, by video conference.
[7] Gawthorpe (2020).   [8] Brand (2020).   [9] Campbell (2020).

Challenging another common view, I argue that such independence cannot be guaranteed by formal institutional design. Since states cannot fully anticipate future threats to national interests and policymaking rules are backed by weak enforcement mechanisms, *de jure* policy autonomy does not always translate into *de facto* policy autonomy.

The true origins of bureaucratic independence instead lie in two characteristics that emerge from the seemingly mundane operational processes through which institutions pursue their mandates. The first is the formation of a deep and wide-ranging network of operational partnerships with actors above and below the state, which enables institutions to build encompassing and durable coalitions for autonomy. The second is the exercise of governance tasks that are costly for states to monitor, which shields institutions against capture by generating information asymmetries that expand and entrench bureaucratic influence at key phases of the policy process. Adopting a martial metaphor, I label the first characteristic *alliances* and the second *stealth*.

I develop this argument in six steps. First, analyzing the strategic incentives facing states and international bureaucrats before and after institutional creation, I explain the riddle of capture as an inevitable corollary of the Jekyll and Hyde problem. Second, I dissect the concept of policy autonomy, distinguishing three core components – agenda-setting powers, the ability to avoid a governmental veto, and access to non-state sources of financing – and highlighting the barriers to attaining them through institutional design. Third, I explore the roots of de facto policy autonomy, detailing the mechanisms by which numerous, deep, and extensive operational alliances and hard-to-monitor governance tasks protect institutions against state meddling. Fourth, I consider the possibility of a reverse causal effect from performance to de facto policy autonomy, arguing that the former can reinforce the latter by altering the political and opportunity costs of capture for states. Fifth, collecting these analytical threads, I tease out the framework's macro- and micro-level observable implications. I conclude the exposition by clarifying scope conditions and discussing the theoretical consequences of relaxing a number of simplifying assumptions.

The Enigma of State Capture

In attempting to understand how international institutions perform, a natural place to begin is with the interests of the two sets of actors who constitute them: member states and bureaucrats. According to the most developed theoretical account of institutional performance, there is an irreconcilable tension between the ends pursued by bureaucrats and the ends institutions are assigned by states. As exemplified by the second epigraph to this chapter, institutions are seen as "Frankensteins" that have shaken off their state-imposed shackles and embarked on a frenzy of transnational destruction.

My framework accepts two premises of the rogue-agency perspective. First, institutions are the product of a deliberate, calculated effort by states to further their shared interests by granting authority to a separate entity. Second, bureaucrats are actors in their own right, with desires and ambitions that may clash with state interests. In sharp contrast to rogue-agency theories, however, I posit that the primary obstacle to effective performance is opportunistic behavior not by bureaucrats but by *states themselves* – the actors who give life and purpose to institutions. In the language of contract theory, it is the principal, not the agent, who experiences the more intense moral hazard problem. This counterintuitive claim follows from two simple insights about the structure of incentives in institutionalized cooperation. First, while bureaucrats are capable of forming and pursuing their own interests, doing so need not come at the expense of attaining institutional objectives. Second, although initially aligned with these goals, state preferences frequently evolve in ways that conflict with and undermine them.

What International Bureaucrats Want

What do international bureaucrats desire? The answer is not obvious. As Barnett and Finnemore point out, international institutions "are often created by the principals (states) and given mission statements written by the principals. How, then, can we impute independent preferences a priori?"[10] The leading paradigms of IR attribute little agency to the manifestations of institutionalized cooperation, treating them as rules, principles, and norms as opposed to living and breathing actors.[11] Encapsulating the realist view, this chapter's first epigraph paints international institutions as vacant, inert vessels through which powerful states pursue domestic political agendas.

Rejecting this characterization of international institutions, the rogue-agency perspective borrows from theoretical traditions outside of IR to fill out bureaucratic interests. Following public choice models, rationalist variants typically assume that bureaucrats strive to maximize their budget, policy authority, prestige, and perquisites.[12] This notion does not seem unreasonable, notwithstanding some clear counterexamples.[13]

---

[10] Barnett and Finnemore (1999, 706).   [11] Barnett and Finnemore (2004).
[12] Miller and Moe (1983); Moe (1984); Niskanen (1971).
[13] Barnett and Finnemore (1999, 706) cite two: "Simply adopting the rather battered

It is far from obvious, though, why performance woes must ensue. Bureaucrats seeking material resources and prestige, for instance, will surely fare better if their institution is perceived as effective by states and other donors – a point acknowledged by some rogue-agency theorists.[14] The same is true of bureaucrats aiming to expand their turf. International institutions typically have to rely on moral suasion rather than centralized enforcement to secure compliance with their dictates. In the absence of democratic accountability, one of their surest paths to legitimacy is, in the words of Allen Buchanan and Robert Keohane, to "effectively perform the functions invoked to justify [their] existence."[15]

Nor are resources, turf, and sweeteners the only – or perhaps even the most significant – objects of bureaucratic yearning. Constructivist variants of the rogue-agency approach place greater emphasis on the role of identity and norms in shaping how bureaucrats form preferences. Here again, there are few grounds for expecting tension with institutional purpose. To the contrary, surveys[16] and ethnographic studies[17] provide evidence that bureaucrats are often genuinely concerned with and driven by their institution's mission. Even rogue-agency theorists concede that these actors tend to be "highly motivated and dedicated to their cause," and that "[l]ofty ideals – such as peace, international cooperation, and solidarity – may play a more prominent role in international organizations than in a national civil service."[18]

Why might international bureaucrats exhibit high levels of intrinsic motivation? Given the "lofty" nature of their mandates, they may develop an attachment to their work through rewarding professional and personal experience. It is also conceivable, as strands of the IR literature suggest, that they internalize an ethos of dedication and loyalty to their mission from their colleagues and wider "epistemic community,"[19] perhaps through processes of bureaucratic socialization.[20] Selection mechanisms could also be part of the story. There is evidence that

Niskanen hypothesis seems less than promising given the glaring anomalies – for example, the opposition of many NATO [North Atlantic Treaty Organization] and OSCE [Organization of Security and Cooperation in Europe] bureaucrats to those organizations' recent expansion and institutionalization." Similar resistance has recently been evident in institutions such as the European Union (EU) and the UN.

14 Hawkins et al. (2006, 65), for example, note: "Agents that are perceived as succeeding in their missions are rewarded with larger budgets . . . Agents that are perceived as failing are punished with smaller budgets, and may even be eliminated entirely."
15 Buchanan and Keohane (2006, 422). Also see Tallberg, Bäckstrand, and Scholte (2018).
16 UN System Chief Executives Board for Coordination (2018); International Civil Service Commission (2008); United Nations (2017). Further examples are provided in Chapters 4 and 5.
17 E.g., Ascher (1983); Barnett (2002); Mathiason (2007); Wade (1996); Zabusky (1995).
18 Vaubel (2006, 137).   19 Haas (1992).   20 Checkel (2005).

individuals who hold cosmopolitan values – such as tolerance, open-mindedness, and progressiveness – are more likely to seek employment in international institutions, as are those who identify with institutional goals.[21] Interestingly, this possibility is consistent with the logic of rogue-agency accounts based on principal–agent theory, which imply that states should screen prospective bureaucrats to ensure that their preferences hew closely to such objectives. Indeed, if bureaucrats are as wayward as these analyses suggest, the persistence of suboptimal screening and selection mechanisms is a major theoretical puzzle for them. In short, there are reasons to believe that, along with material incentives, identity and social norms may lead bureaucrats to attach significant value to effective institutional performance.

The Jekyll and Hyde Problem

On the face of it, specifying state interests is more straightforward. As it is states that give life to institutions, one might expect their interests to match or at least closely approximate institutional objectives. This assumption is consistent with canonical principal–agent models of legislative delegation to bureaucratic agencies in the American politics literature, which imply that only agents (bureaucrats) behave in ways that jeopardize agreed-upon goals – that is, exhibit moral hazard.[22] Subsequent studies, however, have challenged this implication by pointing out that principals (politicians) are often subject to more severe moral hazard problems than agents. In important work on the politics of structural choice, Terry Moe highlights how politicians regularly take actions that impede agency efficiency out of fear that political turnover will enable opponents to enact conflicting policies in the future.[23] More recently, building on the economics literature on time inconsistency in monetary policymaking, Gary Miller and Andrew Whitford have argued that changes in political conditions can cause the same politician to favor different policies at different points in time.[24]

I posit that an analogous time-inconsistency problem characterizes the delegation of authority to international institutions – the Jekyll and Hyde problem. Before institutions are created (period $t - 1$), states have incentives to identify mutual interests and pursue them by means of institutionalized cooperation. Each nation stands to gain

---

[21] Anderfuhren-Biget, Häfliger, and Hug (2013); Ban (2013); Hooghe (2001).
[22] E.g., Weingast (1984); Weingast and Moran (1983). As noted in Chapter 1, these actions entail moral hazard because agents do not bear the full cost of the risks they incur.
[23] Moe (1989, 1990).   [24] Miller and Whitford (2007, 2016).

from delegation – an act that mitigates the cooperation dilemmas highlighted by neoliberal institutionalism while facilitating specialization, collective decision-making, and enforcement – and expects the benefits to outweigh the costs.[25] Once authority has been transferred (period $t + 1$), however, circumstances can evolve in unanticipated ways that encourage states to exploit institutions for narrow national ends rather than broader collective interests – that is, to capture them.[26] Such shifts are sometimes triggered by "endogenous" developments – developments inside institutions – such as operational expansions and bureaucratic initiatives that threaten state interests. They may also arise from "exogenous" events and trends, such as changes in underlying issue characteristics and reorderings of states' foreign policy priorities (for instance, due to the election of a new government).

Why do incentives to pursue parochial interests arise only in period $t + 1$? Three reasons stand out. First, it makes little sense to do so in period $t - 1$. States are unlikely to create an institution with the objective of supplying particularistic benefits to one or a small subset of members. A powerful state could conceivably coerce weaker ones into joining an institution tasked with promoting its particular foreign policy aims. Yet, as Randall Stone points out, institutions are only useful to powerful countries when they elicit *voluntary* participation; if compliance must be compelled using material resources, institutions offer negligible advantage over unilateral action.[27] Second, once established, institutions can facilitate the pursuit of narrow interests in several ways. Institutions provide states with timely and reliable information on the activities, capabilities, and preferences of other nations – a central insight of the neoliberal paradigm.[28] In addition, they enable states to channel a larger pool of resources toward desired ends. Perhaps most importantly for the powerful, they can lend legitimacy to state behavior by virtue of embodying and representing the international community.[29] Third, institutional activities entail distributional consequences, creating winners and losers in ways that are difficult to fully anticipate in period $t - 1$. As illustrated many times throughout this book, adversely affected nations can emerge as a powerful force for capture in period $t + 1$.

---

[25] Abbott and Snidal (1998); Hawkins et al. (2006); Martin (1992).

[26] Not all attempts to influence institutions in period $t + 1$ count as capture, therefore. Efforts to further common interests by updating policies in line with institutional objectives as conditions change, for instance, would not qualify. In practice, such initiatives can usually be distinguished from capture strategies by their (1) high level of coordination among states; and (2) relative infrequency (given the transaction costs of reaching consensus within a large and diverse group).

[27] Stone (2011, 16–19).   [28] Also see Thompson (2010).

[29] Abbott and Snidal (1998); Tallberg, Bäckstrand, and Scholte (2018).

Naturally, states with similar characteristics and interests are more likely to band together to seize control of institutions. In the 1970s and 1980s, for example, a common occurrence in UN agencies was the formation of rival political blocs of industrialized and developing nations. Coordination with other states is not always necessary, however: Powerful nations often possess both the incentives and the means to single-handedly capture institutions – even if this inflicts collateral damage on allied and friendly countries.[30]

In the absence of countervailing forces, the Jekyll and Hyde problem leaves institutions torn between particularistic and collective agendas, unable to formulate, finance, and implement coherent and efficient strategies for advancing their goals. These frictions can cause frustrated bureaucrats to reduce their effort and productivity and, as noted earlier, "loser" states to develop or intensify their own capture strategies.[31] The result, depicted graphically in Figure 2.1, is that the collective goods institutions were established to provide will be undersupplied (quantity C'') relative to their intended level (quantity C'), whereas particularistic goods will be oversupplied (quantity x'' rather than x'). In effect, states have weaker incentives to consider the welfare of other nations in period $t + 1$, reducing the rate at which they are willing to substitute collective goods for particularistic goods (as represented by a flattening of the opportunity set, i.e., the total sum of goods they can obtain). Appendix A.1 presents a formal analysis of this shift in preferences.[32]

If this logic is sound, the evocative supernatural imagery with which rogue-agency theorists depict institutions must be amended: The chief obstacle to effective performance is not institutional Frankensteins but *Jekyll and Hyde states* – states that pursue common interests prior to the creation of institutions (like the well-behaved Dr. Jekyll) but individual interests afterward (like the monstrous Mr. Hyde).

The Power of Policy Autonomy

Is there a solution to the Jekyll and Hyde problem? Relatedly, why do states not anticipate this conundrum before they establish institutions and take steps to mitigate it? A central message of the economics literature on time inconsistency is that governments can make credible

---

[30] Stone (2011).   [31] Junge, König, and Luig (2015).
[32] On the analytical benefits of formalizing conjectures about the performance of international institutions, see Young (2011, 19859). Pertinently, Young suggests that "[a] productive effort of this sort focuses on understanding dilemmas of collective action, like the tragedy of the commons and free ridership in the supply of public goods, as outcomes of interdependent decision making in which participants select strategies that seem rational in individualistic terms but that lead to socially undesirable outcomes."

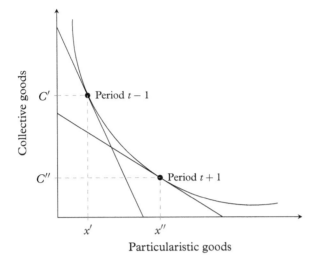

Figure 2.1 State preferences before and after institutional creation

commitments to policies they may be tempted to rescind by delegating authority to an independent agent whose preferences remain close to the desired outcome across all periods.[33] In the context of monetary policymaking, this agent assumes the form of a central bank with a strong aversion to inflation, whose autonomy is assured by a formal legal framework.

Extrapolating this insight to international institutions, we might expect states to "tie their hands" to the initial goals of cooperation by granting formal policy authority to an independent supranational bureaucracy.[34] Even if we accept that institutions are in fact capable of agency, however, the delegation solution suffers from a crucial impediment: Rules-based safeguards on bureaucratic autonomy are difficult to reliably enforce in the international context. As emphasized by the growing literature on informal governance in IR, states – especially the most powerful – routinely behave at variance with formal rules, creating a rift between how institutions are *meant* to function and how they *do* function.[35] In

[33] The delegation solution was first proposed by Rogoff (1985). The classic formulations of the time-inconsistency problem are Barro and Gordon (1983); Kydland and Prescott (1977).

[34] Hawkins et al. (2006); Martin (1992); Schneider and Tobin (2013).

[35] Abbott and Snidal (2000); Christiansen and Neuhold (2012); Christiansen and Piattoni (2003); Kilby (2013); Kleine (2013); McKeown (2009); Stone (2011); Westerwinter, Abbott, and Biersteker (2021).

the "anarchic" realm of international politics, there is no centralized authority above institutions capable of detecting and punishing infringements of policymaking rules. Nor, for similar sovereignty-related reasons, do institutions themselves boast robust mechanisms for enforcing these provisions. A system of decentralized, state-driven enforcement is possible but likely to encounter collective action problems: Compliance is, in effect, a public good for the membership. While civil society groups and other non-state actors can pressure governments to honor international commitments via domestic political channels, violations of policymaking rules tend to be difficult for them to observe and only tenuously connected to their main concerns and priorities.[36] The best hope for enforcement typically lies in the exercise of coercion by powerful states – the actors with the greatest capacity and often the strongest incentives to circumvent formal governance arrangements.

Breaching formal safeguards on policy autonomy is not costless, to be sure. As well as undermining institutional credibility and legitimacy – and thus further compromising performance – it can harm states' own reputation in international engagements.[37] At the design stage, therefore, states should endeavor to strike a balance between giving bureaucrats enough autonomy to successfully pursue institutional goals and retaining sufficient control to protect national interests without contravening policymaking rules.[38]

It is simply not feasible, however, to anticipate all future threats to state interests. Design decisions are made under conditions of uncertainty about the future state of the world, or what contract theorists call "procedural incompleteness." According to IR scholarship on incomplete contracting and rational institutional design, a logical response to this obstacle is to engineer flexibility into formal rules, for instance, in the form of finite duration, renegotiation, and adjustment clauses.[39] Yet in the case of policymaking rules, such provisos are strikingly absent. Rather, amendments typically require the consent of a sizable majority of members – the opposite of flexibility.

It should not be surprising, then, if states misjudge the optimal balance between autonomy and control in period $t-1$ and end up routinely flouting policymaking rules in period $t+1$. As recognized by the informal governance literature, such behavior – despite its costs –

[36] Dai (2005, 2007); Simmons (2009).
[37] Stone (2011). On the role of reputational concerns in motivating state compliance with international commitments, see Downs and Jones (2002); Guzman (2008); Simmons (2000).
[38] Hawkins et al. (2006).
[39] Cooley and Spruyt (2009); Koremenos, Lipson, and Snidal (2001); Koremenos (2016).

often represents the most expedient response to formal governance arrangements that become a hindrance to state interests and are arduous to change.[40] Somewhat surprisingly, though, regular and unanticipated deviations from policymaking rules are not predicted by the most well-developed theory of informal governance, namely, that of Stone.[41] In Stone's telling, powerful states allow formal structures to prevail in ordinary times in return for the right to exercise informal influence when their interests are affected. The implication is that rule violations will be limited, expected, and – forming part of an (implicit or explicit) "inter-temporal exchange" – largely uncontested by weaker states.[42] My framework paints a far more pervasive, unpredictable, and conflictual picture of informal governance.

The emergence of informal policy practices brings into tension an institution's de jure policy autonomy, or the policy autonomy specified in its formal rules, and its de facto policy autonomy, or the policy autonomy it enjoys in practice. By curtailing the scope for opportunistic state interventions, de facto policy autonomy should facilitate the provision of high levels of collective goods and low levels of particularistic goods (close to C' and x', respectively, in Figure 2.1). As de jure policy autonomy offers scant protection against capture, it is neither necessary nor sufficient for de facto policy autonomy: Its presence does not assure freedom from interference; its absence does not preclude the emergence of genuine independence. It should thus be weakly related to both de facto policy autonomy and performance.

Dimensions of Policy Autonomy

What exactly are de jure and de facto policy autonomy? I understand policy autonomy as *the ability of international bureaucrats to determine which mandate-related problems institutions focus on and what measures they take to address such issues in the absence of interference from states.* Similarly to existing definitions of institutional autonomy and related concepts, I identify states as the external actors against whom authority is asserted.[43] Although non-state actors could conceivably intervene in the policy process, their lack of formal representation usually restricts them to indirect influence through advocacy and lobbying activities.[44] In contrast to previous conceptualizations, I emphasize the

---

[40] Abbott and Snidal (2000); Kleine (2013); Westerwinter, Abbott, and Biersteker (2021).
[41] Stone (2008, 2011).   [42] Stone (2011, 14).
[43] For example, Abbott and Snidal (1998); Barnett and Finnemore (1999); Haftel and Thompson (2006).
[44] Tallberg et al. (2013, 2014).

Table 2.1 *Dimensions of policy autonomy*

		Evidence	
Dimension	**Indicators**	**De jure**	**De facto**
Agenda-setting powers	(1) Power to propose new policies (2) Power to prepare budget (3) Power to prepare governing body work program	Agenda-setting and budgetary rules	Real agenda-setting and budgetary practices
Ability to avoid state veto	(1) Decision procedure: ability stronger with majority voting than unanimity (2) Distribution of votes: ability stronger with unweighted than weighted voting	Decision rule (all governing bodies)	Real decision procedure (all governing bodies)
Access to non-state financing	(1) Contributions from non-state actors (2) Independently earned revenue (e.g., investments, interest, service fees)	Budgetary and financing rules	Financial statements

importance of choosing *which* problems institutions tackle as well as *how* to tackle them.

This definition suggests three distinct dimensions of policy autonomy, summarized in Table 2.1. An institution possesses a high degree of de jure policy autonomy if these dimensions are expressed in its formal rules and a high degree of de facto policy autonomy if it exhibits them in practice.

The first dimension is the *power of international bureaucrats to set the policy agenda*. Agenda setting has three main components: (1) the power to propose new programs, projects, regulations, standards, and other kinds of policies; (2) the power to draw up the annual budget; and (3) the power to prepare the governing body's work program.[45] By setting the agenda, bureaucrats define the status quo around which states negotiate with each other. This is important because, assuming at least some heterogeneity in states' policy preferences, bargains that might have been reached under one status quo may not be attainable

---

[45] Hooghe and Marks (2015); Hooghe, Lenz, and Marks (2019).

under another.[46] In other words, agenda-setting powers enable bureaucrats to circumscribe the range of policy choices available to states.

The precise extent to which agenda-setting powers translate into bureaucratic policy influence is determined by a second dimension of policy autonomy: the *ability to avoid a governmental veto*. This is primarily a function of the method by which governing bodies take policy decisions and, if a majoritarian procedure is employed, the distribution of votes. Consensus decision-making, in effect, permits every state to veto policy proposals.[47] Under majoritarian methods, veto power depends on both the decision threshold and the concentration of voting shares. At one extreme, the combination of simple majority voting and equal shares prevents any individual state from blocking proposals. At the opposite extreme, a supermajority requirement with weighted voting commonly confers a veto on states with high shares.[48]

The third dimension is *access to non-state sources of financing*. When states monopolize institutional funding, they can more easily thwart undesired policies by slashing the budget and placing restrictions on how contributions are used – a practice known as "earmarking" – or merely threatening such interventions. Alternative streams of income liberate institutions from this stifling dependency. Two are particularly important: (1) donations from non-state actors; and (2) earnings from investments, loans, services rendered, product sales, and other financial and commercial activities.

In sum, institutions enjoy higher levels of de facto policy autonomy – and thus, according to my argument, more robust protection against capture – when (1) bureaucrats wield agenda-setting powers; (2) individual states are unable veto policy proposals; and (3) nongovernmental sources of financing are available. They possess greater de jure policy autonomy – a markedly less reliable bulwark against capture – when their formal rules stipulate these features.

Alliances and Stealth: The Origins of Policy Autonomy

If policy autonomy cannot be "baked" into institutions through formal design, where *does* it come from? Analyses of the roots of bureaucratic independence mostly come from the institutional design literature in IR,

---

[46] Johnson (2014).
[47] Haftel and Thompson (2006); Hooghe, Lenz, and Marks (2019); Koremenos, Lipson, and Snidal (2001).
[48] The most prominent examples of this configuration are the IMF and the World Bank, in which the United States possesses enough votes to block major policy decisions.

Table 2.2 *Sources of de facto policy autonomy*

Source	Key dimensions	Causal mechanism	
Operational alliances	Quantity of alliances, depth of collaboration, breadth of stakeholders involved	⇒ Partners are willing and able to protect de facto policy autonomy	⇒ Higher political costs of interference for states ⇒ New information and expertise facilitate agenda setting ⇒ Increased material support for institutions
Governance tasks	Designing interventions, allocating resources, implementing operations	⇒ Costly for states to monitor institutions, creating information asymmetries	⇒ Difficult for states to propose new policies, oppose unwanted ones ⇒ Institutions use specialized knowledge to earn own revenue

focusing on the de jure form of the concept and assuming that states by and large respect formal barriers against interference.[49] A notable exception are rogue-agency theories, which, as discussed in Chapter 1, trace autonomy to persistent information asymmetries between states and bureaucrats. Although theoretically cogent, the rogue-agency view raises a series of further questions: Where do information asymmetries themselves originate? Why do they vary across institutions, as must be the case if performance differs? If they are small – and hence states can closely monitor bureaucrats – will autonomy always be limited?

In this section, I propose an alternative account of the origins of de facto policy autonomy that offers clear answers to these questions. My analysis proceeds from a simple premise: Just as institutions are given distinct mandates, they are subject to varying operational demands, in terms of both the functions they are expected to discharge and the resources – material, informational, cognitive, organizational, administrative – they need to do so. My central claim is that the processes through which institutions pursue these requirements – subtle processes often neglected by scholars – have important consequences for their capacity to resist state interference. As summarized in Table 2.2, I posit that de facto policy autonomy is more likely to emerge when

---

[49] Johnson (2014); Haftel and Thompson (2006); Hooghe and Marks (2015); Hooghe, Lenz, and Marks (2019).

institutions exhibit two operational characteristics: (1) they draw support from a strong and extensive network of alliances with subnational and supranational actors; and (2) they exercise governance tasks with high monitoring costs for states. Independence is forged, I submit, with the "hand" of alliances and the "cloak" of stealth.

The Hand of Alliance: Collaboration with Non-State Actors

Operational alliances are sustained patterns of collaboration between international institutions and actors above and below the state – including NGOs, businesses, transgovernmental networks, and other international institutions – involving the shared exercise of authority.[50] Common examples include the recruitment of local NGOs to oversee and deliver humanitarian assistance; the joint development of corporate best practices and codes of conduct with industry associations; the delegation of standard-setting functions to networks of national regulatory agencies; and the co-implementation of development projects with bilateral aid agencies. These arrangements are based on a convergence of goals and interests. Institutions fill "gaps" in their operational capacities with partner resources and skills; partners share institutions' aims and benefit from the material assistance, contacts, normative guidance, public profile, and legitimacy that come with collaboration. Operational alliances are thus a function of both the "demand" for particular capacities by institutions and the "supply" of non-state stakeholders with the willingness and the ability to meet these needs.

While recent IR scholarship has highlighted the potential of operational alliances to enhance institutions' power and authority, it has paid less attention to their crucial role in cultivating and safeguarding policy autonomy.[51] This is perhaps unsurprising, as collaboration is typically initiated outside the regular policy process and framed as a functional solution to institutional capacity deficits.[52] Moreover, as discussed in Chapter 7, scholarship on domestic administrative rulemaking generally

---

[50] Closely related concepts include "orchestration arrangements," "delegated governance," "network governance," "sectoral governance," and "regulatory standard-setting." See Abbott and Snidal (2009a,b); Coen and Thatcher (2008); Héritier and Lehmkuhl (2008); Raustiala (2002); Slaughter (2005). Following Lall (2021), I use "operational alliances" as an umbrella term.

[51] Abbott and Snidal (2009b); Abbott et al. (2015, 2016). However, some of these studies do make the complementary point that alliances allow institutions to "bypass" states by directly supplying public goods to private actors.

[52] Mattli and Seddon (2015).

treats links with societal stakeholders as a constraint on the discretion of bureaucratic agencies.[53]

Operational alliances represent a wholly different form of stakeholder engagement. As well as opportunities to influence institutional activities, they provide partners with material and nonmaterial benefits and facilitate the achievement of shared objectives. Moreover, to the extent that they are visible to the public, they establish reputational links between partners and institutions.[54] Consequently, they give partners a direct stake in institutional performance, incentivizing them to assist bureaucrats in addressing not only the *practical* challenge of undercapacity but also the *political* challenge of state capture. In other words, operational alliances contains the makings of powerful and enduring coalitions for de facto policy autonomy.[55]

In particular, partners can foster de facto policy autonomy in three ways. First, and perhaps most importantly, they can raise the political costs – and thus reduce the overall payoff – of capture for states. This can be achieved via several means, including lobbying policymakers at the domestic level; using frames, symbols, and stories to widen issue resonance and shape preference formation; disseminating information about the costs of capture and the benefits of effective performance; and assembling counter-coalitions of states with opposing interests.[56] Second, partners can ply bureaucrats with information and expertise that strengthen their agenda-setting abilities (particularly when they undertake technically complex functions).[57] Third, partners can provide material support for institutions in the form of financial contributions and payments for products and services, preventing governments from monopolizing funding.

Patterns of operational collaboration are not identical across institutions, however. Rather, they vary in ways that significantly affect the motivation and capacity of partners to pursue autonomy-enhancing strategies. Three alliance characteristics are particularly consequential in this regard:

---

[53] Some studies, however, have argued that such ties in fact enhance bureaucratic autonomy. See Broz (2015); Carpenter (2001).

[54] Lall (2021).

[55] For examples of how alliances with non-state actors can augment the autonomy of international institutions, see Burley and Mattli (1993); Newman (2008, 2010). Akin claims about stakeholder access to institutions are made by Hawkins and Jacoby (2006).

[56] Some of these tactics are used by (domestic and transnational) advocacy groups to influence state behavior. See Keck and Sikkink (1998); Murdie (2014); Risse, Ropp, and Sikkink (1999); Simmons (2009).

[57] Lall (2017).

1. *Depth*. While partnerships between international institutions and non-state actors have become increasingly common in recent years, they sometimes amount to little more than symbolic arrangements formed to satisfy top-down or external pressures for stakeholder engagement.[58] Only when partners partake in the substantive exchange of resources and services at one or more of the five principal stages of the policy process – agenda setting, formulation, monitoring, implementation, enforcement – will they have a serious stake in institutional performance and hence autonomy.

2. *Quantity*. The number of alliances forged by institutions determines the potential size of stakeholder coalitions for autonomy. Other things equal, larger coalitions will be capable of mobilizing more intense pressure on states to refrain from opportunism and of supplying more generous material assistance to institutions.

3. *Breadth*. When alliances involve multiple types of stakeholders – and not exclusively, for instance, civil society groups or businesses – pro-autonomy coalitions will be broader. As stakeholders have different and complementary strengths as guardians of autonomy, this should again reduce the risk of capture. For instance, civil society groups tend to be particularly adept at mobilizing pressure on policymakers and orchestrating publicity campaigns (and are sometimes recruited by institutions for these specific activities);[59] research organizations and fellow international institutions at supplying information and technical knowledge that facilitates bureaucratic agenda setting;[60] and corporations and charitable foundations at furnishing financial resources.[61]

To summarize, operational alliances should provide the strongest protection for de facto policy autonomy when they engage a large and varied set of nongovernmental stakeholders in substantive governance activities.

The Cloak of Stealth: Governance Tasks and Monitoring Costs

The substantive tasks institutions carry out in pursuit of their goals have received surprisingly little attention from scholars. Reflecting the deep intellectual imprint of neoliberal institutionalism, the IR literature has tended to focus on more general and abstract purposes served

---

[58] Abbott et al. (2016).
[59] Most of the literature on domestic political advocacy focuses on NGOs and other civil society actors.
[60] Mattli and Seddon (2015).
[61] Micklewright and Wright (2005); Urrea and Pedraza-Martinez (2019).

Table 2.3 *Common governance tasks performed by international institutions*

Governance task	Example	Monitoring costs
Facilitating agreements	WTO provides a forum for states to formulate and update international trade agreements	Low
Monitoring compliance	ILO requires states to regularly report on their implementation of ratified conventions	Low
Capacity building	UNIDO transfers information, skills, technology, and equipment to developing countries	Low
Designing interventions	IMF attaches binding economic policy conditions to its financial assistance programs	High
Allocating resources	World Bank provides loans to low- and middle-income countries for development projects	High
Implementing operations	UNICEF delivers humanitarian and developmental assistance to children around the world	High

by institutions, such as reducing the uncertainty and transaction costs of international cooperation (see Chapter 1). Even exceptions to this pattern have embraced the paradigm's functionalist spirit, analyzing governance tasks as efficient solutions to cooperation dilemmas confronting states.[62] I argue, in contrast, that some tasks *impede* the pursuit of state interests by exacerbating the classic agency problems of hidden information and hidden action. The key analytical feature of these duties is that they are costly for states to monitor, whether because they involve activities that are difficult to observe and measure or because they require the application of specialized knowledge.

Institutions may be assigned a variety of functions by states, depending on the political priorities and practical possibilities of the era in which they were founded.[63] The following six tasks, whose monitoring costs vary widely for states, are particularly common (see Table 2.3 for a summary):[64]

---

[62] Abbott and Snidal (1998, 2000); Hawkins et al. (2006); Koremenos, Lipson, and Snidal (2001).

[63] One can identify several distinct clusters of institutions created at similar times and assigned similar tasks, such as regional development banks in the 1960s, UN funds and programs in the 1970s, and global health partnerships in the early 2000s.

[64] Abbott and Snidal (1998); Cogan, Hurd, and Johnstone (2016); Hawkins et al. (2006); Koremenos (2016).

1. *Facilitating agreements.* The task of providing a stable forum for states to interact, build consensus, and develop rules, standards, and norms tends to be straightforward for them to monitor. Bureaucrats are mainly required to perform hosting and convening functions, such as providing physical space, administrative assistance, and background information for meetings between government delegates, who can directly observe task execution. Institutions whose primary task is facilitating agreements, such as the World Trade Organization (WTO) and the United Nations Conference on Trade and Development (UNCTAD), therefore tend to have small secretariats (based predominantly at their headquarters) and to describe themselves as "member-driven."[65]

2. *Monitoring compliance.* The provision of information on state compliance with international agreements – traditionally regarded as a central function of international institutions – is also, by its nature, readily observable. Since institutions rarely possess the capacity or authority to directly observe compliance, moreover, this task typically involves soliciting information from states themselves.[66] The International Labour Organization (ILO), for instance, monitors adherence to its conventions by asking ratifying states to periodically submit reports on their legal and practical steps toward implementation.

3. *Capacity building.* A common task among UN institutions is the transfer of information, skills, technology, equipment, and other kinds of human and physical capital to states for capacity-building purposes. This form of support, widely known as "technical assistance," is requested by and implemented jointly with recipient governments, allowing for relatively easy oversight. One of the largest sources of technical assistance in the UN System is the United Nations Industrial Development Organization (UNIDO), which currently supports more than 600 projects spanning almost every developing country.[67]

4. *Designing interventions.* Some institutions go beyond capacity building by directly shaping the content of domestic policy and legislation. This task tends to require more specialized knowledge and broader bureaucratic discretion, rendering it more difficult for states to invigilate. A prominent example are the conditions attached to IMF

---

[65] E.g., https://www.wto.org/english/thewto_e/whatis_e/tif_e/org1_e.htm; https://unctad.org/es/node/2464 [Both last accessed August 11, 2021].

[66] As Stone (2011, 25) points out, "Most intergovernmental organizations, as for example the WTO, rely upon member states to put violations of rules on the agenda: they rely on 'fire alarms' rather than 'police patrols.'" This is also true of most international agreements that contain monitoring provisions. See Koremenos (2016, Ch. 9).

[67] https://open.unido.org/projects [Last accessed March 5, 2020].

loan programs, which are crafted on the basis of complex information about local economic and political circumstances and policy expertise that recipient governments frequently lack.[68]

5. *Allocating resources.* The primary task of international financial institutions (IFIs) (including the IMF) is to pool and allocate material resources for macroeconomic purposes, usually via loans, lines of credit, grants, or investments. This task is also expensive for states to monitor: Identifying and developing viable projects and programs to finance requires issue-specific expertise as well as detailed knowledge of the recipient country or entity, which normally restricts state delegates to a marginal role in the process. The Executive Boards of the IMF and the World Bank, for example, have been repeatedly criticized for "rubber-stamping" staff proposals.[69]

6. *Implementing operations.* The implementation of physical operations in the field, such as peacekeeping and emergency relief missions, is inherently difficult to observe – bureaucratic activities tend to be dispersed and remote from headquarters – and generally requires local information and organizational competences lacked by states, facilitating agency slack. The United Nations Children's Fund (UNICEF), for instance, delivers humanitarian and developmental assistance to children around the world via a network of 155 country offices and seven regional offices, in which 84 percent of its approximately 14,000 staff are based.[70]

Three caveats about this list should be noted. First, it is not intended to be exhaustive. Excluded are tasks exercised by few institutions, such as resolving disputes and authorizing sanctions, as well as essentially passive functions that institutions perform simply by virtue of existing, such as representing the international community and embodying norms. Second, some tasks could be split into a set of narrower functions. Pooling and distributing resources, for instance, are sometimes treated as distinct tasks.[71] I avoid such disaggregation in part for the sake of parsimony and in part because the narrower tasks tend to entail similar oversight challenges for states. Third, even for a single task, monitoring costs can vary over time and across institutions. Some IMF program proposals, to take one example, may be subject to more intense Executive Board scrutiny than others. On the whole, however, I expect the first three tasks to be less costly to monitor than the last three.

---

[68] Martin (2006).   [69] Carin and Wood (2005); Woods (2001).
[70] United Nations System Chief Executives Board for Coordination (2021).
[71] Abbott and Snidal (1998). For a more disaggregated list of tasks, see Koremenos (2016).

How do these differences affect de facto policy autonomy? The mechanism is straightforward. When monitoring costs are high, states will, on average, acquire less information about the design, execution, and impact of operational activities.[72] This expands the scope for hidden bureaucratic action while hindering states' ability to both *propose* new policies and *oppose* proposals that deviate from their interests. Uncertainty about distributional consequences also deters states from imposing severe budgetary penalties on institutions for unwanted behavior, encouraging a more risk-averse approach to resource allocation. Moreover, when monitoring costs arise from the need for task-specific knowledge, bureaucrats may find opportunities to earn independent revenue through the sale of specialized products and services and the provision of expert advice.

This line of reasoning shares a key tenet of the rogue-agency perspective: Information asymmetries between states and bureaucrats weaken the former's capacity to control the latter. In distinction to this view, however, it implies that the consequences for performance are *positive* rather than negative. This difference stems, crucially, from an acknowledgment of the Jekyll and Hyde problem – a recognition that, in the context of delegation to international institutions, the principal faces a more severe moral hazard problem than the agent.

Feedback Effects and Performance Pathways

Up to this point, I have assumed that the direction of causation runs from operational alliances and governance tasks to de facto policy autonomy and then on to performance. But could it flow the other way? That is, could performance influence de facto policy autonomy, which itself influences operational alliances and governance tasks? If so, what are the implications for the overall relationships between these four variables? Acknowledging that performance and de facto policy autonomy are causally complex phenomena that both shape and are shaped by a multiplicity of factors, I argue that their positive association is gradually reinforced by a continuous feedback loop. In contrast, de facto policy autonomy is unlikely to consistently impact either operational alliances or governance tasks.

De Facto Policy Autonomy and Performance

The sustained translation of de facto policy autonomy into effective performance can stimulate further growth in such independence via

---

[72] As Hawkins et al. (2006, 36–37) note, "The function or task assigned to the agent may alter the terms of the contract and the ability of the principal to monitor and sanction that agent."

three mechanisms. First, by advancing the collective interests that originally motivated cooperation, it can raise the *opportunity costs* of capture for states. Second, it enables institutions to develop a reputation for competence, efficiency, and political neutrality – for "getting things done" while remaining "above politics," so to speak.[73] This status increases the *political costs* of capture, which, as noted earlier, can include damage to states' own reputation and credibility in international interactions. Third, improvements in performance increase the "return" on donations to institutions, encouraging non-state actors to provide additional material support.[74]

Although these mechanisms do not eliminate the Jekyll and Hyde problem, they can sufficiently mitigate the net benefits of capture to permit the expansion and consolidation of bureaucratic policy influence.[75] In some instances, they may additionally lead to a broadening of institutional authority, including the assumption of new functional and substantive responsibilities, as states and other stakeholders become increasingly confident in the bureaucracy's ability to execute delegated tasks.

At the other end of the spectrum, when low levels of de facto policy autonomy erode performance, the three converse mechanisms can further suppress discretion. That is, declining performance can reduce (1) the opportunity costs of capture by depressing the collective benefits produced by institutions; (2) the political costs of capture by fostering institutional reputations for incompetence, inefficiency, and politicization; and (3) the gains from financially supporting institutions. Furthermore, it may lead to a form of reverse mission creep whereby core functions migrate to other institutions as stakeholders grow frustrated with persistently suboptimal performance outcomes.

The existence of feedback effects implies that institutions follow distinctive performance pathways as they evolve, illustrated in Figure 2.2. For simplification, I assume that institutions begin ($t = 0$) with

---

[73] On the importance of reputation for international institutions, see Daugirdas (2014, 2019); Johnstone (2010). Interestingly, these studies come from the field of international law rather than IR, which has focused on the reputation of *states*. For an analysis of how reputations for effectiveness can enhance the autonomy of domestic bureaucratic agencies, see Carpenter (2001).

[74] Lall (2021).

[75] Some rogue-agency analyses also suggest that good performance can bolster autonomy, though postulate increased trust in institutions as the causal mechanism. Hawkins et al. (2006, 32), for instance, note that institutions "can demonstrate to states through past successes ... that they can be trusted with new tasks that obviate the need for a new IO. In this way agents can convince states to delegate new authority and resources to them rather than act unilaterally, cooperate without delegating, or delegate to a new IO."

medium levels of performance and de facto policy autonomy.[76] The high-performance pathway starts with rising levels of de facto policy autonomy inducing improvements in performance. In the short ($t = s$) and the medium ($t = m$) term, the two variables positively reinforce each other in a virtuous circle. In the long run ($t = l$), the feedback process exhausts itself – there is an upper limit to each variable – resulting in convergence toward a high-performance, high-autonomy equilibrium. In the low-performance pathway, declining de facto policy autonomy puts downward pressure on performance, with the two variables then progressively weakening each other in a vicious cycle. As feedback eventually diminishes, institutions hone in on a low-performance, low-autonomy equilibrium. Finally, it is possible that de facto policy autonomy remains close to its original level, in which case long-run equilibrium values of each variable should also remain middling (in this stylized example).

The positive association between de facto policy autonomy and performance thus varies in subtle ways over the institutional life cycle. Figure 2.3 plots this relationship over the short, medium, and long runs (corresponding to periods s, m, and l, respectively in Figure 2.2). In the long run, values of de facto policy autonomy and performance lie on the identity ($x = y$) line, which implies that they have the same rate of change. As the timeframe shortens, the slope becomes steeper, meaning that de facto policy autonomy is rising at a faster pace. In addition, as indicated by the solid line segments, the expected range of both variables in the high- and low-performance pathways becomes less extreme. In the medium-performance pathway, by contrast, all values remain near the graph's centroid across the three periods. I describe these relationships formally in Appendix A.2.

Must each pathway begin with changes in de facto policy autonomy? Could, for example, an exogenous increase in performance – an increase precipitated by some variable other than de facto policy autonomy – set institutions on a high-autonomy, high-performance trajectory? From a theoretical perspective, this is unlikely for two reasons. First, since the hypothesized feedback mechanisms depend on stakeholders recognizing a causal connection between performance and de facto policy autonomy, exogenous shocks to the former should make negligible difference to the latter. Second, due to the Jekyll and Hyde problem, such shocks are not guaranteed to last long enough to meaningfully alter the opportunity or political costs of capture. In short, I expect shifts in de facto policy autonomy to be the pivotal catalyst in the long-run evolution of performance.

---

[76] Altering this assumption does not change the overall analytical conclusions.

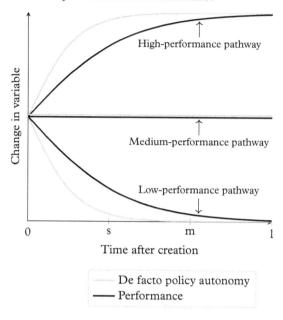

Figure 2.2 Pathways to varying autonomy–performance equilibria

De Facto Policy Autonomy and Its Other Sources

Comparable feedback effects are less likely to characterize the relationship between de facto policy autonomy and its posited operational sources. As noted earlier, the formation of operational alliances mainly reflects the supply and demand of particular capacities required by institutions – variables with little connection to the three dimensions of policy autonomy.[77] Furthermore, since this process usually involves informal interactions with prospective partners and requires no authorization by governing bodies, it is not meaningfully facilitated by regular forms of policy influence. It is conceivable that high levels of de facto policy autonomy could aid the establishment of highly formalized alliances; in general, though, low levels should not present an obstacle to operational collaboration.

Nor is the causal arrow likely to point from de facto policy autonomy to governance tasks. The functional duties initially assigned to institutions tend to be "sticky," exhibiting little responsiveness to the balance of policy influence between states and bureaucrats. Rogue-agency analyses portray autonomous institutions as prone to mission creep, incremen-

---

[77] Abbott and Snidal (2009b); Abbott et al. (2015).

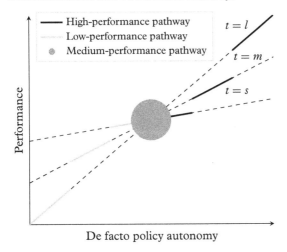

Figure 2.3 Relationship between de facto policy autonomy and performance at different points in time

Notes: The labels refer to the time periods plotted on the *x*-axis in Figure 2.2. In the medium-performance pathway, values of both variables remain within the shaded circular area in all periods.

tally branching out into new activities, issue areas, and territories as their leeway grows. However, it is less common for institutions to assume major new functional responsibilities such as the six tasks delineated by my typology, which are closely tied to their mandates and administrative, operational, and governance structures.[78] Some of these tasks, moreover, are difficult to take on because they are associated with incumbent-favoring network effects (e.g., standard setting) or barriers to entry such as high fixed costs (e.g., allocating material resources) and the need for specialized expertise (e.g., designing policy interventions).[79] In Chapter 3, I provide evidence that task portfolios tend to remain stable over time from the Performance of International Institutions Project (PIIP) dataset.

---

[78] Even regular forms of mission creep are less prevalent than rogue-agency theorists suggest. As Jupille, Mattli, and Snidal (2013, 46) point out, institutions often "actively resist incorporation of [a] new issue (with attendant changes to its architecture, scope or membership) if it is not consistent with its organizational culture or will interfere with its activities."

[79] Lipscy (2017).

Observable Implications

Gathering together these theoretical strands, we can derive a host of observable implications – patterns we should expect to see in the real world – from the framework. To bring some analytical order to these expectations, I distinguish two dimensions along which they vary (see Table 2.4). The first is their *level of analysis* (horizontal axis), which refers to whether they concern the aggregate relationship between variables of theoretical interest (macro-level implications) or the specific behaviors, preferences, and beliefs driving these relationships (micro-level implications). The second is their *explanandum*, which refers to whether they concern the determinants of performance or of de facto policy autonomy. When interacted, these dimensions produce four distinct types of implications, which I elaborate in the rest of this section.

The framework yields three macro-level propositions regarding the sources of performance (top left, cell I in Table 2.4). First, there is a positive relationship between de facto policy autonomy – which is higher when bureaucrats set the policy agenda, governing bodies take decisions by (unweighted) majority voting, and states do not monopolize institutional funding – and performance. Second, there is no association between de jure policy autonomy – which is higher when formal rules specify the three previous characteristics – and de facto policy autonomy. Third, a corollary of the first two hypotheses is that de jure policy autonomy and performance are also weakly related.

These relationships should be underpinned by a series of micro-level behavioral, strategic, and political processes (Table 2.4, top right, cell II). States, especially the most powerful, should predominantly pursue collective interests at the institutional design phase (period $t - 1$) but individual interests once institutions come to life (period $t + 1$), opportunistically attempting to intervene in the policy process with scarce regard for procedural rules. The success of such attempts should be a function of the de facto – not de jure – policy autonomy enjoyed by bureaucrats, whose own preferences and patterns of behavior should more closely reflect institutional objectives. A high degree of de facto policy autonomy should set in motion improvements in performance that eventually reinforce this discretion by elevating the costs of capture for states; a low degree should have the inverse effects.

Turning to the second part of the argument, three macro-level hypotheses regarding the determinants of de facto policy autonomy present themselves (Table 2.4, bottom left, cell III). First, this variable has a positive association with the depth, quantity, and breadth of operational alliances. Second, it has a similar relationship with the exercise of governance tasks that are expensive for states to monitor,

Table 2.4 *Explaining institutional performance: Summary of observable implications*

<table>
<tr><th rowspan="2">Explanandum (what is being explained)</th><th></th><th colspan="2">Level of analysis</th></tr>
<tr><th></th><th>Macro level</th><th>Micro level</th></tr>
<tr>
<td rowspan="1">Performance</td>
<td></td>
<td>(I)

• Positive relationship between DFPA (i.e., bureaucratic agenda-setting powers, ability to avoid state veto, access to non-state financing) and performance
• No consistent relationship between DJPA (i.e., formal rule-based equivalent of DFPA) and DFPA
• No consistent relationship between DJPA and performance</td>
<td>(II)

• States pursue collective interests before institutions are founded but national interests subsequently
• States routinely attempt to interfere in the policy process by flouting formal rules; their success depends on degree of DFPA, not DJPA
• Preferences and behavior of international bureaucrats more closely aligned with institutional goals
• Feedback effects between performance and DFPA (triggered by changes in the latter)</td>
</tr>
<tr>
<td rowspan="1">De facto policy autonomy</td>
<td></td>
<td>(III)

• Positive relationship between depth, quantity, and breadth of operational alliances and DFPA
• Positive relationship between exercise of governance tasks with high monitoring costs (e.g., designing interventions, implementing operations, allocating material resources) and DFPA
• No consistent relationship between exercise of governance tasks with low monitoring costs (e.g., facilitating agreements, monitoring compliance, capacity building) and DFPA</td>
<td>(IV)

• Operational partners pursue anti-capture strategies, e.g., lobbying domestic policymakers, disseminating information, supplying information, expertise, funds
• When governance tasks are costly to monitor, information asymmetries limit state influence at key stages of policy process
• When governance tasks are easy to monitor, states exercise close control and oversight of policy process
• Limited feedback from DFPA to operational alliances or governance tasks</td>
</tr>
</table>

Notes: DFPA = de facto policy autonomy; DJPA = de jure policy autonomy.

such as designing policy interventions, implementing field operations, and allocating material resources. It is weakly associated, on the other hand, with the exercise of easily observable tasks, such as facilitating international agreements, monitoring policy compliance, and providing capacity-building support.

Finally, a sequence of more granular steps should line the causal pathway from operational alliances and governance tasks to de facto policy autonomy (Table 2.4, bottom right, cell IV). When alliances are deep, abundant, and broad, we should observe partners pursuing varied anti-capture strategies, including lobbying domestic policymakers, disseminating information about institutional activities and performance, and equipping bureaucrats with information, expertise, and material resources. The exercise of hard-to-monitor governance tasks should give rise to information asymmetries that limit opportunities for states to table and veto policy proposals and to dictate the allocation of institutional resources. Tasks with low monitoring costs, conversely, should facilitate robust governmental oversight and control of the policy process.

Note on Scope Conditions

Given the framework's emphasis on the dangers of state capture, its observable implications may seem to apply exclusively to intergovernmental organizations (IGOs). It is important to note, though, that it is not only IGOs that are subject to such interference; it is *any* type of institution with which states are actively involved. Such engagement can take several forms, including contributing financial resources; participating in decision-making processes; lobbying or exerting pressure on bureaucrats; and joining operational alliances (or other collaborative arrangements). Although IGOs, by virtue of their membership, engage with states in all these ways, other kinds of institutions may do so to comparable degrees. As discussed in Chapter 3, the PIIP contains a small number of international nongovernmental organizations (INGOs) and public–private partnerships (PPPs) that states have played a central role in establishing, financing, and governing. The argument's implications apply no less to these institutions – an increasingly important part of the global governance landscape – than to the IGOs in the dataset.

Indeed, to the extent that IGOs, INGOs, and PPPs exhibit distinctive operational and policymaking practices, the framework may shed useful light on how membership structures impact performance. Many PPPs and INGOs, for instance, collaborate with and draw significant funding from nongovernmental stakeholders with seats in their governing body. These relationships can encourage the formation of robust operational alliances and dilute governmental agenda-setting and veto powers, expanding bureaucratic room for maneuver in the policy process. Chapter 5's case study of global health institutions offers clear examples of this pattern in the form of Gavi and the Global Fund to Fight AIDS, Tuberculosis and Malaria (GFATM), PPPs that bring together governments, international institutions, civil society groups, pharmaceutical manufacturers, and research bodies.

The theory is less germane to institutions that lack manifestations of bureaucratization and formalization. As noted in Chapter 1, treaties, conventions, protocols, and resolutions cannot meaningfully be described as "actors" with the capacity to deviate from state interests. While some treaties and conventions are administered by a secretariat, this entity is usually part of an associated IGO and restricted to narrow administrative functions, enjoying little (de jure or de facto) policy autonomy. A more ambiguous theoretical fit are so-called informal IGOs such as the G20 and the Proliferation Security Initiative (PSI), which are not legalized through a treaty and rely on individual governments or other IGOs for secretarial support.[80] The argument's applicability to these institutions depends on exactly where they reside on the informal–formal spectrum. In general, the more precisely defined an informal IGO's objectives and the more institutionalized its bureaucratic structure, the more traction the framework will offer analysts.

A second set of scope conditions pertains to the role of formal institutional design. The argument should not be interpreted as dismissing all design features as tangential or irrelevant to performance. To the contrary, the operational demands I have highlighted as a key source of de facto policy autonomy can be understood as a product of design, broadly defined (albeit one whose downstream consequences may not be apparent in period $t-1$). The broader theoretical takeaway is that formal rules are unlikely to have a significant bearing on performance when they are subject to chronic enforcement problems, that is, when they are neither self-enforcing nor backed by strong institutionalized compliance mechanisms.[81] Since rules governing the division of labor between states and bureaucrats in the policy process fall squarely into this category, they should not be expected to spare institutions from performance troubles arising from the Jekyll and Hyde problem.

---

[80] Vabulas and Snidal (2013).
[81] Dispute settlement and sanctioning systems are examples of formal structures with relatively robust enforcement arrangements.

Different Assumptions, Similar Implications

The framework's implications are not contingent upon some of the simplifying assumptions I have made for the purposes of theoretical exposition. Three such premises, in particular, deserve closer scrutiny. First, following rogue-agency theories and other strands of the institutional literature in IR, I have treated states – or at least powerful ones – as holding uniform preferences over policy outcomes in period $t+1$. In reality, of course, preference heterogeneity is far from uncommon, and it is entirely possible that some subset of states consistently favors collectively oriented policies. Nevertheless, so long as at least one powerful state stands to profit from particularistic policies, the argument's implications will remain similar. If only weak states prefer collective goods, powerful ones have little reason to alter their behavior. If some powerful states share this preference, they can benefit from "logrolling" with others, for instance, by trading concessions, issuing side payments, or agreeing to support the policy favored by the most interested party with the expectation of receiving similar treatment when its own preferences are intense – outcomes that are still suboptimal from a performance perspective.[82]

Second, a similar point applies to bureaucratic preferences, which I have also assumed to be uniform. Bureaucrats may have mixed motives such that they derive some utility from policies that damage performance or that some subset always favors these outcomes (for instance, because it includes nationals of a beneficiary country). Provided that bureaucrats are *on average* more supportive than states of policies that promote effective performance – as my analysis of each group's incentives suggests – de facto policy autonomy will remain positively related to performance. Put differently, the theory's implications would only be altered if the proportion of bureaucrats whose preferences substantially deviate from performance-optimal policies were higher than that of states.

Third, the argument has assumed that institutional goals remain constant over time (i.e., throughout period $t + n$). Changes to stated objectives normally require constitutional amendments with high approval thresholds, rendering them rare in practice. While forays into new areas and activities modify the baseline against which we should assess performance, they should not fundamentally alter the incentives facing

---

[82] It is conceivable, as Copelovitch (2010) argues, that all powerful states hold weak policy preferences, creating a void in which bureaucrats enjoy free rein. Such situations are fleeting, however, lasting only until states decide to address a policy issue over which they *do* have intense preferences. Even in this brief window, bureaucrats may refrain from exercising autonomy for fear that their actions will be overturned or punished in the future.

states or bureaucrats. States will still derive benefits from policies that advance particularistic interests; bureaucrats will still have reason to favor policies that further institutional aims – whether they wish to maximize their budget, their authority, or goal attainment itself. Accordingly, the framework's microfoundations should be sufficiently flexible to accommodate mission creep and changes in institutions' operative and process aims.

Finally, one assumption on which my claims about de facto policy autonomy may appear to depend is that institutions are equipped with a substantial bureaucracy. It may seem unrealistic for small secretariats to, for example, exercise agenda-setting powers or cultivate operational sources of autonomy. Although institutions may derive some protection against capture from "strength in numbers," a sizable contingent of staff is by no means a necessary condition for independence. The administrative and substantive knowledge needed to formulate policy proposals and draw up budgets and work programs may be concentrated in a coterie of well-qualified officials. Similarly, provided that a sufficient pool of potential partners exists, the formation of operational alliances is mainly a function of bureaucratic entrepreneurialism and effort rather than size per se. The key resources required for exercising governance tasks with high monitoring costs for states are local information, issue-specific expertise, and specialized organizational capacities (though large numbers of field staff are sometimes essential for implementing operations). Indeed, the case studies presented in Chapters 4 and 5 contain examples both of lean secretariats deploying agenda-setting powers, forging broad operational alliances, and performing hard-to-monitor tasks and of bloated bureaucracies confined to a marginal role in the policy process and failing to collaborate with non-state stakeholders.

It should be noted, however, that *changes* in staff numbers are often a lagging indicator of *changes* in de facto policy autonomy. As discussed previously, performance gains resulting from growth in autonomy may provoke expansions in operational activities and competences, which sometimes necessitate a larger workforce. Conversely, performance problems stemming from shrinking autonomy can precipitate operational and substantive contractions, reducing the need for staff. Furthermore, rogue-agency theorists plausibly observe that states tend to favor smaller secretariats that consume fewer resources, whereas bureaucrats tend to see larger ones as more conducive to their objectives.[83] Accordingly, a shift in the balance of policy influence toward bureaucrats will often be followed by additional recruitment; movement

---

[83] Vaubel (2006); Vaubel, Dreher, and Soylu (2007).

toward states is more likely to result in layoffs and nonreplacements. Again, both scenarios are illustrated in this book's case studies.

Conclusion

This chapter began with two quotations, one portraying international institutions as passive, lifeless vehicles through which powerful nations pursue narrow domestic agendas, the other depicting them as "monsters" capable of behavior that not only strays from expectations but actively damages state interests. The contrasting perspectives that underpin these representations capture important aspects of how institutions function. The realist approach rightly identifies powerful countries as central protagonists in the story of institutional performance and highlights their propensity for exploiting institutions to further particularistic interests. The rogue-agency approach is correct to conceive of institutions as distinct actors with interests and ambitions of their own, the pursuit of which can bring them into conflict with state principals.

I have argued, however, that neither perspective fully captures the reality of how international institutions perform. Institutions are not the mere playthings of powerful states, as realists characterize them; they carry the potential to exert agency in ways that fundamentally challenge their creators' interests. At the same time, assertions of bureaucratic independence do not render institutions "Frankensteins" intent on tearing up their mandates and reaping global destruction, per rogue-agency theories. Somewhat paradoxically, by defying the wishes of powerful states, bureaucrats can bring institutions *closer* to fulfilling their raison d'être.

In particular, two claims distinguish the theoretical framework expounded in this chapter from alternative approaches. First, states have incentives to establish institutions for the purpose of advancing collective interests but then to utilize them in the service of parochial national interests – a dynamic shift I dub the Jekyll and Hyde problem. The degree of de facto policy autonomy wielded by international bureaucrats, whose interests typically remain closer to the original goals of interstate cooperation, is hence a critical determinant of institutional performance.

Second, the Jekyll and Hyde problem cannot be solved by designing institutions to possess high levels of policy autonomy, a tried and tested solution to analogous commitment problems at the domestic level. Owing to the difficulty of both anticipating future threats to national interests and reliably enforcing formal governance arrangements, de jure policy autonomy offers no guarantee of de facto policy autonomy. Instead, the latter emerges when bureaucrats (1) forge robust, copious, and diverse operational alliances with actors above and below the state; and (2) carry out governance tasks that states cannot easily oversee.

An array of observable implications follow from the framework. These include both macro-level hypotheses concerning the relationship between key variables of interest – most notably that de facto policy autonomy has a positive association with performance, the quantity, depth, and breadth of operational alliances, and the costs of monitoring governance tasks – and micro-level, process-related expectations regarding the actions, intentions, and attitudes of states, bureaucrats, partners, and other non-state stakeholders.

The value of a positive theory ultimately hinges on its explanatory power. The next three chapters gauge the framework's empirical purchase, conducting a wide-ranging, multimethod investigation of its observable implications. Chapter 3 evaluates its macro-level propositions, subjecting them to a succession of statistical tests based on the PIIP. The subsequent two chapters pivot from quantitative to qualitative analysis. Chapter 4 presents a detailed comparative case study of the three central institutions of the global food security regime: the Food and Agriculture Organization (FAO), the World Food Programme (WFP), and the International Fund for Agricultural Development (IFAD). Chapter 5 broadens the empirical horizon, undertaking a similar comparison of four major international health institutions – the WHO, the Joint United Nations Programme on HIV/AIDS (UNAIDS), Gavi, and GFATM – the latter two of which are PPPs rather than IGOs. Drawing on a wealth of original and existing sources, including key informant interviews and archival research, these examinations leverage process-tracing and narrative techniques to furnish evidence for the theory's micro-level implications.

3   Learning from Assessment

Quantitative Tests on 54 Institutions

> [T]he process of evaluating the performance of political systems –
> indeed of any system – inescapably requires empirical data, measures,
> and measurements, even if only in the broadest meaning of these terms.
> – Robert A. Dahl, 1967[1]

Political institutions have always been appraised by those under as
well as outside their jurisdiction. Rigorous assessments of their performance, however, have historically been rare. Concerns about mixing
positivist empirical inquiry with normative judgment have dissuaded
some scholars from taking up this enterprise.[2] Others have been put
off by conceptual and methodological conundrums: What are the
principal dimensions of institutional performance? How should they be
operationalized? Should different indicators be aggregated, and if so,
how? As the epigraph to this chapter suggests, tackling such challenges
is essential for understanding how well we and others are governed.

The obstacles to scientifically assessing institutional performance,
though significant, are not insurmountable. Over the past three decades,
social scientists have made considerable progress in measuring the
performance of domestic public institutions – from local governments to
bureaucratic agencies – drawing on surveys, interviews, administrative
data, and multisource evaluations by governments, civil society, and
academics.[3] In recent years, performance assessment has also emerged
as a "hot topic" among stakeholders of international institutions, some

---

[1] Dahl (1967, 168).

[2] As Putnam (1993, 63) noted 30 years ago, "The undeniable admixture of normative
judgments in any inquiry about performance and effectiveness has made most scholars
over the last forty years reluctant to pursue such questions: *de gustibus non disputandum
est*, at least in a value-free, 'objective' social science. Even though political scientists,
as ordinary citizens, are often quite willing to judge a government's performance, the
discipline has too readily relinquished this important patrimony of political science . . .
to political philosophers and publicists."

[3] See footnote 13 in Chapter 1 for key references.

of whom have begun compiling similar sources of data.[4] Yet, thus far, few scholars have sought to take advantage of these developments to improve our empirical understanding of institutional effectiveness – or its determinants.

In this chapter, I undertake statistical tests of my theoretical framework's macro-level propositions using the Performance of International Institutions Project (PIIP), a new dataset on the performance of 54 major international institutions. The PIIP incorporates ratings from six systematic evaluations conducted by donor governments over the past 15 years, which encompass the core dimensions of Chapter 1's definition of institutional performance and are generally regarded as a credible and balanced source of information on this variable.[5] Following scorecards of local and city government performance that are widely used by social scientists, these assessments integrate multiple forms of quantitative and qualitative data and capture the judgments of diverse institutional stakeholders.[6] My explanatory variables are measured with a raft of primary sources, including a unique survey of senior international bureaucrats fielded between 2013 and 2019.

To preview the main results, I find a strong positive association between performance ratings and a survey-based measure of de facto policy autonomy, which holds broadly across evaluations as well as types of performance indicators. In addition, I recover evidence that this relationship is driven by a process of reciprocal causation between the two variables, albeit with the larger and more consistent effect running from de facto policy autonomy to performance. In contrast, there is little sign of a consistent relationship – positive or negative – between performance ratings and de jure policy autonomy, as measured by the content of formal institutional rules.

The results also lend support to my hypotheses regarding the sources of de facto policy autonomy. The depth, quantity, and breadth of operational alliances and the exercise of three common governance tasks with high monitoring costs for states – designing policy interventions, implementing field operations, and allocating material resources – are strong positive predictors of such independence. Conversely, the exercise of three standard tasks with low monitoring costs – facilitating international agreements (low costs), monitoring policy compliance,

---

[4] Gutner and Thompson (2010, 228).   [5] Lall (2017, 246).

[6] Notable examples of subnational assessments include the Government Performance Project (GPP), a 1996–2010 collaboration between academia and civil society that rated American states on their management of money, people, infrastructure, and information; and the Comprehensive Performance Assessment (CPA) carried out by the United Kingdom's Audit Commission between 2002 and 2009 to gauge the performance of local authorities in the country.

and providing capacity-building assistance – is a negative predictor (of varying strength).

In the next section, I outline four basic requirements for a valid measure of institutional performance in the international context, before describing how donor ratings can be combined in ways that credibly satisfy these standards. The second section details the operationalization and measurement of the main explanatory variables: de facto and de jure policy autonomy, operational alliances, and governance tasks. The third section offers preliminary evidence for my framework's posited relationships in the form of descriptive statistics and bivariate correlations. The centerpiece of the chapter is a series of multivariate regression analyses that more rigorously assess these associations. The first set of models regresses my measures of performance and de facto policy autonomy on their hypothesized determinants. The second set addresses the possibility of feedback effects between performance and de facto policy autonomy by means of a simultaneous equations approach, which involves modeling them jointly as a function of more plausibly exogenous variables. The third set implements a battery of robustness checks to deal with other possible threats to sound statistical inference.

Measuring Institutional Performance

A Standard for Performance Measurement

In Chapter 1, I made the case for a subjective approach to conceptualizing the performance of international institutions that focuses on the extent to which they are perceived by stakeholders as achieving sustained and efficient progress toward their stated, operative, and process objectives. In seeking to translate this definition into a concrete performance metric, we confront a number of challenges. I posit that a valid metric must meet four requirements, which together constitute a stringent empirical standard:

1. It must be *inclusive*. International institutions are prone to what Tamar Gutner and Alexander Thompson call the "eye of the beholder" problem: Their performance is judged by a multiplicity of actors, from governments to civil society groups to businesses, whose verdicts may differ sharply.[7] While such variation does not preclude measurement – many quantifiable phenomena are perceived in different ways by observers – it creates a risk that our metric may be skewed by the opinion of an unrepresentative minority. Consequently, it

---

[7] Gutner and Thompson (2010, 233).

must reflect the assessments of stakeholders with diverse affiliations, backgrounds, and relationships to institutions. The more consistent these appraisals, the more confident we can be in the measure.

2. It must be *evidence-based*. A related challenge is that stakeholders may be poorly informed about institutions' policies, operations, and effects, leading to unreliable or biased views about performance. Our metric must accordingly be based on the appraisals of stakeholders with access to accurate and reasonably comprehensive information about institutions, whether in the shape of extensive first-hand observation or more "objective" forms of evidence, such as policy outputs and impact data. Ideally, multiple types and sources of such information should be available to stakeholders. Similarly to before, the higher the degree of evidentiary consistency, the greater the confidence we can place in our measure.

3. It must be *multidimensional*. As discussed in Chapter 1, institutional performance is a many-sided concept that cannot be reduced to any single characteristic. A convincing measure must embrace and express this complexity. In the case of international institutions, my conceptualization suggests, it should encompass indicators of goal attainment, cost-effectiveness, and the quality of internal systems and processes that promote these attributes.[8]

4. It must be *coherent*. A possible pitfall of the multidimensionality requirement is that our metric may not be coherent from an empirical perspective. It is conceivable that institutions excel on different dimensions of performance, with some, for example, making sustained but inefficient progress toward their objectives and others taking limited but efficient strides. In such a scenario, it would make little sense to treat performance as a single latent variable; instead, each dimension should be analyzed separately. This suggests that our measure's constituent indicators must be strongly correlated.[9]

How can we develop a metric that passes these four tests? In the rest of this section, I argue that the recent wave of comparative donor evaluations of international institutions provides the basis for such a construct. I begin by providing an overview of these exercises, before describing their specific performance indicators and my strategy for combining such measures into aggregate performance indices.

---

[8] This is not to deny the value of studying individual dimensions of performance, which may be interesting and important in their own right. Recent studies, for example, offer useful insights into the policy productivity of international organizations. See Tallberg et al. (2016); Sommerer et al. (2021).

[9] This is similar to Putnam's (1993, 64) test of "internal consistency" for a "serious" measure of government performance.

Meeting the Standard: Donor Performance Evaluations

Over the past 15 years, several governments have published comprehensive evaluations of international institutions they financially support. Six of these assessments are publicly accessible and include comparative (numerical or categorical) performance indicators, enabling us to analyze them with quantitative methods. Their main characteristics are summarized in Table 3.1. Five assessments are the work of individual government aid agencies: the Australian Agency for International Development (AusAID), the United Kingdom's Department for International Development (DFID), the Danish International Development Agency (Danida), Netherlands Development Cooperation, and the Swedish International Development Cooperation Agency (Sida).[10] The sixth is by the Multilateral Organisation Performance Assessment Network (MOPAN), an association of 18 donor countries (including the previous five) that appraises the effectiveness of international organizations.[11] The evaluations are ongoing exercises that are periodically updated (with varying frequency).[12]

The origins of the evaluations lie in a long-standing agenda to maximize "results" in international development assistance by improving the monitoring, management, and administration of institutional activities, which gained currency in the donor community following the promulgation of the Millennium Development Goals (MDGs) in 2000.[13] This initiative received fresh impetus from the global financial crisis of 2007–2008, which created pressures for governments to make more efficient use of their multilateral budgets – to increase the "bang for their buck," as one MOPAN official put it.[14] The evaluations were not conceived as a vehicle for articulating, broadcasting, or advancing political interests, therefore. Indeed, branches of government that deal with the more political aspects of international cooperation, such as departments of state and ministries of foreign affairs, have not been directly involved in the evaluation process (despite housing some of the

[10] AusAID was integrated into Australia's Department of Foreign Affairs and Trade in 2013.

[11] The other 13 members are Belgium, Canada, Finland, France, Ireland, Italy, Japan, Luxembourg, Norway, the Republic of Korea, Switzerland, the United Arab Emirates, and the United States. MOPAN was founded in 2002 and is managed by a small secretariat hosted by the Organisation for Economic Co-operation and Development (OECD) in Paris.

[12] Only the AusAID evaluation has yet to be updated. The PIIP includes all updates issued by the end of 2018.

[13] Obser (2007). They can be viewed as part of a broader trend toward the rating and ranking of public and private entities by states. See Kelley and Simmons (2020); Lall (2020).

[14] Author interview #115 with MOPAN policy analyst, September 5, 2018, via video conference. Also see Lall (2021).

Table 3.1 *Overview of donor performance evaluations*

Assessor	Unit	Main sources	Year(s)	Coverage	Selection criteria	Indicators	Scale	Cron. α	r̄ with others
Australia	AusAID	Stakeholder consultations, public submissions, diplomatic feedback, institutional documents, quantitative data (e.g., ATI, Paris monitoring survey)	2011	42 (35 IGOs, 6 PPPs, 1 INGO)	Past funding levels, possibility of future funding, relevance to aid objectives	4 (2 DR, 1 FM, 1 SM)	Categorical (4 values)	0.65	0.55
Denmark	Danida	MOPAN surveys, DFID evaluation	2012, 2013	18 (16 IGOs, 1 PPP, 1 INGO)	Past funding levels	7 (3 DR, 1 FM, 2 SM, 1 KM)	Continuous: 1–6	0.76	0.5
MOPAN	Secretariat	Cross-national stakeholder surveys, institutional documents, interviews with international bureaucrats	2010–2014, 2017, 2019	26 (23 IGOs, 3 PPPs)	Consensus among members	20 (5 DR, 5 FM, 4 SM, 6 KM)	Continuous & ordinal: 1–6 pre-2015, 1–4 post-2015	0.81	0.28
Netherlands	Neth. Develop. Coop.	Diplomatic feedback, MOPAN surveys, DFID evaluation, institutional documents	2011, 2013, 2015, 2017	38 (34 IGOs, 4 PPPs)	Past funding levels	6 (2 DR, 1 FM, 3 SM)	Ordinal: 1–4	0.72	0.51
Sweden	Sida	Diplomatic feedback, institutional documents	2008, 2010–2011	23 (21 IGOs, 2 PPPs)	Past funding levels	2 (1 DR, 1 SM)	Categorical: 6 groups	0.87	0.45
United Kingdom	DFID	Stakeholder consultations, workshops, and interviews, public submissions, field visits, quantitative data (e.g., QuODA, ATI)	2011, 2013, 2016	41 (34 IGOs, 5 PPPs, 2 INGOs)	Past funding levels, possibility of future funding, UK involvement in governance	12 (2 DR, 4 FM, 5 SM, 1 KM)	Ordinal: 1–4	0.85	0.66

Notes: In the seventh column, DR = delivery of results, FM = financial management, SM = strategic management, KM = knowledge management. The ninth column reports the Cronbach's alpha among each evaluation's indicators; the tenth column shows the mean correlation between a composite index based on these indicators and the same index for the remaining five sets of indicators.

bilateral assessor agencies). In interviews, evaluators repeatedly stressed their insulation from political pressures and their overriding aim of delivering an impartial, rigorous appraisal of institutional performance based on reliable empirical evidence.[15]

The evaluations are informed by an eclectic mixture of stakeholders, providing a foundation for performance metrics that fulfil the requirement of inclusiveness. Seeking to "engage at all stages of the assessment process with as wide a range of stakeholders as possible," the British and Australian evaluations solicit the views of governments, civil society groups, private-sector institutions, and international bureaucrats from a heterogeneous set of countries, including some of the smallest and poorest.[16] Importantly, civil society consultees include not only major Western international nongovernmental organizations (INGOs) but also community and grassroots associations in the developing world, which were actively sought out by local donor offices.[17] Feedback is gathered via multiple means, including workshops, interviews, written submissions, surveys, and country visits, which evaluators use "to explore and challenge more general evidence and judgements about the performance of the multilateral organisations."[18]

The Danish, Dutch, and Swedish assessments rely predominantly on input from government ministries, overseas missions, and embassies. The MOPAN evaluation draws on interviews with international bureaucrats and large-scale surveys of developing country "partners" from government, civil society, academia, and the private sector.[19] Like the British and Australian evaluations, these questionnaires include diverse representatives of each stakeholder category, including nongovernmental organizations (NGOs), research institutions, and corporations of widely varying size, scope, and resources.[20] Most of the bilateral evaluations, it should be noted, assign some weight to MOPAN's surveys, usually alongside other cross-national stakeholder questionnaires such as the Survey on Monitoring the Paris Declaration (an international compact for improving aid effectiveness).

With respect to the evidentiary requirement, the evaluations crosscheck stakeholder feedback against two more "objective" sources

---

[15] I conducted five interviews with such officials – from DFID, AusAID, Danida, and MOPAN – between 2012 and 2018, which are listed in Appendix C.

[16] United Kingdom Department for International Development (2011, 140).

[17] Author interview #34 with senior manager, DFID, June 29, 2012, London.

[18] United Kingdom Department for International Development (2011, 213).

[19] MOPAN has been implementing stakeholder surveys since 2003. Until the adoption of its "Common Approach" methodology in 2009, however, they did not compare institutions on a consistent numerical scale.

[20] Author interview #115 with MOPAN policy analyst, September 5, 2018, via video conference.

of information: institutional documents, including policy statements, strategic frameworks, impact studies, financial accounts, and internal audits and reviews; and quantitative data from previous comparative assessments with a more limited conceptual and institutional scope, such as the Quality of Official Development Assistance Assessment (QuODA), the Aid Transparency Index (ATI), the Heavily-Indebted Poor Countries Capacity Building Project (HIPC CBP), and the Common Performance Assessment System (COMPAS). Furthermore, the British and Australian evaluations have been externally peer reviewed – the former by academic development experts, the latter by officials from other government departments with multilateral engagements, a representative of civil society, and a professional consultant – building an additional layer of independent scrutiny into the appraisal process.

Institutions are rated on several aspects of their performance, enabling us to construct holistic multidimensional measures of the concept. In total, the evaluations contain 51 different performance indicators (see Appendix B.3 for a full list). The number of indicators in each evaluation ranges from two (Sweden) to 21 (MOPAN). Essentially all indicators measure one of four dimensions of institutional performance:

1. *Delivery of results*: the achievement of stated and operative objectives (at different organizational and geographical levels), often with a focus on the degree to which results are sustainable and aligned with the needs and priorities of intended beneficiaries.
2. *Financial management*: the presence of institutionalized arrangements for mobilizing and allocating resources in a transparent, cost-effective, and flexible manner.
3. *Strategic management*: the presence of governance structures, policy frameworks, and programming practices that facilitate mandate implementation and the attainment of expected results.
4. *Knowledge management*: the presence of feedback and reporting mechanisms that facilitate the acquisition, dissemination, and utilization of performance information.

In terms of my definition of institutional performance, delivery of results and financial management correspond more or less directly to the attainment of stated and operative objectives and to efficiency, respectively. Strategic and knowledge management approximately capture progress toward process goals, offering valuable insights into the functioning of internal systems and structures that undergird operational activities.

The evaluations are mostly balanced in their coverage of the four dimensions, with a similar number of indicators measuring each. The exception is the Swedish evaluation, whose two indicators solely gauge delivery of results and strategic management. It should be noted that some evaluations additionally include indicators of concepts and characteristics that do not fall under my definition of institutional performance, such as accountability to stakeholders, the promotion of gender equality, and attention to environmental issues. I exclude these from the PIIP, though I later employ the accountability indicators in a separate analysis (see Chapter 6).[21]

Finally, each evaluation's performance indicators are strongly and positively correlated, indicating that the coherence requirement can also be satisfied. Across all waves, the mean correlation among indicators exceeds $r = 0.3$ in the Australian, Dutch, and MOPAN evaluations, $r = 0.4$ in the British and Danish evaluations, and $r = 0.7$ in the Swedish evaluation.[22] Overall, 110 of the 177 individual correlation coefficients (62 percent) are statistically significant at the 10 percent level. In addition, the Cronbach's alpha for each set of indicators – a common measure of internal consistency – comfortably exceeds the conventional acceptability threshold of $\alpha = 0.5$ in all evaluations (mean $\alpha = 0.78$).[23] The strength of these associations suggests that each set of indicators can reasonably be viewed as the expression of a latent performance variable.

Sample Characteristics

The evaluations cover varying subsets of 54 international institutions, a list of which is provided in Appendix B.1.[24] Institutions are selected primarily on the basis of past funding levels – some assessors employ a minimum contributions threshold – and alignment with multilateral cooperation priorities. As indicated in Table 3.1, the Australian and the British evaluations have the broadest coverage of institutions (more than 40), the Danish and the MOPAN appraisals the narrowest (less than 20).[25] Over the 2008–2018 period, the 54 institutions received 421 sets of performance ratings from the six assessors. This translates into 293

---

[21] I also omit summary indices and indicators that only cover a small subset of institutions.
[22] Before 2015, MOPAN indicators were scored on two separate scales: one based on the stakeholder survey and the other based on a review of institutional documents by two consulting firms. In the subsequent analyses, I take an average of the two scales. In addition, I exclude survey-based scores issued in 2010, which, due to methodological changes, are systematically lower than others.
[23] In evaluations where the set of indicators varies across years, I average the alpha for each distinct set.
[24] The collection of documents comprising each evaluation is enumerated in Appendix B.2.
[25] The British evaluation includes a small number of entities that are divisions or departments of other institutions, which I leave out of the PIIP.

separate institution-years, the unit of observation in the PIIP (a pooled cross-sectional dataset).[26]

From an external validity perspective, the PIIP sample entails trade-offs. On the one hand, it is not randomly drawn from the full population of international institutions. The evaluations' selection criteria create a risk that relatively large and prominent institutions will be overrepresented. On the other hand, these institutions also tend to be the most powerful, influential, and studied in global governance, making the sample of considerable interest to academics and practitioners alike. As a recent review of the literature on international organizations observes, scholars have concentrated on "a very few big organizations," including the World Trade Organization (WTO), the International Monetary Fund (IMF), the World Bank, and organs of the United Nations (UN) – of all which appear in the PIIP.[27]

Issue-wise, the sample does appear to be fairly representative of the universe of international institutions. The latest version of the Correlates of War Intergovernmental Organizations (COW IGO) dataset contains dummy (i.e., binary 0/1) indicators for whether intergovernmental organizations (IGOs) deal with political, social, or economic problems.[28] The proportion of IGOs with values of 1 on these three variables is 0.15, 0.34, and 0.51, respectively. The equivalent figures for the PIIP sample are 0.15, 0.41, and 0.44; none of these differences is statistically significant at the five percent level in a one-proportion Z-test.[29] The Yearbook of International Organizations database assigns IGOs to granular subject categories and provides a precise description of their aims, allowing for a more nuanced issue comparison.[30] Using this information, I match both Yearbook IGOs and PIIP institutions – which are included in the Yearbook – to one or more of 20 issue areas from a policy classification scheme developed by Liesbet Hooghe, Tobias Lenz, and Gary Marks.[31] In all but one instance, issue area proportions are similar and statistically indistinguishable between the two sets of institutions (see Appendix B.4 for details).[32] The exception is the domain of humanitarian assistance,

[26] The PIIP goes well beyond the dataset constructed by Lall (2017), which excludes the MOPAN evaluation, covers only the first wave of the other five, and contains one fewer institution. As a result, it has a cross-sectional structure and comprises 53 observations.
[27] Pevehouse and von Borzyskowski (2016, 31).   [28] Pevehouse et al. (2019).
[29] For overlapping institutions, I use the COW IGO value of each indicator; for others, I take the COW IGO value for the most similar institution in this dataset.
[30] https://uia.org/yearbook [Last accessed February 3, 2020].
[31] Hooghe, Lenz, and Marks (2019).
[32] This is true under both the narrow and the broad definition of IGOs used by the Yearbook.

which is slightly overrepresented in the PIIP relative to the Yearbook. I later show that this feature does not drive my statistical findings.

There are also tradeoffs when it comes to the PIIP's composition. The sample mostly consists of IGOs with global memberships, the principal focus of the literature on international institutions. Six institutions have a regional membership (five of which are development banks), seven are public–private partnerships (PPPs), and two are INGOs. There are often good reasons to avoid mixing IGOs, PPPs, and INGOs in datasets of international institutions. At the same time, separating them prevents us from exploring and analyzing the rich institutional diversity of contemporary global governance, in which many important functions and responsibilities are no longer the preserve of IGOs. Furthermore, as discussed in Chapter 2, this book's argument properly applies to *all* international institutions that states actively engage with and thus have the potential to capture. The PPPs and INGOs in the sample fulfil this scope condition: States provide the vast majority of their funding, participate in operational alliances with them, and are represented in almost all of their governing bodies.[33] As not all PPPs and INGOs share these characteristics, of course, caution is warranted when seeking to draw *general* conclusions about them from the sample.

All told, the PIIP provides a solid basis for inference about the types of international institutions that, for good reasons, have traditionally received the lion's share of scholarly and popular attention: global IGOs with relatively ample resources. Care should be exercised, however, if seeking to make generalizations about institutions with small memberships and budgets, such as many of those focusing on individual regions or niche issues. The inclusion of PPPs and INGOs renders the sample more representative of modern global governance and allows us to probe a key theoretical scope condition, though these institutions again may not represent typical members of their own populations.

Constructing Performance Indices

Constructing a composite index of institutional performance from indicators of its different dimensions allows us to capture the concept's richness and complexity while comparing it in a relatively precise manner across institutions. I combine each evaluation's indicators into such a measure using principal component analysis (PCA), a standard

[33] Only the governing bodies of the International Committee of the Red Cross (ICRC) and the International Federation of the Red Cross (IFRC) do not include state representatives.

technique for reducing the dimensionality of multivariate data. The index takes the form of zero-centered predicted scores for the first principal component extracted from the indicators, which accounts for the maximum possible variance.[34] Thus, scores exceeding 0 are above average for the sample and scores under 0 are below average. A considerable proportion of variance is explained by the first principal component in each analysis – 56 percent on average, compared to 18 percent for the second principal component and 11 percent for the third – providing further justification for aggregating indicators.[35] Nevertheless, to examine patterns within different dimensions of performance, I employ individual indicators as well as composite indices in the statistical tests presented later.

The six performance indices – one for each set of evaluation indicators – have a strong positive association with one another. That is to say, institutions that receive high (or low) ratings in some evaluations also tend to receive high (or low) ratings in others. The mean correlation between the indices is $r = 0.49$; all 14 individual coefficients are positive and 11 are significant. These relationships allay potential concerns that the evaluations still reflect some "national bias" in favor of institutions that promote the assessor's particular foreign policy aims.[36] To the contrary, they reveal a high degree of *consensus* among donors – and the varied stakeholders they have consulted – about which institutions are performing effectively and which are faring less well.

Figure 3.1 displays institutions' mean score on each performance index across all years (the absence of a bar indicates omission from the evaluation). As implied by the intercorrelations just described, scores are similar between indices. Only a handful of institutions, for example, have a positive score on one index and a negative score on another. The five institutions with the highest average score on the six indices are, in order, the World Bank; the Private Infrastructure Development Group (PIDG); the International Committee of the Red Cross (ICRC); Gavi, the Vaccine Alliance; and the International Finance Corporation (IFC). The five institutions with the lowest average score are, from lowest to highest, the United Nations Industrial Development Organization (UNIDO); the United Nations Office for Disaster Risk Reduction (UNDRR); the United Nations Educational, Scientific and Cul-

---

[34] Since indicators have an identical scale in each evaluation, they do not require rescaling to the same standard deviation prior to PCA (a common preprocessing step).

[35] Appendix B.3 reports each principal component's explanatory power and correlations with individual indicators (known as factor loadings).

[36] It might be noted, in addition, that this problem is more likely to work *against* rather than for my argument: Biased assessors would presumably assign higher ratings to institutions over which they have greater control – that is, less autonomous institutions.

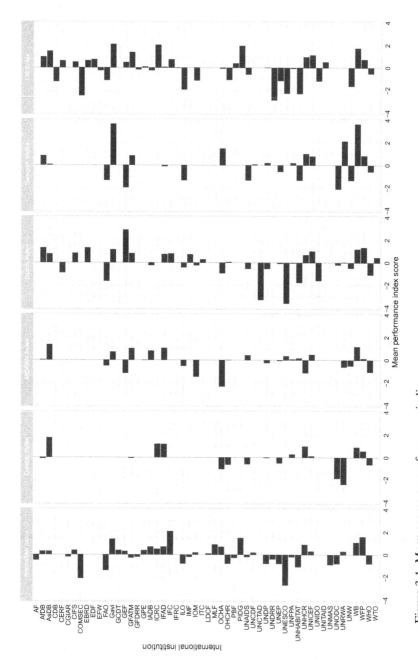

Figure 3.1 Mean scores on performance indices

Notes: The indices are zero-centered predicted scores for the first principal component from a PCA of all performance indicators in a given evaluation (see Appendix B.3 for lists of indicators and factor loadings); scores are averaged across all years in which ratings are issued.

tural Organization (UNESCO); the Commonwealth Secretariat (COM-SEC); and the United Nations Conference on Trade and Development (UNCTAD). As pointed out in Chapter 1, each set of institutions is – on the surface – remarkably heterogeneous.

Explanatory Variables

The explanatory variables are indices of de facto policy autonomy, de jure policy autonomy, and operational alliances; and dummy variables for the exercise of six governance tasks with differing monitoring costs for states. All are measured for every year in which an institution receives a performance rating as well as the previous year (to allow for lagged regression models). Summary statistics on all variables in the PIIP are provided in Appendix B.5.

Policy Autonomy

Chapter 2 noted that previous research on the autonomy of international institutions has mostly focused on the de jure form of the concept, reflecting a long-standing interest among international relations (IR) scholars in questions of institutional design.[37] In consequence, there are no readily available data on de facto policy autonomy covering the PIIP sample. To fill this empirical gap, I designed and implemented a multiyear survey of high-level international bureaucrats – mostly members of the chief of staff's office – in the 54 institutions, achieving a 100 percent response rate. Details on survey methodology, including instruments, sampling strategies, and validation checks, are provided in Appendix D.

The variable *De Facto Policy Autonomy* is a continuous six-point index that aggregates seven indicators (listed in Table 3.2) of the three characteristics of the concept delineated in Chapter 2: agenda-setting powers, the ability to avoid a state veto, and access to non-state funding.[38] The first three indicators focus on agenda setting and are based on responses to the following survey questions:

1. *Does the permanent staff propose new policies (for instance, in the form of programs or projects) or issue draft rules for your organization?* [Response options: *Yes* = 1; *No* = 0]

---

[37] For quantitative measures of de jure policy autonomy and closely related concepts, see Haftel and Thompson (2006); Johnson (2014); Hooghe and Marks (2015); Hooghe, Lenz, and Marks (2019).
[38] Variable names are written in italics throughout the book.

Table 3.2 *Components of policy autonomy indices*

	De Facto Policy Autonomy			De Jure Policy Autonomy		
	Indicator	Scale	Mean (SD)	Indicator	Scale	Mean (SD)
1.	Survey: Do staff propose new policies/rules?	Yes = 1; No = 0	0.71 (0.45)	Formal rules require staff to propose new policies/rules	Yes = 1; No = 0	0.56 (0.50)
2.	Survey: Do staff draft annual budget?	Yes = 1; No = 0	0.72 (0.45)	Formal rules require staff to draft annual budget	Yes = 1; No = 0	0.53 (0.48)
3.	Survey: Do staff set governing body agenda?	Yes = 1; No = 0	0.90 (0.30)	Formal rules require staff to set governing body agenda	Yes = 1; No = 0	0.55 (0.50)
4.	Survey: How does governing body typically make decisions?	MV = 1; SV = 0.5; U = 0	0.25 (0.40)	Formal rule for typical governing body decisions	MV = 1; SV = 0.5; U = 0	0.60 (0.44)
5.	Survey: Are voting shares equally distributed?	Yes = 1; No = 0	0.95 (0.14)	Formal allocation of voting shares is equal	Yes = 1; No = 0	0.90 (0.20)
6.	Proportion of contributions from non-state actors	0–1 (cont.)	0.17 (0.17)	Formal rules permit non-state contributions	Yes = 1; No = 0	0.62 (0.49)
7.	Proportion of income from independent earnings	0–1 (cont.)	0.19 (0.28)	Formal rules permit independent earnings	Yes = 1; No = 0	0.45 (0.50)
	Overall index: 1 + 2 + 3 + (4 × 5) + 6 + 7	0–6 (cont.)	2.90 (1.05)	Overall index: 1 + 2 + 3 + (4 × 5) + 6 + 7	0–6 (cont.)	3.23 (0.50)

Notes: MV = majority voting; SV = supermajority voting; U = unanimity. Scores for indicators 4 and 5 are averaged across all institutional governing bodies.

2. *Does the permanent staff draft your organization's annual budget?* [*Yes =* 1; *No* = 0]
3. *Does the permanent staff prepare the agenda for your organization's governing bodies?* [*Yes* = 1; *No* = 0]

The fourth and fifth indicators, whose values are multiplied together, measure decision-making procedures in institutional governing bodies with responses to two questions:

4. *How are policy decisions typically made in your organization's governing body?* [*Majority voting* = 1; *Supermajority voting* = 0.5; *Unanimity* = 0; scores are averaged across all governing bodies]
5. *If your organization's governing body makes policy decisions by voting, do members have equal shares?* [*Yes/Not applicable* = multiply score for indicator 4 by 1; *No* = multiply score for indicator 4 by 0; multiplied scores are averaged across all governing bodies]

The final two indicators gauge non-state sources of funding using data from institutions' audited accounts, annual reports, and budgetary documents. The sixth is the proportion of an institution's annual contributions that is received from non-state actors. The seventh is the proportion of an institution's total annual income that is independently earned from investments, fees for services rendered, product sales, and other noncontributory sources.

De Jure Policy Autonomy has the same seven indicators as *De Facto Policy Autonomy*, with the sole difference that they are based not on survey data but on formal rules set out in an institution's constitution, charter, treaty, or regulations.[39] A corollary of this difference is that the fifth and sixth indicators are no longer proportions but binary variables measuring whether an institution is formally permitted to receive donations from non-state actors (fifth indicator) and to earn independent revenue (sixth indicator).

In line with the theory, *De Facto Policy Autonomy* and *De Jure Policy Autonomy* have essentially no correlation ($r = -0.05$). As reported in Table 3.2, though the indices have comparable overall means, most of their constituent indicators diverge substantially. On average, de facto scores on the first three indicators are more than 40 percent higher than de jure scores, indicating that international bureaucrats tend to possess more extensive agenda-setting powers in practice than on paper. The opposite pattern holds for the fourth indicator, with almost half of the sample possessing at least one governing body that formally employs a

---

[39] I follow previous indices of de jure autonomy in assigning indicators a value of 0 if the feature they measure is not specified in formal rules.

form of majority voting but actually operates by consensus. De jure and de facto scores on the fifth indicator are comparable. Finally, de facto scores on the sixth and seventh indicators are lower than de jure scores – the average institution draws a modest share of financial resources from nongovernmental and independent sources[40] – though this difference deserves less emphasis because the de facto and de jure versions of these variables are not perfectly equivalent.[41] In a nutshell, formal rules, on their own, paint a strikingly misleading picture of true policy autonomy in PIIP institutions.

Operational Alliances and Governance Tasks

Turning to sources of de facto policy autonomy, *Operational Alliances* is a continuous index comprising indicators of the depth, quantity, and breadth of such arrangements. Each indicator is measured using information from official institutional websites, most of which have a section devoted specifically to "partnerships" or "collaborations."[42] The index is constructed by weighting the quantity of an institution's recorded operational alliances by their individual depth and collective breadth:

$$Operational\ Alliances = \log(Quantity + 1) \times Depth \times Breadth \quad (3.1)$$

where *Quantity* is the number of alliances (1 is added to prevent ln(0) values); *Depth* is the proportion of alliances that involve substantive collaboration at the agenda-setting, formulation, monitoring, implementation, or enforcement stage of the policy process; and *Breadth* is the proportion of five types of stakeholders – NGOs, private-sector actors, IGOs, research bodies, and PPPs – who are members of at least one alliance.[43] Multistakeholder alliances (i.e., alliances with more than two

---

[40] In several institutions, however, this proportion is substantial. During the sample period, eight institutions receive more than a third of average annual contributions from non-state actors, and nine (mostly multilateral development banks) draw more than half of their annual income from independent earnings.

[41] When we exclude these two indicators, ensuring exact de facto–de jure equivalence, the correlation between *De Facto Policy Autonomy* and *De Jure Policy Autonomy* remains modest and negative ($r = -0.19$).

[42] To access older versions of these websites, I use the Internet Archive's Wayback Machine (https://archive.org/web). It is possible, of course, that institutions do not list all of their alliances online. However, alternative data sources are either not available for all PIIP institutions (e.g., partnership catalogues, project databases) or are inconsistent in their coverage of alliances (e.g., annual reports, evaluations). One might add that the space devoted to alliances on an institution's website seems a decent proxy for their importance to its operational activities.

[43] Institutions with no listed alliances are thus assigned a score of 0 on every indicator.

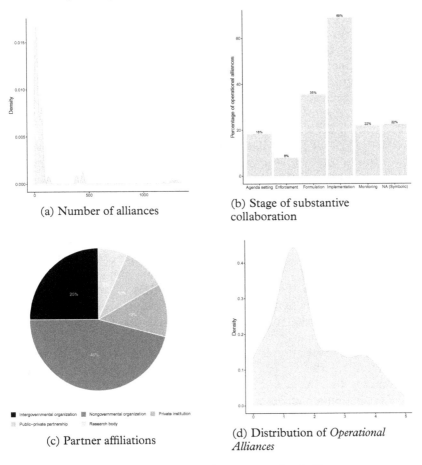

(a) Number of alliances

(b) Stage of substantive collaboration

(c) Partner affiliations

(d) Distribution of *Operational Alliances*

Figure 3.2 Summary information on operational alliances

Source: Author's coding based on information from institutions' official websites.

Note: Multistakeholder alliances are disaggregated into separate dyads between the enlisting institution and each partner.

participants) are disaggregated into separate dyads between the enlisting institution and each partner.[44]

Figure 3.2 summarizes the quantity, depth, and breadth of PIIP institutions' operational alliances. The number of alliances per insti-

[44] In total, 12 percent of alliances are multistakeholder (involving an average of 3.9 partners).

tution varies widely, ranging from 0 to 1,343 (panel a, upper left).[45] Nevertheless, it lies between 10 and 50 for more than half of the sample and between 50 and 100 for almost a quarter. Thus, only a small minority of institutions have less than 10 or more than 100 partnerships. When converted to a logarithmic scale, the distribution assumes a roughly normal (bell curve) shape.

Almost 70 percent of alliances focus on the implementation phase of the policy process (Figure 3.2, panel b, upper right), where non-state actors – in particular NGOs – often possess valuable capacities lacked by institutions, such as local information and access to target actors. More than a third of alliances contribute to policy formulation, while approximately a fifth involve agenda-setting and monitoring activities. Less than 10 percent occur at the enforcement stage, probably reflecting the limited role played by most international institutions in inducing compliance with their policies (see Chapter 2). Around one-fifth entail no substantive collaboration at all and are hence purely symbolic.

Consistent with the high proportion of implementation-stage alliances, almost half of all partners are NGOs (29 percent national, 17 percent international) (Figure 3.2, panel c, lower left). IGOs figure in a quarter of alliances, the majority of which support policy formulation. Private-sector institutions (mostly businesses and professional associations), research bodies, and PPPs make up the remaining quarter of partners, with all three types of actors most commonly assisting in agenda setting and policy formulation.

The distribution of *Operational Alliances* is plotted in Figure 3.2, panel d (lower right). Owing to the logarithmic transformation, it is less skewed than that of the raw number of alliances (panel a). However, it has a trimodal rather than a normal shape, displaying a large peak centered around 1.5 – just below the mean value of 1.83 – and smaller peaks around 2.5 and 4. Two-thirds of the distribution span the 0–2 range.

To measure the second hypothesized source of de facto policy autonomy, I construct dummy variables for whether institutions execute the six governance tasks described in Chapter 2. I draw primarily on information from institutions' websites, annual reports, work programs, budgets, and other policy documents. Figure 3.3 displays the proportion of institutions that perform each task. Averaging across years, nearly two-thirds of institutions provide capacity-building assistance to states (a task with low monitoring costs). Approximately half allocate material resources (high monitoring costs), a third design policy interventions (high costs), a third implement field operations (high costs), a quarter

---

[45] The latter figure is for the World Food Programme (WFP) in 2011.

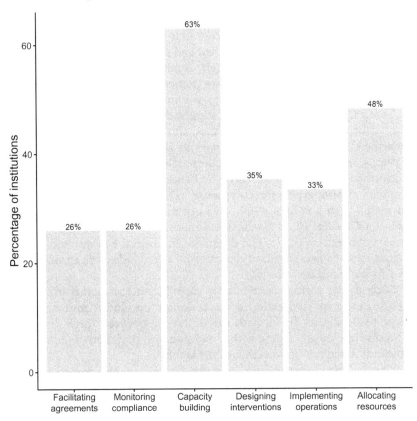

Figure 3.3 Governance tasks exercised by PIIP institutions

Source: Author's coding based on information from institutions' official websites and policy documents.

Note: The percentages represent averages across all sample years.

facilitate international agreements (low costs), and a quarter monitor policy compliance (low costs). Overall, then, the sample is well balanced with respect to the underlying variable of interest: 38 percent of institutions undertake tasks that are easy to monitor and 39 percent undertake tasks that are difficult to monitor.[46]

Descriptive Evidence

I begin the examination of my macro-level propositions by presenting descriptive statistics on the relationships between the variables described

---

[46] Two institutions do not perform any of the six tasks during the sample period.

in the previous two sections. To recap, the main hypotheses are that institutional performance is positively related to de facto policy autonomy but unrelated to de jure policy autonomy; and that de facto policy autonomy is positively related to the number, depth, and breath of operational alliances and to the exercise of governance tasks with high monitoring costs but unrelated to de jure policy autonomy.

Table 3.3 records the mean and standard deviation (in parentheses) of the performance, operational alliances, and governance task measures by quartile of *De Facto Policy Autonomy* and *De Jure Policy Autonomy*. Four patterns stand out, all of which comport with the argument. First, all performance indices rise sharply with bands of *De Facto Policy Autonomy*, implying a strong positive correlation. The mean value of each index increases from less than -0.4 (mean of means $= -1.00$) at the lowest band of *De Facto Policy Autonomy* to more than 0.7 at the highest band (mean of means $= 0.95$). The difference between the lowest and highest values exceeds one standard deviation of every index (mean difference $= 1.59$ standard deviations).

Second, the performance indices vary little across bands of *De Jure Policy Autonomy*, suggesting a weak association. Index means remain close to 0 in every band, with the difference between the highest and lowest values mostly falling within one standard deviation of the variable (mean difference $= 0.76$ standard deviations).

Third, *Operational Alliances* and the three dummies for governance tasks with high monitoring costs – *Designing Interventions*, *Implementing Operations*, and *Allocating Resources* – grow precipitously with bands of *De Facto Policy Autonomy*. The gap between the mean of *Operational Alliances* in the lowest and highest bands is close to 1.5 times its standard deviation. Notably, not a single institution in the lowest band (for at least one year of the sample) designs interventions or implements operations, and only four allocate resources. By contrast, 71 percent of institutions in the highest band design interventions, the same percentage allocate resources, and 65 percent implement operations. As before, values of the three dummies remain similar through bands of *De Jure Policy Autonomy*.

Fourth, the three dummies for governance tasks with low monitoring costs – *Facilitating Agreements*, *Monitoring Compliance*, and *Capacity Building* – vary in a less consistent fashion with bands of *De Facto Policy Autonomy*. The first two dummies have a clearly negative relationship with the latter variable: The proportion of institutions that facilitate agreements and monitor compliance declines from 56 percent and 44 percent at the lowest band of *De Facto Policy Autonomy*, respectively, to six percent and 18 percent at the highest band. The third dummy

Table 3.3 *Descriptive statistics by bands of policy autonomy indices*

Variable	De Facto Policy Autonomy				De Jure Policy Autonomy			
	Low	Low–Mid	High–Mid	High	Low	Low–Mid	High–Mid	High
Australian Perf. Index	-1.11	-0.04	0.28	0.71	-0.08	0.20	0.08	-0.38
	(0.81)	(0.65)	(0.65)	(0.78)	(0.88)	(0.92)	(0.67)	(1.31)
Danish Perf. Index	-0.86	-0.17	-0.14	0.93	-0.11	0.24	-0.41	0.17
	(1.04)	(1.13)	(1.32)	(0.63)	(0.86)	(1.15)	(1.72)	(1.10)
MOPAN Perf. Index	-0.47	0.01	-0.35	1.03	0.05	0.52	-0.89	0.11
	(0.84)	(0.62)	(1.00)	(0.48)	(0.69)	(1.05)	(0.87)	(0.82)
Dutch Perf. Index	-1.18	0.00	0.23	0.90	-0.15	0.45	-0.02	-0.37
	(2.09)	(1.23)	(0.87)	(0.67)	(1.41)	(0.98)	(1.50)	(2.10)
Swedish Perf. Index	-1.38	-0.56	0.82	1.21	-0.07	0.78	-0.32	-0.50
	(0.49)	(1.12)	(0.71)	(1.74)	(1.23)	(1.87)	(1.52)	(0.90)
UK Perf. Index	-1.02	-0.06	-0.02	0.94	0.11	0.10	0.30	-0.40
	(1.26)	(1.17)	(0.83)	(1.09)	(1.45)	(1.31)	(1.47)	(1.05)
Operational Alliances	0.99	1.43	2.22	2.69	1.50	2.18	1.50	1.93
	(0.55)	(1.06)	(1.17)	(1.19)	(1.01)	(1.43)	(0.80)	(1.20)
Facilitating Agreements	0.73	0.34	0.08	0.07	0.38	0.13	0.35	0.45
	(0.45)	(0.48)	(0.28)	(0.25)	(0.49)	(0.34)	(0.48)	(0.50)
Monitoring Compliance	0.62	0.34	0.22	0.18	0.34	0.15	0.65	0.41
	(0.49)	(0.48)	(0.42)	(0.39)	(0.48)	(0.36)	(0.48)	(0.49)
Capacity Building	0.84	0.63	0.86	0.75	0.71	0.76	0.72	0.90
	(0.37)	(0.49)	(0.35)	(0.43)	(0.46)	(0.43)	(0.46)	(0.30)
Designing Interventions	0.00	0.19	0.51	0.81	0.10	0.56	0.33	0.46
	(0.00)	(0.40)	(0.50)	(0.40)	(0.30)	(0.50)	(0.47)	(0.50)
Implementing Operations	0.00	0.21	0.66	0.75	0.15	0.61	0.30	0.46
	(0.00)	(0.41)	(0.48)	(0.43)	(0.36)	(0.49)	(0.47)	(0.50)
Allocating Resources	0.12	0.45	0.27	0.77	0.34	0.65	0.20	0.26
	(0.33)	(0.50)	(0.45)	(0.43)	(0.48)	(0.48)	(0.40)	(0.44)

Notes: Variables means and standard deviations (in parentheses) by quartile bands of *De Facto Policy Autonomy* and *De Jure Policy Autonomy*, i.e., bands corresponding to the lowest quarter, lower–middle quarter, upper–middle quarter, and highest quarter of the distribution.

has a more ambiguous relationship: between 40 percent and 70 percent of institutions in every band deliver capacity-building assistance. Once again, the three dummies exhibit little variation over bands of *De Jure Policy Autonomy*.

Concordant patterns emerge from bivariate correlations between the variables, displayed in Table 3.4. *De Facto Policy Autonomy* has a strong positive association with every performance index. The mean correlation is $r = 0.54$ and all six individual coefficients are significant at the one percent level. *De Jure Policy Autonomy* is weakly associated with the performance indices, with the individual coefficients failing to reach significance at the 10 percent level, fluctuating between positive and negative, and registering a mean of $r = -0.04$.

The correlations also accord with my hypotheses regarding the determinants of de facto policy autonomy. *De Facto Policy Autonomy* is positively associated at a one percent significance level with *Operational Alliances* ($r = 0.59$) and the three dummies for hard-to-monitor governance tasks (mean $r = 0.55$). Conversely, it has a negative correlation with the dummies for easy-to-monitor tasks that ranges from very strong in the case of *Facilitating Agreements* ($r = -0.64$, significant at the one percent level) to strong in the case of *Monitoring Compliance* ($r = -0.35$, significant at the one percent level) to weak in the case of *Capacity Building* ($r = -0.09$, not significant).

Statistical Analysis

The relationships revealed by the descriptive statistics provide initial plausibility for my macro-level propositions. Nevertheless, we cannot rule out the possibility that these patterns are driven by other factors that a descriptive approach cannot "control for." In this section, therefore, I expose my hypotheses to more demanding statistical tests involving the estimation of multivariate regression models.

I begin with a string of baseline ordinary least squares (OLS) specifications in which the dependent variables are (1) the six performance indices and (2) *De Facto Policy Autonomy*. I then relax the assumption of no reciprocal causation between the former and the latter, employing a simultaneous equations approach that attempts to extricate the potentially confounding effects of such feedback. To be sure, neither this nor the baseline analysis can fully uncover the causal structure of the relationships between performance, de facto policy autonomy, and other variables. There is an inevitable tradeoff between empirical scope and inferential credibility when analyzing such a broad and heterogeneous sample, and developing strategies to more cleanly isolate causal effects in individual or small groups of institutions is an important avenue for

Table 3.4 Correlations among main PIIP variables

	Aus. Perf.	Danish Perf.	MOPAN Perf.	Dutch Perf.	Swedish Perf.	UK Perf.	Oper. All.	Fac. Agr.	Mon. Com.	Cap. Build.	Des. Int.	Impl. Oper.	All. Res.	De Facto
Danish Perf. Index	0.32													
MOPAN Perf. Index	0.74†	0.71*												
Dutch Perf. Index	NA	0.52*	0.64*											
Swedish Perf. Index	NA	NA	0.02	0.68**										
UK Perf. Index	NA	NA	0.69**	0.71**	0.81**									
Operational Alliances	0.47**	0.55**	0.49**	0.43**	0.62**	0.53**								
Facilitating Agreements	−0.59**	−0.25	−0.29*	−0.49**	−0.51**	−0.65**	−0.38**							
Monitoring Compliance	−0.35*	−0.35*	−0.42**	−0.24*	−0.26*	−0.21*	−0.21**	0.35**						
Capacity Building	−0.22	−0.09	−0.09	−0.21*	0.02	−0.34**	0.10†	0.36**	0.27**					
Designing Interventions	0.56**	0.62**	0.33*	0.44**	0.46**	0.42**	0.61**	−0.35**	−0.19**	0.17**				
Implementing Operations	0.46**	0.57**	0.20	0.38**	0.55**	0.31**	0.64**	−0.38**	−0.22**	0.33**	0.83**			
Allocating Resources	0.48**	0.41*	0.56**	0.43**	0.28*	0.49**	0.29**	−0.47**	−0.59**	−0.48**	0.37**	0.21**		
De Facto Policy Autonomy	0.67**	0.46**	0.41**	0.54**	0.65**	0.64**	0.59**	−0.64**	−0.35**	−0.08	0.61**	0.62**	0.43**	
De Jure Policy Autonomy	−0.05	0.05	−0.07	−0.01	−0.04	−0.06	0.16**	0.07	0.11†	0.10†	0.26**	0.23**	−0.05	−0.05

Notes: †$p < 0.1$; *$p < 0.05$; **$p < 0.01$. "NA" indicates that a pair of variables has fewer than two shared values. The variable names in the top row are abbreviations of those in the leftmost column.

further research. Even so, the tests shine a precise light on conditional associations that strongly hint at such effects and thus provide the grounds for a meaningful evaluation of the framework's macro-level implications.

Analyzing Institutional Performance

In the first set of baseline specifications, I analyze the relationship between performance and both forms of policy autonomy. The six performance indices and their average value – which approximates the "consensus verdict" among donors and allows us to maximize statistical power – are regressed on *De Facto Policy Autonomy* and *De Jure Policy Autonomy*. Standard errors are adjusted for heteroskedasticity and clustered by institution (except in models with the Australian performance index, of which there is only one wave). I initially control for three possible determinants of institutional performance suggested by previous studies, which are all lagged by one year:[47]

- *# Members* is the logged number of an institution's member states (or partner states in the case of PPPs and INGOs). Sources of membership data are described in Chapter 1 (see the notes to Figure 1.2).[48] The rationale for this control is that smaller groups of states may be capable of deeper, more far-reaching, and hence more effective forms of institutionalized cooperation.[49]
- *Preference Heterogeneity* is the variance of member states' foreign policy "ideal points," as measured by Michael Bailey, Anton Strezhnev, and Erik Voeten's spatial model of UN General Assembly roll-call votes.[50] Institutions characterized by greater homogeneity in foreign policy preferences may find it easier to obtain agreement among member states and thus to avoid collective decision-making failures.[51]
- *Policy Scope* is the number of issue areas in which an institution has substantial involvement, which I select from the policy classification scheme mentioned earlier. An institution is coded as substantially

---

[47] Not all factors proposed by these studies are amenable to operationalization and measurement. For instance, bureaucratic culture, institutional leadership, and the "skill" and "energy" available for devising solutions to institutional problems are difficult to gauge empirically, at least in an objective and precise fashion. See Barnett and Finnemore (1999, 2004); Hall and Woods (2018); Miles et al. (2002); Weaver (2008).

[48] All subsequent membership-based variables draw on these sources.

[49] Miles et al. (2002); Young (2011).

[50] Bailey, Strezhnev, and Voeten (2017). I employ an updated version of the dataset that extends to 2018, available at: https://doi.org/10.7910/DVN/LEJUQZ [Last accessed April 24, 2021].

[51] Copelovitch (2010); Miles et al. (2002); Schneider and Tobin (2013).

involved in a given area if (1) this area is mentioned in its founding document (e.g., treaty, constitution, charter) or online mission statement; (2) at least one of its administrative units (e.g., a division, department, office) is dedicated to this area; and (3) it formulates policies in this area. The larger the number of domains that meet these criteria, the greater the potential risk of "conflicting or complex tasks that are difficult to institutionalize and implement."[52]

Note that these three variables are unlikely to lie on the causal pathway from *De Facto Policy Autonomy* or *De Jure Policy Autonomy* to the performance indices, limiting the risk of posttreatment bias.[53] In robustness checks described later, I incorporate a slew of additional control variables into the analysis.

The results appear in Table 3.5. There is strong evidence for the hypothesized positive relationship between performance and de facto policy autonomy: The estimated coefficient on *De Facto Policy Autonomy* is positive, large, and statistically significant in all seven models. A standard deviation increase in *De Facto Policy Autonomy* is associated with a rise in the average of the performance indices of 0.73, which corresponds to a shift from the median value to the 74th percentile.

The expectation that performance is unrelated to de jure policy autonomy also receives backing, with the coefficients on *De Jure Policy Autonomy* approaching zero and exhibiting mixed signs. A standard deviation rise in *De Jure Policy Autonomy* is accompanied by growth in the average performance index of 0.03, the equivalent of inching up from the median value to the 52nd percentile.

Based on Model 7's estimates, Figure 3.4 plots predicted values of the average performance index, bounded by 95 percent confidence intervals, across all levels of *De Facto Policy Autonomy* (upper left panel) and *De Jure Policy Autonomy* (upper right panel). The difference between the two graphs is stark. The predictions are negative, sizable, and significant at low levels of *De Facto Policy Autonomy*, recording a minimum of −1.32, the 18th percentile of the average performance index; and positive, large, and significant at high levels of *De Facto Policy Autonomy*, peaking at 1.46, the 92nd percentile of the average performance index. Contrariwise, they remain close to and statistically indistinguishable from zero at all values of *De Jure Policy Autonomy*. In other words, whereas the model predicts better performance ratings for institutions with higher levels of *De Facto*

---

[52] Gutner (2005, 11). Also see Blair, Di Salvatore, and Smidt (2022).

[53] Acharya, Blackwell, and Sen (2016); Montgomery, Nyhan, and Torres (2018). I do not include institutions' financial resources as a control variable on account of this risk. However, I later show that the results are robust to controlling for annual income.

Table 3.5 *Relationship between performance and policy autonomy*

	Dependent variable: Index of donor performance ratings						
Perf. Index:	Austral. (1)	Danish (2)	MOPAN (3)	Dutch (4)	Swedish (5)	UK (6)	Average (7)
De Facto Policy Autonomy	0.621**	0.437†	0.279*	0.687**	0.959**	0.937**	0.693**
	(0.138)	(0.242)	(0.138)	(0.155)	(0.201)	(0.134)	(0.106)
De Jure Policy Autonomy	0.012	0.101	0.022	0.022	0.008	0.051	0.020
	(0.100)	(0.086)	(0.055)	(0.100)	(0.105)	(0.106)	(0.062)
# Members (log)	−0.040	−1.093†	−0.934*	−0.390†	0.475	0.229	0.030
	(0.179)	(0.592)	(0.377)	(0.229)	(0.851)	(0.245)	(0.177)
Preference Heterogeneity	−0.547	−0.246	−1.514	−4.680*	−3.776	−2.093*	−1.290†
	(0.904)	(2.136)	(2.630)	(1.795)	(2.693)	(0.872)	(0.718)
Policy Scope	0.086	0.608	0.245	−0.350	−0.474	−0.164	−0.107
	(0.301)	(0.484)	(0.283)	(0.303)	(0.449)	(0.172)	(0.167)
Constant	−1.402	3.213	4.583	3.882	−1.773	−2.357*	−1.188
	(1.179)	(3.767)	(3.607)	(2.465)	(4.698)	(0.997)	(0.914)
Observations	42	33	49	116	64	117	293
R-squared	0.462	0.333	0.286	0.351	0.474	0.477	0.359
Adjusted R-squared	0.387	0.209	0.203	0.322	0.429	0.454	0.348

Notes: †$p < 0.1$; *$p < 0.05$; **$p < 0.01$. OLS estimates with robust standard errors, clustered by institution where performance evaluations have multiple waves, in parentheses. All regressors are lagged by one year.

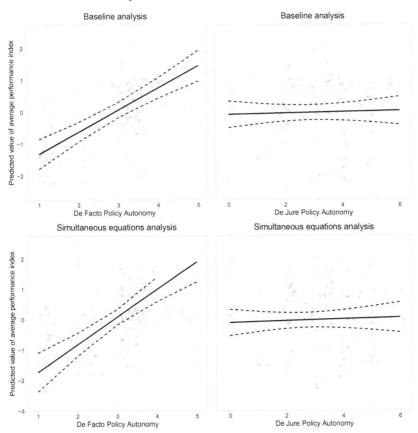

Figure 3.4 Predicted values of average performance index across *De Facto Policy Autonomy* and *De Jure Policy Autonomy*

Notes: Predictions are based on the results of Model 7, Table 3.4 (top panels) and Model 25, Figure 3.6 (bottom panels). The dashed lines represent 95 percent confidence intervals (computed with robust standard errors, clustered by institution). Gray circles denote data points.

Policy Autonomy, it predicts essentially the same rating for institutions at any point on the *De Jure Policy Autonomy* spectrum.

The results for the control variables are generally weak and inconsistent across models. There is little evidence that institutions with smaller memberships or narrower policy portfolios perform better: The coefficients on *# Members* and *Policy Scope* have conflicting signs and mostly fall short of significance. There is stronger, though still not compelling, support for the notion that policy preference alignment among member states increases effectiveness, with the coefficient on

Preference Heterogeneity negative in every model and significant at the 10 percent level in three.

To investigate whether the main findings vary by dimension of institutional performance, I disaggregate each dependent variable into its constituent indicators, generating 51 separate models. The results, summarized in Appendix B.7, are broadly similar across dimensions. Coefficient estimates for *De Facto Policy Autonomy* are positive in 48 of the 51 models and significant in 26. Perhaps reassuringly, a slightly higher proportion of significant estimates occur in models where an indicator of results attainment or financial management – arguably the most central dimensions of institutional performance – is the dependent variable. The estimates for *De Jure Policy Autonomy* are comparable to those in Table 3.5: Almost half are negative and only seven are significant (of which one is negative). In general, there is more consistent support for the hypotheses in models with the Australian, British, Dutch, and Swedish performance indices than in models with Danish and MOPAN indices, a pattern that most likely reflects the larger sample size and higher proportion of results- and efficiency-related indicators in the former set.

Analyzing De Facto Policy Autonomy

The second set of baseline specifications examine the sources of de facto policy autonomy. I regress *De Facto Policy Autonomy* on *De Jure Policy Autonomy*, *Operational Alliances*, and the six governance task dummies (entered in separate models); the control variables are # *Members*, *Preference Heterogeneity*, and *Age*, the logged number of years since an institution's creation. The latter variable features more commonly than *Policy Scope* in statistical analyses of institutional autonomy, on the theoretical grounds that institutions are often characterized by self-reinforcing dynamics that encourage incremental expansions of bureaucratic authority over time.[54] The estimation strategy remains otherwise unchanged.

Table 3.6 exhibits the results. The proposition that de facto policy autonomy is positively predicted by alliance quantity, depth, and breadth and by the exercise of governance tasks with high monitoring costs is borne out. All four measures of these predictors have positive and highly significant coefficients. Averaging across models, a standard deviation rise in *Operational Alliances* pushes *De Facto Policy Autonomy* up by 0.49, lifting an institution from the latter variable's median value to

[54] Haftel and Thompson (2006); Johnson (2014).

Table 3.6 *Sources of de facto policy autonomy*

	Dependent variable: *De Facto Policy Autonomy*					
	(1)	**(2)**	**(3)**	**(4)**	**(5)**	**(6)**
De Jure Policy Autonomy	−0.068 (0.066)	−0.084 (0.089)	−0.093 (0.096)	−0.168[†] (0.090)	−0.138 (0.090)	−0.093 (0.096)
Operational Alliances	0.336** (0.102)	0.487** (0.107)	0.529** (0.104)	0.290** (0.085)	0.301** (0.078)	0.458** (0.106)
Facilitating Agreements	−1.094** (0.298)					
Monitoring Compliance		−0.374 (0.289)				
Capacity Building			−0.183 (0.337)			
Designing Interventions				1.228** (0.274)		
Implementing Operations					1.123** (0.252)	
Allocating Resources						0.510* (0.252)
# Members (log)	−0.179 (0.170)	−0.229 (0.199)	−0.288 (0.207)	0.013 (0.172)	−0.161 (0.160)	−0.129 (0.200)
Preference Heterogeneity	0.110 (0.816)	0.228 (0.925)	0.317 (0.934)	0.585 (0.770)	−0.292 (0.777)	0.096 (0.877)
Age (log)	0.109 (0.128)	−0.028 (0.159)	−0.065 (0.216)	−0.337* (0.158)	−0.295[†] (0.153)	0.018 (0.181)
Constant	3.263** (0.654)	3.480** (0.815)	3.806** (0.932)	3.162** (0.540)	4.396** (0.722)	2.666** (1.018)
Observations	293	293	293	293	293	293
R-squared	0.569	0.427	0.411	0.547	0.551	0.438
Adjusted R-squared	0.560	0.415	0.398	0.537	0.542	0.426

Notes: $^{†}p < 0.1$; $^{*}p < 0.05$; $^{**}p < 0.01$. OLS estimates with robust standard errors, clustered by institution, in parentheses. All regressors are lagged by one year.

its 78th percentile. Designing interventions, implementing operations, and allocating resources are associated with increases in *De Facto Policy Autonomy* of 1.23, 1.12, and 0.51, respectively, which translate into shifts from the median to the 96th, 95th, and 78th percentiles.

Figure 3.5 charts predicted values of *De Facto Policy Autonomy* at varying levels of the four predictors. The predictions rise steeply with *Operational Alliances*, increasing from 1.86 at its minimum value (0), the 21st percentile of *De Facto Policy Autonomy*, to 4.13

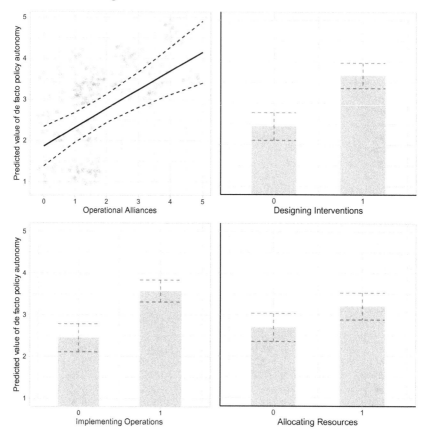

Figure 3.5 Predicted values of *De Facto Policy Autonomy* across *Operational Alliances* and dummies for hard-to-monitor tasks

Notes: Predictions are based on the results of Table 3.6, Model 6 (upper left and lower right panels), Model 4 (upper right panel), and Model 5 (lower left panel). The dashed lines represent 95 percent confidence intervals (computed with robust standard errors, clustered by institution). Gray circles denote data points.

at its maximum value (4.95), the 91st percentile of *De Facto Policy Autonomy* (based on Model 6, Table 3.6, whose estimates are closest to the overall average). Similarly, they become markedly larger as *Designing Interventions, Implementing Operations,* and *Allocating Resources* flip from 0 to 1: The average predicted value is 2.53, the 32nd percentile of *De Facto Policy Autonomy,* when institutions do not perform these tasks and 3.48, the 71st percentile, when they do.

The coefficient on *De Jure Policy Autonomy* is negative in all six models and non-significant in five, substantiating the expectation of a weak de jure–de facto nexus. This finding deserves emphasis: As measured here, the degree of policy autonomy an institution is designed to possess has little – if anything, a slightly adverse – bearing on the degree of policy autonomy it enjoys in practice.

The association between *De Facto Policy Autonomy* and the three dummies for governance tasks that are cheap to monitor is negative and varying in strength. In accordance with the descriptive evidence, the coefficient is sizable and significant at the one percent level for *Facilitating Agreements*, moderate and near significant for *Monitoring Compliance*, and small and nonsignificant for *Capacity Building*. Thus, although easily observable governance tasks are associated with lower levels of de facto policy autonomy, we can only be statistically confident in this relationship in the case of institutions that facilitate international agreements.

The control variables again bring mixed results. There is some evidence that younger institutions enjoy greater de facto policy autonomy: *Age* has a mostly negative coefficient that achieves significance in two models. No clear relationship emerges with membership size or policy preference divergence, as evidenced by the small and nonsignificant estimates for *# Members* and *Preference Heterogeneity*.

Incorporating Feedback: A Simultaneous Equations Approach

The previous specifications were based on the simplifying assumption that de facto policy autonomy influences performance but not vice versa. As my framework recognizes, however, there are good reasons to expect a mutually reinforcing relationship between the two variables. To deal with this possibility, I employ a simultaneous equations strategy that seeks to isolate the component of each variable that is not affected by the other.[55] This approach is commonly used to identify the causal effects of variables that are jointly determined in equilibrium, or *endogenous* variables, given a set of variables determined outside this system, or *exogenous* variables. The canonical example is the supply and demand

---

[55] In doing so, I heed Young's (2011, 19859) call to utilize "methods that can shed light on the role of complex causality as a determinant of effectiveness."

model in economics, in which the price and quantity of goods are endogenous.

A simultaneous equations model comprises a system of structural equations with dependent variables that are a function of one other. Since OLS estimation cannot avoid bias when independent variables are correlated with the error term, the model is usually solved using the technique of two-stage least squares (2SLS). In the first stage of the 2SLS procedure, reduced-form versions of the structural equations – versions that express each endogenous variable in terms of all exogenous variables – are estimated. In the second stage, predicted values from the reduced-form equations are substituted for the endogenous variables in the structural equations. Predictions of each endogenous variable are not "contaminated" by its counterpart, enhancing the credibility of its estimated effect.

I construct a system with two sets of structural equations: one that is identical to the first group of baseline models and another in which *De Facto Policy Autonomy* is regressed on each performance index, *De Jure Policy Autonomy*, the three dummies for governance tasks with high monitoring costs (included in separate models), and the controls from the second group of baseline models. Hence, the endogenous variables in the system are the performance indices and *De Facto Policy Autonomy*; the exogenous variables, on which each endogenous variable is regressed in the first stage of the 2SLS procedure, are *De Jure Policy Autonomy*, # *Members*, *Preference Heterogeneity*, *Policy Scope*, *Age*, *Operational Alliances*, *Designing Interventions*, *Implementing Operations*, and *Allocating Resources*. A more formal description of this system and estimation method can be found in Appendix B.6.

Second-stage coefficients on the policy autonomy variables (from the first set of structural equations) are reported within the right-pointing arrows in Figure 3.6. The estimates for *De Facto Policy Autonomy* remain positive in all seven models and highly significant in six. On average, they are more than a third larger than the corresponding coefficients in the baseline analysis. Notably, a standard deviation increase in *De Facto Policy Autonomy* now comes with a mean boost in the average performance index of 0.95, taking an institution from the median to its 86th percentile. The estimates for *De Jure Policy Autonomy* become positive but stay small and nonsignificant.

The lower panels of Figure 3.4 replicate the prediction plots from the first baseline specification for the simultaneous equation estimates. Predicted values of the average performance index rise even more briskly with *De Facto Policy Autonomy* than before, ranging from -1.73 when *De Facto Policy Autonomy* $= 1$ to 1.89 when *De Facto Policy Autonomy* $= 5$

Policy autonomy   Performance

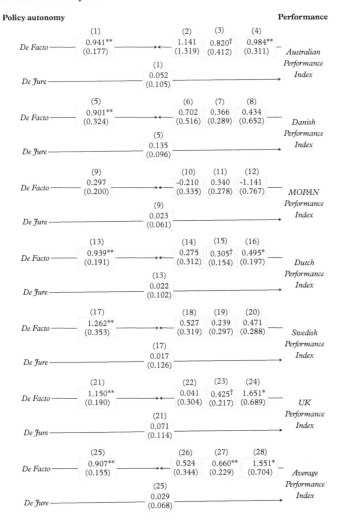

Figure 3.6 Key simultaneous equations results

Notes: † < 0.1; *$p < 0.05$; **$p < 0.01$. Arrows report second-stage 2SLS estimates of the effect of the variable at the tail (the explanatory variable) on the variable at the head (the dependent variable); robust standard errors, clustered by institution where possible, appear in parentheses. In models where a performance index is the dependent variable, the controls are # *Members*, *Preference Heterogeneity*, and *Policy Scope*. In models where *De Facto Policy Autonomy* is the dependent variable, the controls are *Operational Alliances*, # *Members*, *Preference Heterogeneity*, *Age*, and *Designing Interventions* (Models 2, 6, 10, 14, 18, 22, 26), *Implementing Operations* (Models 3, 7, 11, 15, 19, 23, 27), or *Allocating Resources* (Models 4, 8, 12, 16, 20, 24, 28). In the first stage, the opposite dependent variable is regressed on all of the above controls. Regressors are lagged by one year in both stages. For further details, see Appendix B.7.

(lower left panel). As in the baseline results, they vary little across values of *De Jure Policy Autonomy* (lower right panel).

Second-stage coefficients on the six performance indices (from the second set of structural equations) are exhibited inside the left-pointing arrows in Figure 3.6; the left of the three boxes denotes that *Designing Interventions* features as a regressor, the middle box that *Implementing Operations* features, and the right box that *Allocating Resources* features. The results signal a positive but attenuated and less even feedback effect from the performance indices to *De Facto Policy Autonomy*. The coefficients are positive in 19 of the 21 models and significant in eight. The substantive effect is sizable, however: *De Facto Policy Autonomy* grows by an average of 1.12 with each standard deviation of the average performance index, a jump from its median to its 95th percentile. In sum, the findings suggest that the positive relationship between *De Facto Policy Autonomy* and the performance indices reflects a process of mutual causation – albeit one in which the former's impact is stronger than the latter's. In doing so, they corroborate the framework's analysis of dynamic feedback effects, which highlights de facto policy autonomy as the chief force initiating and driving these dynamics.

Alternative Specifications

The results remain in keeping with the argument across a host of alternative specifications, the key estimates from which are reported in Appendix B.7. First, to address possible omitted variable bias, I sequentially add several controls to the baseline models (again lagging them by one year):[56]

1. Dummy variables for the five most common issue areas in the PIIP: economic development (19 institutions), public health (12), humanitarian assistance (nine), the environment (eight), and education (four). Some policy domains may involve cooperation problems or political, social, and economic obstacles that are inherently more difficult for institutions to overcome than those in other areas.[57]
2. An institution's logged annual income in millions of current US dollars, measured using the sources of financial data described in Chapter 1 (see the notes to Figure 1.2). Resource limitations are

---

[56] It is not possible to include all of these variables simultaneously due to the small number of observations in some models.
[57] Miles et al. (2002); Underdal (2010).

frequently cited as an impediment to institutional success.[58] Note, though, that since my argument identifies changes in resources as a potential mechanism linking de facto policy autonomy to performance, controlling for this variable risks absorbing part of the estimated "treatment effect" (and consequently inducing posttreatment bias).

3. The ratio of the real gross domestic product (GDP) of an institution's largest member economy to the combined real GDP of all remaining member economies.[59] Large asymmetries in material capabilities within the membership could facilitate capture by powerful states.[60]

4. The geographical diversity of an institution's member states, measured as $\sum_{i=1}^{M} s_i^2$, where s_i is the share of geographical region i and M is the total number of regions. Regions are defined according to the UN geoscheme.[61] As with preference heterogeneity, wider geographical variation could give rise to more severe coordination problems for states.[62]

5. The average level of democracy among an institution's member states, measured with the widely used Polity2 autocracy–democracy index from the Polity V Project dataset.[63] Institutions with more democratic memberships may enjoy higher levels of compliance with policy decisions – for instance, because they are perceived as more legitimate or because democracies are less likely to violate international commitments – and accordingly achieve superior results.[64]

6. Dummy variables for whether an institution belongs to the two major organizational "families" in the sample, namely, the UN System and the World Bank Group. Members of these families share a distinctive set of historical influences, values, norms, and political dynamics that could shape their performance and autonomy.

Most of these variables have a weak or inconsistent relationship with the performance indices as well as *De Facto Policy Autonomy*. The exceptions are the education issue dummy (negative association with the performance indices), the World Bank Group dummy (positive

---

[58] Abbott and Snidal (2010); Abbott et al. (2015); Gutner and Thompson (2010).

[59] GDP is measured in expenditure-side terms at current purchasing power parity with data from the Penn World Table, version 9.1 (Feenstra, Inklaar, and Timmer 2015).

[60] Conversely, in the hegemonic stability theory tradition, it has been suggested that the presence of a single dominant power is necessary for institutional effectiveness. See Krasner (1983). Note that popular measures of state power, such as the COW Composite Index of National Capability, do not currently cover the PIIP's most recent years.

[61] https://unstats.un.org/unsd/methodology/m49/ [Last accessed April 22, 2018].

[62] Miles et al. (2002). [63] Marshall, Gurr, and Jaggers (2019).

[64] Fearon (1994); Gaubatz (1996); Leeds (1999).

association with the performance indices), and the geographical diversity scale (negative association with *De Facto Policy Autonomy*).

Second, I employ three strategies for addressing temporal trends that could confound the baseline results. First, I include year fixed effects in models where the dependent variable spans multiple years.[65] Second, I control for (1) a linear time trend ($t = 1, 2, ..., T$, where T is the total number of years in the sample) and (2) both a linear and a quadratic time trend ($t + t^2$).[66] Third, I interact the year fixed effects with dummies for whether an institution belongs to the UN System or the World Bank Group.[67] These interactive fixed effects control for family-specific temporal trends.

Third, I examine the robustness of the baseline estimates to the exclusion of different subsets of observations. First, I omit all INGOs and PPPs, which, one might worry, could differ from IGOs in unobserved ways that influence performance and policy autonomy. Second, given the small sample size in some models, I check whether the results are skewed by "influential observations," that is, observations whose removal would significantly alter parameter estimates. Specifically, I exclude from each model all observations with a Cook's Distance of $4/n$, where n is the sample size. Third, I reduce the proportion of humanitarian institutions in the PIIP such that it is statistically indistinguishable (at the five percent level) from that among IGOs in the Yearbook of International Organizations. These institutions are randomly selected for removal.[68]

Finally, I assess the sensitivity of the simultaneous equations results to three modifications that mitigate possible sources of endogeneity in the exogenous variables (from both within and outside the system of equations). First, I exclude *Operational Alliances* from the set of exogenous variables, as it could conceivably be affected by the endogenous variables (see Chapter 2). Second, I restrict this set to variables that are a direct product of institutional design, such as *De Jure Policy Autonomy* and *Policy Scope*. Third, I lag all first-stage regressors to their values in 2007, the year before the first wave of performance ratings was released.

---

[65] I do not control for institution fixed effects due to the short time period covered by the PIIP, during which there is minimal within-institution variation in any variable.

[66] As a strategy for addressing unobserved time-specific heterogeneity, year fixed effects are generally preferable to time trends because they capture potentially confounding temporal patterns of any functional form.

[67] Grigorescu (2010).

[68] Three institutions are excluded: UNICEF, the UN Office for the Coordination of Humanitarian Affairs (OCHA), and the UN Central Emergency Response Fund (CERF). Re-randomizing yields similar results.

Conclusion

The quantitative evidence presented in this chapter furnishes consistent support for my theoretical framework's macro-level propositions. Ratings from a recent wave of methodical, evidence-based donor evaluations of international institutions – probably the most reliable source of comparative data on institutional performance – are positively associated with de facto policy autonomy, as measured by responses to a multifaceted bureaucratic survey. Statistical tests suggest that this relationship is the product of both a strong and sizable effect running from de facto policy autonomy to performance and a weaker and less uniform effect in the opposite direction. Performance scores have negligible association, by contrast, with a parallel measure of de jure policy autonomy based on official design rules, reflecting a stunning gap – often ignored by scholars – between institutions' formal governance arrangements and true modus operandi.

A similar bifurcation characterizes the findings on the roots of de facto policy autonomy. Institutions that boast deeper, more numerous, and broader operational alliances and that exercise governance tasks with lofty monitoring costs for states, such as designing policy interventions and implementing field operations, tend to enjoy wider latitude in the policy process. The reverse is true of institutions whose tasks are amenable to close and sustained governmental oversight, of which monitoring policy compliance and facilitating international agreements are clear examples. Both sets of results emerge unscathed from a succession of robustness checks involving alternative controls, samples, and estimation methods, reducing the chances that they are artifacts of idiosyncratic modeling choices.

The evidence marshaled in this chapter does not constitute the final word on the determinants of institutional performance and autonomy in global governance. Given the donor evaluations' recency and focus on major institutions, the PIIP currently comprises a fairly modest number of cases and years. This limits the statistical power of the chapter's tests and the generalizability of their results both to smaller and less influential institutions and to earlier time periods. In addition, it prevents us from analyzing how performance and de facto policy autonomy co-evolve over extensive periods of time, an important facet of my argument.[69] More

---

[69] As more comparative performance evaluations – and waves of existing ones – are published, these limitations will become less severe. A notable development in this regard is the passage of the Multilateral Aid Review Act of 2020 in the United States – the largest donor to many international institutions – which established a presidential task force to undertake such assessments.

generally, the data are not sufficiently fine-grained to allow for tests of the theory's micro-level implications, which concern the causal processes that tie together performance, de facto policy autonomy, operational alliances, and governance tasks.

In the next two chapters, therefore, I conduct in-depth case studies of seven institutions in the PIIP – the Food and Agriculture Organization (FAO), the World Food Programme (WFP), and IFAD in Chapter 4 and the World Health Organization (WHO), the Joint United Nations Programme on HIV/AIDS (UNAIDS), Gavi, and the Global Fund to Fight AIDS, Tuberculosis and Malaria (GFATM) in Chapter 5 – which shed valuable complementary light on the causal mechanisms and temporal dynamics postulated by my framework.

4   Performing for Scraps

Comparing the FAO, the WFP, and IFAD

> The hungry people of the world wanted bread, and they were to be given statistics.
>
> – John Boyd Orr, first director-general of the Food and Agriculture Organization, 1966[1]

> The work of the World Food Programme to the benefit of humankind is an endeavour that all the nations of the world should be able to endorse and support.
>
> – Announcement of the Nobel Peace Prize, 2020[2]

> Since its earliest days, the International Fund [for Agricultural Development] has achieved an exemplary form of cooperation and co-responsibility between nations at different stages of development.
>
> – Pope Benedict XVI, 2009[3]

In the ancient world, Rome was the center of a powerful empire that straddled much of Europe, North Africa, and Western Asia. Today, it plays host to a very different transnational governance complex with an even larger jurisdiction: the global food security regime. The core institutions of this system are the Food and Agriculture Organization (FAO), situated in the historical heart of the city overlooking the Circus Maximus and the Baths of Caracalla; the International Fund for Agricultural Development (IFAD), located in the southern business district of Esposizione Universale Roma amid a sea of austere fascist-era architecture; and the World Food Programme (WFP), which lies several kilometers to the southwest of IFAD in Magliana, a humdrum urban neighborhood.

Besides their location and issue area, the FAO, IFAD, and the WFP resemble each other in several respects, from their membership to their governance structure. Puzzlingly, however, they are widely recognized as performing at very different levels, with the FAO plumbing the depths of the effectiveness spectrum and the WFP and IFAD scaling

---

[1] Orr (1966, 162).   [2] Norwegian Nobel Committee (2020).   [3] The Holy See (2009).

the heights – differences reflected in the three epigraphs to this chapter.[4] As such, they represent an attractive set of cases for assessing this book's theoretical framework, helping us to hold constant numerous potential determinants of institutional performance and de facto policy autonomy and thus to isolate the relationship and causal pathways between them.

In this chapter, I undertake an extended comparative case study of the FAO, the WFP, and IFAD. Drawing on key informant interviews, policy documents, archival records, expert evaluations, and other primary and secondary sources, I trace each institution's performance over its full lifecycle and the role of de facto policy autonomy in molding this trajectory.[5] Equally important, I explore the roots of such independence, paying special attention to (1) feedback effects arising from over-time trends in performance; (2) the quantity, depth, and breadth of operational links with non-state actors; and (3) the costs states incur in monitoring governance tasks.

The examination corroborates the framework's main observable implications, most notably those concerning the micro-level processes that connect the dependent and explanatory variables. In all three cases, institutionalized cooperation between states was motivated by a common interest in bolstering global food security that subsequently gave way to narrower national priorities – the Jekyll and Hyde problem. There are few signs, in contrast, of the wide and enduring discrepancy between bureaucratic preferences and institutional goals suggested by rogue-agency theories. Quite the reverse: Bureaucrats exhibit a staunch and lasting commitment to the advancement of such objectives that impels them, time and again, to contest opportunistic governmental interventions in the policy process.

Critically, I find that short-, medium-, and long-run trends in performance closely follow those in de facto policy autonomy. The FAO's paltry discretion in policy initiation, development, and delivery – a far cry from its creators' intentions – has enabled powerful nations, in particular the United States, to consistently frustrate collectively oriented bureaucratic initiatives while skewing policy outcomes toward particularistic ends. The more ample freedom from interference enjoyed by the WFP and IFAD, in contrast, has afforded bureaucrats the space and time to develop innovative interventions that assure food security for many of the world's most vulnerable people. Over time,

---

[4] As a well-known volume on international food politics summarizes, "Of the Rome-based UN [United Nations] food organizations, the WFP and IFAD are frequently praised for their work, and the FAO is frequently criticized" (Paarlberg 2010, 181). More than three decades ago, Talbot and Moyer (1987, 362) offered a remarkably similar précis of the general consensus among stakeholders.

[5] For further details on the interviews conducted for this and the next chapter, including a full list, see Appendix C.

these performance patterns have, in turn, reinforced and amplified differences in autonomy, with the FAO's shortcomings encouraging deeper governmental encroachment and the WFP and IFAD's successes furnishing an additional "shield" against interference.

As well as performance itself, alliances and stealth emerge from the examination as central determinants of de facto policy autonomy. The FAO's failure to wrest itself from state domination can be traced both to its weak and narrow operational ties with non-state actors and to its tripartite role as an agreement facilitator, a compliance monitor, and a capacity builder – functions that require close interaction with governments and thus lend themselves to easy top-down oversight. The WFP and IFAD's capacious autonomy, on the other hand, has been forged on a foundation of strong and broad operational alliances, especially with civil society groups, and the exercise of complex, capacity-intensive tasks that are difficult to closely monitor: delivering emergency food aid in the WFP's case and financing policy interventions in IFAD's case.

In the next section, I enumerate the similarities and differences between the FAO, the WFP, and IFAD, providing a more precise description of the case selection strategy and what it allows us to "control for." The rest of the chapter comprises three sections – one per case – that proceed in order of institutional creation. In each section, I begin by providing an overview of the institution's origins, establishment, and principal design features. I then chart the evolving relationship between performance and de facto policy autonomy, partitioning the narrative into historical phases characterized by common trends in the two variables. Finally, I turn to the central hypothesized sources of de facto policy autonomy, exploring whether and how operational alliances and governance tasks have shaped the balance of influence between states and bureaucrats.

Case Selection: Comparing Institutional Characteristics

This book's case studies, as explained in Chapter 1, are based on a "most similar systems" design that matches institutions on as many characteristics as possible *other* than their performance and de facto policy autonomy, the main dependent and explanatory variable, respectively. Although no two institutions are identical, greater likeness in these attributes increases our confidence that processes and pathways linking de facto policy autonomy to performance are causal rather than spurious.

Table 4.1 summarizes a number of key similarities and differences between the FAO, the WFP, and IFAD. The top panel shows that the three institutions have similar average values of the 14 control variables

Table 4.1 *Matched trio: The FAO, the WFP, and IFAD compared*

Characteristic	FAO (Mean)	WFP (Mean)	IFAD (Mean)	St. dev. in PIIP
Control variables				
Age (log)	4.24	3.97	3.62	0.74
Mean Democracy	4.17	4.17	4.01	1.11
Geographical Diversity	1273.32	1249.03	1413.79	832.93
GDP Asymmetry	0.21	0.21	0.23	0.11
# Members (log)	5.25	5.25	5.09	0.60
Policy Scope	2	2	2	0.57
Preference Heterogeneity	0.74	0.74	0.68	0.12
Development Issue	0	0	1	0.48
Education Issue	0	0	0	0.27
Environment Issue	0	0	0	0.30
Humanitarian Issue	0	1	0	0.40
Health Issue	0	0	0	0.42
UN System	1	1	1	0.47
World Bank Group	0	0	0	0.21
Other characteristics (as of 2020)				
Focus on food security	Yes	Yes	Yes	
No. of executive body members	49	36	36	
Executive body term length	3 years	3 years	3 years	
Type of institution	IGO	IGO	IGO	
Scope of activities	Global	Global	Global	
Headquarters	Rome	Rome	Rome	
Performance indices				
Australian Performance Index	−1.38	1.61	0.70	0.95
Danish Performance Index	NA	0.57	1.18	1.19
MOPAN Performance Index	−0.51	0.14	1.05	0.98
Dutch Performance Index	−1.64	1.34	0.74	1.54
Swedish Performance Index	−1.34	0.84	−0.10	1.48
UK Performance Index	−1.13	0.72	0.07	1.31
Average Performance Index	−0.84	0.81	0.40	1.23
Explanatory variables				
De Facto Policy Autonomy	1.22	3.53	3.82	1.05
De Jure Policy Autonomy	5.00	5.67	4.50	1.37
Operational Alliances	1.05	4.65	2.75	1.22
Facilitating Agreements	1	0	0	0.46
Monitoring Compliance	1	0	0	0.47
Capacity Building	1	1	1	0.42
Designing Interventions	0	1	1	0.49
Implementing Operations	0	1	1	0.49
Allocating Resources	0	0	1	0.49

Notes: Italicized variables are defined in Chapter 3. Values are averaged across all evaluation years.

in Chapter 3's statistical analysis.[6] The gap between their highest and lowest values is less than half a standard deviation of 11 variables and less than one standard deviation of 12 variables – all but *Development Issue* and *Humanitarian Issue*. Neither of the latter variables were strong predictors of the performance indices or *De Facto Policy Autonomy* in Chapter 3. Moreover, they diverge between the WFP and IFAD, both of which exhibit high levels of performance and de facto policy autonomy (discussed below), and therefore cannot fully explain the variation of interest in this chapter.

As indicated in the second panel, the three institutions also share several features that were not analyzed in Chapter 3. They all focus on food security issues; are governed by an executive body in which representatives of around a fifth of member states serve three-year terms; are intergovernmental organizations (IGOs) belonging to the United Nations (UN) System; conduct operations in essentially every region of the world; and are headquartered in Rome.[7]

When we inspect scores on the seven performance indices, exhibited in the third panel, the affinities come to an abrupt end. On the six indices that cover all three institutions, the range of mean values exceeds one standard deviation in every case, 1.5 standard deviations in three cases, and two standard deviations in one case. In percentile terms, the FAO lies below the lower tertile of the Performance of International Organizations Project (PIIP) sample on five indices and the 15th percentile on three indices. At the other end of the scale, IFAD sits above the upper tertile on five indices and the 85th percentile on two indices. The WFP occupies even more rarefied air, surpassing the upper quartile on six indices and the 85th percentile on three indices.

An analogous split occurs in the explanatory variables, listed in the bottom panel. The FAO's mean value of *De Facto Policy Autonomy* is 2.21 standard deviations smaller than the WFP's and 2.48 standard deviations smaller than IFAD's; the three values represent the 13th, the 74th, and the 82nd percentile of the distribution, respectively. The gap is even larger for *Operational Alliances*, with the FAO's mean value (26th percentile) 2.96 standard deviations less than the WFP's (99th percentile) and 1.4 standard deviations less than IFAD's (77th

---

[6] I exclude *Income*, which, as noted Chapter 3, could be considered a mediating rather than a control variable.

[7] The similarity of their goals is emphasized by the food policy expert D. John Shaw (2009, 1–2): "They all work for or with food. They seek to end hunger and alleviate poverty. They subscribe to contributing to the achievement of the MDGs [Millennium Development Goals] established by world leaders at the UN Millennium Summit in 2000 ... [T]he mission statements of all institutions show a close similarity."

percentile). With respect to governance functions, the FAO has a value of 1 on all dummies for tasks with low monitoring costs and of 0 on all dummies for tasks with high monitoring costs; the WFP and IFAD score 1 on only one of the former set of tasks but at least two of the latter set.

The three institutions are more comparable in terms of *De Jure Policy Autonomy*, on which their means fall within a range of 1.12 standard deviations. From an institutional design perspective, therefore, the WFP and IFAD's advantage in *De Facto Policy Autonomy* is somewhat surprising. This disparity is even more puzzling given that, as discussed subsequently, the two institutions began life with markedly *lower* levels of de jure policy autonomy than the FAO.

In brief, in a similar fashion to the statistical tests, the case selection strategy holds constant a host of factors that could jointly influence institutional performance and de facto policy autonomy. In doing so, it enables us to more credibly identify the causal connections between these variables, operational alliances, and governance tasks – albeit by qualitative rather than quantitative means. It is this undertaking to which I now turn.

The Food and Agriculture Organization

The FAO was founded shortly after the Second World War as a specialized agency of the newly created UN. The war left scarring experiences of hunger and malnutrition across Europe and other parts of the world, prompting discussions among the Allied powers about a multilateral scheme to boost and more efficiently allocate food supplies. Particularly interested was American president Franklin Roosevelt, one of whose chief goals – outlined in his famous 1941 State of the Union Address – was to ensure "freedom from want" for all citizens of the world.[8] In 1943, at Roosevelt's initiative, the UN held an international conference on food and agriculture in Hot Springs, Virginia. Delegates from 44 nations agreed to appoint an interim commission to draw up plans for a new IGO that would become the FAO.

The constitution of the FAO, signed in Quebec on October 16, 1945, committed member nations to "raising levels of nutrition and standards of living of the peoples under their respective jurisdictions; securing improvements in the efficiency of the production and distribution of all food and agricultural products; bettering the condition of rural populations; and thus contributing towards an expanding world economy and

---

[8] Roosevelt (1941).

ensuring humanity's freedom from hunger."[9] More concisely, the FAO's website describes its mission as "to achieve food security for all and make sure that people have regular access to enough high-quality food to lead active, healthy lives."[10]

Although responsible for some notable achievements, the FAO is generally judged to have fallen well short of this mandate. The Organization has long been viewed as "ineffectual" and "bloated" by public and private stakeholders, and countless studies and appraisals have highlighted deficiencies in key aspects of its performance.[11] The most comprehensive independent assessment of the FAO, the 2007 *Independent External Evaluation* (*IEE-FAO*), diagnosed "a serious state of crisis which imperils the future of the Organization."[12] This verdict, as discussed earlier, has been echoed in the comparative donor evaluations analyzed in Chapter 3. As a 2013 report by the Center for Global Development, a prominent think tank, sums up, "The *IEE-FAO* and the large comparative evaluations find serious limitations on FAO's effectiveness."[13] This section seeks to make analytical sense of the Organization's persistent underperformance.

Tracing Policy Autonomy and Performance over Time

To assess my framework's explanatory power, I trace the coevolution of policy autonomy and performance over the FAO's near 80-year history. The examination naturally divides itself into three phases: (1) the period from the FAO's establishment until around 1970, during which it lost its initially wide-ranging policy discretion and came to be dominated by industrialized food-producing nations; (2) the 1970s and 1980s, which saw the Organization experience its first major crisis and increasingly come under the sway of developing countries, leading to policy gridlock and financial decline; and (3) the three decades since then, during which self-reinforcing feedback processes have accelerated these declining trends, trapping the FAO in a low-autonomy, low-performance equilibrium.[14] Table 4.2 summarizes the three components of de facto and de jure policy autonomy in each phase.

[9] Food and Agriculture Organization (1945, 1288). The FAO was provisionally headquartered in Washington, DC, after its establishment. In 1951, it was relocated to Rome permanently.
[10] www.fao.org/about/en/ [Last accessed December 12, 2020].
[11] Jarosz (2009, 38). Also see Jarosz (2009); Marchisio and Di Blasé (1991); Paarlberg (2010); Shaw (2009); Staples (2006); Talbot (1990); Talbot and Moyer (1987).
[12] Food and Agriculture Organization (2007, 9).
[13] Center for Global Development (2013, 5).
[14] For a similar historical demarcation, see Shaw's (2007) authoritative history of world food security.

Table 4.2 *Summary of the FAO's policy autonomy*

Dimension	Indicator	De jure	De facto
Agenda-setting powers	Power to propose new policies	Delegated to director-general	Primarily exercised by Conference and Council since early 1950s
	Power to prepare budget	Delegated to director-general	Shared by secretariat and Council committees in recent decades
	Power to prepare governing body program	Delegated to director-general	Primarily exercised by Council committees in recent decades
Ability to avoid state veto	Decision procedure: 1. Conference	Majority voting for most issues	Consensus for most issues (since early years)
	2a. Executive Committee (1945–1947)	Majority voting for most issues	Consensus for most issues (since early years)
	2b. Council (executive body: 1947–present)	Majority voting for most issues (since early years)	Consensus for most issues (since early years)
	Distribution of votes	Unweighted	NA (consensus norm)
Access to non-state financing	Non-state contributions	Unspecified	Always received; high until 1970s, declining since then
	Independent earnings	Permitted in 1999	Always made; generally low

Bread, Damned Bread, and Statistics

The severity of the global food security situation after the Second World War – "half the people in the world lacked sufficient food for health," as Sir John Boyd Orr, the FAO's first director-general, later recounted – convinced states that the Organization would require a strong and authoritative secretariat.[15] At the design stage, therefore, the balance between institutional autonomy and member control was struck resolutely in favor of the former.

The FAO was created with a two-tier governance structure common to UN specialized agencies. The highest governing body was the Conference, which comprised one delegate from every member state and was responsible for determining general policy, approving the budget, and electing a director-general to run the secretariat. Supervision of day-to-day work was delegated to an Executive Committee composed not of governments but – uniquely among IGOs – of 9–15 independent individuals "qualified by administrative, experience or other special

[15] Orr (1966, 163).

qualifications to contribute to the attainment of the purpose of the Organization."[16]

Subject to the membership's oversight, the director-general was granted "full power and authority to direct the work of the Organization."[17] This included the right to "formulate for consideration by the Conference and the Executive Committee proposals for appropriate action in regard to matters coming before them"; to draft the Programme of Work and Budget; and to draw up the provisional agenda of the Conference and the Executive Committee.[18] The latter bodies were required to take regular decisions by simple, unweighted majority voting, denying veto power to any individual state. When considering the admission of new members, constitutional amendments or suspensions, and the approval of conventions and recommendations, a two-thirds majority was necessary. This proviso was later extended to decisions on agreements with member governments, the level of the budget, and the in-session addition of agenda items.[19]

It did not take long for the bureaucracy to test its extensive formal powers. In 1946, Orr proposed the creation of an FAO-administered "World Food Board" to stabilize agricultural commodity prices, manage a global food reserve for emergencies, and allocate food surpluses to needy countries, among other things. Anxious that states might be tempted to "escape from the ... difficult task of outlining measures for increasing the world food supply," Orr saw the body as a device to "get governments to give [the FAO] the necessary power" to accomplish its mission.[20] Although initially sympathetic, the United States came out strongly against the proposal at the second session of the Conference, fearing that it would depress prices for commercial agricultural exports, prevent the use of food aid for political purposes, and interfere with ongoing plans for a multilateral trade organization.[21] The United Kingdom soon followed, expressing conflicting concerns that a World Food Board would raise the price of agricultural imports by stimulating global demand. In essence, as Orr put it, "Britain and America were not prepared to give either funds or authority to an organization over which they had not got full control."[22] Orr attributed the United States' about-face to President Roosevelt's death and succession by Harry Truman the

[16] Food and Agriculture Organization (1945, 1291).
[17] Food and Agriculture Organization (1945, 1292).
[18] Food and Agriculture Organization (1945, 1292).
[19] Most of these extensions were made in the FAO's first few years.
[20] Orr (1966, 168, 166). Orr wished to completely exclude states from the World Food Board, preferring that it consist of business people representing all areas of the world working under the UN's general supervision.
[21] Hambidge (1955).   [22] Orr and Lubbock (1953, 57).

previous year. "The American government under President Truman," he lamented, "had swung to the right and come under the influence of big business which had always been opposed to Roosevelt's 'New Deal' ideas."[23]

To ensure that the World Food Board proposal was not put to a vote, the Anglo-American alliance demanded the establishment of an intergovernmental commission to further scrutinize its implications. The commission firmly rejected the scheme, instead recommending that the more sympathetic Executive Committee be replaced by a Council of 18 nations. Executive Committee members vigorously opposed this idea, arguing in an impassioned report that the Council would be "swayed by consideration of the special interests of the countries represented on it."[24] Their objections fell on deaf ears: The Council was inaugurated as the FAO's executive body at the Conference's third session in 1947. As Sergio Marchisio and Antonietta Di Blasé note, "This institutional modification was clearly of major importance to FAO's structural equilibrium, for it eliminated any expert influence at the Organization's decision-making level."[25]

The limits of bureaucratic influence were exposed again in 1949. Seeking to salvage key elements of the World Food Board scheme while assuaging Anglo-American apprehensions, the secretariat published a proposal for an International Commodity Clearing House to reallocate food surpluses without disrupting commercial markets. In the short term, the Clearing House would purchase surpluses using dollars and sell them at concessionary prices to deficit countries for currencies not convertible into dollars or gold; in the longer run, it would build up buffer stocks to smooth out fluctuations in food prices. In spite of broad support from agricultural experts, the plan was blocked by major food producers in the Conference. Resistance was led by the United States, Canada, Australia, New Zealand, and France, which claimed that the Clearing House's functions "either could be performed by governments and existing international agencies or might create as many problems as they solved."[26] With consensus decision-making becoming increasingly common in the Conference and the Council, proposals that were unpopular among even small subsets of the membership had little hope of success.[27]

As a more palatable alternative to the Clearing House, the Conference established the Committee on Commodity Problems, an intergovernmental body that would collect information about food surpluses and issue recommendations on their disposal. A clear pattern was

[23] Orr (1966, 194).   [24] Quoted in Staples (2006, 94).
[25] Marchisio and Di Blasé (1991, 20).   [26] Food and Agriculture Organization (1949).
[27] Marchisio and Di Blasé (1991, 185–186).

crystallizing: Bureaucratic attempts to introduce an efficient mechanism for managing food surpluses and relieving shortages would trigger a sequence of opaque political maneuvers in the Conference or the Council that ultimately shifted authority to a state-dominated body. "As was the case with the World Food Board," Amy Staples observes, "[member states] feared losing control over their food aid programs to a strong FAO that might override national policies ... [T]his series of proposals and counterproposals again shifted the focus of decision making from a powerful international organization ... to a coordinating body of national representatives."[28]

Rather than proposing measures to direct surpluses to deficit regions, the Committee on Commodity Problems developed a set of guidelines – the *Principles of Surplus Disposal*, published in 1954 – specifying the minimum volume of food countries had to commercially import before receiving aid. These rules were heavily criticized by economists and development practitioners, who pointed out that food assistance should allow recipients to *reduce* commercial imports; indeed, maintaining existing levels could have the perverse effect of lowering local prices and impoverishing farmers.[29] Not by coincidence, 1954 was also the year in which the United States passed the Agricultural Trade Development and Assistance Act (known as PL480), which institutionalized the deployment of food aid "[t]o increase the consumption of United States agricultural commodities in foreign countries."[30]

The migration of policy powers to consensus-based intergovernmental organs relegated the secretariat to a largely passive role managing administrative affairs, compiling statistics and classifications, and fulfilling technical assistance requests. The chasm between the FAO's ambitious objectives and modest authority was not lost on its leadership, as illustrated by Orr's epigraphic lament – expressed in his 1966 memoir, *As I Recall* – that the world's hungry people needed bread yet received statistics. Even during his tenure, Orr bemoaned that "the resources and powers entrusted to FAO are woefully limited in relation to these far-reaching objectives. It cannot order particular policies to be adopted; it can only advise, educate, and persuade. It cannot embark on the executive function of purchase and procurement in order to stimulate

---

[28] Staples (2006, 98).   [29] Hopkins (1992).
[30] (United States Congress 1954, 454). On the use of PL480 food aid for political ends by different administrations, see Uvin (1992).

output and equalize distribution; it can only recommend, demonstrate, and discuss."[31]

Little changed with the election of the first director-general from a developing country, the Indian civil servant Binay Ranjan Sen, in 1956. Sen saw clearly that "the major powers were not prepared to establish some form of world food security arrangement under the control of a multilateral organization," and that "a different strategy was therefore required that would be more acceptable to them but would also keep the goal of eliminating hunger alive."[32] His approach was two-pronged. First, backed by developing nations, the secretariat scaled up its capacity-building activities by tapping new sources of UN technical assistance funding, principally the Expanded Programme of Technical Assistance (EPTA), the United Nations Special Fund (UNSF), and from 1965 onward the United Nations Development Programme (UNDP), an amalgamation of the previous two schemes. Second, Sen launched the worldwide Freedom from Hunger Campaign in 1960 to raise awareness of hunger, malnutrition, and possible solutions to them.

The United States "failed to fully back Sen's campaign, because not only did it depart from [American] plans for postwar political and economic dominance through disbursement of its grain surpluses, but also because this new direction promised a greater and more powerful role for the FAO in addressing world hunger."[33] In 1961, to prevent Sen from cooking up other initiatives that might threaten its foreign policy interests, the United States sponsored an amendment to the FAO's constitution limiting the director-general's length of office.[34] Sen's succession in 1967 by Addeke Hendrik Boerma, a Dutch agricultural economist, "represented a victory for the industrialized countries, which had sought the post of Director General by promising magnificent gifts to the Organization's voluntary programmes."[35]

The secretariat's failure to enact the measures it deemed necessary to alleviate food shortages and stimulate production also found expression in stagnant agricultural yield and nutrition trends at the international level. World food output per capita rose by just 1.1 percent annually in the 1950s and 0.8 percent in the 1960s.[36] Moreover, this growth was largely concentrated in the industrialized world, with the most food-insecure nations often enjoying the smallest gains. Africa's per capita growth rate, for example, was *negative* in the 1950s (−0.2 percent) and only marginally above zero in the 1960s (0.1 percent). According to one conservative estimate, the combined number of undernourished people

---

[31] Quoted in Staples (2006, 94).   [32] Shaw (2007, 77).   [33] Jarosz (2009, 43–44).
[34] Food and Agriculture Organization (1961a).
[35] Marchisio and Di Blasé (1991, 68).   [36] Grigg (1986, 246).

in Africa, Asia, and Latin America rose from 550 million in the 1948–1950 period to 650 million between 1960 and 1965.[37] Globally, the proportion of such people was almost identical in the two periods. It is no surprise, then, that "developing Member Nations became increasingly disenchanted with the organization during [the years from 1946 to 1970]."[38]

Nor did the FAO succeed in efficiently allocating resources during the first phase of its life. Financial records obtained from the Organization's Rome archives indicate that, on average, 22 percent of annual expenditures between 1945 and 1969 were consumed by administrative costs, such as office, travel, communications, meeting, accounting, and pension expenses (see upper right panel of Figure 4.1).[39] In several early years, this figure exceeded 40 percent.

Ironically, the only dimension of policy autonomy on which the FAO excelled in the first phase was the one *not* specified in its formal rules: access to non-state sources of financing. Organizational regulations did not explicitly permit donations from non-state actors or independent earnings by the secretariat; all funding needs, the FAO's founders anticipated, would be met with assessed (i.e., mandatory) contributions by member states. Yet, as shown in the lower right panel of Figure 4.1, approximately half of average annual contributions from 1945 to 1970 came from nongovernmental sources (the largest being EPTA and the UNSF). Independent earnings were more modest, making up only a few percent of total income over this quarter-century.

The Empire Strikes Back

The second chapter of the FAO's story begins with the world food crisis of the early 1970s, which was precipitated by a perfect storm of inclement weather, fertilizer shortages, and the first global oil shock. Food stocks plummeted and prices rocketed around the world, with especially devastating consequences for the Sahel region of Africa and Bangladesh, which suffered severe famines that left hundreds of thousands dead. The FAO was condemned for neither predicting nor forcefully tackling the crisis, and a sense that it had "failed to achieve its mandate" became prevalent among donor countries.[40] Boerma accepted that the Organization had done "far from enough when measured

---

[37] Grigg (1985). The threshold for undernourishment is 1.2 × the basal metabolic rate. In contemporary calculations (discussed subsequently), it varies by individuals' physical characteristics and is thus more context-sensitive.

[38] Marchisio and Di Blasé (1991, 67).

[39] I exclude salaries from administrative costs, as they directly contribute to the FAO's substantive activities.

[40] Ross (2011, 95).

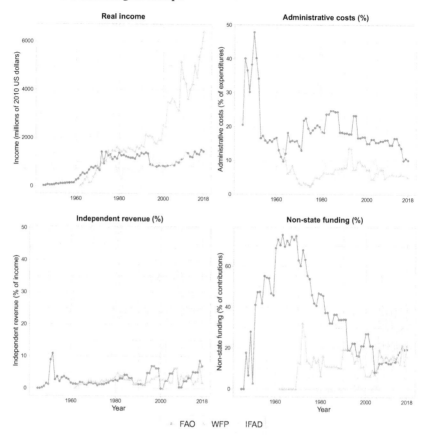

Figure 4.1 Financial trends: The FAO, the WFP, and IFAD

Sources: FAO audited accounts, David Lubin Memorial Library, Rome; WFP audited accounts, WFP Library, Rome; IFAD audited financial statements, IFAD Library, Rome.

Notes: Income data are adjusted for inflation using the United States Consumer Price Index, with 2010 as the base year. Biennial data are divided by two to produce annual values.

against present world needs," placing the blame squarely on member states: "FAO has struggled unceasingly to have its independent ideas ... accepted by its member states. The point I am trying to make is that, all along, we have found ourselves ultimately circumscribed by the limits of political will."[41]

[41] Boerma (1975, 100).

Critics also ascribed the FAO's shortcomings to its efforts to promote the technology-driven "Green Revolution" in the late 1960s and early 1970s, which, they alleged, had distracted it from the challenges facing food producers on the ground. Green Revolution innovations – which included high-yielding crops, chemical fertilizers, pesticides, and new irrigation techniques – had been strongly endorsed by industrialized nations, above all the United States, whose scientists, philanthropists, and corporations played a leading role in developing and commercializing them. The world food crisis, however, demonstrated that they were no panacea. "The Green Revolution had not averted the food crisis," Lucy Jarosz points out, "because it could not address either the proximate causes, such as declining terms of trade or the price of oil, or the larger political and economic dimensions that structured the grains trade and global food flows."[42] What is more, while sometimes improving agricultural productivity, the technologies carried an array of less desirable consequences, such as damaging the environment, raising production costs, increasing inequality among farms, and dispossessing small tenants.[43]

With little faith in the FAO's ability to solve the crisis, Henry Kissinger, the American secretary of state, turned to the UN General Assembly to coordinate a multilateral response. At Kissinger's behest, the UN convoked a World Food Conference in 1974 to "discuss ways to maintain adequate food supplies, and to harness the efforts of all nations to meet the hunger and malnutrition resulting from natural disasters."[44] Participants adopted more than 20 resolutions concerning food production, management, research, and aid, many of which overlapped with existing FAO initiatives. The most significant decision was the foundation of two new international institutions with mandates that directly challenged the FAO: IFAD, which would "finance agricultural development projects primarily for food production in the developing countries";[45] and the World Food Council, a UN body that would "provide over-all, integrated and continuing attention for the successful co-ordination and follow-up of policies concerning food production, nutrition, food security, food trade and food aid, as well as other related matters, by all the agencies of the United Nations system."[46]

---

[42] Jarosz (2009, 48).   [43] George (1977); Patnaik (1990); Pearse (1980).

[44] Kissinger (1973). The conference was held in Rome but not under the FAO's auspices, a decision "seen, implicitly, as a sign of lack of confidence in FAO to deal with the world food crisis" (Shaw 2007, 137).

[45] United Nations (1974, 13).

[46] United Nations (1974, 18). The World Food Council was permanently suspended in 1993.

This bout of institution-building accelerated an ongoing shift in substantive authority away from the FAO, eroding its focal position in global food security governance. In 1971, supporters of the Green Revolution movement set up the Consultative Group for International Agricultural Research (CGIAR), a collection of scientific institutes that soon took over many of the FAO's research activities.[47] During the 1970s, the World Bank substantially expanded its funding for agricultural and rural development projects, briefly becoming "agriculture's most active and generous official international promoter";[48] the UNDP and UNCTAD emerged as major sources of agriculture-related technical assistance; and, as discussed later, the WFP came to play a central role in delivering emergency food assistance. Unsurprisingly, these developments caused consternation within the FAO. At the Conference's 1975 annual session, Gonzalo Bula Hoyos, the chairman of the Council, posed an alarming question to other delegates: "Have we considered the danger that in this way FAO may find itself isolated, reduced to impotence, immured in its ivory tower like a cold technical relic?"[49]

In a bid to reassert the FAO's leadership, Boerma called on the World Food Conference to adopt a global food policy involving an "International Undertaking on World Food Security" – a commitment by states to build up food stocks sufficient to cover production shortfalls – and a global grain reserve to stabilize prices and prevent shortages of the commodity. Neither part of the proposal ultimately succeeded. The Undertaking was endorsed by the World Food Conference and adopted by the FAO Council later in the year, yet only a small number of signatories – and even fewer large agricultural exporters – instituted food reserve policies.[50] Tentative negotiations over an international grain reserve took place at the World Food Conference but collapsed by the end of the decade, mainly due to objections from developing nations about the proposed price of accessing supplies.[51]

The demise of the grain reserve plan reflected a fundamental restructuring of power relations in the FAO that had commenced in the 1960s. As the last European empires crumbled and newly independent countries across Asia, Africa, and beyond entered the multilateral system, the FAO's membership rose from 75 in 1960 to almost 150 by the end of the 1970s. Developing nations came to represent a sizable majority in the Conference, even if they continued to supply a small share of

---

[47] Revealingly, the FAO initially opposed CGIAR's establishment due to fears about institutional competition, but was eventually persuaded to change its stance by peer institutions.

[48] Shaw (2009, 112).   [49] Food and Agriculture Organization (1975).

[50] Marchisio and Di Blasé (1991, 110–111).   [51] Hopkins (1990, 188).

the budget. Amplifying their influence was a high degree of consensus on food security and broader development issues, fostered in part by widespread membership of the Group of 77 (G77) nonaligned nations and adherence to the redistributive ideology of the New International Economic Order. What followed was an antagonistic "North–South" split over the FAO's programs, spending priorities, and overall direction that has by and large persisted to the present day.[52]

Another sign of the developing world's newfound clout was the 1976 election of Edouard Saouma – a Lebanese FAO official who saw the G77's agenda as the best means of restoring the Organization's authority – as director-general over the United States' preferred candidate. Saouma proved a willing agent of the G77, executing their wishes to boost technical assistance for developing countries, increase the number of field staff, and allocate more resources to agricultural investment projects. According to James Ingram, the WFP's executive director for most of the 1980s, "FAO under Saouma was regarded by the G77 as their agency."[53] Policy proposals during this era often originated not in the Conference or the Council but in the G77's secretariat at FAO headquarters, which regularly invited Saouma to its meetings.[54] So satisfied was the group with Saouma's contributions to its cause that, having reversed the 1962 constitutional amendment restricting the director-general's tenure, it ensured his reelection for two more six-year terms.

The G77's interventions put it on a "collision course" with the United States and other industrialized nations, which favored maintaining the FAO's more limited informational and administrative role.[55] From the developing world's perspective, any possibility of the FAO becoming an effective guardian of global food security had been dashed long ago by the excessive meddling of wealthy nations. The G77's overriding aim, as one South American Conference delegate recalled, was thus "to use its policy influence to redistribute benefits to developing countries – even if the price was discord, waste, and programmatic incoherence."[56] That is, poor performance seems to have encouraged states to pursue capture

---

[52] Such a divide was not unique to the FAO. Hopkins (1990, 178) describes the period from 1973 to 1981 as the "structural conflict wave" in the UN, during which "coalitions of southern or G77 states sought to control issues, agendas, and budgets ... in order to exercise power and extract resources from industrialized states."

[53] Ingram (2007, 95).

[54] Marchisio and Di Blasé (1991, 178).

[55] Shaw (2009, 97). Marchisio and Di Blasé (1991, 107) elaborate: "As [industrialized] countries saw it, FAO was a universal organization and, as such, should – despite the new international economic order issue – keep to its traditional mandate, which basically consisted in promoting the exchange of food and agriculture information."

[56] Author interview #46 with FAO Conference delegate, January 19, 2015, Rome.

strategies that further stifled de facto policy autonomy – an early example of the negative feedback processes postulated by my framework.

Unable to regain control of the policy apparatus, industrialized countries began contemptuously abstaining from votes on – and occasionally rejecting – the Programme of Work and Budget submitted to the Conference. In the early 1980s, they went a step further, insisting on zero real growth in the budget and repeatedly delaying or withholding contributions, practices that continued throughout the decade. The money they saved was often redirected to trust funds "earmarked" for specific sectors and themes that aligned more closely with their foreign policy agendas. Deliberations in the Conference and the Council became increasingly fractious and politicized, with industrialized countries and the G77 almost permanently at loggerheads – frequently over diplomatic controversies with little connection to food security – and becoming less trusting of the secretariat.[57] North-South tensions were also reflected in mounting hostility toward the FAO in Western policy circles and media outlets, especially those partial to the United States' Reagan administration.[58] With most non-budgetary decisions still taken unanimously, the upshot was a state of severe policy paralysis. As Marchisio and Di Blasé observe, "FAO was yet again placed in a contradictory position, for on the one hand it was required to abide by the principles of the new international economic order, whilst on the other it was deprived of the legal and financial means to implement these principles."[59]

The resource gap opened up by the FAO's budget freeze was not plugged by other sources of funding. Although remaining fairly high throughout the second phase, the average proportion of contributions received from non-state actors fell from 62 percent in the first five years (1970–1974) to 35 percent in the last five (1985–1989) (see lower right panel of Figure 4.1). This drop was mainly a consequence of the UNDP's pivot toward non-agricultural technical assistance and domestic project implementation in the early 1970s, a decision widely perceived

---

[57] In 1990, for instance, the United States further slashed its contribution because of the FAO's perceived support for the Palestine Liberation Organization.

[58] Several pro-Reagan think tanks and media outlets delivered blistering rebukes of the FAO around this time, including the Heritage Foundation and the *Daily American*, a Rome-based newspaper that published two lengthy dossiers of criticism. Talbot (1990, 37) summarizes the *Daily American*'s "indictment" as follows: "(1) FAO is 'an arrogant, overbudgeted, and rarely effective bureaucracy'; (2) FAO has failed in its 'most fundamental task,' which is 'to keep the hungry from starving'; (3) it is 'impossible for outsider observers to check and monitor where funds are spent and how'; (4) FAO is 'ethically contemptible' and demands 'increased contributions,' but reneges on 'basic promises and duties'; (5) FAO is 'unwilling or unable to accept these criticisms and equally unwilling to consider major structural changes.'"

[59] Marchisio and Di Blasé (1991, 224).

as reflecting dissatisfaction with the FAO's performance and partnership behavior – another instance of negative feedback from performance to de facto policy autonomy.[60] Independent earnings continued to account for just a few percent of revenues in the second phase (lower left panel of Figure 4.1). Worryingly, therefore, a declining trend was taking hold in the one dimension of de facto policy autonomy on which the FAO still fared well.

Hampered by the loss of core competences, shrinking resources, and entrenched policy stalemate, the FAO failed to make deeper inroads toward its outcome objectives during the second phase. According to its own estimates, plotted in Figure 4.2, the global count of undernourished people barely budged between 1970 and 1990, remaining in the region of 850 million.[61] The Organization's resource efficiency also left much to be desired: Administrative costs made up one-fifth of annual expenditures, on average (upper right panel of Figure 4.1).

Short Summits, Long Troughs

The end of the Cold War, followed soon after by the election of a new director-general – the Senegalese diplomat Jacques Diouf – briefly ignited hopes that the FAO could reverse its deteriorating performance trajectory. Diouf pledged to streamline operations and administration – the FAO's total number of staff had remained close to 6,000 since the 1970s, up from around 4,000 in the early 1960s – and to return food security to the top of the international community's agenda.[62] To the latter end, he convened the 1996 World Food Summit, "a forum at the highest political level to marshal the global consensus and commitment needed to redress a most basic problem of humankind – food insecurity."[63] The Plan of Action adopted by the 182 states in attendance enumerated 27 objectives, most of which, detractors noted, were "only a restatement of commitments acceptable to every government rephrased in the sustainable, participatory, gender-sensitive, anti-poverty, environmentally friendly terms of the moment."[64] One of the few indisputably new aspirations was to halve the number of undernourished people in the world to roughly 400 million by 2015, a target that seemed eminently achievable in view of recent successes in

---

[60] Crittenden (1981).
[61] Undernourishment is defined as consuming less than the minimum daily energy requirement, that is, the number of calories needed for light activity and a minimum acceptable weight given one's height.
[62] For staff numbers from 1963 to 1999, see the Yearbook of the United Nations, available at https://unyearbook.un.org [Last accessed April 12, 2020]. There is no consistent reporting of such figures before this period.
[63] Food and Agriculture Organization (1995).
[64] Shaw (2007, 353).

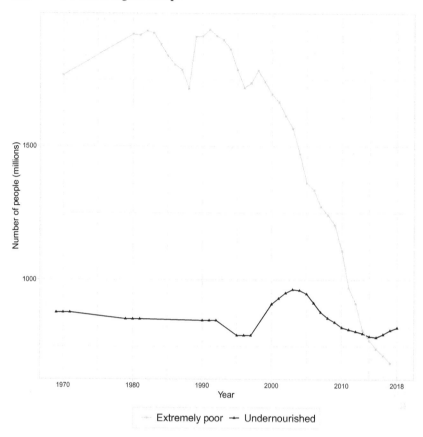

Figure 4.2 Number of undernourished and extremely poor people in the world, 1969–2018

Sources: FAO online hunger statistics (undernourishment 1969–1997), accessed at:
https://web.archive.org/web/20130929070556/http://www.fao.org/hunger/en/;
FAO *State of Food Security and Nutrition in the World* reports (undernourishment 2000–2018); Bourguignon and Morrisson (2002) (extreme poverty 1970, averaged across the authors' two time series); World Bank PovcalNet online database (extreme poverty 1980–2017), accessed at: http://iresearch.worldbank.org/PovcalNet/home.aspx.

reducing poverty in Asia and other parts of the world. A modified version of this goal – halving the 1990 proportion of undernourished people by 2015 – was incorporated into the UN's Millennium Development Goals (MDGs) in 2000.

Conspicuously missing from the Plan of Action was any intention to declare food a human right, a move strongly advocated by civil society groups in the run-up to the World Food Summit. As stressed by the NGO Forum on Food Security, a gathering of more than 1,200 nongovernmental organizations (NGOs) from 80 countries held in parallel to the meeting: "International law must guarantee the right to food, ensuring that food sovereignty takes precedence over macroeconomic policies and trade liberalization. Food can not be considered as a commodity, because of its social and cultural dimension."[65] Despite being backed by much of the FAO's membership, an explicit commitment to this right was vetoed by the United States, which worried that it would generate additional "international obligations" to provide food aid and trade concessions to developing countries.[66]

The subsequent years saw neither sustained progress toward the World Food Summit's objectives nor an easing of the FAO's internal strife, policy impasse, and financial troubles. To the contrary, a growing loss of confidence in the Organization appeared to exacerbate these problems, encouraging industrialized nations to make deeper budgetary cuts and pursue even more particularistic agendas. One long-serving FAO planning officer singled out the declining cost of interference for states as a key mechanism behind this feedback process:

A perverse dynamic arose in the late 1990s whereby some rich nations saw the FAO's problematic performance and reputation as justification for overtly political interventions. The thinking was: "If the Organization is already failing to do what we want – already compromised, in a sense – why shouldn't we use it for our own narrow purposes?" The growth in earmarked funding during the 1990s was an obvious example ... Of course, this strategy played well at home – think about how the FAO was perceived in America at the time, for example.[67]

To take stock of the situation, the FAO Council called a follow-up conference, the World Food Summit: Five Years Later, in 2002. Speaking at the opening ceremony, UN Secretary-General Kofi Annan warned participants that they were in serious danger of missing their undernourishment target, deeming progress "far too slow."[68] Echoing Boerma's frustrations almost three decades earlier, Diouf laid culpability at the door of governments: "[S]ix years after the World Food Summit 1996, death continues to stalk the multitude of hungry people on our planet. Promises have not been kept. Worse, actions have not reflected words. Regrettably, the political will and financial resources have not matched the mark of human solidarity."[69] Once more, though, few meaningful

[65] NGO Forum on Food Security (1949).
[66] Food and Agriculture Organization (1997, 50).
[67] Author interview #49 with FAO planning officer, January 20, 2015, Rome.
[68] Food and Agriculture Organization (2002, Annex 1).
[69] Food and Agriculture Organization (2002, Annex 1).

commitments were made; the centerpiece of the conference's official declaration was a largely rhetorical call for public and private stakeholders to forge an "international alliance against hunger" to meet the undernourishment goal.[70] Brushing off renewed pressures from civil society, the United States again quashed a proposed resolution endorsing a right to food, maintaining that trade liberalization and investment in biotechnology were more promising strategies for tackling hunger and malnutrition.[71] An NGO Forum held alongside the meeting expressed its "collective disappointment in, and rejection of, the official Declaration."[72]

Shortly after the World Food Summit: Five Years Later, the FAO Council adopted a joint proposal by the United States and Canada for a "comprehensive external evaluation ... that considers FAO's performance and impact and how effectively and efficiently it is discharging its mandate."[73] This exercise, which evolved into the *IEE-FAO*, drew on a wide array of sources, including more than 2,500 internal and external interviews, 12 surveys of bureaucrats and state delegates, several field visits, and specially commissioned working papers on major policy initiatives and organizational departments. As noted by the lead authors, a team of six food policy and development experts, it represented not only the first independent assessment of the FAO but also "probably the largest and most ambitious evaluation ever attempted of a global intergovernmental organization."[74]

The *IEE-FAO*, as mentioned earlier, delivered a damning indictment of the FAO's performance. The "serious state of crisis" it highlighted took two forms. The first was a financial crisis stemming from real budget cuts and delayed contributions over the preceding 25 years. The resulting shortfall was not offset, it emphasized, by the concurrent growth in earmarked funding for states' "own priorities," which "frustrates attempts by FAO management to design a coherent strategy."[75] The second crisis was a programmatic one caused by the Organization's tendency to "[dissipate] resources, providing products and services with few significant outcomes or impacts and in areas where it no longer has comparative advantage" and to make "small, non-strategic

---

[70] Food and Agriculture Organization (2002, Appendix).
[71] The United States has enjoyed some success in making the case for biotechnology. In 2004, the FAO published a controversial report emphasizing the potential of genetically modified crops to "meet the needs of the poor" (Food and Agriculture Organization 2004a). An open letter to the Organization signed by more than 850 NGOs and 800 individuals from 83 countries called the report "a declaration of war on the farmers [the FAO] is pledged to support" (GRAIN 2004).
[72] Food and Agriculture Organization (2002, Annex 3).
[73] Food and Agriculture Organization (2004b, 1).
[74] Food and Agriculture Organization (2007, 6).
[75] Food and Agriculture Organization (2007, 181, 38).

interventions with little, if any, prospect of replication elsewhere or of generating sustainable benefits."[76] Together, these two predicaments had progressively diminished the FAO's standing in global food security governance: "Issues of trade in agricultural and food products have become principally the purview of the WTO. Agricultural research as an international public good now resides unquestionably with the CGIAR. Much of the governance of natural resources for food and agriculture has migrated over the past two decades to new environmental agreements. Legislative leadership in issues of animal health, including epidemic diseases which may spread to humans (zoonoses), reside principally with the World Organisation for Animal Health."[77]

The *IEE-FAO* ascribed these woes chiefly to "low levels of trust and mutual understanding between Member Nations themselves and between some Member Nations and the Secretariat," which encouraged politicization and impeded productive cooperation and rational decision-making.[78] This was linked, it argued, to the "low levels of delegated authority relative to comparator organizations," which "creates and reinforces a rigid, risk-averse, and centralized organizational culture" and hence "greatly limits FAO's potential for development effectiveness in meeting the needs of its Members."[79] Within the secretariat, authority was highly concentrated in the director-general – the official closest to member states and governing bodies – whose approval is required for even routine processes. Other members of senior management, such as division directors, enjoyed "few independent powers of decision-making."[80] In the *IEE-FAO*'s main staff survey, only 17 percent of respondents believed that decisions were made at a level that makes their work effective and 13 percent considered the Organization successful in delegating appropriate levels of authority and responsibility.[81]

Interestingly, the *IEE-FAO* rejected any connection between performance problems and bureaucratic motives or preferences. In the staff survey just mentioned, 84 percent of respondents reported being proud to be an FAO employee and 93 percent strongly supported the Organization's goals and objectives.[82] Around three-quarters cited factors other than pay as their motivation to do a good job, higher than

[76] Food and Agriculture Organization (2007, 10).
[77] Food and Agriculture Organization (2007, 39).
[78] Food and Agriculture Organization (2007, 9).
[79] Food and Agriculture Organization (2007, 3).
[80] Food and Agriculture Organization (2007, 313).
[81] While the response rate is not disclosed, "[s]urvey respondent demographics were compared with the overall demographics of FAO to ensure responses were representative" (Food and Agriculture Organization 2007, 220).
[82] Food and Agriculture Organization (2007, 225).

the average proportion in a sample of 50,000 comparable surveys of public, corporate, and nonprofit institutions. In a follow-up interview one official described the FAO as possessing a "dream mandate," an opinion "shared by a number of focus groups."[83] The report sums up: "The overwhelming consensus of staff at all levels is that FAO's mission, goals and objectives are noble and that these merit the full commitment of staff."[84] Tellingly, it was only "[w]hen asked to consider how the overarching principles of FAO translate into day-to-day activity" that "staff responses [became] far less positive."[85]

The *IEE-FAO* proposed a lengthy list of reforms to the FAO's management strategy, governance procedures, administrative systems, budget, and technical assistance programs, which were accepted by the Conference. A Conference committee was formed to draw up an "Immediate Plan of Action" based on the proposals, whose implementation has continued under the two most recent directors-general: José Graziano da Silva, a Brazilian agronomist; and Qu Dongyu, a Chinese agricultural official.[86] These efforts have generally been well received by the Organization's now 3,000 staff and 194 member states, and have succeeded in arresting its long-standing decline in contributions and total income (see upper left panel of Figure 4.1).

The reform process has left the FAO's de facto policy autonomy largely untouched, however. As one member of senior management reflected: "The rules say one thing, but member states do something else – they dominate every aspect of the policy process. In that respect, the *[IEE-FAO]* hasn't changed a thing."[87] Programs, projects, and rules still tend to be put forward by state delegates rather than bureaucrats, with the Council's seven standing committees – which deal with program, finance, constitutional and legal matters, commodity problems, agriculture, forestry, and fisheries – playing a pivotal agenda-setting role.[88] The Conference and the Council continue to operate mostly by consensus, a practice that has even extended to budgetary decisions in recent years.[89]

Nor have the reforms checked the FAO's growing reliance on governmental sources of financing: Non-state actors supplied an average of 21 percent of annual contributions from 1990 to 2006 and 16 percent from

---

[83] Food and Agriculture Organization (2007, 225).
[84] Food and Agriculture Organization (2007, 225).
[85] Food and Agriculture Organization (2007, 225).
[86] Food and Agriculture Organization (2008).
[87] Author interview #51 with FAO senior manager, January 19, 2015, Rome.
[88] Author interview #47 with FAO Council delegate, January 19, 2015, Rome. While the secretariat drafts the budget, spending proposals are heavily vetted by the Council's Programme Committee and Finance Committee.
[89] Author interview #49 with FAO planning officer, January 20, 2015, Rome.

2008 to 2018 (lower right panel of Figure 4.1). Independent earnings have remained a tiny fraction of total income (lower left panel of Figure 4.1), even though the FAO's constitution was amended in 1999 to permit the secretariat to sell and license products and services and to invest surplus funds.[90]

As my framework would predict, therefore, improvements in institutional performance have been difficult to discern. Soon after the *IEE-FAO*'s release, the FAO came under fire for failing to anticipate and avert a spike in food prices that wrought economic and social turmoil across large parts of the developing world. Abdoulaye Wade, the president of Senegal, went as far as to call for the Organization's abolition, berating it as a "bottomless pit of money largely spent on its own functioning, with very little effective operations [sic] on the ground."[91] Criticism intensified with the publication of the comparative donor evaluations and the growing realization that the World Food Summit's undernourishment target was well out of reach: Almost exactly the same number of people were undernourished in 2015 as in 1996 (see Figure 4.2). By way of comparison, the number of people living in extreme poverty fell by almost 60 percent over this period. The MDG of halving the 1990 proportion of undernourished people by 2015 was also missed, albeit by a smaller margin.[92] The related MDG of halving the 1990 proportion of extremely poor people was achieved five years ahead of schedule.

Finally, the upper right panel of Figure 4.1 shows that, despite attempts to improve organizational efficiency in the wake of the *IEE-FAO*, the FAO's administrative outlays have remained elevated in recent years, averaging 17 percent of annual expenditures in the 1990–2006 period and 14 percent over the next 12 years.

Sources of De Facto Policy Autonomy

Why has the FAO failed to preserve the high degree of policy discretion enshrined in its constitution? In accordance with the framework, the Organization's limited de facto policy autonomy is linked to both its exercise of governance tasks with modest monitoring costs for member countries and its dearth of robust operational ties with actors above and below the state.

Governance Tasks

The FAO is often described as serving both a "normative" and an "operational" role. In terms of the governance tasks delineated in

[90] Food and Agriculture Organization (1999).   [91] Ba (2008).
[92] United Nations (2015).

Chapter 2, the former mainly involves facilitating and monitoring international agreements, while the latter entails delivering capacity-building assistance to developing countries.

Industrialized nations have traditionally viewed the FAO first and foremost as a forum for exchanging views, sharing information, and formulating international regulations, standards, and guidelines on food security. In this capacity, the Organization arranges and provides administrative support for sessions of the Conference and the Council, compiles cross-national agricultural data, and conducts background research to inform policy decisions. These activities are largely costless for states to observe, restricting the scope for autonomous bureaucratic action. In the opinion of one evaluation officer: "The FAO is above all a vehicle for bringing together states and helping them to develop rules, standards, and other kinds of normative instruments … Governments are in the driving seat; the bureaucracy – though reasonably large by the standards of international organizations – supports and enables negotiations. The whole process takes place under the noses of government delegates in Rome, so staff don't have many opportunities to independently influence policy."[93]

The FAO is also charged with monitoring the implementation of legal instruments agreed under its auspices, such as the *International Treaty on Plant Genetic Resources for Food and Agriculture* and binding decisions made by specialized regional commissions (such as the General Fisheries Commission for the Mediterranean). This task entails soliciting and publicizing compliance information from state parties to these instruments. The monitoring mechanism for the *International Treaty on Plant Genetic Resources for Food and Agriculture*, for instance, requires signatories to submit regular reports on implementation measures to a Compliance Committee of legal and scientific experts, which synthesizes them for the agreement's governing body.[94] Since states lie at both ends of the monitoring "information loop," it is relatively straightforward for them to oversee the mechanism's operation.

Developing countries have, for the most part, been more interested in the FAO's capacity-building work – its provision of policy advice, expertise, skills, and equipment via technical assistance projects – than its normative pursuits. Member governments formally request such support from the Organization and then work closely with its country offices to execute projects, providing them with information about local agricultural and economic conditions, facilitating their communications

---

[93] Author interview #48 with FAO evaluation officer, January 19, 2015, Rome.
[94] See www.fao.org/plant-treaty/areas-of-work/compliance/faqs/en/ [Last accessed July 25, 2020].

with relevant government agencies and nongovernmental stakeholders, and often co-financing their activities. Consequently, though taking place far from headquarters, staff activities can still be easily tracked by states. In this regard, Ross Talbot and H. Wayne Moyer point out, the FAO's in-country operations differ significantly from projects conducted by international financial institutions (IFIs), whose design bears a strong bureaucratic imprint: "FAO is severely constrained in its policy autonomy in that its resources are primarily technical rather than financial. Unlike the World Bank and IFAD, FAO cannot carry out development projects, but can only provide technical support."[95] That the costs of such assistance are often shared with recipient governments presents a further constraint: "FAO activities must remain very closely tied to the projects funded by [donors] ... FAO must do what the donors want, if it is to retain access to this funding."

Operational Alliances
The struggle to cultivate and maintain strong operational ties with non-state stakeholders has been a recurring theme in the FAO's history. In the Organization's early years, the supply of potential partners was the principal constraint. Few NGOs existed, let alone focused on food security, and the FAO was the sole international institution operating in this issue area. Among institutions in the broader development policy space, only EPTA and the UNSF – and later the UNDP – expressed an interest in joining forces with FAO staff.

Supply-side constraints eased in the 1970s and 1980s, as civil society blossomed across much of the world, new food-focused international institutions were established, and development finance agencies began to pay more attention to agriculture and rural poverty. Demand for partners became the limiting factor: The FAO repeatedly spurned opportunities to work with other actors in the growing food security ecosystem due to fears about competition and the loss of authority. In a wide-ranging critique published in 1988, the Heritage Foundation, an American think tank, lamented that the Organization was "unwilling to give up any bureaucratic turf."[96] In support of this charge, it quoted the chairman of the Danish FAO National Committee, an official liaison body, calling the FAO "an unwilling partner in international cooperation." Nor was this unaccommodating attitude well received by the few partners the Organization *did* have, as illustrated by the UNDP's decision to scale down collaboration in the late 1970s.

---

[95] Talbot and Moyer (1987, 354).   [96] Pilon (1988, 5).

By the third phase of the FAO's history, it had acquired, in the *IEE-FAO*'s telling, a "bad name" as a partner and a "narrow" and "territorial image."[97] The report was especially scathing about the secretariat's weak operational ties with the private sector, the "biggest player in much of the global agricultural landscape in the 21st century," and at the country level, where it "has few resources, in terms of engaging with other development agencies, NGOs, and the private sector."[98] In a survey of member states, 78 percent of respondents blamed the difficulties encountered by the Conference and the Council in performing their global governance role on "poor links and institutional relationships with other global bodies," the highest share of the four response options.[99] Noting that the FAO "has neither a strategy nor specific plans for partnerships," the *IEE-FAO* offered a spate of recommendations for broadening and solidifying these arrangements.[100] According to the comparative donor evaluations, however, the Organization continues to lack diverse and productive partnerships.

Data from the FAO's website substantiate this assessment.[101] In the years it has received performance ratings from donors, the Organization has listed an average of 36 operational partners, well below the sample mean of 66. More than 60 percent of these collaborators had a purely symbolic affiliation with the FAO, almost three times the mean. The vast majority of partners were IGOs (42 percent) or NGOs (53 percent), with only a small fraction hailing from the private sector (five percent).

The relative paucity and shallowness of the FAO's operational alliances have severely curtailed the external political and material support available to bureaucrats for resisting capture. As one partnerships coordinator bemoaned, "Given the wide range of public and private actors who are interested in food security issues, we should have more, broader, and stronger partnerships than we do. Unfortunately, the relationships we *have* formed are too often PR [public relations] exercises that, if you look closely, don't involve much meaningful collaboration. Nobody is invested enough in our performance to put real pressure on governments to stop misbehaving – something I've seen done in our sister agencies."[102] Nor, as detailed in

---

[97] Food and Agriculture Organization (2007, 215).
[98] Food and Agriculture Organization (2007, 63, 216).
[99] Food and Agriculture Organization (2007, 172). All member states were surveyed, of which around half responded.
[100] Food and Agriculture Organization (2007, 216).   [101] Extracted from links provided at: www.fao.org/partnerships/en/ [Last accessed January 2, 2019].
[102] Author interview #50 with FAO partnerships coordinator, January 20, 2015, Rome.

the previous section, have partners helped to shore up policy autonomy by reducing the FAO's reliance on governmental contributions.

World Food Programme

A joint initiative of the FAO and the UN, the WFP was founded in 1961 for a three-year trial period, after which it was made permanent. The Programme was born out of a timely convergence of interests between the FAO, which had been attempting to create a mechanism for allocating surplus agricultural commodities to food-deficit countries since its inception, and the United States, whose new Kennedy administration believed that such a device would legitimize, ease the burden on, and improve the efficiency of the country's massive bilateral food aid scheme. After reading a report by Director-General Sen on the hunger-alleviating potential of agricultural surpluses in April 1961, George McGovern, the director of the United States' Office of Food for Peace, presented a proposal for a temporary multilateral food distribution program to the FAO. Receiving widespread assent, the document formed the basis for parallel FAO and UN resolutions formally establishing the WFP later in the year.

In light of the WFP's experimental character – it was only expected to last until food surpluses were disposed of – its founding documents did not articulate a definitive set of objectives. The clearest summary of its priorities was provided in the FAO's resolution, which mentioned that attention would be paid to "meeting emergency food needs" and promoting "economic and social development, particularly when related to labor-intensive projects and rural welfare."[103] In 1996, the WFP became the first UN body to adopt an official mission statement, at the core of which were three goals: "(a) to use food aid to support economic and social development; (b) to meet refugee and other emergency and protracted relief food needs; (c) to promote world food security in accordance with the recommendations of the United Nations and FAO."[104] The Programme's website describes its aims as "delivering food assistance in emergencies and working with communities to improve nutrition and build resilience."[105]

In contrast to the FAO, the WFP is credited with making significant headway toward its objectives, averting countless famines, saving millions of lives, and meaningfully advancing economic and social development across the globe through the provision of multilateral food

---

[103] Food and Agriculture Organization (1961b, paragraph 10).
[104] World Food Programme (1996b, Annex).
[105] www.wfp.org/overview [Last accessed December 14, 2019].

assistance.[106] The Programme was awarded the 2020 Nobel Peace Prize "for its efforts to combat hunger, for its contribution to bettering conditions for peace in conflict-affected areas and for acting as a driving force in efforts to prevent the use of hunger as a weapon of war and conflict."[107] WFP operations are renowned among stakeholders for their impact and efficiency, an image scholars and food aid experts have found to be well justified.[108] Although a comprehensive independent evaluation of the Programme has yet to be carried out, internal and external appraisals of its activities have been consistently effusive.[109] For instance, a 2007 review of the WFP's management and administration by the Joint Inspection Unit (JIU), the UN's oversight arm, described it as playing a "primary, critical role in fighting hunger and ensuring food security worldwide" and highlighted its reputation as "a dynamic organization that fulfils its mandate and delivers fast, effective aid and assistance to its beneficiaries."[110] As discussed in the second section, similarly positive conclusions have been reached by the comparative donor evaluations.

Tracing Policy Autonomy and Performance Over Time

The WFP's de facto policy autonomy and performance have evolved in two distinct phases: the period from its creation until the early 1990s, in which structural constraints on bureaucratic leeway were gradually dismantled, yielding rich performance dividends; and the past two decades, in which high levels of de facto policy autonomy (see Table 4.3) have laid the ground for – and been reinforced by – impressive performance outcomes.

Food Fights for Freedom

As a shared FAO–UN undertaking rather than a stand-alone agency, the WFP was designed with little room for bureaucratic policy maneuver. Per its founding resolutions and Basic Texts, the Programme was governed by an Intergovernmental Committee composed of 20 member

[106] Barrett and Maxwell (2005, 123–124) note that emergency food aid, of which the WFP is the principal international manager and distributor, has "protected the life and health of hundreds of millions of emergency-affected people over the past fifty years."
[107] Norwegian Nobel Committee (2020).
[108] E.g., Barrett and Maxwell (2005); Clay and Stokke (2013); Paarlberg (2010); Ross (2011); Shaw (2001, 2011). Encapsulating the academic consensus, Clay describes the WFP as "unquestionably a success story within the UN system" (2003, 707).
[109] E.g., Federal Ministry for Economic Cooperation and Development (Germany) (2005); Chr. Michelsen Institute (1994); United Nations Joint Inspection Unit (2001).
[110] United Nations Joint Inspection Unit (2001, 2).

Table 4.3 *Summary of the WFP's policy autonomy*

Dimension	Indicator	De jure	De facto
Agenda-setting powers	Power to propose new policies	Delegated to secretariat in 1991	Exercised by secretariat since mid-1970s
	Power to prepare budget	Delegated to secretariat in 1991	Exercised by secretariat since 1991
	Power to prepare governing body program	Delegated to secretariat	Always exercised by secretariat
Ability to avoid state veto	Decision procedure: 1. Intergovernmental Committee (1961–1976)	Majority voting for most issues	Consensus for most issues (since early years)
	2. Committee on Food Aid Policies and Programmes (1976–1996)	Majority voting for most issues	Consensus for most issues (since early years)
	3. Executive Board (1996–present)	Consensus	Consensus
	Distribution of votes	Unweighted	NA (consensus norm)
Access to non-state financing	Non-state contributions	Permitted in 2000	Always received; low until ≈1970, moderate thereafter
	Independent earnings	Permitted in 2000	Always made; consistently low

states of the UN and the FAO, half of whom would be elected by the FAO Council and the other half by the UN Economic and Social Council (ECOSOC).[111] On paper, this body normally employed simple, unweighted majority voting and took decisions on "important" issues, such as the approval of projects and the allocation of budgetary resources, by a two-thirds vote. In practice, it tended to operate by consensus.[112]

The WFP was administered by a small unit within the FAO secretariat – equivalent in status to a department – that was entrusted with few agenda-setting powers. The head official, the WFP's executive director, was appointed by and reported to both the UN secretary-general and the FAO director-general, whose (individual or collective) approval was required for a wide range of decisions, including senior staff

[111] World Food Programme (1963). Membership increased to 23 in 1963.
[112] Author interview #52 with WFP senior manager, January 21, 2015, Rome.

appointments, the adoption of management rules, and the disbursement of emergency food aid.[113] While the executive director was tasked with preparing the Intergovernmental Committee's agenda, responsibility for drafting the budget was shared between the secretariat, the FAO Finance Committee, and the UN Advisory Committee on Administrative and Budgetary Questions. The WFP's administrative and accounting services were provided by the FAO on a reimbursable basis, resulting in a nontrivial fiscal transfer to the latter each year.[114] Funding took the form of voluntary contributions from states – pledged at special conferences that only the UN secretary-general and the FAO director-general could call – with no formal provision for non-state donations or bureaucratic revenue-generating activities.

Kept on a tight leash by a troika of the Intergovernmental Committee, the UN, and the FAO, the WFP struggled to make an independent impact in its first decade. During the experimental period, the Programme responded rapidly to an earthquake-induced humanitarian emergency in northern Iran and launched moderately successful development projects in Sudan and Togo, convincing donors that it deserved to be extended. However, lacking a proprietary stockpiled food reserve, sizable cash supplies, and control over the deployment of such resources, it was unable to build on and extend this progress in the ensuing years. Emergency operations were allocated an ever smaller share of the budget by the Intergovernmental Committee, in large part because the United States feared the misuse of quickly disbursed funds,[115] and development projects often failed to yield either short-term nutritional or long-term economic benefits.[116] As a result, the WFP remained "a largely marginal actor in the global food aid system," handling only five percent of such assistance by end of the 1960s.[117]

The WFP's role dramatically grew over the next two decades, transforming it into the focal institution of multilateral food aid. An initial catalyst was the world food crisis of the early 1970s. The WFP made a decisive contribution to mitigating famine in Africa's Sahel region, leveraging an innovative combination of cargo aircraft, trucks, and camel trains to dispatch food aid to 25 million people.[118] Recognizing its potential to make similarly impactful interventions elsewhere, the World Food Conference delegated the Programme a host of additional responsibilities. First, it was handed administrative control over a new International Emergency Food Reserve stocked with 500,000 tons of cereals. Second, its mandate was broadened to include "promoting world

---

[113] The executive director was appointed in consultation with the Intergovernmental Committee.
[114] Charlton (1992).   [115] Hopkins (1990, 193).   [116] Clay (2003, 702).
[117] Charlton (1992, 632).   [118] Barrett and Maxwell (2005).

food security in accordance with the recommendations made to it by the United Nations and the FAO."[119] Third, the Intergovernmental Committee was reconstituted as the Committee on Food Aid Policies and Programmes, a more powerful body with 30 members and a remit to deal with *all* aspects of short- and long-term food aid policy.

These developments equipped the WFP with a ready supply of commodities and cash – as the recognized international authority on food aid, it attracted increased contributions – eliminating the key operational constraints on its emergency response capability. Equally important, they eased the *political* constraints on its work by enabling the secretariat to play a more proactive role in the policy process. While their formal agenda-setting powers remained modest, bureaucrats began discreetly crafting proposals for emergency operations as well as regular development projects, which they would then submit to the Committee on Food Aid Policies and Programmes on behalf of recipient governments.[120] Despite taking decisions by unanimity, the Committee almost never rejected project proposals and only occasionally requested modifications to their terms.[121] "Unless the WFP leadership decides to withdraw a project," one observer reported in 1990, "all projects are approved."[122]

Project authorization was another area in which the bureaucracy's policy space expanded. At the end of the experimental period, the Intergovernmental Committee had, in the interests of rationalizing its workload, permitted the executive director to unilaterally approve projects with a food value up to $750,000 and revisions to existing project budgets worth a maximum of $100,000. Following the world food crisis, these thresholds were raised multiple times, by the early 1980s reaching $1.5 million for project approvals and 10 percent of project food value for budget revisions (with a ceiling of $1.5 million per year per project).[123]

The WFP's burgeoning discretion empowered it to preempt and deflect attempts by powerful nations to manipulate its assistance for narrow political purposes. At the height of the Cold War, the secretariat defied the United States to push through much-needed development projects in Soviet allies such as Cuba, Ethiopia, Nicaragua, and Vietnam.[124] The WFP executive director, James Ingram, was committed

[119] World Food Programme (1978, 21).
[120] Author interview #63 with WFP government partnerships officer, January 27, 2015, Rome.
[121] Talbot (1990, 61); Talbot and Moyer (1987, 357).   [122] Hopkins (1990, 192).
[123] World Food Programme (2004, 8). Projects involving refugee populations had a $2 million food value limit.
[124] Uvin (1994, 149). In most cases, the United States opted against blocking consensus in the Committee on Food Aid Policies and Programmes, anticipating that it would be defeated in a majority vote.

to both ensuring "political even-handedness in the distribution of our assistance ... by 'standing up' to the US and others" and resisting "donor efforts to radically cut back the list of countries eligible for WFP assistance."[125] This pledge did not always lead to confrontation with major donors; the secretariat exhibited considerable skill at averting and defusing political tensions by modifying project terms and offering concessions to disgruntled parties.[126] The WFP's growing reputation for political neutrality during the 1980s, not to mention the broad support among member states for Ingram's reelection in 1986, attest to a high degree of success in delivering on his commitment.[127]

In response to popular demand, the WFP also used its widening latitude to ramp up emergency operations. In the 1980s, it led the international response to a string of high-profile famines, including in Ethiopia (1983–1985), where it dispatched two million tons of food, and Sudan (1989), where it released 1.5 million tons from 20 aircraft in what remains the largest humanitarian airdrop in history. The positive publicity garnered by these interventions stimulated further growth in contributions, which, in turn, facilitated further operational expansion.[128] Archival financial data show that the WFP's annual real income more than doubled between 1970 and 1990, overtaking that of the FAO, its parent organization (upper left panel of Figure 4.1). The secretariat grew from less than 800 staff in the early 1980s to almost 2,000 a decade later.[129]

These developments fueled a sharp surge in WFP food deliveries. Figure 4.3 illustrates how the metric tonnage of food distributed by the Programme increased from 900,000 in 1975 to more than 2.3 million in 1990 (left panel), raising its total number of beneficiaries from less than 15 million to almost 45 million (right panel). By the early 1990s, a quarter of global food aid and a third of all UN development assistance flowed through the WFP, with the majority allocated to

[125] Ingram (2007, 310).
[126] For instance, Ingram placated opposition to a set of projects in Grenada, Rwanda, Senegal, and Madagascar from the United States and Canada, which were uncomfortable with the proposed approach of selling food to finance general government budget assistance, by promising to study the consequences of this practice. A staff report published the next year found it to carry no adverse consequences for recipient countries. Hopkins (1990, 193).
[127] Hopkins (1990, 196–197).
[128] Charlton (1992, 631).
[129] WFP annual reports of the executive director (1963–2013), accessed from the WFP Library, Rome.

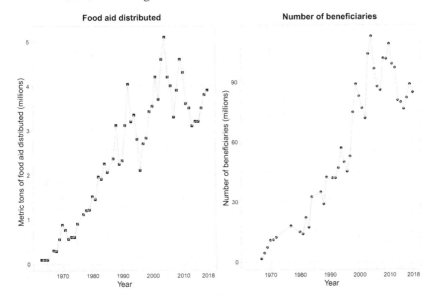

Figure 4.3 WFP food aid deliveries, 1963–2018

Sources: Annual reports of the WFP executive director (1963–2013), WFP Library, Rome; annual WFP performance reports (2014–2018), accessed at: www.wfp.org/publications?f%5B0%5D=publication_type%3A2149.

emergency operations rather than development projects. Commendably, the secretariat was able to maintain a high level of efficiency while scaling up its activities: Administrative spending accounted for an average of six percent of annual disbursements over the 1975–1990 period, less than a third of the FAO's figure (upper right panel of Figure 4.1).[130]

Bureaucratic independence was not without limits, nevertheless. The WFP remained, for all intents and purposes, a department of the FAO, which insisted on vetting policy papers, authorizing emergency aid allocations, and micromanaging financial administration and hiring decisions – often, Ingram protested, in ways that exceeded its formal powers.[131] During the 1970s and 1980s, these intrusions typically served as a conduit for political tensions simmering in the FAO at the time. Ingram complained that the Committee on Food Aid Policies and Programmes, "ostensibly an intergovernmental technical body," sometimes "became a political body where issues were not considered on

---

[130] A 1992 assessment of the European Commission's food aid transportation costs identified the WFP as its most cost-effective aid partner. TecnEcon (1992).
[131] Ingram (2007).

their merits but in terms of North-South politics."[132] The small share of funding the WFP derived from nongovernmental sources compounded these problems: On average between 1975 and 1990, three percent of annual income came from independent earnings (lower left panel of Figure 4.1) and 12 percent of annual contributions were supplied by non-state actors (lower right panel).

Upon assuming office, Ingram sought to rein in the FAO's – and, by extension, the G77's – influence by appealing to the UN, the WFP's other parent, for support. The entreaty quickly bore fruit: In the mid-1980s, a legal opinion by the UN Office of the Legal Counsel and reports by the JIU and a special UN task force corroborated Ingram's assertion that the FAO had exceeded its de jure authority, suggesting the need for a clearer separation between the two institutions. In addition, the UN secretary-general's ex-officio representative on the Committee on Food Aid Policies and Programmes became a more vocal presence in its deliberations, repeatedly advocating broader bureaucratic discretion and urging members to give the executive director "the support which he will need to discharge his responsibilities effectively."[133] UN backing emboldened Ingram, who began to regularly dispense with illicit practices and norms that entrenched the FAO's policy influence, such as its prescreening of documents submitted to the Committee.[134] In 1990, Ingram persuaded the Committee to commission a more fundamental review of the WFP's governance arrangements and relationship with the FAO. The report, published later in the year, proposed a series of far-reaching reforms that would transform the Programme into a fully independent institution, including giving the executive director sole authority over its administrative and financial affairs and increased control over its staffing and emergency allocations; converting it into a distinct legal entity; moving it to its own headquarters; and giving the Committee, whose membership would increase to 42 nations, exclusive powers of oversight. The proposals were adopted by the Committee in 1991.

Two years later, the WFP's governing body was restructured yet again, albeit this time thanks to developments outside the institution. In the

[132] Ingram (2007, 96). He added, though, that "[w]ithin the FAO Finance Committee and the FAO Council consideration was even more overtly political." This is consistent with Talbot's (1990, 61) reading: "In contrast to the FAO, however, the WFP secretariat is less captured by the leadership and agenda of the Group of 77."
[133] Ingram (2007, 88).
[134] Charlton (1992, 641). Ingram later reflected that his "predecessors had unnecessarily acquiesced in FAO control over their personnel and financial management of the Program, control which was stifling progress in the use of food aid for development and emergencies" (2007, 88).

early 1990s, a combination of the end of the Cold War, deepening inter-dependence between nations, and growing linkages between economic, social, and political issues prompted reflection in the international community about the future of the sprawling UN System. Resolving that UN funds and programs would benefit from greater structural and organizational coherence, the UN General Assembly passed a 1993 resolution converting their governing bodies into identical executive boards comprising 36 (rotating) nations from five regional groups.[135]

When revised to incorporate this change, the WFP's Basic Texts further extended the secretariat's de jure policy autonomy. In addition to the powers acquired in the 1991 reforms, the executive director would bear full responsibility for preparing a Management Plan (a comprehensive biennial program of work) and a longer-term Strategic Plan; for drafting the budget; and for setting the new Executive Board's agenda. The upper limit for unilateral project approvals and budget revisions (per year per project) was lifted to $3 million in food value. Executive Board decisions would be taken unanimously, though a majority vote would be required if consensus could not be attained. Decisions about amendments to the Basic Texts and mid-session changes to the agenda would require the consent of a two-thirds majority. With respect to non-state funding, the WFP would be permitted to both accept donations from "intergovernmental bodies, other public and appropriate non-governmental, including private, sources" and earn its own income from investments.[136]

More Food, More Honor

Since its restructuring and separation from the FAO, the WFP has succeeded in sustaining a high degree of policy independence *in practice* as well as on paper. The Programme's secretariat, which now numbers almost 8,000, is the chief architect of its Management Plan, Strategic Plan, and budget.[137] Furthermore, it is the source of almost all project proposals and reports submitted to the Executive Board, which, in the words of one official, is largely confined to a "rubber-stamping role."[138] As Sandy Ross remarks, "[T]he dynamics of donor control are complicated by the capacity of the WFP secretariat to work up proposals for projects with one or more recipient countries, lobby for support

---

[135] Members of the WFP Executive Board would still be elected in equal share by the FAO Council and ECOSOC.
[136] World Food Programme (2000a, 20).
[137] United Nations System Chief Executives Board for Coordination (2021, 1).
[138] Author interview #64 with WFP resource management officer, January 28, 2015, Rome.

amongst EB member-states (and NGOs who it may well contract with to deliver the aid), and put forward a proposal at the Board. The Board dynamics are such that donors are usually reluctant to be seen to be opposing well-prepared project proposals, and it would be a mistake to equate donor power with control over WFP activities."[139]

Executive Board decisions are usually made by consensus, in line with the Basic Texts, though majority voting is common on politically sensitive matters.[140] Since the early 2000s, country programs have been approved on a "no-objection basis," and the executive director has enjoyed budgetary authority over protracted relief and recovery operations – a key category of WFP assistance – with a food value of $20 million and below. While the majority of the Programme's resources still flow from states, it has received a higher proportion from independent and non-state sources than the FAO in many recent years (lower left and right panels of Figure 4.1, respectively).[141]

With a firm grasp on the policy machinery, the secretariat has continued to scale up emergency operations – which now account for more than 90 percent of WFP expenditures – while resisting opportunistic interventions in the aid allocation process. On numerous occasions, senior management has persuaded large donors to set aside political misgivings to assist relief efforts in rival nations. During the North Korean famine of the 1990s, for example, the WFP's executive director, Catherine Bertini, successfully lobbied skeptical American policymakers to contribute food aid to its mission in the country.[142] By 1999, food shipments from American shores had reached almost 600,000 tons, making them the largest form of foreign aid to North Korea.[143] Three years later, the United States was swayed by Bertini to send a generous food assistance package to Zimbabwe, another country with which it had hostile relations. Over the next five years, it delivered more than 700,000 tons of food to Zimbabwe via the WFP, the most of any nation.

When combustible situations have arisen, the WFP secretariat has maintained its adeptness at pacifying and placating concerned parties. In 2002, for instance, the Programme's efforts to prevent a looming famine in southern Africa were almost derailed after several recipient countries discovered that its food shipments contained genetically mod-

---

[139] Ross (2011, 203).
[140] Author interview #65 with WFP Executive Board member, January 28, 2015, Rome.
[141] Contributions from non-state actors reached more than a fifth of the total in 2018.
[142] Ross (2011, 134).
[143] More recently, the WFP convinced South Korea to fund a program addressing acute malnutrition among babies and mothers in North Korea, to which it had refused to provide any food aid for several years. It continues to send such assistance through the WFP, including 50,000 tons of rice in 2019.

ified organisms (GMOs), an innovation they strongly opposed. Their concerns were swiftly put to rest when WFP staff arranged for the food to be locally milled, which all but one of them found acceptable; a non-GMO substitute was sourced for the holdout country (Zambia).[144] The next year, the Programme adopted a policy of guaranteeing that food aid meets the health and safety standards of both donor and recipient countries. Another example is the decision to avoid following the FAO into the controversial debate over whether there is a human right to food – despite the obvious connection to the WFP's work. As Ross argues, endorsing this right "could have caused bitter political struggles on the [Executive Board], and almost certainly a decline in US support."[145] More generally, Ross highlights the success of WFP officials in "depoliticizing" decision-making throughout the 1990s by decentralizing operational processes and embedding potentially controversial project proposals in policy frameworks endorsed by the Executive Board.[146]

Econometric studies of WFP assistance offer more systematic evidence of the limited influence of politics in its operations. Analyzing data on food aid flows to 114 countries between 1975 and 1998, Christopher Barrett and Kevin Heisey find that WFP allocations were highly sensitive to local (nonconcessional) food availability – a key indicator of recipient need – whereas bilateral allocations from the United States were essentially unresponsive.[147] A follow-up study by Eric Neumayer shows that during the 1990s the Programme's assistance was positively associated with several other measures of local need, such as poverty and reliance on food imports, but largely unrelated to proxies for donors' political interests, such as their food exports to and distance from recipient nations.[148] Similarly to before, bilateral allocations – particularly from the United States – have a weaker correlation with indicators of recipient need and a stronger one with indicators of donor interest. These results are consistent with the WFP's own needs-oriented criteria for apportioning aid – including those articulated in its 1996 mission statement and 2004 "Humanitarian Principles" – as well as donor perceptions of the process.[149] As Christopher Barrett and Daniel Maxwell summarize, there is a "widespread belief within the donor community that multilateral assistance is more effective in reaching intended recipients in a timely and cost-effective manner, partly because it is allocated more according to recipients' needs than donors' needs."[150]

---

[144] Clapp (2005).   [145] Ross (2011, 219).   [146] Ross (2011, 124).
[147] Barrett and Heisey (2002). The latter finding is also reported by Barrett (2001).
[148] Neumayer (2005).   [149] World Food Programme (1996b, 2000b).
[150] Barrett and Maxwell (2005, 63).

The WFP has also demonstrated responsiveness to the requirements of recipient countries in *how* it procures aid. Traditionally, food has been shipped from donor to recipient countries, where it is either handed out to beneficiaries or monetized, that is, sold on the open market to finance budgetary support for the government or NGO development projects. Since at least the 1970s, this model has been criticized by development experts for its slow response time, high transportation costs, and propensity to depress local agricultural prices, with censure intensifying in the late 1990s and early 2000s.[151] In response, despite resistance from donors that benefit from a multilateral outlet for discarding surplus food – in particular the United States – the WFP has altered its procurement system in four notable ways. First, since the mid-1970s, it has purchased more food from developing countries, which now account for more than 80 percent of total procurement. Second, over the past 15 years, it has experimented with aid modalities that give greater agency to beneficiaries, such as the provision of vouchers and electronic cards for local food purchases. Third, to facilitate the previous two strategies, it has urged donors to replace in-kind contributions with (unearmarked) cash. Fourth, it ended monetization outside of "exceptional circumstances" in 1997.[152]

The development of robust needs-based procurement and allocation systems has yielded remarkable results in the WFP's post-independence era. By the turn of the millennium, the Programme had grown into the world's largest humanitarian agency, supplying 95 percent of multilateral food aid and more than half of all such assistance. In total, it had fed no less than a billion people.[153] Since 2000, the WFP has delivered an average of almost four million metric tons of food to over 90 million people per year (see Figure 4.3), leveraging an enormous logistical network that coordinates 5,600 trucks, 30 ships, and nearly 100 planes on any given day.[154] In doing so, it has succeeded in preventing numerous likely famines – including in Afghanistan (2001), southern Africa (2001), the Sahel region (2012), South Sudan (2014), Nigeria (2017), and Yemen (2019) – and in substantially mitigating serious humanitarian crises in Iraq (2004), Haiti (2010), Somalia (2011), Syria (since 2011), and elsewhere.

These achievements have been made possible by a motivated workforce that appears genuinely committed in advancing the WFP's goals. In a recent global staff survey, 86 percent of respondents reported that

---

[151] For extended discussions of the critique and the evidence behind it, see Barrett and Maxwell (2005); Clapp (2012).
[152] World Food Programme (1997, 10).   [153] Ross (2011, 132).
[154] www.wfp.org/overview [Last accessed November 2, 2020].

their mission makes them feel that their work is important and 88 percent expressed pride in their association with the Programme.[155] Presenting these results in a recent annual report, David Beasley, the current executive director, described the WFP's staff as its "greatest asset."[156]

Success has also been facilitated by – and contributed to – sustained growth in institutional resources. Real annual income has almost quintupled since 2000 (upper left panel of Figure 4.1), equipping the WFP with the largest regular budget of any multilateral development institution. The secretariat has continued to make economical use of these funds, keeping administrative costs at just six percent of total expenses on an average annual basis from 2000 to 2018 (upper right panel of Figure 4.1). This figure is the lowest among operational UN agencies and likely to compare favorably with any multilateral development or humanitarian organization.[157]

According to several officials and Executive Board members, the WFP's accomplishments have been instrumental in safeguarding and reinforcing its hard-won independence. In particular, they highlighted how effective performance heightened the risks of political interference by fostering domestic support for the Programme's work and forcing states to choose between competing foreign policy goals. These feedback mechanisms, one WFP oversight officer opined, helped to explain the absence of state opposition to bureaucratic agenda setting since the end of the Cold War:

WFP's independence and apolitical character are central reasons for its consistently strong results. What's sometimes overlooked, though, is that the relationship goes both ways: Effectiveness has made it easier for us to stay above the political fray. We have a reputation for saving lives, which makes it harder for governments to interfere with our decisions; there's a price to pay at home. There's also a cost in foreign policy terms. Food security is a major goal for most donors. If WFP is working well, states have to ask themselves: Is it worth risking this progress for some conflicting priority?[158]

As evidence of feedback from performance to policy autonomy, some interviewees cited the secretariat's growing powers of project approval over the past two decades, which they linked to Executive Board respect

---

[155] World Food Programme (1996a, 4). Eighty-five percent of staff completed the survey, the highest ever rate for a large UN agency.
[156] Food and Agriculture Organization (2019, 5).
[157] To my knowledge, there are no comparable panel data for such institutions. However, according to estimates by Easterly and Williamson (2011), only a few multilateral aid agencies had a ratio of administrative costs to total development assistance below six percent in 2008 (the mean was 29 percent).
[158] Author interview #54 with WFP oversight officer, January 22, 2015, Rome.

for its track record of proposal screening, design, and preparation. A key impetus for this expansion was a 2000 report by the Working Group of Governance – a committee of member state delegates later renamed the Governance Group – that emphasized "the Board's confidence in the ability of the Secretariat to design and implement effective projects and operations within a robust policy framework."[159] More recently, the Executive Board has considered allowing the executive director to unilaterally approve and revise a wide range of emergency operations, country strategic plans, and service provision activities as part of a new policy framework designed to "reinforce the effectiveness and efficiency of WFP's operations."[160] One Executive Board member wryly noted that enthusiasm for this proposal "dramatically increased" following the announcement of the 2020 Nobel Peace Prize.[161]

Sources of De Facto Policy Autonomy

Effective performance is by no means the only source of the WFP's expansive de facto policy autonomy. Even more significant have been the high costs of monitoring emergency food assistance for (donor and recipient) governments and the vast and diverse web of operational alliances with non-state actors the Programme has spun to carry out this function.

Governance Tasks

The WFP's primary duty during its first 15 years – delivering aid projects to improve nutritional and health outcomes with a view to promoting socioeconomic development – is a form of capacity building that presents few monitoring difficulties for states. As in the FAO, governments submit technical assistance requests to the secretariat and work closely with it to design, organize, and implement projects.

Distributing emergency food aid across the globe is a considerably harder task for states to oversee. The WFP manages a complex, highly decentralized supply chain that comprises several stages: (1) planning the aid intervention; (2) procuring food from governments or commercial producers, sometimes spread across disparate geographies; (3) checking the food's quality, if necessary processing and fortifying it, before packaging and labeling it; (4) transporting the food to the target area by air, sea, or land (or some combination thereof); (5) depositing the food in warehouses or mobile storage units; and (6) dispensing the

---

[159] World Food Programme (2000c, 8).   [160] World Food Programme (2019, 2).
[161] Author interview #142 with WFP Executive Board member, November 3, 2020, via video conference.

food to beneficiaries.[162] The supply chain is administered by teams of logistics experts that operate in and move between multiple countries and regions, preventing states from easily tracking their activities. The Executive Board is only directly involved in the planning stage (of relatively large operations), and even there oversight is inhibited by the time pressures of emergency response and the technically challenging nature of global supply chain management.[163] These monitoring difficulties have been underscored in several independent reviews of the WFP's oversight arrangements in recent decades.[164] Executive Board members interviewed for a 2012 report on internal WFP controls by the United States Government Accountability Office (GAO), for example, "described oversight as difficult because they lacked sufficient resources and expertise" as well as "sufficient time."[165]

It is not by accident, then, that the WFP's de facto policy autonomy remained circumscribed until emergency response became its primary focus in the 1980s and 1990s. As one logistics manager recounted, "For the secretariat, the shift toward emergency assistance meant not only a change in its day-to-day work but also – maybe even more saliently – greater freedom from the dictates of member states ... Emergency operations are more devolved and complex than regular development projects, which effectively shelters staff from governing body scrutiny. That's why the Intergovernmental Committee was able to take a more hands-on approach to governance than its successor."[166] Nor is it a coincidence that independence further flourished following the decentralization reforms of the 1990s, which transferred key decision-making and operational powers away from headquarters – the easiest location for states to monitor their exercise.[167]

Operational Alliances

The WFP's operational links with non-state actors stretch back to its experimental years. To build support for its continuation, field staff made a concerted effort to involve humanitarian NGOs, agribusinesses,

---

[162] Author interview #58 with WFP logistics manager, January 23, 2015, Rome. The WFP's supply chain even has its own annual report. See www.wfp.org/publications/wfp-supply-chain-annual-report-2019 [Last accessed February 2, 2020].

[163] Lall (2017, 274–275).

[164] World Food Programme (2000c, 2005); United States Government Accountability Office (2012); World Food Programme (2020). In response to these assessments, the Executive Board has taken steps to streamline its agenda and bolster its technical expertise. The impact of these efforts is not yet clear; many interviewees felt that oversight problems are likely to persist because they are inherent in the WFP's operational structure.

[165] United States Government Accountability Office (2012, 15).

[166] Author interview #58 with WFP logistics manager, January 23, 2015, Rome.

[167] See Ross (2011).

and religious groups in planning and delivering projects.[168] A fully-fledged network of operational alliances, however, did not materialize until the WFP expanded its emergency operations more than a decade later. Unable to single-handedly manage all stages of the food aid supply chain, the secretariat enlisted the logistical and technical support of a multitude of subnational and supranational actors. Among the WFP's closest partners were private shipowners and insurers, who helped to meet its transportation needs; other UN institutions and IGOs, including the UNDP, the United Nations High Commissioner for Refugees (UNHCR), the United Nations Children's Fund (UNICEF), the European Commission, and the World Bank, with which it pooled resources, expertise, and experience; and local and international NGOs, which dispensed food at the final stage of the supply chain.[169]

The WFP's budding network of partners formed a loose but increasingly influential coalition for policy autonomy in the 1980s and 1990s. Logistical and policy expertise supplied by institutional, civil society, and private-sector partners put the secretariat in a position to seize control of key agenda-setting powers.[170] In addition, as discussed earlier, the UN's legal and political support was crucial to Executive Director Ingram's successful departure from FAO-biased policy norms and crusade for self-determination. Ingram cultivated the UN as an ally by participating in meetings of its senior officials, entering the Joint Consultative Group on Policy – a forum for its development agencies to coordinate their activities – and "seeking out more opportunities for collaborative projects" with its funds and programs.[171] Central to these efforts was the WFP's liaison officer with the UN, Tekle Tomlinson, who Ingram praised as "highly respected by the secretariat and delegates alike" and a "superb lobbyist for the program."[172]

NGO partners also emerged as important advocates for policy autonomy during Ingram's tenure, albeit with member states rather than the UN. Among the most influential were global humanitarian charities – in particular CARE, Mercy Corps, Save the Children, and World Vision – many of which were members of the Coalition for Food Aid, a Washington-based lobby group established in 1985. Exploiting their close ties to Capitol Hill, these organizations repeatedly dissuaded

---

[168] Johnson (2014). In his 1965 petition to make the WFP permanent, the first executive director, Addeke Hendrik Boerma (a previous FAO director-general), expressed particular gratitude to "other agencies in the United Nations family and the nongovernmental organizations with which the Program has been cooperating so fruitfully" (Food and Agriculture Organization 1965, v).

[169] Shaw (2001).

[170] Author interview #53 with WFP program manager, January 21, 2015, Rome.

[171] Ingram (2007, 311).   [172] Ingram (2007, 65).

American policymakers from vetoing project proposals in the Committee on Food Aid Policies and Programmes on purely political grounds.[173] Many of the largest were personally courted by Ingram. After being introduced in New York by Tomlinson, for instance, Ingram developed "an enduring friendship extending into my retirement" with a senior representative of Church World Service, a faith-based American humanitarian organization.[174]

As emergency assistance came to dominate the WFP's activities in the 1990s, collaboration with civil society mushroomed. The roster of NGO partners soared from 170 in 1988 to 1,120 a decade later, with the vast majority local or national in scope.[175] This expansion, which turned charity workers into the "face" of the WFP to its beneficiaries, broadened and deepened the coalition for autonomy, particularly in developing countries. An additional boost came with the 1995 establishment of the nonprofit Friends of the World Food Program – renamed World Food Program USA in 2007 – to raise funds for the Programme from private American sources. Within a few years, Friends of the World Food Program had not only mobilized millions of dollars in donations but also morphed into a powerful advocate for the WFP's work. An early example of the organization's influence, which has stemmed in large part from its well-connected Board of Directors, was its successful drive to coax American policymakers into supporting the WFP's aid package for North Korea in 1997.[176]

The WFP's partnership network has maintained its breakneck pace of growth over the past two decades, becoming the largest of any international institution. Today, it encompasses approximately 1,300 NGOs, 50 businesses, 20 IGOs, and 15 research institutes. Online data indicate that an annual average of 87 percent of partnerships involved substantive collaboration in the decade leading up to 2018, predominantly at the implementation stage of the policy process.[177]

The breadth and depth of this network has further consolidated and reinforced de facto policy autonomy. Local knowledge shared by grassroots civil society groups, which account for most of the network's recent growth, has deepened information asymmetries between WFP field staff and the Executive Board, bolstering bureaucratic agenda-

[173] Author interview #59 with WFP partnerships and advocacy officer, January 23, 2015, Rome.
[174] Ingram (2007, 65).
[175] WFP Committee on Food Aid Policies and Programmes and Executive Board session reports (1988–1998), accessed from the WFP Library, Rome.
[176] Author interview #11 with employee of World Food Program USA, May 11, 2012, Washington, DC.
[177] The data were collected from www.wfp.org/partners [Last accessed February 23, 2019].

setting powers. International institutions (such as UNICEF and the UNHCR) and humanitarian NGOs (such as members of the Coalition for Food Aid, now known as the Alliance for Global Food Security) have maintained intense pressure on major donor states to endorse projects and programs put forward by the secretariat. Recent examples include successful campaigns for a massive emergency assistance program in Syria following the outbreak of civil war in 2011 – despite many donors' suspension of diplomatic relations with the country; for local and regional food purchase schemes beginning in 2008; and for the inclusion of funding for global food security in national COVID-19 relief legislation, most notably the American Rescue Plan Act of 2021.

The introduction of local and regional purchases was seen as a particularly significant event in the international aid community, in light of the United States' firm historical commitment to in-kind food aid – a commitment central to the WFP's own creation.[178] As one partnerships and advocacy officer explained, the coalition for autonomy was a central force behind this development: "When states try to derail WFP programs for the sake of national interests, partners step in with vital financial support and launch intense lobbying campaigns at the domestic level. Pressure from NGOs such as CARE and Save the Children, for instance, has been instrumental in persuading the US to reverse its long-standing opposition to local and regional purchases in recent years ... Given the WFP's origins, many of us thought this shift would never happen."[179]

World Food Program USA has also continued to play an important advocacy role in the American context, building strong and enduring cross-party support for the WFP's work through information dissemination and lobbying activities (including congressional testimonies and submissions).[180] A sizable resource base – since 2000 it has received more than $300 million dollars in donations – and access to the upper echelons of political power have been crucial to its success.[181] Recent members of World Food Program USA's Board of Directors range from prominent Capitol Hill lobbyists to former politicians with "blue chip, bipartisan credentials," including secretaries of agriculture, senators,

---

[178] Moreover, the American NGO community had traditionally favored this mode of procurement. Their stance began to shift in the mid-2000s, largely in response to growing evidence of its damaging consequences for recipient countries.

[179] Author interview #59 with WFP partnerships and advocacy officer, January 23, 2015, Rome.

[180] For examples of testimonies, see www.wfpusa.org/explore/food-security-policy-page/ testimonies [Last accessed January 20, 2020].

[181] Form 990 tax filings for Friends of the World Food Program/World Food Program USA, 2001–2019, available at projects.propublica.org/nonprofits/organizations/ 133843435 [Last accessed April 18, 2020].

and congressional representatives from both the Democratic and the Republican Parties.[182] From 2011 to 2015, the Board was chaired by Hunter Biden, a lawyer whose father, Joe Biden, then served as vice president of the United States.

Interestingly, World Food Program USA's advocacy efforts have framed support for the WFP as a means of not only promoting the United States' humanitarian and development goals but also protecting its national security. In 2017, for instance, it published a report linking hunger to nine different types of global "instability," including interstate conflict, civil war, and terrorism.[183] "At a time of unprecedented need, and as the U.S. Government considers funding levels for international food assistance programs," World Food Program USA president, Rick Leach, stressed, "it is vital that these decisions are informed by a clear understanding of how ensuring food security abroad is in our national security interests."[184] Similarly, when recently thanking the Biden administration for allocating billions of dollars to such programs in the American Rescue Plan Act, Leach declared preventing hunger to be in the United States' "moral, economic and national security interests."[185]

Finally, partners have limited the WFP's reliance on state financing by providing most of the near $12 billion in nongovernmental contributions it has welcomed since 2000. The largest partner donations have come from the European Commission ($6.5 billion between 2000 and 2018), other UN institutions ($2.9 billion), and private donors ($1.1 billion, of which close to $250 million is due to World Food Program USA).

International Fund for Agricultural Development

IFAD, as discussed earlier, is a progeny of the World Food Conference of 1974. Declining agricultural output in the developing world was widely seen as a central cause of the ongoing food crisis, and delegates to the meeting had little confidence in the FAO's capacity to turn the tide. Flush with cash from the recent oil price spike and facing pressure to help other developing countries shoulder the burden of higher energy costs, members of the Organization of the Petroleum Exporting Countries (OPEC) proposed the creation of a multilateral fund to boost food production in poor rural areas. While the United States and a few

---

[182] Ross (2011, 133).
[183] World Food Program USA (2017).
[184] www.wfpusa.org/news-release/new-report-highlights-hunger-as-a-driver-of-instability/ [Last accessed January 12, 2021].
[185] www.wfpusa.org/news-release/wfpusa-statement-inauguration-biden-harris/ [Last accessed February 3, 2021].

other members of the Organisation for Economic Co-operation and Development (OECD) were initially reluctant to sanction the creation of another food-focused international institution, they were won over by assurances that it would not become an "operational" agency.[186] The World Food Conference passed a resolution to launch IFAD as soon as possible, which was swiftly endorsed by the UN General Assembly. A formal treaty establishing IFAD as a specialized agency of the UN was adopted in June 1976 by an international conference held at the FAO's headquarters.

IFAD's foremost objective, according to its founding agreement, is "to mobilize additional resources to be made available on concessional terms for agricultural development in developing Member States."[187] In pursuing this goal, the treaty elaborates, it should "provide financing primarily for projects and programmes specifically designed to introduce, expand, or improve food production systems and to strengthen related policies and institutions within the framework of national priorities and strategies."[188] Along similar lines, IFAD's website defines its mission as "to transform rural economies and food systems by making them more inclusive, productive, resilient, and sustainable," including by helping rural populations "increase their productivity and access markets," "create and access jobs and rural economic growth," "increase their incomes, move out of poverty and improve their food and nutrition security," and "build their resilience in the face of a changing climate and manage the natural resource base sustainably."[189]

IFAD is generally agreed by observers and stakeholders to have consistently and cost-effectively delivered on its mandate. Despite beginning with modest means, the Fund has mobilized considerable sums for agricultural development – by 2019, it had contributed to the financing of almost 1,000 projects worth more than $50 billion – ameliorating living standards and access to food in many of the world's most deprived rural communities.[190] The enduring impact and creative design of these projects have given IFAD a reputation for being "dynamic, experienced, resourceful, innovative," characteristics also highlighted by academic appraisals of its performance (of which there are fewer than in the previous cases).[191] The one comprehensive external assessment of IFAD's performance, the 2005 *Independent External Evaluation*

---

[186] Talbot (1990, 103).
[187] International Fund for Agricultural Development (1976, 4).
[188] International Fund for Agricultural Development (1976, 4).
[189] www.ifad.org/en/vision [Last accessed March 2, 2020].
[190] International Fund for Agricultural Development (2020, 26).
[191] Talbot and Moyer (1987, 359). See Hopkins (1990); Martha (2009); Shaw (2007, 2009); Talbot (1982, 1990, 1991).

Table 4.4 *Summary of IFAD's policy autonomy*

Dimension	Indicator	De jure	De facto
Agenda-setting powers	Power to propose new policies	Delegated to secretariat	Exercised by secretariat since early 1980s
	Power to prepare budget	Delegated to secretariat	Always exercised by secretariat
	Power to prepare governing body program	Unspecified	Exercised by secretariat since early 1980s
Ability to avoid state veto	Decision procedure:		
	1. Governing Council	Majority voting for most issues	Consensus for most issues (since early years)
	2. Executive Board	Majority voting for most issues	Consensus for most issues (since early years)
	Distribution of votes	Weighted by state category and contributions	NA (consensus norm)
Access to non-state financing	Non-state contributions	Some forms permitted	Always received; low until ≈1970, moderate thereafter
	Independent earnings	Permitted	Always made; high but volatile

(*IEE-IFAD*), found a high proportion of its projects to be relevant to its mission and soundly executed, while noting some areas for improvement.[192] This finding chimes with the recent donor evaluations as well as a wave conducted in the 1980s that focused solely on IFAD.[193]

Tracing Policy Autonomy and Performance Over Time

IFAD closely resembles the WFP in the trajectory of its de facto policy autonomy and performance over its lifecycle. The Fund was designed with tight constraints on bureaucratic leeway in the policy process, which it succeeded in gradually dismantling by the mid-1990s, unleashing tangible gains in performance. Over the past quarter-century, de facto policy autonomy and performance have maintained their steady upward gradient, with the former benefiting from continuous positive reinforcement by the latter (see Table 4.4).

[192] International Fund for Agricultural Development (2005*b*).
[193] For an overview of the latter, see Talbot (1990, 124–127).

Breaking and Entering the Cycle

To assuage OECD concerns about institutional proliferation, IFAD was not endowed by its creators with a powerful bureaucracy. The founding treaty vested supreme decision-making powers in a Governing Council on which all member states had a seat. Responsibility "for the conduct of the general operations of the Fund" was delegated to an Executive Board of 18 nations elected by the Governing Council.[194] Three categories of member states, representing IFAD's major economic blocs, would elect six representatives each: category I, contributing developed countries (essentially the OECD); category II, contributing developing countries (essentially OPEC); and category III, potential recipient countries (the rest of the world). Both governing bodies would take decisions by weighted majority voting, with states' shares determined by a combination of their membership category and their financial contributions. Regular business would require a simple majority of ballots cast; high-stakes issues, including membership, financing, the adoption of bylaws and regulations, treaty amendments, and the election of the president (the head of the secretariat), would be settled by a two-thirds majority.

The president would manage administrative affairs, prepare the budget, and, "under the control and direction of the Governing Council and the Executive Board ... be responsible for conducting the business of the Fund."[195] As in other IFIs, this remit included identifying, designing, and preparing projects for consideration and approval by the Executive Board. Unlike these institutions, however, IFAD was not permitted to participate in the second half of the "project cycle": supervision, monitoring, follow-up, and evaluation.[196] This limitation was a "definite political decision made at the insistence of OECD nations" led by the United States, which determined that since "IFAD's principal responsibility is to provide additional capital for development projects in rural areas ... most of the functions of the project cycle should be handled by existing international institutions."[197] For similar reasons, IFAD's secretariat was kept small and lean. Even a decade after its establishment, the Fund employed just 84 professionals and 106 support staff.[198]

---

[194] International Fund for Agricultural Development (1976, 13).

[195] International Fund for Agricultural Development (1976, 14). The power to prepare the Governing Council and the Executive Board's work program was not mentioned in the founding treaty.

[196] International Fund for Agricultural Development (1976, 18). IFAD's role in the project cycle was described in detail in the first iteration of its *Lending Policies and Criteria*, adopted in 1978. See International Fund for Agricultural Development (1978).

[197] Talbot (1990, 109, 107).

[198] Talbot (1990, 107).

Another difference between IFAD and existing IFIs was that it would be financed solely by voluntary contributions, which would be replenished at three-year intervals. In other words, it could neither obligate member states to supply stable and predictable resource flows nor borrow from them or international markets – a major source of funding for IFIs such as the World Bank and the International Monetary Fund (IMF).[199] Permission was, nonetheless, given to draw "special contributions" from non-state actors and "funds derived from operations and otherwise accruing to the Fund."[200]

In its earliest years, IFAD had negligible involvement in *any* stage of the project cycle. Lacking experience conceiving and crafting projects, it was mostly restricted to co-financing those originated by other (multilateral and bilateral) aid agencies. In this capacity, it functioned more or less as the "add-on" institution desired by OECD nations.[201] As the secretariat observed and formed deeper partnerships with co-financing and implementing agencies, however, it soon became familiar with the basics of project identification, design, and preparation, enabling it to "exert some modest influence" over these processes.[202]

By the early 1980s, staff had gained enough knowhow to become directly involved in the first half of the project cycle. A pipeline of IFAD-originated projects began to flow, many of which pioneered new financial instruments and development strategies, such as the Grameen Bank's microcredit approach in Bangladesh (whose creator, Muhammad Yunus, was later awarded the Nobel Peace Prize).[203] Projects were formulated through a rigorous multistage process. First, a country program manager based in the recipient nation would draw up a project proposal in consultation with government representatives (and sometimes nongovernmental stakeholders). This document would be submitted to a Technical Review Committee chaired by the head of the Project Management Department, which would scrutinize and revise it before forwarding it to a Program and Project Review Committee chaired by the president for further examination. At this stage, the country program manager would be required to mount an oral defense of the proposal "while defects and other deficiencies are likely pointed out" by the president and other members of senior management."[204] Based on the comments received during this grilling, the proposal would then be revised and resubmitted to the Program and Project Review Committee. If approved at this point, it would finally be presented

[199] Martha (2009, 459).
[200] International Fund for Agricultural Development (1976, 6).
[201] Talbot (1990, 107).   [202] Talbot (1990, 107).   [203] Shaw (2009, 141).
[204] Talbot (1990, 110.).

by the president to the Executive Board (usually alongside a financing agreement between IFAD and the recipient country).

As this description suggests, states had little direct involvement in project planning. Nor were they apt to carefully scrutinize the secretariat's recommendations during Executive Board sessions. Remarkably, according to Talbot, the Executive Board had not turned down a single project proposal as of 1990: "The board has a veto power, but (like Thomas Jefferson said of the impeachment clause in the US Constitution) it is a 'rusty shotgun behind the door.' I believe it is accurate to state that no project sent by the secretariat to the board has ever been denied, although one was returned for minor amendment, then subsequently approved."[205] Talbot's overriding impression was of a policy apparatus in the tight grip of bureaucrats: "What needs to be emphasized concerning IFAD's policy process is the crucial role played by the secretariat, both in technical and political issues."[206]

IFAD's de jure and de facto policy autonomy grew increasingly at variance. "The realities of power within IFAD are quite different ... from the constitutional requirements," Talbot and Moyer observed in 1987.[207] First, the Governing Council ceded most of its formal authority to the Executive Board, offering little direction to or oversight of the Fund during its annual session – "an exercise in ceremony and rhetoric" to many onlookers.[208] Second, as detailed earlier, the Executive Board itself delegated the task of project development to the secretariat, primarily serving as a "reacting institution."[209] Third, Board members generally took decisions by consensus rather than any form of majority voting.[210] Fourth, the secretariat – "with some subtlety" – began making tentative forays into the second half of the project cycle, in particular by incorporating monitoring and evaluation provisions into selected project agreements.[211]

These trends were attended by palpable improvements in performance, as recognized in a series of glowing donor assessments throughout the 1980s. A 1981 report by the GAO concluded that IFAD "has performed according to its Articles of Agreement and has satisfied the objectives upon which the US based its contribution."[212] A comparative examination of internal evaluation systems published by the JIU in the same year applauded the Fund's "solid start toward determining

---

[205] Talbot (1990, 106).
[206] Talbot (1990, 110). As early as 1982, Talbot commented that "the real decision makers are the top-level officials in the IFAD bureaucracy" (1982, 218).
[207] Talbot and Moyer (1987, 359).   [208] Talbot (1990, 106).
[209] Talbot and Moyer (1987, 367).
[210] Author interview #67 with IFAD senior manager, January 29, 2015, Rome.
[211] Talbot (1990, 109).   [212] General Accounting Office (1981, 4).

and progressively improving the results and impact of its work," a verdict echoed three years later in a program review by the United States Agency for International Development (USAID).[213] Studies commissioned in the mid-1980s by the German Ministry for Economic Cooperation and jointly by the World Bank and the IMF highlighted IFAD's innovative operational techniques, with the former calling it a "pioneer institution."[214] A 1984 appraisal of the Fund's monitoring and evaluation arrangements by the Canadian International Development Agency (CIDA) deemed it "an institution deserving of continuing donor support ... because it deals in a relatively cost-effective manner with priority needs of the Third World's poorest rural populations."[215] The upper right panel of Figure 4.1 adduces further evidence of such efficiency: IFAD's annual ratio of administrative costs to total expenses averaged only seven percent between 1980 and 1990.

Bureaucratic discretion was augmented by swelling revenues from lending and investment activities. As shown in the lower left panel of Figure 4.1, independent earnings accounted for almost a third of IFAD's income during the 1980s.[216] This revenue stream fueled sustained growth in its resource base (upper left panel) despite little increase in contributions from governments or non-state actors (lower right panel) over the period.

At the same time, IFAD's exclusion from key stages of project cycle was creating operational frictions that threatened to derail its encouraging start. Implementing agencies typically possessed broader development-centered mandates that extended well beyond agriculture. Consequently, from IFAD's perspective, their "project designs did not give sufficient focus to the needs of the poorest rural groups."[217] Another problem, noted in the USAID assessment, was that the secretariat's guidelines for project monitoring and evaluation were not always respected by implementers.[218] As one operations manager summed up, IFAD's progress was being "limited" by its "lack of operational responsibility for the crucial later phases of the project cycle, coupled with

[213] Joint Inspection Unit (1981, XIV); United States Agency for International Development (1984).
[214] Federal Republic of Germany Ministry for Economic Cooperation (1984, 121); Cassen and Associates (1986).
[215] Canadian International Development Agency (1984, 45).
[216] The sharp year-to-year fluctuations are a product of IFAD's three-year replenishment cycle, in which pledged contributions are paid in irregular and uneven instalments.
[217] International Fund for Agricultural Development (2005b, 2).
[218] "IFAD has articulated an ambitious and comprehensive approach to monitoring and evaluation, but has not successfully institutionalized monitoring and evaluation at the project level," the report concluded. United States Agency for International Development (1984, 35).

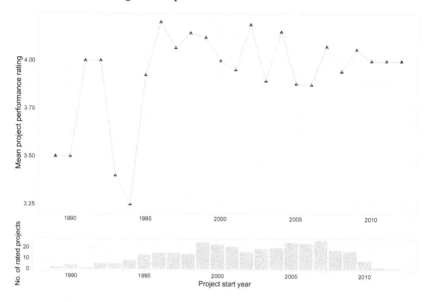

Figure 4.4 Number and performance ratings of assessed IFAD projects, 1989–2012

Source: IFAD ARRI Database, available at www.ifad.org/en/web/ioe/w/ifad-s-independent-evaluation-ratings-database.

Notes: The rating scale ranges from 1 to 6. The earliest project in the database is excluded due to differences in assessment methodology (which results in an anomalously high score).

the need for producing projects more or less acceptable to established IFIs."[219] "These factors," the official regretted, "may have made IFAD less innovative in practice than it might have been if given a freer hand."[220]

These problems were reflected in the relatively low performance ratings awarded by IFAD's Office of Evaluation – an operationally independent arm of the secretariat – to projects initiated in the late 1980s and early 1990s. These scores, much like the comparative donor assessments, are based on a mixture of interviews, field visits, focus groups, and stakeholder surveys and cover multiple dimensions of project performance, including impact, efficiency, sustainability, relevance, and innovation.[221] As plotted in Figure 4.4, though few in number (lower panel), projects commencing prior to 1995 mostly received ratings of less than 3 out

[219] King (1985, 18).   [220] King (1985, 18).
[221] International Fund for Agricultural Development (2015).

of 6, the Office of Evaluation's threshold for "satisfactory" performance (upper panel).

In the early 1990s, the secretariat began exerting intense pressure on the Governing Council to expand IFAD's participation in the project cycle, even conducting detailed studies on the adverse performance consequences of its confinement to the first half.[222] A key breakthrough came in 1996, when the secretariat commissioned a *Joint Review of Supervision Issues in IFAD Financed Projects* in collaboration with four implementing institutions: the World Bank, the United Nations Office for Project Services (UNOPS), the Arab Fund for Economic Social Development (AFESD), and the African Development Bank (AfDB). Reaffirming the operational strains identified by earlier evaluations and inquiries, the report made five recommendations, the most significant of which was the establishment of an experimental direct supervision program covering 15 projects.[223] The proposals were endorsed in 1997 by the Governing Council, which justified derogating from the founding treaty's prohibition on direct supervision on the grounds that the decision was supported by the same majority required for treaty amendments (i.e., two-thirds). This maneuver, which was questioned but not directly challenged by American and British delegates, was "somewhat remarkable," as Rutsel Martha, a former IFAD general counsel and director of legal affairs, has observed: "There is no precedent in other organizations whereby any organ of an international organization took recourse to waiving one or more the limitations imposed by the constituent instrument on the activities that the organization may engage in."[224]

Sowing Seeds, Reaping Harvests

The direct supervision experiment inspired a fresh assertiveness and ambition in the bureaucracy. Strategic frameworks crafted by senior management in the late 1990s and early 2000s broadened IFAD's operative goals to include developing the skills and capacities of the rural poor, strengthening local institutions, and improving access to productive natural resources, technology, financial services, and markets.[225] Wary of growing bureaucratic activism, OECD nations called for a full-scale independent evaluation of IFAD in 2002, which was launched by the Governing Council the following year. The *IEE-IFAD*, which was

---

[222] For a summary, see International Fund for Agricultural Development (2013*a*, 113).

[223] Evaluators reported that "not even the strongest [cooperating institutions] are meeting IFAD's requirements for an impact-oriented supervision" and "serious disadvantages had arisen from [IFAD's] inability to learn, even to a limited extent, from direct supervision experience." International Fund for Agricultural Development (2004, 1).

[224] Martha (2009, 469).

[225] International Fund for Agricultural Development (1998, 2002).

undertaken by an international team of development consultants, on the whole painted a positive picture of the Fund's performance. Analyzing a random sample of projects, it found two-thirds to either have substantially achieved or be likely to achieve their main objectives; 65 percent to target the right people; and 100 percent to be relevant to recipient country needs and IFAD strategic objectives. The overall portfolio was praised as "broadly pro-poor," with evaluators estimating that around half of IFAD's assistance was allocated to low-income countries.[226]

These accomplishments were closely linked, the *IEE-IFAD* contended, to the high degree of independence enjoyed by staff, in particular country program managers: "A cornerstone of [IFAD's] approach … remains the freedom of action granted to CPMs [country program managers], under which they [control] the relationship with the country, the identification of projects, the technical design process, and the relationships with government and the cooperating institution during implementation."[227] The Governing Council and the Executive Board, by comparison, were found to occupy a peripheral position in the policy process. The former entrusted its guidance and oversight functions to the latter, whose "crowded agenda and infrequent meetings" and dearth of "tools and training" prevented it from properly discharging them.[228]

IFAD's performance was not deemed perfect. Some programs were judged to lack "strategic coherence," overlapping with those of other IFIs and failing to appropriately adapt policy instruments to local contexts and requirements.[229] Although not yet able to assess the Direct Supervision Pilot Programme, the *IEE-IFAD* added weight to the conclusions of the *Joint Review of Supervision Issues in IFAD Financed Projects*, drawing attention to "problems with project supervision, particularly the 'arms-length model' of supervision which contrasts strongly with the more hands-on approach of the World Bank and most other IFIs."[230]

Two months after the *IEE-IFAD*'s release, the Office of Evaluation *did* publish a review of the Direct Supervision Pilot Programme. The findings were overwhelmingly positive, with directly supervised projects rated as outperforming partner-supervised ones on virtually every indicator of implementation performance. The overarching conclusion was that, "compared with supervision by [cooperating institutions], direct supervision has greater potential to contribute to better development effectiveness at the project level and, at the same time, allows for more

---

[226] International Fund for Agricultural Development (2005*b*, 22).
[227] International Fund for Agricultural Development (2005*b*, 8).
[228] International Fund for Agricultural Development (2005*b*, 7).
[229] International Fund for Agricultural Development (2005*b*, 52).
[230] International Fund for Agricultural Development (2005*b*, 29).

attention to IFAD's broader objectives at the country programme level, such as policy dialogue and partnership building."[231] With the enthusiastic backing of senior management, the Office of Evaluation urged the Governing Council to introduce an official policy permitting direct project supervision under appropriate and clearly defined circumstances.

The *IEE-IFAD* and Direct Supervision Pilot Programme assessment set in motion a series of institutional reforms that have further bolstered IFAD's performance over the past 15 years. In 2006, the Governing Council amended the founding treaty to allow the Executive Board to authorize direct project supervision – "one of the most far-reaching changes since the Fund was established," in the words of the Independent Office of Evaluation (which the Office of the Evaluation was renamed in 2011).[232] Later in the year, the Board adopted a *Supervision and Implementation Support Policy* clarifying IFAD's approach to project implementation and specifying detailed criteria for choosing among supervision modalities.[233] Acknowledging the benefits of active in-house oversight, the policy set an ambitious target of raising the proportion of directly supervised projects from five percent to three-quarters within a decade.

At the same meeting, the Executive Board approved a strategic framework aimed at addressing criticisms of IFAD's operational coherence and sensitivity to local context.[234] To reduce overlap with other IFIs, performance management at the project, country, and corporate levels would be integrated into a single system. In addition, a new results-based policy tool – the country strategic opportunities program (COSOP) – was introduced to promote unified country programs that "operationalize the corporate hierarchy of development objectives in the specific national conditions and context" and are "located within, and ... supportive of, the government's priorities and policies, institutions and programmes for rural poverty reduction."[235]

Subsequent evaluations, both internal and external, suggest that these reforms have largely achieved their aims. A 2013 study of the *Supervision and Implementation Support Policy* by the Independent Office of Evaluation revealed that the percentage of directly supervised projects had reached the 75 percent target in 2009 – seven years ahead of schedule – and now exceeded 90 percent.[236] Importantly, these projects were found

---

[231] International Fund for Agricultural Development (2005*a*, vii).
[232] International Fund for Agricultural Development (2012*b*, iii).
[233] International Fund for Agricultural Development (2006*a*).
[234] International Fund for Agricultural Development (2006*b*).
[235] International Fund for Agricultural Development (2006*b*, 14).
[236] International Fund for Agricultural Development (2013*b*, iii).

to "fare better than those supervised by cooperating institutions against almost all performance indicators, but particularly those that matter to IFAD's target group the most, such as targeting, food security, gender and institution-building."[237] Similarly, Independent Office of Evaluation reports on topics ranging from rural finance policy to field offices document marked progress in enacting the *IEE-IFAD*'s recommendations on strategic coherence.[238] One such assessment, for example, concludes that "[o]ver the past decade, IFAD has made major efforts, including expanded country presence, to go beyond projects and to assure that its project and non-project interventions are embedded in coherent country strategies."[239] This verdict is echoed by the comparative donor evaluations, which have awarded IFAD among the highest scores on indicators of strategic management.[240]

Project outcomes, too, tell a story of improving performance. Average project success ratings have been consistently higher since the mid-1990s, exceeding 3 in most years (see upper panel of Figure 4.4). In the two years preceding the *IEE-IFAD*, they began a downward trend that lasted until 2006. The reforms that followed the report helped to reverse this decline, with a particularly sharp upturn in indicators of goal attainment, sustainability, and innovation. Ratings of projects beginning after 2008 have leveled off, though the small sample size cautions against drawing firm conclusions (see lower panel). As illustrated in the upper right panel of Figure 4.1, project performance gains have not come at the expense of overall resource efficiency: IFAD's administrative outlays have remained modest since 1995, averaging 12 percent of expenditures per year.[241]

Several sources point to IFAD's enterprising and dedicated workforce as an integral element of its effectiveness. In staff questionnaires conducted since the *IEE-IFAD*, the percentage of respondents who report being "positively engaged in IFAD objectives" across six areas of the work environment has risen from 66 percent to around three-quarters.[242] MOPAN surveys provide evidence that stakeholders also

[237] International Fund for Agricultural Development (2013*b*, iii).
[238] A list of these evaluations is available at www.ifad.org/en/web/ioe/cle [Last accessed July 2, 2020].
[239] International Fund for Agricultural Development (2013*b*, 42). Almost a third of IFAD's workforce is now stationed in one of its 40 country offices.
[240] IFAD has received either the highest or the second highest score on the 10 indicators of strategic management in the evaluations (listed in Appendix B.3).
[241] In Easterly and Williamson's (2011) dataset on aid agency overhead costs in 2008, IFAD's ratio of administrative costs to total development assistance (13 percent) is well below average for multilateral institutions (29 percent).
[242] See Reports on IFAD's Development Effectiveness 2008–2019, available at www.ifad.org/en/financial-documents [Last accessed June 3, 2021].

view IFAD officials in a positive light, with the majority of respondents strongly agreeing that they are "sufficiently skilled and experienced"[243] and almost 30 percent pinpointing the Fund's "openminded, creative and knowledgeable staff members" as "one of its key strengths."[244] Along similar lines, evaluators have regularly highlighted the secretariat's professionalism and loyalty to its mandate – before as well as after the *IEE-IFAD*. One of the principal conclusions of a 2002 review of IFAD's promotion of replicable innovations, for example, was that "staff are highly committed to the organization's mandate and to the search for innovative solutions"[245]

Improvements in performance have fortified the political barricades around IFAD's bureaucracy, which today numbers more than 700 officials.[246] As one program manager emphasized, opportunistic interventions now carry heightened risks for states: "In the past, some states used issues with project supervision and program coherence to justify bringing foreign policy considerations into allocation and disbursement decisions. Today, there's no excuse for such behavior. The major impediments to performance have been removed. IFAD stands tall in the international development community, so governments know that political meddling could lead to a public backlash."[247] Expressing a common view among donor nations, one Governing Council member argued that the secretariat's "successful response to the *Independent External Evaluation* and experience with the supervision pilot demonstrate that there are collective benefits to giving staff a larger and more autonomous role in the project cycle."[248] Indeed, when explaining its decision to endorse direct supervision in 2005, the Executive Board explicitly cited evidence of improved operational effectiveness under the pilot scheme.[249]

In addition, IFAD has become a more attractive "investment" for partners and other nongovernmental donors, in particular rapidly expanding co-financing agencies such as the Global Environment Facility (GEF) and the Least Developed Countries Fund (LDCF). The average share of annual contributions received from non-state actors rocketed from two

---

[243] Multilateral Organisations Performance Assessment Network (2019, 125). The response rate is not disclosed.

[244] Multilateral Organisations Performance Assessment Network (2013, 16).

[245] International Fund for Agricultural Development (2019, 2).

[246] United Nations System Chief Executives Board for Coordination (2021, 1).

[247] Author interview #60 with IFAD program manager, January 26, 2015, Rome.

[248] Author interview #69 with IFAD Governing Council member, January 30, 2015, Rome.

[249] International Fund for Agricultural Development (2012c, 4).

percent in the decade before the *IEE-IFAD* to 28 percent between 2006 and 2018 – almost double the figure for the FAO and the WFP (lower right panel of Figure 4.1). With independent earnings still constituting nearly a quarter of income in this period (lower left panel), this has delivered a salutary boost to IFAD's real financial resources (upper left panel), which have risen by an average of almost a third per annum.

Sources of De Facto Policy Autonomy

Taking a longer and broader view, there is also an intimate connection between IFAD's extensive de facto policy autonomy and (1) the specialized nature of its governance tasks – designing, financing, and supervising agricultural development projects – which render them difficult for states to monitor; and (2) its strong and wide-ranging operational bonds with non-state stakeholders throughout the project cycle.

Governance Tasks

While IFAD offers comparable forms of technical assistance to the FAO and the WFP, it is unique in undertaking large-scale, resource-intensive policy interventions that fundamentally restructure rural economies. Given the scope and complexity of these projects, a deep understanding of local conditions, economic and agricultural policy, and development assistance more generally are essential for identifying, crafting, and delivering them. Accordingly, IFAD field officers typically possess an advanced academic degree in a field related to agriculture, economics, or finance as well as several years of experience with rural development programs.[250] Similarly, staff in the Technical Advisory Division, which works closely with country offices, are renowned for their "technical expertise in agronomy, livestock, rural infrastructure, rural finance, natural resource management, the environment, gender, public health and nutrition, household food security, and sustainable livelihoods."[251] Specialized educational qualifications are also held by a high proportion

---

[250] A recent job posting for a country director position specified the following minimum qualifications: "Advanced university degree from an accredited institution in rural development, agriculture, economics, rural finance, development policy or other job related fields; Eight years of progressively responsible international experience [in international organizations, rural development/financial institutions or government services], preferably in area of implementation and supervision of rural development programmes of which at least two years' experience working in an international organization." www.devex.com/jobs/country-programme-manager-569586 [Last accessed September 12, 2019].
[251] Shaw (2009, 86).

of senior management, including, as of 2020, four of IFAD's five department heads (two of whom have doctorates in economics).[252]

The rich array of materials prepared by staff in the course of project identification and development also attests to the informational and epistemic demands of IFAD's work. The COSOPs introduced in response to the *IEE-IFAD* embed projects in comprehensive policy frameworks – frequently exceeding 100 pages and containing several technical appendices – that seek to harmonize and synergize IFAD interventions at the country level.[253] Drawing on stakeholder consultations and interviews, local agricultural and socioeconomic data, and technical analysis, COSOPs review the rural poverty situation on the ground, reflect on lessons from IFAD's previous activities in the country, define a set of strategic objectives, describe arrangements for program implementation, and present concept notes for specific projects. The latter documents detail basic project characteristics (e.g., location, cost, time frame), the rationale and "theory of change" behind the intervention, policy instruments and operational activities, monitoring and evaluation arrangements, supervision modalities, financing arrangements, and implementation risks.

Populated mostly by career politicians and diplomats with wide-ranging responsibilities and busy schedules, IFAD's governing bodies are rarely equipped to closely scrutinize and appraise these materials. The resulting asymmetries in project-related information between states and bureaucrats explain several features of Executive Board practice noted earlier, including its very rare exercise of veto powers; its short and infrequent sessions; and its persistent struggles to conduct robust oversight of the secretariat. As one Board member conceded, "Our ability to seriously inspect and evaluate the staff's work is more limited than many of us would like to admit. The complex nature of IFAD's interventions creates significant monitoring challenges … You can't design effective projects without in-depth knowledge of agricultural conditions at the grassroots level and what types of interventions are likely to work in those settings. Only field officers have that kind of information and expertise."[254]

Finally, as noted earlier, IFAD's function as a lender and a grantmaker has generated a sizable (albeit volatile) stream of independent income in the shape of interest and investment earnings. Defying the financial rule-book, it has supplemented this revenue by borrowing from sovereigns and, more recently, international capital markets.

---

[252] See IFAD's online directory of "expert staff," available at www.ifad.org/en/experts [Last accessed May 16, 2020]. Similar data for the year 2011 are compiled by Lall (2017).

[253] For examples, see www.ifad.org/en/cosop [Last accessed May 10, 2021].

[254] Author interview #70 with IFAD Executive Board member, January 30, 2015, Rome.

Operational Alliances

Unlike the FAO and the WFP, IFAD was compelled by its limited mandate to search for operational partners from the outset. In its initial co-financing role, the Fund learned valuable project identification and design skills from more established aid agencies and IFIs, facilitating a swift transition into the first half of the project cycle. As a project originator, IFAD depended on these partners for supervision, monitoring, and evaluation services, working especially closely with UNOPS, the World Bank, and regional development banks.

In the early 1980s, IFAD began enlisting the support of local and international NGOs at the design, monitoring, and evaluation stages of the project cycle. These actors were valued, in particular, for their capacity to reach the most marginalized rural populations, devise creative solutions to development problems, and directly involve beneficiaries in project implementation.[255] Collaboration strengthened with the establishment of the External Relations Division, a focal point for civil society interaction within the secretariat, in 1985; an IFAD/NGO Extended Cooperation Programme for financing innovative NGO interventions in 1990; and an annual NGO policy consultation and associated IFAD/NGO Advisory Group in the same year.[256] By the end of 1993, 150 NGOs were participating in 81 IFAD projects.[257]

Operational links with development finance institutions and NGOs gave rise to an emergent coalition for policy autonomy that steadily grew in influence throughout the 1980s. A pivotal contribution came during negotiations over IFAD's second replenishment in 1984. Irked by OPEC's recent decision to cut its share of contributions and increasingly mistrustful of the UN System more broadly, the Reagan administration publicly threatened to withdraw from IFAD – an act that "would have meant zero resources and, quite possibly, the collapse of the organization."[258] IFAD appealed for support to USAID and the United States Department of Agriculture, which instigated a vociferous lobbying campaign that was soon joined by other IFIs and influential humanitarian NGOs, including Bread for the World and the Hunger Project. By January 1986, Reagan officials had come around to the replenishment, only modestly reducing the United States' funding share. The coalition enjoyed similar success in other major donor countries. For instance,

[255] These benefits were highlighted in an influential background paper on IFAD's relations with NGOs presented to the Executive Board in 1984. International Fund for Agricultural Development (1984).
[256] The Advisory Group comprised six NGO representatives (elected during the consultation for three-year terms) and three IFAD officials.
[257] Bouloudani (1994).   [258] Hopkins (1990, 194).

pressure from the World Development Movement, a London-based anti-poverty NGO, helped to secure a £10 million increase in the United Kingdom's contribution to the replenishment.[259]

The coalition's efforts to win over American policymakers were abetted by the UN's assignment of a full-time staff member to support IFAD's interests on Capitol Hill. According to one admiring American official, "[H]er success rate in 'educating' key members of Congress and the congressional staff has ... been phenomenal."[260] In 1988, the Senate Committee on Appropriations, which just a few years earlier had voiced serious reservations about the Fund, confidently declared itself to have "repeatedly found that IFAD plays a unique and needed role in the provision of development assistance for the world's poorest people."[261] Over the next decade, the coalition recurrently harnessed this goodwill to persuade the United States against launching politically motivated interventions in the Executive Board, succeeding on several occasions in averting the rejection of proposed projects in Soviet-friendly countries.[262] In some instances, this was achieved by assembling counter-coalitions of OPEC and other developing nations eager to check American influence in IFAD's policy process.

Another valuable contribution, mentioned earlier, was the backing provided by implementing partners in the struggle over direct supervision, most notably in the form of the *Joint Review of Supervision Issues in IFAD Financed Projects*. Although these agencies derived financial benefits from performing supervisory functions for IFAD, they shared its view that dividing the project cycle across multiple institutions undermined operational coherence, favoring a more flexible approach to collaboration that was tailored to each project's specific requirements. Note, in addition, that many implementing partners collaborated with IFAD staff on project identification, design, and planning, sharing information and expert knowledge that were critical to the expansion of bureaucratic agenda-setting powers.

Over the past two decades, the coalition for policy autonomy has become broader and deeper, expanding its political reach and influence. IFAD has now teamed up with more than 1,000 NGOs, hundreds of which are currently involved in projects.[263] In addition, it has established co-financing partnerships with around 60 bilateral and multilateral aid agencies; become an implementing agency for the GEF; inaugurated and hosted global forums for policy dialogue between agricultural

---

[259] Bouloudani (1994). The organization changed its name to Global Justice Now in 2015.
[260] Talbot (1990, 119).   [261] United States Congress (1990, 73).
[262] Author interview #67 with IFAD senior manager, January 29, 2015.
[263] Author interview #68 with IFAD partnerships officer, January 30, 2015, Rome.

producers, civil society, and governments, such as the Farmers' Forum and the International Land Coalition; and worked with corporations at the community level to improve access to capital markets and new technologies.[264] According to data gleaned from IFAD's website, 87 percent of its operational alliances between 2007 and 2018 entailed substantive rather than tokenistic collaboration, most of which occurred at the formulation and implementation stages of the policy process.[265] Around two-thirds of partners are IGOs and NGOs, the remainder business entities and public–private partnerships (PPPs).

NGO collaborators continue to lead advocacy efforts on IFAD's behalf, most importantly in the United States, where they work closely with its Americas Liaison Office.[266] A key coordinating role is played by the NGO Working Group on IFAD and Rural Poverty, an informal alliance of some 40 food-focused nonprofits – including Bread for the World, the Congressional Hunger Center, and ACDI/VOCA – that seeks to strengthen American support for IFAD. The Working Group's activities tend to intensify around replenishment negotiations, when it meets and organizes letter-writing campaigns to members of Congress to encourage political and financial patronage of the Fund. Senior figures in the Working Group have also been invited to submit statements and testimony to congressional committees considering the United States' engagement with IFAD. During a 2006 hearing of the House of Representatives Subcommittee on Domestic and International Monetary Policy, Trade, and Technology, for example, the president of Bread for the World, the Reverend David Beckman, recounted how his organization had "come to love IFAD" for its "resolute focus on the rural poor" and "real efforts to empower groups of farmers, women's groups, and other groups in rural areas so that they can take part in the design of [its] interventions."[267] Beckman went on to underscore IFAD's role in promoting the United States' commercial interests as well as its

---

[264] Shaw (2009, 148).

[265] www.ifad.org/partners/ [Last accessed September 8, 2019].

[266] A recent advertisement for a position in this office mentions that the holder "develops and maintains strong relations with U.S. based advocacy groups" and "ensures the effective and efficient implementation the outreach and advocacy strategy with the U.S. Congress and the U.S. Administration, identifying and cultivating champions, promoting increased awareness of IFAD and its mandate, highlighting synergies and complementarities with the U.S. position and strategy vis-à-vis issues of mutual relevance." https://job.ifad.org/psc/IFHRPRDE/EMPLOYEE/HRMS/s/WEBLIB_IFA_FORM.ISCRIPT1.FieldFormula.IScript_IFADSimulation?route=viewJobPosting&joid=1604 [Last accessed October 3, 2020].

[267] United States Congress (2006). When introducing Bread for the World, Beckman proudly shared that "[w]e mobilize about a quarter of a million letters to Congress every year on issues that are important to hungry and poor people in our own country and around the world."

development and humanitarian objectives: "[I]n the long haul, nothing is more important to U.S. farmers than the expansion of markets in developing countries. When people in East Asia were able to get out of poverty and hunger to some extent, that was good for agriculture in Oklahoma." He closed by inviting representatives "to enthusiastically support IFAD and, specifically, to support its policies of resolute focus on the rural poor and empowerment of the rural poor."

Similar lobbying drives, albeit smaller in scale, have targeted other OECD nations – in particular the United Kingdom, which hosts a number of prominent humanitarian NGOs – as well as recipient countries. In the latter, they have often been orchestrated by IFAD itself as part of a conscious effort to build alliances for domestic policy change, a central component of its official *Partnership Strategy*.[268] A recent meta-evaluation identified several examples of IFAD "influencing policy through partnerships," stressing the "importance of an enabling policy environment to support and accelerate agriculture and rural development" and the Fund's role "as a broker and facilitator to achieve better inputs into policy engagement at country level."[269] A senior partnerships coordinator elaborated: "Fostering support for progressive policy change in borrower countries is central to IFAD's approach to rural development. Civil society groups are critical advocacy partners because they're able to both observe how policies affect remote populations and assemble broad-based coalitions for change from the grassroots level upwards … They are instrumental in shaping government preferences on agricultural and development policy."[270]

Finally, aid agencies and other international development institutions remain vocal cheerleaders for IFAD's work and mission – particularly during replenishment deliberations – as well as productive partners in project formulation and implementation. In the past few decades, they have also come to represent a significant source of revenue for the Fund, mostly on account of their rising co-financing contributions. Since 2000, development agencies have provided approximately $1.5 billion in donations, around a fifth of the total and essentially all funding received from non-state actors.

Conclusion

It is perhaps a twist of historical irony that of the three global food security institutions based in Rome, the one residing closest to the city's

---

[268] International Fund for Agricultural Development (2012*a*).
[269] International Fund for Agricultural Development (2018, 35).
[270] Author interview #68 with IFAD partnerships coordinator, January 30, 2015, Rome.

ancient center of power is also the one afflicted most by opportunistic political interference. Despite beginning life with a relatively free hand, the FAO has found itself suffocated by stringent governmental control since its earliest years, leading to policy choices and substantive outcomes that too often serve the parochial interests of powerful nations at the expense of collective food security goals. Despite their affinities with the FAO, the WFP and IFAD have evolved in entirely different directions. By breaking out of the restrictive formal constraints initially saddled on their bureaucracies, both institutions have succeeded in carving out and sustaining ample policy autonomy vis-à-vis states, providing the basis for rational, balanced, and innovative action in pursuit of their objectives.

Several of the theoretical framework's observable implications are borne out in this chapter's case comparison, as précised in Table 4.5. At the macro level (upper panel), the three cases exhibit the predicted relationships between variables of theoretical interest: a positive association between de facto policy autonomy and performance, variables with low values for the FAO and high values for the WFP and IFAD; a weak association between de jure policy autonomy – high in the FAO and mixed in the WFP and IFAD (due to governance reforms) – and both de facto policy autonomy and performance; a positive association between the number, depth, and breadth of operational alliances – low for the FAO and high for the WFP and IFAD – and de facto policy autonomy; and a positive association between the costs of monitoring governance tasks – low for the FAO and high for the WFP and IFAD – and de facto policy autonomy.

The chapter's distinctive contribution, however, lies in its exploration of the framework's micro-level implications (lower panel). Five patterns that emerge from the examination are noteworthy in this regard. First, each case is characterized by an unmistakable manifestation of the Jekyll and Hyde problem, with states endeavoring to further common interests at the design stage but more parochial purposes once institutions have been brought to life. This is reflected in both the public-spirited mandate handed to each institution and the habitual attempts by states to subsequently intervene in and capture the policy machinery in defense of particularistic agendas – attempts more successful in the FAO than in the WFP or IFAD.

Second, I find few signs of the systematic divergence between bureaucratic interests and institutional objectives expected by rogue-agency theories. On the contrary, evidence from surveys, interviews, and policy documents suggests that a high proportion of bureaucrats are sincerely motivated by and committed to their institution's stated, operative, and process goals and make good-faith efforts to further them.

Table 4.5 *Support for theoretical implications: Case comparison of global food security institutions*

Observable implication	Case 1: FAO	Case 2: WFP	Case 3: IFAD
Macro level			
Positive relationship between DFPA and performance	Low DFPA, low performance	High DFPA, high performance	High DFPA, high performance
Weak relationship between DJPA and DFPA	High DJPA, low DFPA	Mixed DJPA, high DFPA	Mixed DJPA, high DFPA
Weak relationship between DJPA and performance	High DJPA, low performance	Mixed DJPA, high performance	Mixed DJPA, high performance
Positive relationship between alliance number, depth, breadth and DFPA	Few, shallow, narrow alliances, low DFPA	Numerous, deep, broad alliances, high DFPA	Numerous, deep, broad alliances, high DFPA
Positive relationship between costs of monitoring governance tasks and DFPA	Three easy-to-monitor tasks, low DFPA	One easy-to-monitor task, two hard-to-monitor tasks, high DFPA	One easy-to-monitor task, three hard-to-monitor tasks, high DFPA
Micro level			
States experience Jekyll and Hyde problem	Major food producers block proposals to expand and efficiently allocate supplies	United States attempts to veto politically sensitive projects during Cold War	OECD nations periodically attempt to veto projects on political grounds
Bureaucratic interests aligned with institutional objectives	Survey, interview, policy-based evidence of alignment	Survey, interview, policy-based evidence of alignment	Interview, evaluative, policy-based evidence of alignment
Feedback from performance to DFPA	Feedback effects from mid-1970s	Feedback effects from ≈ 2000	Feedback effects from ≈ 2000
Alliances provide protection against opportunistic state interference	NA (few, shallow, narrow alliances)	Partners mitigate interference by providing expertise, advocacy, financial support	Partners mitigate interference by providing expertise, advocacy, financial support
Higher costs of task monitoring weaken state control	Tasks require close interaction with states, facilitating oversight	Remote, logistically complex nature of tasks impedes oversight	Need for expertise and local information impedes oversight

Notes: DFPA = de facto policy autonomy; DJPA = de jure policy autonomy.

Third, in the long run, performance outcomes loop back into de facto policy autonomy by altering the opportunity and political costs of capture for states. In the FAO, this process began in the mid-1970s and culminated in deeper governmental penetration of the policy apparatus. In the WFP and IFAD, it started in the 2000s and shored up the bureaucracy's already robust insulation against interference. Indications of a bidirectional relationship between de facto policy autonomy and either governance tasks or operational alliances are less apparent, in contrast.

Fourth, the hypothesized mechanism linking governance tasks to de facto policy autonomy is on clear display across the cases. The relative ease of observing the FAO's normative and operational functions, which are undertaken in close proximity to and collaboration with government representatives, have left little room for independent bureaucratic action. Conversely, the monitoring challenges associated with the WFP and IFAD's activities, which take place at a distance from oversight bodies and require considerable technical expertise and local knowledge, have shrouded the secretariat in a "cloak of stealth" that decisively tips the balance of policy influence its favor.

Finally, when operational alliances are numerous, deep, and broad, as with the WFP and IFAD, they lay the foundation for a powerful and enduring constituency for de facto policy autonomy. Partners of both institutions have facilitated and amplified bureaucratic agency by supplying information and specialized knowledge, engaging in political advocacy with states, and contributing financial resources. No such "hand" of support has been extended to the FAO, whose comparatively weak and narrow alliances have afforded scant protection against capture.

While demonstrating the plausibility of the framework's posited causal processes, the case study has not established that they extend beyond the realm of food security. It remains possible that distinctive political, strategic, institutional, and other features render this issue area a uniquely good fit for the argument, and that a different set of performance dynamics characterize other domains. To address this risk, the next chapter broadens the scope of the qualitative investigation by presenting analogous evidence from another significant slice of the global governance architecture, namely, the international public health regime.

5   The Performance of Life

Comparing the WHO, UNAIDS, Gavi, and GFATM

> Health administrators and medical scientists in all the organs of WHO
> [World Health Organization] – Assembly, Board, and Secretariat –
> complain that if only the politicians would get out of their way, WHO
> could *really* put on a program for world health.
>
> – Charles S. Ascher, 1952[1]

The United States' disengagement from and recommitment to the
World Health Organization (WHO) during the coronavirus (COVID-
19) pandemic – the vignette that opened Chapter 2 – offers a dramatic
illustration of the tension between narrow political expediency and
broader institutional purpose. But is this episode characteristic of the
dynamics shaping the WHO's performance over the past seven decades?
Or does it represent an anomalous intrusion of politics into an impartial
scientific technocracy, reflecting perhaps the febrile atmosphere of the
pandemic or the volatile temperament of the Trump administration?
More generally, does this book's theoretical framework illuminate the
causal processes and pathways underlying the performance of global
health institutions? As emphasized in Chapter 1, gathering qualitative
evidence from multiple issue areas is essential for assessing the generalizability of hypothesized causal mechanisms.

This chapter presents a second case comparative study that transports
us from the hilly interior of the Italian peninsula to the verdant southwest
shores of Lake Geneva, the home of four major international health institutions: the WHO; the Joint United Nations Programme on HIV/AIDS
(UNAIDS); Gavi, the Vaccine Alliance; and the Global Fund to Fight
AIDS, Tuberculosis and Malaria (GFATM). The examination, which is
informed by a similar range of sources to Chapter 4, furnishes additional
support for the theory, most notably its micro-level, process-related
implications. An initial ambition among each institution's founders
to further common public health goals has come into conflict with
more parochial national interests after its creation, frequently pitting

---

[1] Ascher (1952, 40).

opportunistically minded states against mandate-oriented international bureaucrats. These frictions have been resolved in starkly different ways across the four cases. Low levels of de facto policy autonomy have left the WHO and UNAIDS vulnerable to persistent political interference, impeding bureaucratic efforts to identify and implement enduring solutions to the problems that motivated their creation. Gavi and GFATM's expansive discretion, in contrast, has enabled them to mobilize and direct substantial resources toward efficient, high-impact interventions that have dramatically improved health and socioeconomic outcomes in many of the world's most deprived regions. The chapter's detailed process-tracing analysis indicates that these divergent trajectories have been progressively reinforced by feedback effects from performance to de facto policy autonomy.

The investigation also points to alliances and stealth as crucial bases of de facto policy autonomy. Underlying the WHO's susceptibility to interference and capture has been both a failure to engage in productive operational collaboration with its diverse stakeholders and an amenability to close oversight stemming from its state-facing governance tasks: building international consensus, monitoring treaty compliance, and providing technical assistance. Similarly, UNAIDS' brittle operational alliances and easily observable coordination and capacity-building functions go a long way toward explaining its stunted policy independence. Gavi and GFATM's more ample discretion has originated in a dense and wide-ranging web of operational alliances, most significantly with civil society groups and United Nations (UN) agencies, and a mandate to identify large-scale health interventions for financial support, a task that requires information and technical expertise typically unavailable to government delegations.

The chapter follows a parallel structure to the previous one. To ground the case selection strategy and clarify what it holds constant, the next section compares the four institutions on the dependent, explanatory, and control variables from Chapter 3's statistical inquiry. The rest of the chapter is organized in three parts, the first focusing on the WHO, the second on UNAIDS, and the third on Gavi and GFATM (which are grouped together on account of their similarity on key variables of interest and their comparatively brief lives). As before, each section begins with an overview of institutional origins and design, proceeds to trace the trajectory of performance and de facto policy autonomy over time, and concludes by exploring the role of governance tasks and operational alliances in molding such independence.

Case Selection: Comparing Institutional Characteristics

This chapter's case selection strategy, like the previous one's, seeks to identify institutions that are as similar as possible in all respects other than their performance, the main dependent variable, and de facto policy autonomy, the main explanatory variable.[2] Table 5.1 replicates Chapter 4's statistical comparison of institutional characteristics for the WHO, UNAIDS, Gavi, and GFATM. As reported in the upper panel, the institutions register similar mean values of almost every control variable in Chapter 3. The cross-institutional range of such values is less than half a standard deviation for nine of the 14 variables and 0 for seven of the eight dummy variables. The five controls with larger ranges were all weakly associated with the performance indices and *De Facto Policy Autonomy* in Chapter 3. Only one – *UN System* – fits this chapter's pattern of variation in performance and de facto policy autonomy (described subsequently). Gavi and GFATM's exclusion from the UN System is closely related to their status as public–private partnerships (PPPs), which I discuss shortly.

The additional characteristics enumerated in the second panel of Table 5.1 exhibit similarly little cross-institutional variation. All four institutions are governed by an executive board with 28–38 members who serve two- or three-year terms; are global in their operational scope; and are headquartered in Geneva. The only significant difference between the institutions is the nature of their membership: The WHO and UNAIDS are composed solely of states, whereas Gavi and GFATM also include civil society groups, private-sector actors, research institutes, and other nongovernmental stakeholders. This variation, it was noted in Chapter 1, presents a useful occasion to examine the framework's applicability to institutions beyond intergovernmental organizations (IGOs). In addition, as elaborated below, it complements and enriches the theoretical explanation for Gavi and GFATM's extensive de facto policy autonomy, some aspects of which are connected to their public–private status.

Mean performance index scores, shown in the third panel, *do* differ markedly between the four institutions. The within-group range of the six indices covering every institution exceeds one standard deviation in all cases, 1.5 standard deviations in five cases, and two standard deviations in four cases. In percentile terms, the WHO and UNAIDS lie below

2 The comparison excludes Unitaid, another Geneva-based health agency in the Performance of International Organizations Project (PIIP) dataset, for two reasons. First, it is relatively small and specialized, focusing on the provision of grants – of which fewer than 50 have been disbursed – for late-stage research and development (R&D) activities concerning a handful of diseases. Second, it was founded in 2006, leaving only a short period over which to examine its performance.

Table 5.1 *Matched quartet: The WHO, UNAIDS, Gavi, and GFATM compared*

Characteristic	WHO (Mean)	UNAIDS (Mean)	Gavi (Mean)	GFATM (Mean)	St. dev. in PIIP
Control variables					
Age (log)	4.19	2.97	2.70	2.50	0.74
Mean Democracy	4.13	4.17	3.89	4.30	1.11
Geographical Diversity	1262.45	1247.78	2123.71	1486.76	832.93
GDP Asymmetry	0.21	0.21	0.32	0.22	0.11
Membership Size (log)	5.25	5.25	4.53	5.05	0.60
Policy Scope	1	1	1	1	0.57
Preference Heterogeneity	0.74	0.75	0.75	0.69	0.12
Development Issue	0	0	0	0	0.48
Education Issue	0	0	0	0	0.27
Environment Issue	0	0	0	0	0.30
Humanitarian Issue	0	0	0	0	0.40
Health Issue	1	1	1	1	0.42
UN System	1	1	0	0	0.47
World Bank Group	0	0	0	0	0.21
Other characteristics (2020)					
Executive body members	34	38	28	28	
Executive body term length	3 years	3 years	2 years	3 years	
Type of institution	IGO	IGO	PPP	PPP	
Scope of activities	Global	Global	Global	Global	
Headquarters	Geneva	Geneva	Geneva	Geneva	
Performance indices					
Australian Performance Index	−0.79	−0.20	1.40	−0.29	0.95
Danish Performance Index	−0.63	−0.58		−0.07	1.19
MOPAN Performance Index	−1.07	0.44	0.71	1.03	0.98
Dutch Performance Index	−1.09	−0.56	1.15	0.81	1.54
Swedish Performance Index	−0.57	−1.34	3.65	0.84	1.48
UK Performance Index	−0.54	−0.61	2.08	1.38	1.31
Average Performance Index	−0.49	−0.57	1.49	0.83	1.23
Explanatory variables					
De Facto Policy Autonomy	1.39	1.10	3.61	3.16	1.05
De Jure Policy Autonomy	4.0	4.50	2.00	2.00	1.37
Operational Alliances	1.61	1.39	3.22	3.52	1.22
Facilitating Agreements	1	1	0	0	0.46
Monitoring Compliance	1	0	0	0	0.47
Capacity Building	1	1	0	0	0.42
Designing Interventions	0	0	0	0	0.49
Implementing Operations	0	0	0	0	0.49
Allocating Resources	0	0	1	1	0.49

Notes: Italicized variables are defined in Chapter 3. Values are averaged across all evaluation years.

the bottom tertile of the Performance of International Organizations Project (PIIP) sample on four of the seven indices; Gavi and GFATM score above the upper tertile on five and six indices, respectively, with the former also surpassing the top decile on four indices.

A similar split marks most of the explanatory variable means, displayed in the bottom panel. In terms of *De Facto Policy Autonomy*, the WHO and UNAIDS sit in the lowest fifth of the PIIP sample, GFATM near the median, and Gavi in the top quarter. The average of Gavi and GFATM's means is more than two standard deviations higher than that of the WHO and UNAIDS' means. This gap extends to *Operational Alliances*, on which Gavi and GFATM rank in the top fifth and the WHO and UNAIDS around the median, a combined average of 1.2 standard deviations lower. Among the governance task dummies, Gavi and GFATM score 1 only on *Allocating Resources*, a task with sizable monitoring costs for states; the WHO and UNAIDS do so on three and two of the tasks with low monitoring costs, respectively.

The bifurcated pattern extends to *De Jure Policy Autonomy*, albeit in a direction that implies a modest negative relationship with performance: The WHO and UNAIDS occupy the top quarter of the distribution, an average of 1.64 standard deviations above Gavi and GFATM, which languish in the bottom third. In this respect, the four cases might be seen as a difficult test for the argument: The two high-performing institutions are designed to possess a relatively low level of policy autonomy, while the two low-performing institutions are designed to possess a relatively high level of policy autonomy.

All in all, the dictates of the "most similar systems" design guiding my case selection strategy appear to be broadly satisfied. The WHO, UNAIDS, Gavi, and GFATM share a significant number of characteristics aside from their values of the dependent and explanatory variables (even if not quite as many as the FAO, the WFP, and IFAD). The most salient difference between them – the nature of their members – is consistent with the framework's logic and offers a window into one of its key scope conditions.

World Health Organization

The WHO's story begins, in the same way as the FAO's, with the Second World War, which left in its wake pervasive health problems and shattered medical systems in combatant nations, creating a serious threat of deadly epidemic outbreaks. Fearing that the patchwork of existing transnational health institutions, such as the International Sanitary Conventions and the Office International d'Hygiène Publique, would prove inadequate to meet these challenges, the recently established UN called a conference in 1946 "to consider the scope of, and the appropriate machinery for, international action in the field of public health and proposals for the establishment of a single international health organization of the United Nations."[3] Over five weeks of a sweltering New York summer, delegates drew up a 19-page constitution for a new specialized agency of the UN – the WHO – which was signed by representatives of 61 states (including, in a first for such an agency, all UN members).

Entering into force on April 7, 1948 – celebrated ever since as World Health Day – the WHO's constitution declared its mission as nothing less than "the attainment by all peoples of the highest possible level of health," defined as "a state of complete physical, mental and social well-being and not merely the absence of disease or infirmity."[4] To pursue this objective, the WHO was delegated 22 more specific responsibilities, including "to act as the directing and coordinating authority on international health work," "to furnish appropriate technical assistance," "to stimulate and advance work to eradicate epidemic, endemic, and other diseases," and "to propose conventions, agreements, and regulations, and make recommendations with respect to international health matters."[5]

These aspirations were widely applauded. In one of the first issues of *International Organization*, the American scholar Charles E. Allen hailed "an extraordinary advance in the evolution of international health institutions," describing the WHO's constitution as "the broadest and most liberal concept of international responsibility for health ever officially promulgated."[6] Yet, similarly to the FAO, the WHO has struggled to effectively discharge this mandate over its long and checkered history. Rather than the public health pioneer and leader envisaged by its creators, it has come to be seen as a "highly politicized" and "fragmented organization with cumbersome governance"[7] "that does many things poorly and few things well."[8] These shortcomings have been exhaustively catalogued in studies and commentaries by social scientists, historians, and medical practitioners in recent decades.[9] In addition, they are the subject of numerous independent assessments commissioned by member states – often in response to performance problems – as well as

[3] United Nations (1946b).   [4] United Nations (1946a, 3,2).
[5] United Nations (1946a, 3–4).   [6] Allen (1950, 30).   [7] Bloom (2011, 144).
[8] Collier (2011, 1575).
[9] For example, Bloom (2011); Chorev (2012); Clinton and Sridhar (2017); Cueto, Brown, and Fee (2019); Godlee (1994b,a); Kohlmorgen (2007); Lee (2009); Siddiqi (1995); Youde (2012).

the ongoing wave of comparative donor evaluations.[10] As we shall see, the WHO's response to COVID-19 has – even setting aside the Trump administration's unwelcome intervention – brought into focus and added weight to long-standing critiques of its performance.

Tracing Policy Autonomy and Performance Over Time

The arc of the WHO's de facto policy autonomy and performance comprises three distinct phases that closely resemble those partitioning the FAO case study: the 25 years from the Organization's creation to the early 1970s, in which initially expansive bureaucratic discretion was steadily eroded by industrialized countries, above all the United States; the 1970s and 1980s, which saw the rise of developing countries as a powerful political bloc – and force for capture – resulting in persistent North–South frictions and financial crisis; and the past three decades, during which performance problems have not only become more severe but also reinforced the bureaucracy's subordinate position in the policy process, entrenching a low-performance, low-autonomy equilibrium. Table 5.2 details the individual components of policy autonomy over the three phases.

Noble Ambitions – But Politicians Get in the Way

Given the complexity of the postwar reconstruction effort and the traditional influence of medical practitioners in international health cooperation, the WHO was designed to be an autonomous technical agency. Two bodies would govern the Organization. The World Health Assembly, representing all member states, would determine policies and regulations, review operational activities, approve the budget, consider applications for membership, and elect the director-general (the head of the secretariat). The Executive Board, made up of 18 states from different regions, would execute the Assembly's decisions, prepare its agenda, and draw up a general program of work for the Organization.[11] Unlike delegates to the Assembly, members of the Executive Board were required to be "technically qualified in the field of health" and to serve in a personal capacity (rather than as representatives of the states designating them).[12] The director-general would enjoy "considerable power,"[13]

---

[10] Among the major independent evaluations are Danish International Development Agency (1993); Joint Inspection Unit (1993); Nordic UN Project (1990); Moon et al. (2015); National Research Council (2016); The Independent Panel for Pandemic Preparedness and Response (2021); United Nations (2016); World Health Organization (1992, 2015, 2021a,b).
[11] The Executive Board has expanded multiple times. As indicated in Table 5.1, it currently has 34 members.
[12] United Nations (1946a, 9).   [13] Cueto, Brown, and Fee (2019).

Table 5.2 *Summary of the WHO's policy autonomy*

Dimension	Indicator	De jure	De facto
Agenda-setting powers	Power to propose new policies	Delegated to Executive Board	Primarily exercised by governing body committees since early 1950s
	Power to prepare budget	Delegated to director-general	Shared by director-general and governing body as well as regional committees since 1970s
	Power to prepare governing body work program	Delegated to director-general and Executive Board	Primarily exercised by governing body committees since 1970s
Ability to avoid state veto	Decision procedure: 1. World Health Assembly	Majority voting for most issues	Consensus for most issues (since early years)
	2. Executive Board	Majority voting for most issues	Consensus for most issues (since early years)
	Distribution of votes	Unweighted	NA (consensus norm)
Access to non-state financing	Non-state contributions	Permitted	Always received; slow growth over time
	Independent earnings	Permitted	Always made (mainly investments); invariably low

authorized to draft the budget, oversee technical and administrative functions, and set the Executive Board's agenda.[14]

De jure policy autonomy was further bolstered by decision-making and financing rules. The World Health Assembly and the Executive Board would take regular decisions by a simple majority vote and settle "important questions," including the adoption of agreements, conventions, and constitutional amendments, with the backing of a two-thirds majority (both unweighted).[15] The WHO would be financed by assessed contributions from member nations, which would be calculated biennially based on the size of their economy and population. In addition, it was permitted to "accept and administer gifts and bequests"[16] and to earn income from investing "monies not needed for immediate requirements."[17]

Constitutional ambitions met a match in the first director-general, the Canadian psychiatrist and health official Brock Chisholm. Chisholm believed that the WHO could only fulfil its mission by embracing an

---

[14] World Health Organization (1948).   [15] United Nations (1946a, 15).
[16] United Nations (1946a, 15).   [17] World Health Organization (1950a, 7).

ambitious and wide-ranging agenda that addressed several health challenges at once – including malaria, tuberculosis, maternal and child care,
population control, and mental health – while recognizing their deep
connection to broader socioeconomic conditions, a central insight of the
incipient field of "social medicine." Critical to institutional success, he
maintained, would be a dedicated staff of "world citizens" willing to set
aside national identity for the cause of global public health.[18] To this end,
officials were recruited on the basis of "competitive examination scores
in order to ensure the highest possible level of technical expertise"[19]
and obliged to take a professional oath: "I solemnly swear to exercise in
all loyalty, discretion and conscience the functions entrusted to me as a
member of the international service of the World Health Organization . . .
and not to seek or accept instructions in regard to the performance
of my duties from any government or other authority external to the
Organization."[20] On the rare occasions Chisholm felt that officials had
betrayed their "objectivity as a scientist," he responded by "taking [them]
to task" and "giv[ing them] a stiff talking to" – and sometimes even
refusing to renew their contracts.[21]

For a brief time, the spirit of impartial internationalism cultivated
by Chisholm seemed to pervade the WHO's policy organs, especially
the Executive Board. In 1948, even as Cold War rivalries were sharp-
ening, the American representative on the Board commended Eastern
European colleagues for their "entirely professional" approach that
nurtured a "real atmosphere of professional friendship."[22] Individuals
who simultaneously served on both WHO governing bodies were known
to regularly reverse their vote in the Board, and one country – the
Netherlands – even selected a foreign national to fill its seat on the latter
organ.[23]

It did not take long for politics to throw a wrench in Chisholm's
plans. In 1950, frustrated with their lack of control over the Executive
Board, industrialized nations proposed converting it into a regular
intergovernmental body. While Chisholm narrowly defeated the proposal
by threatening to resign, it sent an ominous message to both Board
members (particularly those doubling up as delegates to the World
Health Assembly) and the secretariat. In the subsequent years, escalating
Cold War tensions made the United States increasingly suspicious of

---

[18] Chisholm (1947, 115).   [19] Staples (2006, 145).
[20] World Health Organization (1953a, 134). On multiple occasions during the "Red
Scare," Chisholm rejected attempts by the United States to institute a national loyalty
test for American WHO officials.
[21] Quoted in Staples (2006, 145).   [22] Quoted in Staples (2006, 145).
[23] Ascher (1952, 45).

social medicine approaches to public health, which "had a ring of 'socialism' and [were] closely associated with growing concerns about the rise of Communism."[24] Instead, American delegates insisted on narrower technical solutions to specific problems, a business-friendly "biomedical" strategy premised on the notion that poor health stems above all from the absence of appropriate medical technology and supplies. The knock-on effect was to restrict the WHO's range of programs, reduce its field presence, and concentrate its energies on activities that could be undertaken from headquarters, such as compiling statistics, providing public information, and formulating regulations and guidelines. As it "moved closer to US foreign policy and became partially captive to US resources and priorities," Marco Cueto, Theodore Brown, and Elizabeth Fee observe, the Organization "abandoned dreams of a collaborative community of nations and began coming to terms with new international political realities."[25]

This shift had far-reaching repercussions. A few months before the second session of the World Health Assembly, the Soviet Union led a withdrawal of nine Eastern Bloc countries from the WHO motivated by concerns about American domination.[26] The group did not reengage with the Organization until Cold War tensions eased following the death of Joseph Stalin several years later. In 1952, exasperated by "the United States' heavy hand in the organization," Chisholm declined to serve a second term as director-general.[27] His final address to the World Health Assembly struck a somber tone, admitting that "[t]he hopes we had five years ago that WHO, as a non-political body, could be spared the frustrating effects of a politically and psychologically divided world community have unfortunately not been realized."[28] Nevertheless, he expressed optimism that "[a] harmonious relationship between a world-minded Assembly, an independent Executive Board and a free and reliable Secretariat can overcome practically all handicaps which might interfere with the fullest realization of WHO's potentialities."[29]

---

[24] Lee (2009, 9). Another study points out that "a social medicine perspective, if taken seriously, implied questioning the inequality of land ownership in rural areas and the multitude of inequities that produce poor housing, misery, and illness in urban areas" (Cueto, Brown, and Fee 2019, 63).

[25] Cueto, Brown, and Fee (2019, 62).

[26] As the Polish health minister bemoaned, the WHO had "surrendered to the imperialistic States and in particular to the United States." World Health Organization (1950b, 324).

[27] Cueto, Brown, and Fee (2019, 70).

[28] World Health Organization (1953b, 119). "We must admit," he added, "that we have so far failed to live up to the great hopes men and women throughout the world have placed in us" (p. 120).

[29] World Health Organization (1953b, 119).

Yet under Chisholm's successor, the Brazilian doctor Marcolino Gomes Candau, the two governing bodies became even less "world-minded" and "independent." Members of the Executive Board, whose expert character Chisholm had so vigorously defended, yielded with increasing regularity to government pressures to serve as national representatives.[30] Given the Board's constitutional role as agenda setter for the World Health Assembly, this trend significantly amplified state influence in the policy process. Furthermore, both bodies began to take regular decisions by consensus rather than majority voting, allowing powerful nations to single-handedly block undesired policy proposals that *did* make it onto the agenda.[31]

Perhaps the clearest imprint of American influence lay in the WHO's biomedically inspired attempts to use recent advances in pharmaceutical technology and logistics to eradicate major infectious diseases, some of which were feared to be fueling the spread of communism in the developing world. The most prominent examples are the unsuccessful campaigns against tuberculosis (1947–1951), malaria (1955–1970), and yaws (1955–1970), which were beset by a combination of unanticipated drug resistance, high rollout costs, inadequate consultation with affected populations, and underdeveloped local health infrastructure.[32] These problems pointed to fundamental limitations in the strategy of "promoting global solutions to local problems by relying on technological fixes rather than the improvement of social and economic conditions."[33] The failure of the malaria campaign, hitherto the WHO's largest and most expensive undertaking, was especially damaging to its reputation, emanating an "obvious sense of organizational crisis."[34]

From the mid-1950s onward, wariness of bureaucratic ambitions led the United States to consistently oppose augmenting the WHO's resources. Since the vast majority of member states favored operational expansion – and budgetary decisions were still taken by majority voting – this stance only mildly tempered funding growth. Total organizational income rose from less than $5 million in 1948 to $19 million in 1960 to $81 million in 1970, an inflation-adjusted growth rate of around 40

---

[30] In hindsight, one biography of Chisholm reflects, his faith in the Board's capacity to resist these pressures was perhaps naïve: "[Chisholm] must have also known that these same professionals, when faced with issues that touched on the power, influence, and prestige of their own countries or on their own religious dogmas, would act as chauvinistically as anyone else. Perhaps in theory, expert committees and delegates to the WHO might behave somewhat apolitically when faced with strictly medical issues, but to divide the work of the WHO into strictly apolitical medicine on one hand and the political on the other was not possible; the two would always collide." Farley (2009, 204).

[31] Beigbeder (1998).   [32] Chorev (2012, 67).

[33] Cueto, Brown, and Fee (2019, 59).   [34] Siddiqi (1995, 210).

percent per year (see upper left panel of Figure 5.1). The number of staff leapt from a few hundred to almost 3,500, with the fastest rise occurring in the first few years – the period when the secretariat enjoyed the greatest autonomy.[35] On average, 15 percent of annual expenditures supported administrative rather than operational activities over the 22-year period, indicating a comparatively inefficient use of resources.

The WHO enjoyed limited access to nongovernmental sources of financing during its first phase. On average, just six percent of annual contributions between 1948 and 1970 came from non-state actors (lower left panel of Figure 5.1), with the Expanded Programme of Technical Assistance (EPTA) and the United Nations Special Fund (UNSF) accounting for the largest shares (as for the FAO in this period). Independent earnings, mostly in the form of interest on investments in government securities, represented a tenth of revenues (lower right panel).

A New (International Economic) Agenda

The decolonization wave of the 1950s and 1960s, together with the sense of institutional dissatisfaction that followed the failed malaria campaign, ushered in a second phase in the WHO's history marked by a more influential role for the Global South. Four occurrences, in particular, transformed developing countries into leading protagonists in the policy process, capable of curtailing the influence of staff – an early example of negative feedback from performance to de facto policy autonomy – as well as formerly ascendant industrialized countries. First, they came to constitute a sizable majority in the World Health Assembly, which still took some "important" decisions by majority voting: The WHO's membership surged from near 70 states in 1950 to almost 130 two decades later. Second, developing countries formed an "exceptionally stable coalition, so that they were consistently unified in how they voted."[36] This was achieved through regular meetings under the auspices of the Group of 77 (G77) and the Arab League, whose outputs would not be disclosed to other WHO members in advance of governing body sessions. One internal American memorandum from the late 1970s bemoaned: "We are often in the dark about G-77 or Arab League closed-door decisions in the course of the World Health Assembly until they suddenly appear as conference documents. Our ability ... to influence the actions of those delegations once the caucus has reached a decision is limited."[37] As in the FAO, the "glue" that

---

[35] Staffing figures from 1963 to 1999 are recorded in the Yearbook of the United Nations, available at https://unyearbook.un.org [Last accessed April 12, 2020].
[36] Chorev (2012, 144).   [37] Quoted in Chorev (2012, 43).

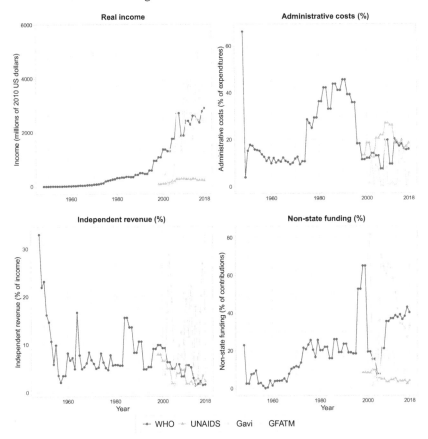

Figure 5.1 Financial trends: The WHO, UNAIDS, Gavi, and GFATM

Sources: WHO financial reports, WHO Library, Geneva; UNAIDS financial reports, acquired from www.unaids.org/en/resources/publications/all and through personal communications with staff; Gavi financial reports, available at www.gavi.org/news-resources/document-library/financial-reports; GFATM annual reports, available at www.theglobalfund.org/en/archive/annual-reports/. *Notes:* Income data are adjusted for inflation using the United States Consumer Price Index, with 2010 as the base year. Biennial data are divided by two to produce annual values.

bound together this heterogeneous set of nations was the ideology of the New International Economic Order, which implied the need for a massive expansion in the WHO's resources and in-country capacities as well as a more holistic focus on health systems and the socioeconomic contexts in which they are embedded. Third, Assembly committees comprising small subsets of the membership, such as the Committee on Programme and the Committee on Administration and Finance, became heavily involved in setting the body's agenda, impinging on the Executive Board's constitutional prerogative.[38] Fourth, the WHO's regional offices for Africa, Southeast Asia, and the Western Pacific, which are governed by Regional Committees dominated by national health ministries, also emerged as active instigators of policy proposals and budgetary items.

The developing world's rising clout found most visible expression in the WHO's Alma-Ata Declaration of 1978. Explicitly endorsing principles of the New International Economic Order, this proclamation identified primary healthcare rooted in community institutions and practices as the key to attaining Health for All by the Year 2000, a new objective defined as "the attainment by all peoples of the world by the year 2000 of a level of health that will permit them to lead a socially and economically productive life."[39] When attempting to introduce the social medicine policies advocated by the Declaration, however, the secretariat encountered stiff resistance from industrialized nations, which dismissed them as idealistic, costly, and excessively taxing on public health systems in the developing world.[40] An exasperated Halfdan Mahler, the third director-general, opened the 1987 session of the World Health Assembly by asking the membership: "Is WHO to be the Organization you have decided it should be, the Organization that will lead the people of this world to health for all by the year 2000? Or is not to be that kind of Organization? Is it to be merely a congregation of romanticists talking big and acting small; or just another international group of middlemen, giving pocket money to ministries of health and keeping a percentage for its own survival?"[41]

As a compromise with the biomedical paradigm favored by the United States, the WHO ended up embracing a "selective" primary healthcare approach that privileged disease-specific, scalable interventions such as growth monitoring, oral rehydration, breastfeeding, and immunization. Although cost-effective, this strategy fell well short of the comprehensive reforms needed to strengthen primary healthcare systems across the globe – let alone to attain Health for All by the Year 2000. The bold vision laid out in the Alma-Ata Declaration swiftly disintegrated, a failure

---

[38] Siddiqi (1995, 83).

[39] World Health Organization (1978, 3). Primary healthcare is generally understood as "essential health care based on practical, scientifically sound and socially acceptable methods and technology made universally accessible to individuals and families in the community through their full participation and at a cost that the community and country can afford to maintain at every stage of their development in the spirit of self-reliance and self-determination."

[40] Chorev (2012).   [41] World Health Organization (1987a, 11).

that saw the WHO "[lose] much of its international stature" and "[gain] a reputation as overly idealistic and too political."[42]

Discord between developed and developing countries led to mounting politicization of the policy apparatus. Against Mahler's pleas, the World Health Assembly routinely descended into point-scoring on contentious political issues with tenuous links to the WHO's mandate, from national liberation struggles to economic sanctions to nuclear weapons. After one heated debate over the treatment of Arabs in Israeli-occupied territories in 1976, the American ambassador to the UN remarked: "The absence of balance, the lack of perspective, and the introduction by the WHA [World Health Assembly] of political issues irrelevant to the responsibilities of WHA do no credit to the United Nations. Indeed, this is precisely the sort of politicized action which decreases respect for the U.N. system."[43] Several years later, a draft Assembly resolution censuring Israel over the same issue was derided as "entirely political" by the country's delegate, Ephraim Dowek, who raged that "[i]n any normal procedure respectful of law and legality, this draft resolution would have been deemed irreceivable for being in blatant breach of the Constitution of WHO and its noble goals."[44] Expressing serious concerns about the Organization's performance, Dowek appealed "to all countries that strive to keep politics out of WHO to vote against the draft resolution – not for the sake of Israel, but for the sake of WHO itself and of the millions of human beings who rely upon it."[45] In the late 1980s, the WHO agreed in principle to admit the Palestine Liberation Organization as a member state, prompting the United States to threaten withdrawal. After a series of tense diplomatic confrontations, the application was indefinitely postponed.

In the early 1980s, at the behest of the "Geneva Group" of large donors led by the United States and the United Kingdom, the World Health Assembly introduced a policy of zero real growth in the regular budget. The WHO's financial woes deepened when, a few years later, the Geneva Group to withhold and defer assessed contributions in protest at the G77's attempts to push social medicine policies through the

---

[42] Youde (2012, 40, 39). Health for All by the Year 2000 was quietly phased out of the WHO's agenda. In 1993, an Executive Board working group conceded – with some understatement – that "the Organization and Member States had perhaps not been entirely successful in defining and implementing the goals and programmes set." The chairman of the Board concluded that there was "a consensus that the present situation was untenable and that some rethinking of the goal of health for all by the year 2000 was necessary." World Health Organization (1993, 180, 189).

[43] United States Department of State (1976, 37).

[44] World Health Organization (1985, 242).

[45] World Health Organization (1985, 242).

Assembly. In 1985, for instance, the United States refused to pay its entire contribution – a quarter of the regular budget – on the grounds that an *Essential Medicines List* recently published by the Organization harmed American pharmaceutical producers. After failing to alter the decision, Mahler could not conceal his frustrations from the Assembly: "For more than a year now your Organization has been held financial hostage due to uncertainty about payments of assessed contributions ... What crimes has WHO committed against those who are withholding mandatory contributions? Surely it cannot be the influence of commercial lobbies who falsely believe that WHO is blocking their expansion, whereas in fact adding resources for the health underprivileged as part of WHO's value system could open up new markets in the most ethical of ways."[46] To this day, state-backed opposition from American and European pharmaceutical manufacturers has continued to thwart the WHO's efforts to widen access to essential medicines, a notable recent example being its failed proposal for a binding international agreement on the financing and coordination of research and development (R&D) activities.[47]

In an attempt to reassert its leadership within the Organization, the United States used the threat of further funding cuts to secure a string of procedural reforms that, in effect, required both governing bodies to approve the budget by consensus.[48] The upshot was that "the Member States with the highest budgetary contributions could control the level of expenditures of the next budgets."[49] In addition, the United States and other large donors began delivering their funding in the form of voluntary contributions earmarked for particular purposes. As one European aid official explained, "We invest in these programmes because we have control over what we invest in. If we don't like what happens we can vote with our cheque book."[50] As the scale of earmarked donations soared – by the early 1990s they exceeded assessed payments – they came to be seen as a threat to the coherence of organizational activities and the balance of influence among member states. "Rich countries' voluntary contributions helped prevent financial disarray," Nitsan Chorev points out, "but ... deepened the dependence of the WHO secretariat on rich countries' resources and weakened the procedural influence of poor member states."[51]

---

[46] World Health Organization (1987*b*, 3).   [47] Beigbeder (2018, 133–144).
[48] This was achieved by amending the World Health Assembly's budgetary approval process and empowering the Executive Board's Programme Committee to screen and make unanimous recommendations on the director-general's budgetary proposals.
[49] Beigbeder (1998, 154).   [50] Quoted in Godlee (1995, 178–179).
[51] Chorev (2012, 141).

Voluntary contributions kept the WHO's overall resources on a growth path during the second phase, albeit a less steep one than before. Income reached $300 million in 1980 and almost $500 million in 1990, which translates into a subdued inflation-adjusted growth rate of five percent per annum between 1971 and 1990 (upper left panel of Figure 5.1). The secretariat added only 500 employees to its existing contingent of 3,500 over this period, a similarly modest expansion. Reflecting the difficulty of efficiently allocating resources to disparate and conflicting policy agendas, a rising share of annual expenditures – 31 percent, on average – was allocated to administrative activities.

In terms of funding sources, non-state actors accounted for approximately a fifth of contributions in the second phase (lower left panel of Figure 5.1), thanks mainly to a rise in technical cooperation grants from UN partners such as the United Nations Development Programme (UNDP) and the United Nations Population Fund (UNFPA). The share of independent earnings in annual income dipped marginally to an average of eight percent (lower right panel). Hence, nongovernmental income streams did not meaningfully offset shortfalls in other dimensions of de facto policy autonomy during this era.

The one significant achievement of the second phase was the successful 1967–1980 campaign to eradicate smallpox – the only time an infectious disease has been wiped out through human intervention. Interestingly, this episode represented one of the few occasions in the WHO's history when staff "gained relative autonomy and overcame the tradition ... of being subservient to political powers as they increasingly exercised legitimate international authority."[52] This discretion was the product of an unusual set of circumstances, including détente between the United States and the Soviet Union – which briefly encouraged forbearance toward the WHO – and the leadership of an entrepreneurial and resourceful group of officials who made it a priority to forge robust operational partnerships with "political and medical leaders, tribal chiefs, and local vaccinators."[53] Even under these favorable conditions, not everything went smoothly. The membership had rejected the secretariat's original proposal for a smallpox eradication program in the early

---

[52] Cueto, Brown, and Fee (2019, 145). A less well-known example is the series of onchocerciasis (river blindness) control programs undertaken since the mid-1970s. A 1990 evaluation of one such scheme pinpointed its "high degree of autonomy" and devoted staff with "a sense of honor and pride in one's work and in the mandate of the Program as a whole" as particular strengths. World Health Organization (1990, 6, 7).

[53] Cueto, Brown, and Fee (2019, 145). In addition to Candau and Mahler, these officials included Donald A. Henderson, the head of the WHO's smallpox program; Ciro de Quadros, the program's chief epidemiologist in Brazil; and Mahendra Dutta, a senior official in the Indian health ministry's smallpox eradication department.

1950s as unrealistically ambitious, unnecessarily delaying the campaign by more than 15 years, and later offered only half-hearted backing for it.[54] As the WHO's official history of the campaign acknowledges, "Since smallpox was such a good candidate for global eradication, it is surprising that the commitment to undertake such a programme was so long delayed and, even after being accepted by the WHA, so ill-supported both within WHO and by most Member States."[55] Owing to this lack of support, the head of the program later admitted, "eradication was achieved by only the narrowest of margins."[56]

Crisis, Competition, and Pandemic Politics

By the 1990s, with the afterglow of smallpox eradication fading, political quarrels incapacitating the policy machinery, and resource constraints imperiling basic programs, the WHO's role as the leading global health authority was being widely questioned. A series of assessments by member states, the UN, and medical experts crystallized an emerging consensus that the Organization was in the throes of an existential crisis and required fundamental reform.[57] The WHO could only fulfil its mandate, one *British Medical Journal* (*BMJ*) analysis concluded, if it were "seen to be above national politics and free from divisive internal wranglings."[58] The direction of travel was clear to the secretariat: In a survey of headquarters staff fielded in 1993, more than half of respondents rated organizational performance as worse than in previous years, while almost three-quarters said the same of staff morale.[59]

Dwindling confidence in the WHO had two key consequences. First, it exacerbated the Organization's financial difficulties. In 1993, the Geneva Group tightened its regular budget policy from zero real growth to zero nominal growth. The following year, it strengthened its control over resource allocations by establishing an Administrative, Budget, and Finance Committee under the Executive Board to oversee and recommend improvements to the secretariat's budget preparation process – another instance of negative feedback from performance to de facto policy autonomy. Second, an "authority crisis" arose as states turned to other institutions to tackle issues within the WHO's remit.[60] The World Bank grew into a large-scale financier of health programs during the

[54] Lee (2009, 55).   [55] Fenner et al. (1988, 418).   [56] Henderson (1998, 17).
[57] Danish International Development Agency (1993); Godlee (1994b,a); Joint Inspection Unit (1993); Nordic UN Project (1990); Walt (1993).
[58] Godlee (1994b, 1428).
[59] McGregor (1993, 1205). The response rate was 34 percent.
[60] Chorev (2012, 147). Some scholars trace the origins of this crisis back to the foundation of the UNFPA in 1969, which occurred, they argue, because "the WHO was not fully trusted to conduct family planning." Cueto, Brown, and Fee (2019, 160).

1990s, using structural adjustment loans to promote liberalizing reforms that often contradicted WHO policy advice. Even more damaging was the 1996 creation of UNAIDS to address the rampant HIV/AIDS epidemic. "From the perspective of the WHO," Kelley Lee notes, "the creation of UNAIDS was a significant blow to the organization's leadership over a global health issue that should have been a clear call for it to assert its mandate. In large part, it was a vote of non-confidence more generally in an organization struggling in the 1990s with its own internal political and bureaucratic problems."[61] The WHO was initially slow to recognize the seriousness of HIV/AIDS, viewing it as a problem chiefly for wealthy countries and hence a distraction from the more urgent business of primary healthcare. The Global Programme on AIDS eventually launched by the Organization was generously funded but hamstrung by inefficiency and poor coordination, ultimately making little difference to disease transmission on the ground. The global number of AIDS-related deaths rocketed from around 50,000 in 1985 to a million a decade later (see Figure 5.2). With UNAIDS in the picture, the WHO has largely been relegated to "a side role in the governance of HIV/AIDS."[62]

The emergence of Gavi and GFATM in the early 2000s – a response to the WHO's failure to bring pervasive infectious diseases under control – struck a further blow to its authority. GFATM was charged with addressing the "big three killers" (see Figure 5.2): AIDS, deaths from which continued to mushroom in the new millennium; malaria, which reached "epidemic proportions" by the 1990s;[63] and tuberculosis, which underwent a resurgence since the 1980s.[64] Gavi, meanwhile, would focus on a host of vaccine-preventable diseases with lower – yet still significant – mortality rates that had barely budged for decades, including hepatitis B, meningitis, measles, and typhoid. As Chelsea Clinton and Devi Sridhar write, donor countries simply "did not trust preexisting institutions, particularly WHO, to steward amplified efforts to close the vaccine gap or defeat HIV/AIDS, TB [tuberculosis], or malaria."[65] This was ironic, they add, considering that "the donor countries heavily influenced, if not actually controlled, the [agenda] of WHO."

Under pressure from the Geneva Group, the WHO responded to the challenge of institutional competition by slashing expenses,

---

[61] Lee (2009, 62).   [62] Harman (2012, 104).   [63] Lee (2009, 49).

[64] This was in part because the WHO recommended "unsound treatment for MDR-TB [multidrug-resistant tuberculosis] patients in poor countries, instead of the standard, more expensive treatment successfully used in rich countries." Cueto, Brown, and Fee (2019, 291).

[65] Clinton and Sridhar (2017, 40).

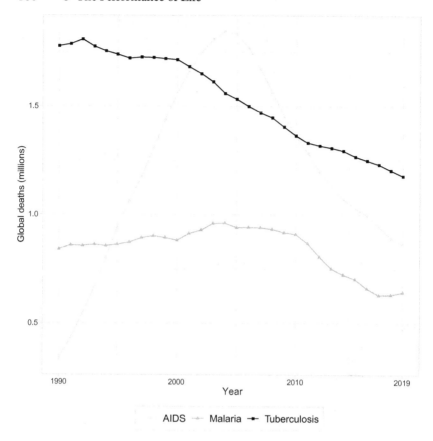

Figure 5.2 Global deaths from AIDS, malaria, and tuberculosis, 1990–2019

Source: Global Burden of Disease Study 2019 online database, available at http://ghdx.healthdata.org/gbd-results-tool.

consolidating administrative structures, and improving transparency. As plotted in the lower right panel of Figure 5.1, the proportion of administrative expenditures fell from an annual average of 22 percent between 1991 and 2005 to 15 percent between 2006 and 2018. The secretariat, which numbered close to 6,000 officials by the late 2000s, shrunk by a tenth in the subsequent years.[66] Organizational resources

---

[66] UN System Chief Executives Board for Coordination reports on personnel statistics, available at https://unsceb.org/reports [Last accessed November 3, 2020]. In recent years, states have allowed staff numbers to recover in an effort to improve performance.

were kept lean by the absence of nominal growth in the regular budget, to which many states were still delaying payments. In 2006, a combination of declining real income (upper left panel) and membership arrears of almost $150 million – more than 15 percent of the biennial budget – forced the secretariat to use voluntary contributions to cover some essential running costs. These donations have continued to grow in importance over the third phase, despite increasing awareness of their risks. A 1995 expert study commissioned by Australia, Norway, and the United Kingdom found that – particularly when earmarked – voluntary funds distorted the balance among operational activities, undermined cohesion across programs and levels of the Organization, and hindered long-term planning.[67] In a series of financing dialogues with donors since 2013, the WHO's senior management has repeatedly attested to these problems, emphasizing "the critical role of assessed contributions in ensuring the security and stewardship of the programme budget as a whole."[68] Nonetheless, as of the 2018–2019 biennium, assessed funding still made up just 17 percent of all contributions.

Rising voluntary contributions sustained the sluggish upward trajectory in aggregate income, which touched $1.4 billion in 2000, $2.4 billion in 2010, and $2.9 billion in 2018. Adjusting for inflation, this corresponds to an annualized growth rate of eight percent, roughly the same as during the second phase. Earlier trends in access to alternative sources of financing have also persisted. The average proportion of annual contributions received from non-state actors edged up to 31 percent, mostly as a result of major subventions from the Bill and Melinda Gates Foundation and Gavi. Independent earnings slipped slightly to an average of six percent of annual income.

Importantly, the WHO's competition-induced reforms left agenda-setting powers firmly in governmental hands. The World Health Assembly and the Executive Board continue to operate predominantly by consensus, while states retain key proposal powers. As a recent analysis of WHO governance summarizes, "Member states demand faithfulness to their often-conflicting demands. They elect the director-general, chart the work plan, approve the budget, and steer the overall direction. Such tight control can chill the Secretariat from acting as the moral leader for world health and advocating passionately on behalf of the most disadvantaged."[69] It is understandable, then, that Margaret Chan, the director-general from 2006 to 2017, often described the WHO as the "servant" of its membership. Several recent proposals for improving

[67] Vaughan et al. (1995).   [68] World Health Organization (2016c, 2, 4).
[69] Gostin, Sridhar, and Hougendobler (2015, 2).

its effectiveness have explicitly called for greater independence vis-à-vis states.[70]

Nor did the reforms heed bureaucratic calls to expand the WHO's field presence and scale up its programs for tackling infectious disease and strengthening health systems in developing countries. With the Geneva Group lurking menacingly in the background, Gro Harlem Brundtland, director-general from 1998 to 2003, rejected any notion that the Organization would become a "field agency," instead prioritizing its traditional functions of providing information, promoting research, and developing standards and regulations.[71] Even these activities have been plagued by performance problems. For instance, despite being constitutionally empowered to promulgate hard international law, the WHO has only ever managed to produce three binding instruments: rules on the statistical categorization of diseases and causes of death, which have evolved into the *International Classification of Diseases*; the *International Health Regulations* (*IHR*), first adopted in 1969, which govern the response to transnational public health risks; and the *Framework Convention on Tobacco Control*, effective since 2005, which sets standards for the consumption, marketing, and sale of tobacco. For Clinton and Sridhar, "This represents a missed opportunity, as law can be a powerful public health tool. Just as the Framework Convention and *IHR* were justified by the fact that tobacco and health security as relates to infectious diseases transcend borders, so too do a range of major health challenges, including alcohol overconsumption and antimicrobial resistance, both areas that WHO has called greater attention to in recent years."[72] As with proposals for a treaty on R&D, attempts to tackle these and other issues (such as marketing practices and salt and sugar consumption) via legal means have been met with vigorous resistance from major donor nations.[73]

The WHO's performance again came under scrutiny in the mid-2010s, when it became apparent that several health-related Millennium Development Goals (MDGs) – including reducing the 1990 under-five and maternal mortality rates by two-thirds and three-quarters, respectively, and providing universal access to reproductive healthcare and affordable essential medicines – would be missed by a wide margin. This failure was made starker by the Organization's previous enthusiasm for the MDGs and insistence on treating them as a yardstick for its performance. In one 2005 report on the targets, for instance, it

---

[70] E.g., Clinton et al. (2020); Gostin, Sridhar, and Hougendobler (2015); Moon (2014); Reddy, Mazhar, and Lencucha (2018).
[71] World Health Organization (1998).   [72] Clinton and Sridhar (2017, 187).
[73] Beigbeder (2018).

declared that, "while the MDGs do not reflect the entirety of WHO's work, they are central to its agenda in assisting Member States, and represent important milestones against which the Organization's overall contribution to health development can be measured."[74] Subsequent efforts to downplay the miss were met with skepticism by stakeholders.[75] "[T]he glass is not half full," the People's Health Movement, a global network of grassroots activists, nongovernmental organizations (NGOs), and academics, warned: "The picture ... is that of a global health crisis" that would not be solved by the WHO's "charity model with new vertical disease programs seeking to apply technical solutions to palliate the effects of an unfair global dispensation rather than progressing the necessary structural reforms."[76]

Performance problems have been most harshly exposed, however, by what has emerged as the foremost public health challenge of the twenty-first century: pandemics. Three major pandemics have occurred since 2000. The first, the 2009 H1N1 influenza outbreak first detected in the United States, spread widely but ultimately caused fewer deaths than the seasonal flu. The WHO was panned for overstating the seriousness of the pandemic and providing inconsistent information and guidance to the public. A 2011 evaluation of its response by a committee of health experts reiterated these criticisms while rebuking states for failing to meet *IHR* capacity requirements for detecting, assessing, and reporting public health threats.[77] The "lack of enforceable sanctions," the committee concluded, was the "most important structural shortcoming of the IHR."[78] Warning – remarkably presciently – that "the world is ill-prepared to respond to a severe influenza pandemic or to any similarly global, sustained and threatening public-health emergency," it issued 15 recommendations, including boosting *IHR* compliance, developing advance agreements for vaccine development and delivery, and establishing a $100 million reserve fund and associated workforce to be rapidly deployed in crisis situations.[79] Few of the proposals received serious consideration from the WHO's governing bodies.

The Organization received even stronger censure for its handling of the 2014–2016 West African Ebola outbreak, with some critics even calling for it to be replaced.[80] This time, it was faulted for reacting too slowly: Ebola was not designated a "Public Health Emergency of International Concern" (PHEIC), thereby mandating a rapid international response under the *IHR*, until more than 1,000 people had lost their lives.

[74] World Health Organization (2005a, 3, 10).
[75] World Health Organization (2005b).   [76] People's Health Movement (2015, 42).
[77] World Health Organization (2012).   [78] World Health Organization (2012, 13).
[79] World Health Organization (2012, 12).   [80] DeCapua (2014); McInnes (2015).

A central reason for this delay, many observers believed, was the WHO's excessive deference to West African member governments, which had initially sought to play down the outbreak. Several independent reviews published over the ensuing years validated these charges, calling for far-reaching reforms to organizational systems for preventing and responding to disease outbreaks.[81] Once again, they also took states to task for failing to comply with *IHR* standards, equip the WHO with an adequate regular budget, and support the secretariat's efforts to strengthen in-field technical capacities. Indeed, at the height of the pandemic in September 2014, Director-General Chan stressed that the WHO could not be a "first responder" in the same way as "international N.G.O.'s ... who are working on the ground to provide, you know, direct services," bemoaning that its budget was "highly earmarked, so it is driven by what I call donor interests."[82] With little funding earmarked for pandemics and a wilting regular budget, the Organization had been forced to downsize its emergency response unit from 94 staff to 34 over the five years preceding the outbreak.[83] In addition, powerful member states were widely blamed for refusing to back organizational reforms recommended after the H1N1 pandemic that would have enabled a more effective response to Ebola, such as the emergency reserve fund and workforce and advance agreements for drug development and sharing.[84] Assessments of the Ebola debacle put forward many of the same proposals; *The Lancet*, a leading medical journal, expressed "little confidence" that WHO governing bodies would take heed.[85]

This brings us to COVID-19, perhaps the sternest test in the WHO's history. The chargesheet against the Organization is lengthy: It waited an entire month to declare a PHEIC after receiving reports of cases in Wuhan in late December 2019, by which time the disease had spread to 18 countries; took a similar amount of time to warn of human-to-human transmission, despite clear evidence of this possibility in early January 2020; did not use the word "pandemic" until March 11, when 118,000

---

[81] For example, Moon et al. (2015); National Research Council (2016); United Nations (2016); World Health Organization (2015). In her last speech to the World Health Assembly in 2017, Director-General Chan admitted that "WHO was too slow to recognize that the virus, during its first appearance in West Africa, would behave very differently than during past outbreaks in central Africa, where the virus was rare but familiar and containment measures were well-rehearsed." World Health Organization (2017*a*).

[82] Fink (2017). In December 2015, Chan proclaimed that the WHO must become "a fully operational emergency organization." Chan (2015*b*, 818).

[83] Renwick and Johnson (2014). The regular budget fell by around $1 billion – more than 20 percent – between the 2009–2010 and 2014–2015 bienniums.

[84] Clinton and Sridhar (2017).

[85] *The Lancet* (2015).

cases in 114 countries had been recorded; opposed travel restrictions that might have significantly slowed cross-border transmission; and has still yet to discover the origins of the SARS-CoV-2 virus. Some of these shortcomings have, once more, been attributed to the WHO's inability to stand up to member states – in this instance China, which has been accused of refusing to share all available information about the Wuhan outbreak. "Much of the criticism of WHO," one commentator sums up, "asserts that it failed to exercise global health leadership and instead became a tool of Chinese politics, power, and propaganda."[86]

The WHO's blunders presented the Trump administration with a convenient opportunity to draw attention away from its own difficulties tackling COVID-19, as noted in Chapter 2. Although President Biden swiftly reversed the United States' notice of withdrawal and funding freeze, the episode bears signs of a far-reaching shift in the distribution of power within the WHO – one that could generate even sharper operational frictions going forward. As Tana Johnson remarks, "The World Health Organization found itself caught between two powerful and competing member-states – it was able to raise the alarm, but it could not single-handedly answer the call."[87]

At the time of writing, two evaluations of the WHO's response to COVID-19 have been published, one by an Independent Panel for Pandemic Preparedness and Response convened by the World Health Assembly and the other by an *IHR* review committee. Both reports find that the Organization should have declared a PHEIC and warned of the potential for a pandemic sooner than it did; advised countries to assume human-to-human transmission before this possibility was scientifically confirmed; and recommended stricter travel restrictions in the early stages of the outbreak.[88] Some of the blame is attributed to the slow and cumbersome nature of the WHO's pandemic alert system, a consequence, according to the Independent Panel, of the fact that "the legally binding *IHR* (2005) are a conservative instrument as currently constructed and serve to constrain rather than facilitate rapid action."[89] In a familiar pattern, the evaluations also condemned states' persistent lack of compliance with the *IHR* – particularly in the area of preparedness – and failure to implement recommendations from previous pandemic response assessments. "When steps have been explicitly recommended," the Independent Panel laments, "they have

[86] Fidler (2020).   [87] Johnson (2020, E153).
[88] The Independent Panel for Pandemic Preparedness and Response (2021); World Health Organization (2021b).
[89] The Independent Panel for Pandemic Preparedness and Response (2021, 26).

been met with indifference by Member States, resulting in weakened implementation that has severely blunted the original intentions."[90]

Significantly, the Independent Panel identifies political interference as a key constraint on the WHO's ability to exercise the discretion necessary for addressing urgent public health challenges such as COVID-19 – discretion stipulated in its own formal rules:

While the WHO Director-General nominally has many of necessary formal and legal authorities to make decisions, and guide and communicate with the world concerning pandemics and health at large, in practice there are challenges to the use of that authority. Global health is inevitably a politically charged domain and it is vital that WHO as an institution is strong enough to be able to perform with maximum independence. The same degree of independence is also desirable for other institutions across the multilateral system.[91]

Accordingly, one of the Independent Panel main recommendations is to "[f]ocus and strengthen the independence, authority, and financing of the WHO."[92] Among the means it suggests are increasing the regular budget, strengthening the secretariat's decision-making powers, extending the director-general's tenure, and eliminating *IHR* requirements that prevent staff from responding "immediately and independently" to emergencies.[93] In sum, as in previous pandemics, there is evidence that the prioritization of particularistic interests by member nations has hindered the WHO's efforts to mount an effective response to COVID-19.

Several interviewees felt that the WHO's dearth of autonomy during the third phase has been deepened and reinforced by performance deficiencies. According to one World Health Assembly delegate, "Member nations feel there's less to lose from meddling in an organization that's already coming up short and has a poor reputation. It's almost as if they're thinking: What more could go wrong?"[94] One WHO governance coordinator described the Organization as "trapped in a downward spiral" whereby "excessive [state] interference leads to unsatisfactory results, which are then used to justify further incursions."[95] The official added that, while most colleagues remain passionate about their work – the majority of staff agreed that "employees are highly motivated" in a

---

[90] The Independent Panel for Pandemic Preparedness and Response (2021, 16).

[91] The Independent Panel for Pandemic Preparedness and Response (2021, 48–49).

[92] The Independent Panel for Pandemic Preparedness and Response (2021, 46).

[93] The Independent Panel for Pandemic Preparedness and Response (2021, 16).

[94] Author interview #138 with World Health Assembly delegate, October 15, 2020, by video conference.

[95] Author interview #117 with WHO governance coordinator, June 9, 2020, by video conference.

recent internal survey[96] – many found the situation "so frustrating that they have simply left – in some cases to one of the newer, less politicized [global health] agencies, like the Global Fund or Gavi."

Sources of De Facto Policy Autonomy

Why did the expansive policy autonomy legislated by the WHO's creators fail to endure in practice? Despite its technocratic design and earnest efforts to remain free from politics, the Organization has consistently lacked the two sources of de facto policy autonomy highlighted by my framework, exercising governance tasks that are readily observable by governments and maintaining tenuous operational ties with actors above and below the state.

Governance Tasks

The WHO, not unlike the FAO, is often described as bearing a dual identity as a "normative" and a "technical" agency. In the former guise, it facilitates and monitors compliance with international agreements; in the latter, it conducts capacity-building operations, primarily in developing countries.

The WHO's normative role involves bringing states together to share information, knowledge, and experience, coordinate policies, and formulate international regulations and standards. In support of these activities, the secretariat arranges and hosts sessions of the World Health Assembly and the Executive Board, pools and standardizes national health data, and catalyzes and synthesizes medical research. As they necessitate close interaction with government delegates and national health agencies, these functions can be observed and scrutinized in real time, minimizing potential informational asymmetries in favor of bureaucrats.[97] As one Executive Board member explained, "The normative work done at headquarters involves a continuous exchange with member state representatives and national health authorities. Although staff have some leeway in crafting normative products, most activities require explicit governmental approval or occur within clearly defined parameters set by the governing bodies ... There aren't many surprises from the secretariat's end."[98]

A less widely appreciated side of the WHO's normative identity is its responsibility for verifying compliance with its two principal legal

---

[96] World Health Organization (2021a, 42). The response rate was relatively low, though "the survey respondent profile closely mirrored that of the overall staff profile" (p. 8).
[97] For details on the interactive process, see World Health Organization (2017b).
[98] Author interview #134 with WHO Executive Board member, October 15, 2020, by video conference.

instruments, the *IHR* and the *Framework Convention on Tobacco Control*. Both monitoring systems are based on self-reporting. The *IHR* require states to provide the World Health Assembly with annual compliance updates featuring a set of detailed benchmarks.[99] Similarly, parties to the *Framework Convention* must send the treaty's governing body a biennial reporting instrument containing a core implementation questionnaire.[100] Both sets of documents are compiled by the secretariat and published (in full or summary form) on the WHO website. With information solicited directly from states, this process again lends itself to relatively straightforward oversight.

The crux of the WHO's technical assistance activities is providing policy advice, expertise, and information to governments; helping health ministries design and implement strategies and programs; training health workers; and delivering equipment and supplies.[101] Although the officials who furnish such support are mostly based in the field and hold specialized medical qualifications, their latitude is circumscribed by the narrow purview and demand-driven nature of technical assistance, which is requested by member states to address specific deficits in their public health capacities. Projects are typically co-implemented and co-financed by recipient governments and yield readily observable outputs, facilitating top-down monitoring of local WHO teams. As per official technical assistance guidelines, "[O]perational staff are placed at the disposal of governments concerned and carry out their duties under the administrative control of the government concerned."[102] This is corroborated by, a recent evaluation of the WHO's "presence in countries" by an international development consultancy, which drew attention to its intimate working relationship with – and sensitivity to the needs of – health ministries: "As well as WHO's technical expertise, the closeness of WHO's relationship with the Ministry of Health is highly valued and the HWO [Head of WHO Offices in Countries, Territories, and Areas] and country team are seen as very closely aligned to the Ministry of Health's needs and responsive to the Ministry's requests and priorities."[103]

Operational Alliances

The absence of constructive operational collaboration with other inhabitants of the global public health space has been a consistent feature of the WHO's story. In a pattern reminiscent of the FAO, the

---

[99] World Health Organization (2008).
[100] https://fctc.who.int/who-fctc/reporting [Last accessed August 12, 2020].
[101] On the whole, the WHO has fared little better here than in other endeavors. Beigbeder (1998, 122) summarizes: "Criticisms have been addressed to the lack of effectiveness of programmes, their inadaptation to the particular conditions of specific countries, to the excessive employment costs of international 'experts', to the excessive number of poorly-financed projects, to the mismanagement of funds, of fellowships, etc."
[102] Beigbeder (1998, 117–118).   [103] World Health Organization (2016a, 20).

constraint during the first phase came from the "supply side": Civil
society was small and unorganized in most countries, the healthcare
industry was still in its infancy, and only a handful of international
institutions – mainly the United Nations Children's Fund (UNICEF),
ETPA, and the UNSF – took an interest in public health issues.[104]
In a sign of things to come, relations with the latter agencies were
plagued by suspicion and mistrust on the WHO's part. UNICEF's
maternal and child health programs in the late 1940s and early 1950s
were perceived as "stepping into WHO territory."[105] At the WHO's
insistence, a UNICEF-WHO Joint Committee on Health Policy was
formed in 1948 to coordinate their activities. The Committee stipulated
that all medical programs undertaken by UNICEF required approval
by the WHO, which it exalted as "the highest international authority in
the [health] field."[106] Similarly, while initially welcoming the technical
assistance funds made available by EPTA, the WHO soon adopted
an attitude of "firm resistance in any instance when the interests or
the autonomy of the Organization appeared to be in question."[107]
This stance impeded the effective execution of EPTA-financed projects,
which "were not integrated in a coherent country programme" and "did
not always respond to countries' real needs."[108] In a further example of
reverse causation from performance to de facto policy autonomy, EPTA
responded by downsizing its allocations from the 1970s onward. One
WHO partnerships coordinator opined that, in addition to hampering
its operational activities, the Organization's reluctance to share authority
deprived it of valuable allies in its pursuit of policy independence:
"The WHO got off on completely the wrong foot with its UN siblings,
with the consequence that governments became its chief 'partner.' This
had lasting implications for its autonomy: Close relationships with peer
institutions could have provided a powerful and legitimating base of
support for the secretariat's own agenda."[109]

During the second phase, supply-side constraints were relaxed as
civil society became denser and more organized and the healthcare

[104] "WHO was almost alone in the global public health area for many years after its
founding in 1948," notes Beigbeder (2018, 10).
[105] Cueto, Brown, and Fee (2019, 58).
[106] Cueto, Brown, and Fee (2019, 58). In Beigbeder's (2001, 90) telling, "WHO initially
opposed the creation of UNICEF and then tried to limit its activities by placing it
in the UN secretariat under close supervision of the UN specialized agencies. When
these attempts failed, WHO has constantly insisted on its leadership in public health
policies."
[107] Beigbeder (1998, 109). For instance, the WHO adamantly opposed any involvement
of EPTA's governing bodies in the design of technical assistance projects.
[108] Beigbeder (1998, 109).
[109] Author interview #122 with WHO partnerships officer, June 10, 2020, by video
conference.

industry expanded in many countries. Yet WHO demand for operational assistance from stakeholders remained just as weak. Staff continued to engage primarily with health ministries at the country level, only sporadically involving civil society in projects and programs. This "top-down approach," in the view of the partnerships officer mentioned earlier, "not only resulted in worse health outcomes on the ground but also entrenched the dominance of member states back at headquarters."[110] Private-sector institutions, particularly pharmaceutical manufacturers, were regarded as a threat to public-minded health policy.[111] As discussed earlier, one of the only instances in which the WHO overcame its apprehensions about collaborating with non-state actors – the triumphant smallpox campaign – was also one of the only times it achieved genuine operational autonomy.[112]

Interactions with other UN institutions continued to be beset by tensions over authority and territory. A "powerful rivalry" broke out between the WHO and UNICEF, as William Muraskin has documented: "Conflict and competition between UNICEF and WHO had grown severe ever since UNICEF in the early 1980s had declared the 'Children's Revolution' and entered the area of promoting children's health in a direct way – resulting in an increase in turf issues between the two organizations as well as disagreement on style and approach in numerous cases."[113] These strains led to low levels of communication and coordination between the two institutions in the field, where UNICEF staff enjoyed considerably "more autonomy" than their WHO counterparts.[114] Relations with the UNDP, the successor to EPTA and the UNSF, became "a source of professional and personal conflict" as it began to pay more attention to the nexus between socioeconomic development and health.[115] In the judgment of a 1992 evaluation by health experts, these problems directly contributed to the failure of the WHO's Global Programme on AIDS, which was dogged by squabbles and overlap with other international institutions.[116]

[110] Author interview #122 with WHO partnerships officer, June 10, 2020, by video conference.
[111] Cueto, Brown, and Fee (2019, 284) comment that "[y]ears of rancorous exchanges" with these companies "had by the mid-1990s ended all friendly communication," and that "many officers considered the pharmaceutical industry an enemy bound to sabotage the WHO's attempts to implement rational drug policies."
[112] The Organization's autonomous onchocerciasis control programs (see footnote 52) similarly involved extensive collaboration with community groups, NGOs, international development agencies (such as the World Bank and the UNDP), private foundations, and pharmaceutical companies (such as Merck & Co.). See Beigbeder (2018, 93–98).
[113] Muraskin (1998, 35).   [114] Beigbeder (1998, 189).   [115] Lee (2009, 61).
[116] World Health Organization (1992). As Morse and Keohane (2014, 404) conclude, "WHO was simply unable or unwilling to work collaboratively with other UN agencies to address the full impact of AIDS on societies."

In response to this and other criticism of its engagement with non-state actors, the WHO has made a concerted effort to build deeper and wider operational alliances in recent decades. In the late 1990s, the Organization established a dedicated office "to build partnerships and alliances with other key actors such as other UN agencies, NGOs and the private sector."[117] Soon after, a Civil Society Initiative was launched to study and propose measures for strengthening relations with civil society. In addition, the WHO founded and hosted a variety of public–private governance schemes to combat major infectious diseases, including Roll Back Malaria, the Stop TB Partnership, and the 3 by 5 Initiative (which was co-managed by UNAIDS).

These efforts have borne little fruit. Dealings with the private sector remain cool; Clinton and Sridhar note that "the number of companies working with the WHO has been quite limited and their donations unimpressive."[118] The Civil Society Initiative's recommendations "never made it past WHO member states, and thus remain in a coma, ignored and unimplemented," reports one NGO.[119] The public–private governance schemes were derailed by the WHO's abiding aversion to sharing authority. An independent assessment of Roll Back Malaria by medical professionals, for instance, found that its "loose" governance structure made it "more and more like a WHO programme with friends, rather than a true partnership of equals, all of whom are committed to specific roles and responsibilities."[120] An analysis by the *BMJ* echoed this conclusion, highlighting partner concerns that "WHO was using its new alliances to get back in the driver's seat in international health policy making."[121] "WHO speaks a language of partnership," one senior official from another global health institution told the journal, "but the reality is of insecurity and control-freakery."[122] As well as a loss of territory, the secretariat feared that "bringing new actors into the organization would lead to an institutional capture and weaken the autonomy of the WHO."[123] My argument suggests a rich irony to these fears.

Similar concerns reared their head in 2011, when an initiative by Director-General Chan to mobilize more contributions from non-state actors was thwarted by staff concerns about "tensions between financing arrangements that permit non-governmental contributions, particularly from the commercial sector, and the ability to maintain institutional

---

[117] World Health Organization (1998).   [118] Clinton and Sridhar (2017, 198).
[119] Third World Network (2012).
[120] World Health Organization (2002, 17). In part for these reasons, Roll Back Malaria has been rebranded as the RBM Partnership to End Malaria and moved from the WHO to the United Nations Office for Project Services (UNOPS).
[121] Yamey (2002*a*, 1237).   [122] Yamey (2002*a*, 1237).   [123] Chorev (2012, 194).

autonomy."[124] Two years later, a Chan-backed proposal for a multi stakeholder forum to "bring together Member States, global health funds, development banks, partnerships, NGOs, civil society organizations, and the private sector ... to shape the future global health agenda in a way that is relevant to all" was dropped due to a lack of internal support.[125]

The West African Ebola pandemic, in which insufficient communication and collaboration with non-state actors was widely perceived to have impeded the WHO's response, brought fresh scrutiny of its partnership behavior. One expert evaluation identified "a number of places where poor partnership with other stakeholders complicated and delayed the response to the crisis."[126] Shortly after the outbreak, the WHO adopted a *Framework of Engagement with Non-State Actors* to strengthen its operational alliances while managing risks arising from conflicts of interest and undue external influence.[127] The document's recommendations have yet to be fully implemented.

Despite efforts to expand and strengthen them, therefore, the WHO's operational alliances have maintained their limited character throughout the third phase. The Organization's website lists an average of 62 alliances in the years it has received donor performance ratings, just below the mean in the PIIP sample. Almost half of these arrangements were symbolic rather than substantive, more than double the PIIP mean. IGOs were the most common collaborators (48 percent of alliances), followed by PPPs (28 percent), NGOs (19 percent), and research institutes (five percent). In practice, governments and health ministries remain the WHO's true partner of choice.[128]

Joint United Nations Programme on HIV/AIDS

UNAIDS traces its origins to the WHO's struggle to check the devastating spread of the HIV/AIDS epidemic in the late 1980s and early 1990s. The ineffective inter-institutional collaboration highlighted by the 1992 assessment of the Global Programme on AIDS implied the need for a distinct, stand-alone mechanism for pooling resources and coordinating interventions. Evaluators recommended the formation of a WHO-led working group to explore this possibility over the following

---

[124] Reddy, Mazhar, and Lencucha (2018, 3).   [125] Richter (2012, 142).
[126] World Health Organization (2015, 24).   [127] World Health Organization (2016b).
[128] According to Lee (2010, 3), "Many CSOs [civil society organizations] continue to lament the difficulties of working with WHO, the closed nature of its activities, and allegedly blind romance with public-private partnerships."

year. Concurring with their diagnosis, the working group proposed a new UN program on HIV/AIDS to be cosponsored by the WHO, the UNDP, UNICEF, the UNFPA, the United Nations Scientific, Educational and Cultural Organization (UNESCO), and the World Bank. The United Nations Economic and Social Council (ECOSOC) endorsed the idea in 1994, calling on the proposed cosponsors to bring it to fruition within the next two years. After extended negotiations over details of the cosponsoring arrangement, UNAIDS was formally established on January 1, 1996.

The ECOSOC resolution authorizing UNAIDS' creation specified several objectives for the Programme, which can be summarized as providing global leadership in responding to HIV/AIDS; building consensus on approaches to tackling the disease; strengthening in-country capacities to develop and implement HIV/AIDS policies, programs, and monitoring systems; and fostering broad-based social mobilization and political commitment to addressing the epidemic at the national and international levels.[129] A more succinct mission statement published in 2010 describes UNAIDS as "an innovative partnership that leads and inspires the world in achieving universal access to HIV prevention, treatment, care and support."[130]

Despite the best intentions of its founders, UNAIDS has suffered from many of the same performance problems as the Global Programme on AIDS. While credited with raising the international profile of HIV/AIDS, UNAIDS is viewed by many stakeholders as lacking a clear purpose and comparative advantage, exacerbating duplication and coordination problems between aid agencies, and failing to improve prevention and treatment outcomes on the ground. This perception is substantiated by a succession of external assessments published over the past two decades[131] – including the comparative donor evaluations – as well as a small but expanding academic literature.[132] In recent years, a growing chorus of stakeholders has called on donor governments and cosponsor agencies to consider phasing out UNAIDS.

Tracing Policy Autonomy and Performance over Time

Three distinct trends characterize policy autonomy and performance over UNAIDS' 25-year existence: the emergence of a gap between the

---

[129] United Nations Economic and Social Council (1994).
[130] Joint United Nations Programme on HIV/AIDS (2010).
[131] Global Review Panel on the Future of the UNAIDS Joint Programme Model (2017); Joint United Nations Programme on HIV/AIDS (2002, 2009b, 2020); UNAIDS Leadership Transition Working Group (2009).
[132] For example, Chin (2007); Clinton and Sridhar (2017); Kohlmorgen (2007); Lee (2009); Pisani (2008); Youde (2012).

Table 5.3 *Summary of UNAIDS' policy autonomy*

Dimension	Indicator	De jure	De facto
Agenda-setting powers	Power to propose new policies	Delegated to executive director	Primarily exercised by donor states and cosponsor governing bodies since early years
	Power to prepare budget	Delegated to executive director	Primarily exercised by donor states since early years
	Power to prepare governing body work program	Delegated to executive director	Primarily exercised by donor states and cosponsor governing bodies since early years
Ability to avoid state veto	Decision procedure: Programme Coordinating Board	Consensus	Consensus
	Distribution of votes	Unweighted	NA (consensus norm)
Access to non-state financing	Non-state contributions	Permitted	Always received; consistently low
	Independent earnings	Unspecified	Always made; consistently low

bureaucracy's copious de jure policy autonomy and meagre de facto policy autonomy (see Table 5.3); mounting performance problems as state interference in the policy process has steadily intensified over time; and negative feedback from performance to de facto policy autonomy, dragging UNAIDS toward a low-autonomy, low-performance equilibrium.

Recognizing the trickiness of coordinating six large and diverse cosponsor agencies – a task once likened by the head of the Global Programme on AIDS to "walking six cats on a leash"[133] – UNAIDS' designers resolved that a healthy dose of bureaucratic independence would be needed.[134] The institution's governing body, the Programme Coordinating Board, would meet biannually to determine policies and strategies, monitor program planning and implementation, and approve the work plan, budget, and other proposals submitted by the executive director (the chief of staff).[135] The Board would include 22 states and – in a first for a UN agency – allow five NGOs (three from developing countries, two from developed countries or transition economies) to participate in its sessions without voting. This innovation was motivated

[133] Balter (1998, 1864).   [134] Johnson (2014).
[135] Joint United Nations Programme on HIV/AIDS (1999).

by "a clear recognition of the crucial importance of activists, whose main weapon was moral outrage, to keep government accountable."[136] In addition to proposal and budgetary powers, the executive director was assigned the role of agenda setter and secretary for the Board. The latter body would "endeavour to adopt its decisions and recommendations by consensus," taking a simple (unweighted) majority vote when such efforts failed.[137]

In keeping with other UN funds and programs, UNAIDS was only permitted to accept voluntary contributions. No restrictions were placed on their source: The 1994 ECOSOC resolution invited cosponsor agencies to "contribute to the resource needs of the programme,"[138] and a follow-up resolution the next year later appealed "to all Governments, international institutions, non-governmental organizations and the private sector to support the Programme with adequate contributions to its resources."[139] The founding documents made no mention of supplementing these donations with independent earnings by the secretariat, though.

Headed by the Belgian microbiologist Peter Piot, the few hundred staff constituting the secretariat began with sufficient autonomy to pursue advocacy strategies, promulgate international guidelines on the relationship between human rights and HIV/AIDS, and gather new information on the extent of the epidemic.[140] In the field, however, it struggled to manage cosponsor agencies, whose member states grew increasingly concerned that the more coherent response to HIV/AIDS they had previously desired could interfere with other foreign policy priorities. Within each country, operations were organized by a UN Theme Group on HIV/AIDS (convened by the existing UN resident coordinator), which contained representatives of every cosponsor with a ground presence and was usually assisted by an adviser from the UNAIDS secretariat. Rather than integrating their activities into the Theme Group's unified work plan, cosponsors largely continued to operate in isolation – even if they overlapped with or undercut one another. These problems were extensively documented in an independent *Five-Year Evaluation of UNAIDS* published in 2002, which singled

[136] Cueto, Brown, and Fee (2019, 223).
[137] Joint United Nations Programme on HIV/AIDS (1999, 4).
[138] United Nations Economic and Social Council (1994, 3).
[139] United Nations Economic and Social Council (1995, 2).
[140] A recent UN Joint Inspection Unit (JIU) report surmises: "During this early period, the context may have allowed UNAIDS and its secretariat the latitude to function with a more flexible organizational construct in terms of its governance, administrative, oversight and accountability structures compared with other United Nations system organizations." United Nations Joint Inspection Unit (2019, iii).

out the failure to "develop a genuinely integrated approach" as a central constraint on the Programme's effectiveness.[141]

Efforts to rein in cosponsors via the Programme Coordinating Board were stymied by the secretariat's lack of *de facto* influence in the policy process. The Board's agenda was, in practice, set by major donor nations and cosponsor governing bodies, which sought to exclude "any proposals that down the road could lead to an expansion of the secretariat's authority on the ground."[142] Even when such schemes did make it onto the agenda, they were usually vetoed or heavily diluted thanks to the practice of consensus decision-making. The *Five-Year Evaluation* noticed a recurring lack of dialogue on "hard-hitting questions" during Board meetings, a pattern it linked to "the consensual nature of decision-making that buries the hard choices that need to be made."[143] Overall, the assessment rated UNAIDS as successfully progressing toward just one of the several objectives defined in the 1994 ECOSOC resolution: providing global leadership to stakeholders. Perhaps not by coincidence, this was also the area of its mandate where the secretariat had managed to carve out the greatest discretion. "It is probably realistic," evaluators reflected, "that achievements have been greatest at global level and in those areas under the direct influence of the Secretariat."[144]

The epidemic marched ruthlessly on, its annual global death toll rising from 1.06 million when UNAIDS was founded to 1.66 million in 2001 (see Figure 5.2). This alarming trend, coupled with UNAIDS' skillful advocacy work – praised by the *Five-Year Evaluation* as "a strength of the Secretariat in particular" – sparked growing interest in HIV/AIDS among international development donors.[145] UNAIDS itself, however, barely benefited from the resulting deluge of resources for combating the disease: Real annual income remained in the region of $100 million throughout the Programme's first five years (see upper left panel of Figure 5.1), far less than what experts believed it needed. Nor, the *Five-Year Evaluation* pointed out, did cosponsors receive any kind of windfall, hampering their ability to alleviate UNAIDS' financial difficulties: "Financial arrangements brought cosponsors neither benefits in the form of extra funds, nor their support through commitments to fund. In that sense, the word cosponsor is a complete misnomer."[146] As discussed subsequently, much of the new funding for HIV/AIDS was

---

[141] Joint United Nations Programme on HIV/AIDS (2002, xi).
[142] Author interview #128 with UNAIDS program officer, July 22, 2020, by video conference.
[143] Joint United Nations Programme on HIV/AIDS (2002, 39).
[144] Joint United Nations Programme on HIV/AIDS (2002, xiii).
[145] Joint United Nations Programme on HIV/AIDS (2002, xi, xiv).
[146] Joint United Nations Programme on HIV/AIDS (2002, ix).

instead directed to GFATM in a "deliberate effort to bypass the existing UN institutions, including UNAIDS."[147] Even Executive Director Piot conceded that GFATM's creation could be viewed as a "vote of no confidence in the UN's ability to deal with the AIDS epidemic."[148] Following in the WHO's footsteps, UNAIDS saw its role in HIV/AIDS governance become "increasingly second" to that of other international institutions.[149]

The expansion of bilateral HIV/AIDS programs in the early 2000s also undermined UNAIDS' authority. By far the largest was the President's Emergency Plan for AIDS Relief (PEPFAR) launched by the United States in 2003, whose scale and scope rendered it a powerful instrument for bringing UNAIDS into line with President George W. Bush's "compassionate conservativism" agenda. As PEPFAR began disbursing funds, soon becoming the largest ever international health program targeting a single disease, UNAIDS was roundly criticized for bowing to American pressures to distance itself from evidence-based interventions such as needle exchange services (providing drug users with sterile needles and syringes), condom distribution, broader access to HIV treatment for sex workers, and permissive abortion laws.[150] The background paper for a 2009 evaluation of UNAIDS by the Center for Global Development summarizes: "[C]ritics of UNAIDS allege that since the Bush administration came to power the leadership of UNAIDS has had clear parameters from the US on what they could or could not say on certain topics that did not align with US policy."[151] Stakeholders interviewed for the report gave a frank assessment of the consequences of such pressure, citing the "emasculation" of institutional authority, "dreadfully weakened rigor" on scientific issues, and policy stances "dominated by political/ideological/'activist'-related concerns, more so than actual science."[152]

American influence was also evident in UNAIDS' refusal to challenge the adoption of ideologically motivated domestic policies by several African countries receiving PEPFAR support, including the criminalization of homosexuality, the exclusion of sex workers and illegal drug users from health services, and the prioritization of abstinence programs. One disappointed civil society delegate to the Programme Coordinating Board lamented that "governments are corrupt, and have different priorities, they can be against homosexuality ... [The Board] could kick

[147] McInnes et al. (2014, 36).   [148] Yamey (2002b, 1294).
[149] Harman (2012, 105).
[150] UNAIDS Leadership Transition Working Group (2009, 16).
[151] Sridhar, Kuczynski, and Latulippe (2008, 13).
[152] Sridhar, Kuczynski, and Latulippe (2008, 13–14).

them off the UNAIDS delegation but they never do."[153] The consensus norm was again identified as a key culprit, ensuring that decisions "depended on the agreement of conservative states resistant to . . . rights-based responses to the epidemic."[154]

Another ramification of state meddling was the sustained neglect of HIV prevention as a strategy for containing the epidemic. A 2008 *The Lancet* analysis deemed this oversight "[p]erhaps the biggest failure in the response to HIV/AIDS."[155] The official *Second UNAIDS Evaluation*, which covered the 2002–2008 period, reached a similar verdict, emphasizing that "UNAIDS leadership and support for effective HIV prevention policies and programmes has been inadequate."[156] Some prevention measures, such as condoms, clean needles, and education programs for marginalized groups, clashed with ideological agendas pushed by the United States and likeminded African countries. Others, such as male circumcision and pre-exposure antiretroviral therapy, were simply overlooked as staff scrambled to satisfy disparate state and cosponsor demands. When UNAIDS finally approved some of the latter strategies, the main effect was to foment uncertainty and suspicion. In 2008, for instance, the scientist Daniel Halperin complained that UNAIDS' "very sudden" endorsement of circumcision as a prevention measure "understandably left many African Ministries of Health feeling confused, and mistrustful," adding that "[i]f UNAIDS had showed technical leadership on this issue years ago, then programmes/service delivery might be currently occurring at a much faster rate."[157]

Nor did matters improve at the country level, where many stakeholders started to "hold UNAIDS itself responsible for the cooperation and coordination problems . . . and criticize UNAIDS for creating a duplication of structures and for being ineffective."[158] A 2005 assessment by a public–private Global Task Team on Improving AIDS Coordination Among Multilateral Institutions and International Donors drew further attention to these deficiencies: "The UN System's response to AIDS at country level is, at the moment, unevenly coordinated, despite the existence of [UNAIDS]. In many countries, the UN Theme Group on HIV/AIDS has not succeeded in establishing a truly joint programme that includes the AIDS activities of all UNAIDS Cosponsors."[159]

Similar issues afflicted the 3 by 5 Initiative launched jointly with the WHO in 2003, which fell well short of its target to provide antiretroviral

---

[153] Smith (2014, 150).   [154] Smith (2014, 129).
[155] Das and Samarasekera (2008, 2101).
[156] Joint United Nations Programme on HIV/AIDS (2009*b*, xx).
[157] Das and Samarasekera (2008, 2101).   [158] Kohlmorgen (2007, 141).
[159] Joint United Nations Programme on HIV/AIDS (2009*a*, 14).

therapy to three million people with HIV/AIDS by the end of 2005.[160] An independent review published in 2006 singled out dysfunctional coordination mechanisms as a key contributor to this outcome.[161] *The Lancet*'s editorial board caustically quipped that "2005 is likely to be remembered more for the 3 million deaths and almost 5 million new infections it heralded than for the 300,000 lives saved through treatment for HIV."[162]

Coordination problems repeatedly resurfaced in subsequent evaluations, most of which recommended more robust bureaucratic authority over cosponsor agencies, whose number rose to 11 in 2012.[163] Stakeholders consulted by assessors were frequently unable to identify UNAIDS' distinctive role at the country level. The background paper for the Center for Global Development appraisal saw this as a significant problem for the Programme: "Arguably, the greatest challenge ... is to clarify the value added of UNAIDS in light of the fact that observers often ask, 'What does UNAIDS actually do?' As one respondent remarked, 'It is hard for most people to describe what UNAIDS is.'"[164]

To its credit, the secretariat has assiduously implemented evaluation recommendations that fall within its scope while, survey evidence suggests, remaining committed to UNAIDS' mission.[165] States have been far less receptive to these suggestions – particularly the idea of strengthening bureaucratic authority. To the contrary, performance failings appear to have to provoked deeper and more regular intrusions into the policy process. In the opinion of one UNAIDS planning officer, the publication of the comparative donor evaluations has compounded these feedback effects: "States have used donor ratings to justify a more domineering stance in the Programme Coordinating Board, dictating to staff what our priorities should be, how we should allocate resources, how we should spend our time, and so on. The problem is that these diktats don't always align with the Programme's needs. Many governments, for example, have been on the wrong side of the debate over prevention versus treatment and access for marginalized groups, and haven't done anything to improve inter-agency coordination on the ground."[166]

---

[160] Only 1.6 million people were receiving such treatment by the deadline.
[161] World Health Organization (2006).   [162] The Lancet (2005).
[163] Joint Inspection Unit (2007); Joint United Nations Programme on HIV/AIDS (2009b); UNAIDS Leadership Transition Working Group (2009).
[164] Sridhar, Kuczynski, and Latulippe (2008, 10).
[165] In a 2018 staff questionnaire, 89 percent of respondents agreed that "what motivates them to come to work each day is their commitment to the AIDS response." Joint United Nations Programme on HIV/AIDS (2018, 4). Two-thirds of the secretariat completed the survey.
[166] Author interview #33 with UNAIDS planning officer, June 12, 2012, Geneva.

More recent assessments indicate that old ghosts continue to haunt UNAIDS. A 2019 review of its management and administrative systems by the UN Joint Inspection Unit (JIU) reported "frustrations at various levels about coordination and communication, programme delivery, funding, and reporting processes," noting that "the most substantive rift seems to be between the cosponsors and secretariat in addressing how UNAIDS is delivering at various levels, what it will look like in the future and how it will be staffed to meet its future needs."[167] Along similar lines, an *Independent Evaluation of the UN System Response to AIDS in 2016–2019* drew attention to performance problems stemming from "poor interaction" between the secretariat and cosponsors, a lack of clarity about UNAIDS' role, and an inadequate budget.[168]

The latter problem is reflected in consistently lethargic growth in UNAIDS' resources since the turn of the millennium. After peaking at almost $290 million in the late 2000s, annual income declined to less than $220 million in 2018, an inflation-adjusted annual growth rate of just four percent (see upper left panel of Figure 5.1). Staff numbers have followed a similar course, rising to more than 900 in 2011 before sliding to 680 at the end of 2018.[169] Administrative outlays have absorbed an annual average of 19 percent of expenditures over the full 1996–2018 period, lending succor to charges of institutional inefficiency (upper right panel of Figure 5.1).

Nor has UNAIDS succeeded in broadening its resource base by tapping nongovernmental sources of financing. On an average basis, states supplied 94 percent of annual contributions up to 2018 (lower left panel of Figure 5.1), with the lion's share coming from the United States, Sweden, the Netherlands, and the United Kingdom. Independent earnings accounted for just four percent of annual income (lower right panel).

Sustained underperformance, thrown into sharp relief by the tangible progress made by other international institutions in combating HIV/AIDS during the 21st century (discussed shortly), have led many stakeholders to question whether UNAIDS is still needed today.[170] A clear consensus is yet to emerge on this issue, with proposals ranging "from increasing the Secretariat's technical role and providing invest-

---

[167] United Nations Joint Inspection Unit (2019, 9).
[168] Joint United Nations Programme on HIV/AIDS (2020, 46).
[169] United Nations Joint Programme on HIV/AIDS (2019, 4).
[170] Joint United Nations Programme on HIV/AIDS (2020). Calls for UNAIDS to be dismantled began as early as 2008. See England (2008). They intensified following a 2018 sexual harassment scandal that eventually led to the executive director's resignation. See Cohen (2018).

ment advice to countries to phasing out the Secretariat by 2030 now that most Cosponsors have incorporated HIV in their work."[171]

Sources of De Facto Policy Autonomy

Aside from performance-induced feedback effects, two factors have been integral to UNAIDS' depressed levels of de facto policy autonomy: the relatively low cost to governments of overseeing its consensus-building and technical assistance functions; and its sparse and fractious operational linkages with subnational and supranational stakeholders.

Governance Tasks

While not every task entailed by UNAIDS' unique mandate fits neatly into Chapter 2's typology, most of them can be classified as forms of agreement facilitation or capacity building.[172] The Programme's consensus-building functions are exercised at two levels. At the headquarters level, UNAIDS organizes and provides administrative support for sessions of the Programme Coordinating Board; brings together stakeholders in panels, workshops, conferences, and others forums to deliberate on policy issues; and compiles cross-national HIV/AIDS information. As states are the dominant constituency on the Board, the main source of HIV/AIDS data, and pivotal to any viable approach to tackling to the epidemic, they are privy to all these activities. One Board member described consensus building as "by necessity, a government-centered task that leaves little space for bureaucratic expression."[173] "It's in large part for this reason," the delegate continued, "that UNAIDS has never become a truly autonomous agency – notwithstanding its creators' wishes."

At the national level, UNAIDS develops strategies for harmonizing cosponsor operations through participation in UN Country Teams – the current incarnation of the UN Theme Group on HIV/AIDS – and conducts advocacy for increased political attention and a more robust policy response to the disease. While harder for the Programme Coordinating Board to observe, these functions involve direct exchanges with host governments, which are represented in UN Country Teams and the primary target of advocacy campaigns. They are thus no less amenable to state oversight than the secretariat's headquarters-based activities.

---

[171] Joint United Nations Programme on HIV/AIDS (2020, 39).
[172] UNAIDS' advocacy work, in particular, does not clearly correspond to any component of the typology.
[173] Author interview #130 with UNAIDS Programme Coordinating Board member, July 24, 2020, by video conference.

The bulk of UNAIDS' in-country technical assistance concentrates on four areas: the formulation of policies and strategic frameworks for addressing HIV/AIDS; the monitoring, evaluation, and implementation of projects and programs; the strengthening of health systems and institutions; and the collection and synthesis of information on the national epidemiological situation. Support is solicited by UN member states and delivered by small teams of local UNAIDS staff (based in country or regional offices) working intimately with National AIDS Councils – coordinating bodies usually housed within health ministries – or other government authorities.[174] UNAIDS accordingly emphasizes that technical assistance projects are "country-owned, country-led, and demand-driven," buttressing rather than independently shaping the national HIV/AIDS response.[175] Recipient government monitoring is, in effect, built into their structure, leaving few avenues for bureaucrats to exploit information asymmetries in pursuit of their policy goals.

Operational Alliances

As a vehicle for bringing together international institutions, civil society groups, and other HIV/AIDS stakeholders, UNAIDS was always intended to leverage operational alliances to advance its objectives. It is surprising, therefore, that the secretariat's relationships with non-state actors have for the most part remained weak and distant, especially at the country level.

Engagement with cosponsor agencies has been consistently strained, an outcome for which both sides share blame. As the implications of UNAIDS' proposed leadership and coordination role became clearer in the late 1990s, cosponsors began to jealously protect their turf and resources. According to one UNAIDS official at the time, "The Programme has failed to co-ordinate its co-sponsors because they have no desire to be coordinated ... They all compete with one another for funding, attention, and kudos and UNAIDS is obliged to kowtow to them. Consequently, UNAIDS lacks independence."[176] The WHO, still resentful of its waning authority, was especially difficult to work with: "Piot was like a nursery school teacher trying to get all children to play nicely together in the sand pit. It wasn't easy because the WHO, the biggest kid in the AIDS class, was still sulky about having its toys taken away and given to the other agencies to play with."[177] The *Five-Year Evaluation of UNAIDS* found evidence of deep concerns about the secretariat's authority among cosponsors:

---

[174] Management consultants, medical practitioners, and civil society groups are regularly contracted to assist in the implementation of technical assistance projects.
[175] Joint United Nations Programme on HIV/AIDS (2007).
[176] Das and Samarasekera (2008, 2101).   [177] Pisani (2008, 5).

The unsettled relationship between cosponsors and Secretariat at the country level creates animosity in regard to any action that may be construed to reinforce the Secretariat's institutional presence at the country level. Given that CPAs [Country Programme Advisers] are paid by the Secretariat the suspicions weigh on his/her relationships with the cosponsors ... For many of the same reasons, cosponsors watch the size of CPA offices with suspicion as it may indeed create the impression of an agency in its own right. The creation of a Country Support Division within the UNAIDS Secretariat has again created suspicion that UNAIDS was to assume more of an independent role at the country level.[178]

A similar attitude has been detected in more recent assessments. The *Second Independent Evaluation of UNAIDS* mentions cosponsor concerns about UNAIDS becoming "a potential competitor for funding" and "a de facto agency rather than functioning as a secretariat to the cosponsors."[179] The *Independent Evaluation of the UN System Response to AIDS* cites "territoriality around technical issues" and "the lack of 'co-ownership' by the Cosponsors" as sources of tension with the Programme.[180]

At the same time, UNAIDS has – despite promising early signs – been reproached for failing to show effective leadership in interactions with cosponsors. Many stakeholders, the Center for Global Development evaluation discovered, see this shortcoming as the root of its coordination and duplication problems: "In the view of many individuals consulted at both global and national levels, inadequate leadership by UNAIDS has resulted in power struggles among the various UN bodies and a joint work plan that does not adequately delineate responsibility. This causes some issues to have multiple owners – for example, prevention of mother-to-child transmission (MTCT), which falls under the mandate of a number of cosponsors. The result has been duplication of effort, unhealthy competition for funding, and gaps in some areas."[181] The absence of institutional leadership has been felt most keenly on the ground, where UNAIDS has been accused of refusing to fully engage with cosponsor agendas, integrate their activities into its plans, and participate in interagency forums.[182] The result, one field support officer from a cosponsor argued, was "a significant missed opportunity to cultivate relationships that could have bolstered the secretariat's authority both in the field and at headquarters."[183]

---

[178] Joint United Nations Programme on HIV/AIDS (2002, 36–37).
[179] Joint United Nations Programme on HIV/AIDS (2009*b*, 66).
[180] Joint United Nations Programme on HIV/AIDS (2020, 46).
[181] UNAIDS Leadership Transition Working Group (2009, 19).
[182] Multilateral Organisations Performance Assessment Network (2005).
[183] Author interview #42 with UNICEF field support officer, January 10, 2014, by telephone.

Collaboration with civil society, an influential force in the fight against HIV/AIDS, has been decidedly uneven. At the global level, the secretariat has forged potent advocacy coalitions with transnational civil society associations such as Oxfam, the Global Network of People Living with HIV, the Clinton Health Access Initiative, the Elton John AIDS Foundation, and AIDS Action Europe.[184] These alliances have deployed a host of "effective tools for 'going loud' on contentious issues and shaming states into action," including demonstrations and protests, lobbying drives (usually targeting health ministries), letter-writing campaigns, and the dissemination of information and research.[185] In doing so, one UNAIDS external relations coordinator observed, they have "restricted the range of policies states can propose – or, equally important, veto – in the PCB [Programme Coordinating Board]."[186] The *Second Independent Evaluation* adds: "At the global level, civil society involvement is considered to provide an important reality check, to bring a different perspective to policy debates and to play an important role in agenda setting."[187] Hence, in accordance with my argument, the secretariat has enjoyed the most pronounced policy influence where it has fashioned the strongest partnerships with non-state stakeholders.

On the ground, engagement with civil society has been less fruitful. "Civil society influence at the global level is clear," notes the *Second Independent Evaluation*, "but it is harder to find good examples at country level."[188] Efforts to incorporate NGOs into technical assistance projects have been patchy, in part due to the absence of an overarching strategy or framework for such collaboration, and the secretariat's Civil Society Partnerships unit is "reported by staff and external stakeholders to be overstretched" and "to lack institutional support."[189] The *Independent Evaluation of the UN System Response to AIDS* indicates that these problems have yet to be solved: "There continues to be a degree of discontent among some stakeholders about the quality and level of CSO

---

[184] Harman (2011). The secretariat has used liaison committees, the Programme Coordinating Board, consultations, and workshops to foster these relationships. The UN secretary-general's special envoys for HIV/AIDS, who are recommended by UNAIDS and often drawn from civil society, have also played a role in alliance building.

[185] Harman (2011, 442).

[186] Author interview #127 with UNAIDS external relations officer, July 21, 2020, by video conference.

[187] Joint United Nations Programme on HIV/AIDS (2009*b*, xxvii).

[188] Joint United Nations Programme on HIV/AIDS (2009*b*, xvii). Kohlmorgen (2007, 138) observes that "CSO involvement prevails mainly at the global level and is encouraged mainly by the UNAIDS Secretariat, whereas the involvement (and sometimes also the cooperation) at the country level differs from country to country and is often not very far-reaching."

[189] Joint United Nations Programme on HIV/AIDS (2009*b*, 86).

[civil society organization] and community involvement – particularly at the country level. A number of KIs [key informants] interviewed articulated mixed assessment of the Joint Programme's level of community involvement at the country level, with many saying the approach was too ad hoc and not aligned with the level of engagement across the Joint Programme at the global level."[190]

Besides facilitating advocacy partnerships, civil society participation in the Programme Coordinating Board has made little perceptible difference to UNAIDS' de facto policy autonomy. Although members of the NGO delegation "see eye to eye" with the secretariat on many policy issues, to quote one external relations officer, their lack of enfranchisement renders them "impotent allies when it comes to actually influencing Board outcomes."[191] Informal practices introduced by the Board chair (a voting member), such as inviting NGOs to speak last and requiring unanimous consent for their nomination, have further "prevented them from having any substantive effect on power relations or altering the state-centric nature of the policy recommendations."[192] Behind the scenes, the NGO delegation is routinely pressured into watering down or withdrawing its demands, particularly during confrontations with socially conservative states.[193] It is perhaps no surprise, then, that many watchers of the Board believe that "civil society groups merely serve as window dressing to make UNAIDS appear more inclusive than it really is."[194]

Ties with other kinds of nongovernmental stakeholders have been even weaker. A 2017 report on UNAIDS' joint program model by a panel of high-ranking health officials and other policymakers identified five types of "key stakeholders with limited opportunities for interaction" with the secretariat: (1) the private sector, in particular antiretroviral manufacturers; (2) private foundations, now one of the largest sources of funding for international HIV/AIDS programs; (3) the scientific community and research institutes; (4) bilateral donor agencies and UN

[190] Joint United Nations Programme on HIV/AIDS (2020, 50).
[191] Author interview #127 with UNAIDS external relations officer, June 21, 2020, by video conference.
[192] Youde (2012, 71). Relatedly, Smith (2014, 139) describes ardent Board resistance to taking substantive decisions during "thematic" sessions on special topics such as human rights and gender equality, in which "the NGO Delegation and observers play a particularly crucial and active role."
[193] Smith (2014, 150).
[194] Youde (2012, 71). More broadly, one director of a major NGO's harm reduction program notes: "UNAIDS is constrained by governments. It is hanging by a thread. It can't do anything to jeopardize its relationships with governments ... It talks about civil society and strategic involvement, but since [it] serve[s] at the pleasure of rogue governments, it is reluctant to criticize them." Chan (2015a, 161–162).

entities (other than cosponsors); and (5) young people "whose future is at stake."[195] This analysis is consistent with information provided on UNAIDS' website, which lists only cosponsors and a handful of NGOs as partners – a network of operational alliances far smaller and narrower than average for the PIIP sample.[196] Collaboration is mostly substantive rather than tokenistic, occurring at the agenda-setting stage of policy process with NGOs and across all stages with cosponsors.

Finally, collaboration problems are evinced by the low share of contributions received from nongovernmental sources – of which partners account for less than half in most years – and by (internal and external) questionnaires and interviews. In a survey of 657 stakeholders conducted for the *Second Independent Evaluation*, a worryingly large proportion of NGO networks (28 percent), faith-based groups (31 percent), and organizations representing people living with HIV (41 percent) disagreed or strongly disagreed with the statement that the secretariat "has been able to support, engage with, and address the concerns of civil society."[197] Nine stakeholder interviews conducted for the *Independent Evaluation of the UN System Response to AIDS* discussed the extent of civil society participation in UNAIDS' work, of which six judged it "too low" and four "particularly low at the country level."[198] In addition, several hundred UNAIDS and cosponsor staff were surveyed on how well the Programme promoted the involvement of communities and civil society in the HIV response; 44 percent answered "adequately" and almost a fifth "somewhat inadequately" or "inadequately."[199] Finally, a sample of 1,100 staff and stakeholders was asked how effectively UNAIDS worked with other "major stakeholders," such as the Global Fund and PEPFAR. The distribution of responses is similar for the two surveyed groups, with "adequately" accounting for around 40 percent and "somewhat inadequately" and "inadequately" for a combined 20 percent.[200]

---

[195] Global Review Panel on the Future of the UNAIDS Joint Programme Model (2017, 33).
[196] www.unaids.org/ [Last accessed January 12, 2020]. The website does not contain a dedicated partnerships section.
[197] Joint United Nations Programme on HIV/AIDS (2009*b*, 86). The response rate was around one-third (the exact size of the survey distribution list is not known).
[198] Joint United Nations Programme on HIV/AIDS (2020, 50).
[199] Joint United Nations Programme on HIV/AIDS (2020, 51). The response rate was close to 35 percent (only approximate sample numbers are disclosed).
[200] Joint United Nations Programme on HIV/AIDS (2020, 45).

Gavi, the Vaccine Alliance, and the Global Fund to Fight AIDS, Tuberculosis, and Malaria

Gavi and GFATM represent, in some sense, the culmination of the story thus far, the expression of enduring frustrations with the lack of progress made by the WHO, UNAIDS, and other UN institutions in combating widespread infectious diseases. By the new millennium, public health experts had come to believe that a substantial increase in funding would be required to gain the upper hand over these ailments. Large donor states, were adamant, however, that existing global health institutions – and the UN System more generally – were too cumbersome and politicized to be trusted with more resources.[201] As an alternative, they sought a flexible and efficient institutional architecture that could rapidly direct significant sums to the most impactful epidemiological interventions. Over a series of conferences and meetings, they gradually converged around the idea of a public-private partnership among a small number of donor and recipient governments, civil society groups, industry actors, research organizations, and other stakeholders.

Inaugurated in 2000 at the World Economic Forum, Gavi would seek, per its *Guiding Principles*, "to save children's lives and protect people's health through the widespread use of safe vaccines, with a particular focus on the needs of developing countries."[202] The institution's *Statutes*, adopted in 2008, articulates the more specific goals of "(i) providing vaccines and the means to deliver such vaccines to people in the poorest countries; (ii) facilitating the research and development of vaccines of primary interest to the developing world; and (iii) to provide support in connection with achieving the foregoing purposes by helping to strengthen health care systems and civil societies supporting such purposes in the developing world."[203] GFATM was established two years after Gavi to, in the words of its *Framework Document*, "attract, manage and disburse additional resources . . . that will make a sustainable and significant contribution to the reduction of infections, illness and death, thereby mitigating the impact caused by HIV/AIDS, tuberculosis and malaria in countries in need."[204] Since effective vaccines do not yet exist for AIDS, tuberculosis, and malaria – a key reason why they remain

---

[201] Barnes and Brown (2011, 56). One senior American official involved in founding GFATM disparaged the UN – with some irony – as "terribly bureaucratic and overly political," comparing it to "a wild horse without saddle and reigns, circling without a competent rider."

[202] Global Alliance for Vaccines and Immunization (2000, 64).

[203] The GAVI Alliance (2008, 1).

[204] Global Fund to Fight AIDS, Tuberculosis and Malaria (2001*a*, 91).

the "big three killers" – the two mandates have not overlapped much in practice.

Stakeholders widely credit Gavi and GFATM with making considerable strides toward their objectives over their relatively brief lives. Both institutions have won plaudits for catalyzing an unprecedented increase in the resources available for combating infectious disease and for channeling them to cost-effective programs and initiatives that have saved millions of lives. These achievements have been recognized both in policy circles – Clinton and Sridhar cannot identify a single example of a policymaker contesting the institutions' effectiveness[205] – and by a growing body of scholarship on global public–private health partnerships.[206] Numerous external assessments have also extolled Gavi and GFATM's performance, drawing particular attention to their impact on health outcomes – from vaccination rates to treatment coverage to deaths averted – and their mobilization of resources and public interest in the battle against infectious disease.[207] Finally, they have received among the highest ratings in the comparative donor evaluations as well as surveys of policymakers and civil society leaders in the low- and middle-income countries they support.[208]

Tracing Policy Autonomy and Performance over Time

Policy autonomy and performance have evolved in a similar and straightforward fashion in Gavi and GFATM. De facto policy autonomy robustly expanded throughout their first 15 years – unconstrained by a highly restrictive set of formal rules (see Tables 5.4 and 5.5) – spurring a sharp upward trend in performance. In the past few years, this discretion has been sustained and strengthened by continued performance gains, establishing the conditions for a high-autonomy, high-performance equilibrium.

Already apprehensive about giving non-state actors a full "seat at the table," Gavi and GFATM's creators were not willing to risk further dilution of their policy influence by a powerful international bureaucracy. A multistakeholder governing Board would decide on funding applications submitted by eligible countries and formulate

[205] Clinton and Sridhar (2017, 19).
[206] For example, Bartsch (2007); Buse and Harmer (2007); Buse and Tanaka (2011); Clinton and Sridhar (2017); Harman (2012); Hill (2011); Smith (2014); Walker (2012); Youde (2012, 2018).
[207] CEPA LLP (2010); Chee et al. (2008); Euro Health Group (2020); Global Fund to Fight AIDS, Tuberculosis and Malaria (2009b); Global Fund to Fight AIDS, Tuberculosis, and Malaria (2015, 2017b).
[208] See the *Listening to Leaders* report series, available at www.aiddata.org/ltl [Last accessed July 2, 2021].

Table 5.4 *Summary of Gavi's policy autonomy*

Dimension	Indicator	De jure	De facto
Agenda-setting powers	Power to propose new policies	Delegated to Working Group and secretariat (2000–2008); Executive Committee and secretariat (2008–2017); secretariat only (2017–)	Primarily exercised by secretariat since mid-2000s
	Power to prepare budget	Delegated to Working Group, secretariat, Board chair (2000–08); secretariat (2008–)	Primarily exercised by secretariat since mid-2000s
	Power to prepare governing body work program	Delegated to Working Group, secretariat, Board chair (2000–08); secretariat, Board chair and vice chair (2008–)	Primarily exercised by secretariat since early 2000s
Ability to avoid state veto	Decision procedure: Board	Consensus	Consensus but majority voting not uncommon
	Distribution of votes	Unweighted (when consensus not reached)	Unweighted (when consensus not reached)
Access to non-state financing	Non-state contributions	Permitted	Always received; consistently high
	Independent earnings	Not permitted	Always made; reasonably high

broad plans and strategies. The Gavi Board would have 15 members representing the Bill and Melinda Gates Foundation, UNICEF, the World Bank, the WHO, developing country governments, donor country governments, the vaccine industry in both industrialized and developing countries, civil society, technical health agencies, and research institutes. Decisions would be taken by consensus or, if disagreement persisted, a two-thirds majority vote. A Working Group comprising delegates of most Board constituencies and the chief of staff – the executive secretary, later renamed the chief executive officer – would formulate specific policy proposals and prepare work plans and budgets "in close collaboration" with the secretariat.[209] The Board's agenda would be drawn up by its chair in consultation with the executive secretary and the Working Group.

The GFATM Board would include 18 voting members drawn from developing countries, donor countries, civil society, and the private sector and five nonvoting members representing people with AIDS, tuberculosis, or malaria, the WHO, UNAIDS, the World Bank (the

[209] Global Alliance for Vaccines and Immunization (2000, 69).

Table 5.5 *Summary of GFATM's policy autonomy*

Dimension	Indicator	De jure	De facto
Agenda-setting powers	Power to propose new policies	Delegated to Board (2002–2011); secretariat (2011–);	Primarily exercised by secretariat since mid-2000s
	Power to prepare budget	Delegated to Board (2002–09); secretariat (2011–)	Exercised by secretariat since late 2000s
	Power to prepare governing body work program	Delegated to secretariat, Board chair and vice chair	Primarily exercised by secretariat since mid-2000s
Ability to avoid state veto	Decision procedure: Board	Consensus	Consensus, but majority voting not uncommon
	Distribution of votes	Unweighted (when consensus not reached)	Unweighted (when consensus not reached)
Access to non-state financing	Non-state contributions	Permitted	Always received; consistently modest
	Independent earnings	Unspecified	Always made; consistently low

institution's trustee), and Switzerland (for legal purposes).[210] In addition to making funding decisions and general policy and strategy, the body would be responsible for setting "operational guidelines, work plans and budgets."[211] Decisions would be made by consensus or, failing that, a two-thirds majority of (1) the group encompassing donor and private-sector seats; and (2) the group encompassing developing country and NGO seats. The Board's agenda would be set jointly by its chair, its vice chair, and the secretariat, which would be headed by an executive director. Beyond this duty, the secretariat was only entrusted with limited administrative chores, such as collecting and summarizing grant applications, preparing background materials for Board meetings, and publicizing Board decisions.

Gavi and GFATM would be financed exclusively by voluntary contributions from partner constituencies, that is, from both public and private sources. Neither institution is formally permitted to generate independent earnings, and Gavi's *Guiding Principles* expressly forbid the secretariat from mobilizing resources for "its own activities."[212]

---

[210] The allocation of nonvoting seats to the WHO and UNAIDS is generally regarded as an expression of donor dissatisfaction with these institutions. See Cueto, Brown, and Fee (2019); Kohlmorgen (2007).

[211] Global Fund to Fight AIDS, Tuberculosis and Malaria (2003, 7).

[212] Global Alliance for Vaccines and Immunization (2000, 69). GFATM's by-laws require the secretariat to support the Board in raising funds but do not specify whether it

In the institutions' first few years, as administrative and operational arrangements were still being ironed out, donor governments and UN agencies were effectively the only participants in the policy process. In addition to being delegated few agenda-setting powers, the two secretariats were kept small – Gavi began with six full-time employees and GFATM with 12 – and confined entirely to headquarters as a "political compromise" to secure the participation of existing global health institutions.[213] Furthermore, they were housed, physically and administratively, within other agencies: UNICEF in Gavi's case and the WHO in GFATM's case. As with the WFP in its first two decades, this hosting arrangement severely circumscribed their control over appointments, procurement, finances, and other managerial affairs.

As grants began to flow and programs were rolled out at the country level, bureaucrats found opportunities to exercise greater agency in the policy process. Gavi's secretariat assumed a host of proposal powers initially exercised by the Working Group (and ad-hoc task forces established by the Board) and began to manage an increasing share of analytical work.[214] As one member of the Working Group remarked in 2008, "Now, Gavi is an entity. The governance structure changed ... [Staff] wanted control of the working group, and a more advisory role for the task forces. Much more power to the secretariat. More professional reporting, more professional management."[215] Staff also gained authority over new institutional units established to support Gavi's burgeoning operations, including those associated with the International Finance Facility for Immunisation (IFFIm), a funding mechanism launched in 2006 that converts long-term donor pledges into Vaccine Bonds to be sold on international capital markets. Requiring extra manpower to handle this workload, the secretariat grew to 20 employees in 2005 and almost 100 in 2008.[216] The first comprehensive assessment of Gavi, the consultant-led *Evaluation of the Gavi Phase 1 Performance (2000–2005)*, looked favorably on these developments, describing the secretariat as a place where "good science took precedence over political and turf issues."[217]

With a solid foothold in the policy process, the Gavi secretariat exhibited an "emerging activism" that elicited unease among donor countries.[218] A case in point was its skilful maneuvering of programs for holistically strengthening national health systems through the Board. This agenda was first advocated by Julian Lob-Levyt, Gavi's executive

can earn its own income. Global Fund to Fight AIDS, Tuberculosis and Malaria (2003, 9).
213 Bruen (2018, 220).   214 Bruen (2018, 221).
215 McNeill and Sandberg (2014, 338).   216 Bruen (2018, 220).
217 Chee et al. (2008, 94).   218 Naimoli (2009, 11).

secretary and chief executive officer from 2005 to 2010, who saw functional and well-equipped health systems as essential for sustaining high vaccination coverage. As one former colleague put it, Lob-Levyt recognized "the absurdity of vaccine campaigns that consume four weeks to plan, implement and clean up and that, when repeated eight times a year, totally paralyse the health system."[219] While strongly endorsed by the medical community, health systems support was at odds with the more targeted, technologically-oriented interventions traditionally favored by the United States. To overcome this tall hurdle, the secretariat used a combination of "agenda setting, technical and procedural decision-making, and conflict resolution" to secure the adoption of an official health systems strengthening policy via a narrow Board vote in 2005 – a notable, though not uncommon, deviation from the body's unanimity norm. Bemused Board members were left, to quote the American health official Joseph F. Naimoli, "to wonder whether they have become extensions of the Secretariat."[220] The policy has earned "much public praise" for promoting training programs, facility upgrades, public information campaigns, and other measures that have broadened access to immunization and related critical health services.[221]

Around the same time, GFATM staff also acquired a raft of new policy responsibilities, including negotiating, drafting, and entering into grant agreements with recipient countries – key agenda-setting powers;[222] reviewing requests for grant extensions; and deciding whether and when to consolidate new and existing grants to improve operational efficiency.[223] To keep pace with its expanded remit, the secretariat ballooned from 200 officials in 2005 to almost 500 three years later.[224] A palpable sense of purpose and confidence pervaded its ranks, as reflected in the results of a 2006 internal survey on GFATM's working environment, which indicated that "staff are highly motivated by the mission and overall potential of the organization."[225]

Steps toward de facto policy autonomy became leaps when Gavi and GFATM became organizationally sovereign in the late 2000s. Technically, Gavi began life as two separate entities – the Global Alliance for Vaccines and Immunization, an operational institution, and the Vaccine Fund, a financing institution – with parallel governance structures. In 2008, they were consolidated into a single institution, the

[219] Storeng (2014, 868).   [220] Naimoli (2009, 11).   [221] Storeng (2014, 876).
[222] These agreements cover issues such as budget allocations, disbursement schedules, performance metrics, and grounds for termination.
[223] Clinton (2014).
[224] Global Fund to Fight AIDS, Tuberculosis and Malaria (2009b, 11).
[225] Global Fund to Fight AIDS, Tuberculosis and Malaria (2006, 6). The survey was returned by 71 percent of staff.

Gavi Alliance (subsequently renamed Gavi, the Vaccine Alliance), to reduce duplication and raise brand awareness. As part of the merger, the Working Group was replaced by an Executive Committee with a similar composition but less involvement in the budgetary process.[226] The secretariat relocated to its own headquarters, took over the administrative and financial services furnished by UNICEF, and expanded to more than 200 staff. Soon after, it became more involved in managing grants at the country level, taking over monitoring and fiduciary risk management functions from multilateral partners (such as UNICEF and the WHO) and thus becoming an "effective proxy manager for donors."[227] In short, what emerged was an "expanded and vastly strengthened Secretariat now at the centre of Gavi operations."[228]

This transformation did not go unnoticed. One official from another global health agency recalled the secretariat "developing more control over what happens" following Gavi's independence, such that the policy process no longer felt like "equals dividing up the tasks."[229] A 2012 assessment of the relationship between Gavi and the World Bank published by the latter's Independent Evaluation Group was more direct: "The Gavi Secretariat changed and grew in size after the reorganization … The Secretariat has become an effective independent organization, operating like a corporation."[230] Highlighting the "advanced marketing and advocacy capabilities" now enjoyed by staff, evaluators characterized Gavi's operating model as increasingly "Secretariat-driven."[231]

GFATM gained organizational independence in 2009, when its Board came to the conclusion that the WHO's administrative and fiduciary services were no longer needed. Along with these duties, the secretariat was handed responsibility for preparing budgets and work plans for all departments and policy organs.[232] Additional powers soon followed. In early 2012, the executive director began not only negotiating but also executing agreements with implementing partners. A few months later, staff became involved in designing funding proposal guidelines and overseeing grant implementation, "a significant departure from the Secretariat's historic passivity in grant application and management."[233] By mid-2012, the preponderance of the secretariat's human and financial resources were being allocated to management-related activities, with every grant assigned a dedicated point person.[234]

---

[226] GAVI Alliance (2008).   [227] Bruen (2018, 257).   [228] Bruen (2018, 257).
[229] Bruen (2018, 222).   [230] World Bank (2014, 40).   [231] World Bank (2014, 40).
[232] Global Fund to Fight AIDS, Tuberculosis and Malaria (2009a, 2011).
[233] Clinton (2014, 36).   [234] Clinton (2014, 35).

Another component of Gavi and GFATM's de facto policy autonomy are the specialized bodies of medical practitioners, epidemiologists, economists, lawyers, and other experts they rely on to appraise funding applications. Gavi's Independent Review Committee, which is divided into three teams of between eight and 18 individuals, reviews all proposals for new grants (not renewals) based on technical criteria and advises the Board on their suitability. The Committee's recommendations, which have been found technically sound and appropriate by external assessors, are virtually always accepted by the Board, giving it an important form of "gatekeeping" power. [235] Some of this influence, several interviewees pointed out, is shared with the secretariat, which nominates the Committee's members, appoints its chair, organizes its schedule, and often participates in its sessions.[236] Since 2014, the secretariat and the Committee have, for all intents and purposes, jointly determined annual funding renewal decisions through participation in a High Level Review Panel tasked with assessing grant performance.

GFATM's equivalent of the Independent Review Committee, the Technical Review Panel, has up to 40 members and also issues funding recommendations that are invariably endorsed by the Board.[237] The exhaustive *Five-Year Evaluation of the Global Fund*, undertaken by two consortia of academics, health officials, and consultants, judged the Panel a "robust" mechanism for assessing the quality of funding proposals.[238] Similarly, Aidspan, a nonprofit watchdog, has found its decisions to promote interventions with "a meaningful impact on preventing further infections."[239] Beyond its appraisal role, the Panel has actively shaped policy decisions – most notably regarding the grant application process – by serving in an advisory capacity to the Board. In one study's reckoning, "It would be difficult to overstate the impact the TRP's [Technical Review Panel's] feedback had on [the] Board's decisions, particularly relating to application guidelines and the TRP's own terms of reference."[240] Similarly to their Gavi counterparts, GFATM staff have derived significant policy influence from their relationship with the Panel. As well as shaping its composition by soliciting and short-listing membership applications,[241] they screen and select the funding

---

[235] Donoghue et al. (2010). In Gavi's first decade, just two out of several hundred recommendations were rejected.

[236] Until recently, the secretariat directly appointed Committee members.

[237] According to Clinton (2014, 225), "There is no record in any Board Meeting Report of any Board Member asking for changes beyond those the TRP [Technical Review Panel] already had proposed as conditions for Board approval or had flagged for the Secretariat to include in its subsequent negotiations with the principal recipients."

[238] Ryan et al. (2007, 67).   [239] Garmaise (2010, 9).   [240] Clinton (2014, 220).

[241] Global Fund to Fight AIDS, Tuberculosis and Malaria (2017a).

proposals it considers, manage its logistics and communications, and collaborate with it in regulating proposal development and review, preparing grant agreements, and learning lessons from intervention outcomes.[242]

Funding trends have further shored up the two institutions' de facto policy autonomy, particularly in Gavi's case. Averaging over the 2001–2018 period, non-state actors accounted for 43 percent of annual contributions to Gavi and 12 percent to GFATM (bottom left panel of Figure 5.1). The corresponding figures for the WHO and UNAIDS are 29 percent and five percent, respectively. The Bill and Melinda Gates Foundation was the largest nongovernmental donor to both Gavi and GFATM and the largest donor of any kind to the former. GFATM's top benefactor was the United States, which ranked third for Gavi (behind the United Kingdom).[243] On average, independent earnings have, amounted to 14 percent of income for Gavi, more than triple the figures for the WHO and UNAIDS, and a more comparable four percent for GFATM (bottom right panel).

Closely controlled by a coalition of bureaucrats – who currently number approximately 200 in Gavi and 700 in GFATM – and technical experts, the two institutions have earned a widespread reputation for operating in an "apolitical" fashion free from "state-centric brinkmanship."[244] There are few documented instances of political considerations affecting funding decisions or other policies and activities. One GFATM grant manager alluded to pressures from the United States and some African nations to deny funding to countries pursuing "politically controversial" HIV prevention measures, but stressed that the Technical Review Panel "has never caved in."[245] Systematic analyses of funding data show that grants have predominantly been allocated and renewed according to recipient countries' disease burden and ability to attract external financing – that is, their *need*.[246] One review of the literature on GFATM's grantmaking process reports "no robust pre-existing work showing evidence of political [factors] rather than evidence or performance influencing Fund decision-making."[247] Tellingly, on the rare occasions political disputes over Gavi or GFATM's work *have*

---

[242] Global Fund to Fight AIDS, Tuberculosis and Malaria (2019*b*).
[243] Gavi has received almost as much from the proceeds of IFFIm and the Advance Market Commitment, another innovative financing mechanism based on donor pledges. This income is transferred to Gavi from the World Bank, the treasurer for both schemes.
[244] Barnes and Brown (2011, 59).   [245] Author interview #121 with GFATM grant manager, June 9, 2020, by video conference.
[246] Clinton (2014); McCoy and Kinyua (2012); Tagem (2017); Theiner (2012).
[247] Clinton (2014, 201).

arisen, they have been aired in the WHO's governing bodies rather than either institution's Board.[248]

This operational model has yielded remarkable results. Exceeding even their founders' hopes, Gavi and GFATM have mobilized massive resources for the fight against infectious disease in a short space of time. The institutions' annual revenues – which, as indicated earlier, are composed mostly of contributions – began at a high level and have grown briskly over time, averaging close to $3 billion for Gavi and $4 billion for GFATM between 2010 and 2018 (see upper left panel of Figure 5.1 for inflation-adjusted figures). Cumulatively, Gavi had raised almost $40 billion and GFATM more than $50 billion by 2018. As early as 2013, only a decade or so after their establishment, they had overtaken the WHO and the World Bank as the two largest sources of multilateral health financing, collectively accounting for around a quarter of all health-related Official Development Assistance (ODA).[249] GFATM currently supplies 25 percent of international financing for HIV programs, 77 percent for tuberculosis programs, and 56 percent for malaria programs.[250] Commendably, the vast majority of funds raised by the two institutions have been utilized for operational purposes: Administrative costs amounted to an average of only six percent of Gavi's annual expenditures and three percent of GFATM's up to 2018.

The institutions' sizable resource base has been put to impressive use. As illustrated in Figure 5.3, programs financed by Gavi immunized 764 million children (left panel) and averted 13.8 million deaths (right panel) between 2000 and 2018.[251] Basic vaccine coverage in Gavi-supported countries, as measured by the proportion of children who have received three doses of the diphtheria–pertussis–tetanus (DPT3) vaccine, has risen from 59 percent in 2000 to more than four-fifths today.[252] These achievements have been made possible both by an extensive grant portfolio that currently covers 77 countries hosting 60 percent of the global birth cohort – meaning that Gavi protects nearly half of the world's children through vaccination – and by aggressive efforts to expand the reach of existing vaccines and stimulate the development of more

---

[248] "With Gavi distributing the vaccines," Chorev (2012, 219) notes, "the WHO was left with the minimal role of serving as a stage for member states to air their frustrations."

[249] Valentine et al. (2015). Among bilateral donors, only the United States contributes more health-related ODA than both institutions.

[250] www.theglobalfund.org/en/results/ [Last accessed October 20, 2021].

[251] Several independent studies (not undertaken or funded by Gavi) also find that these programs have markedly improved immunization and mortality rates. See Ikilezi et al. (2020); Jaupart, Dipple, and Dercon (2019); Lu et al. (2006).

[252] Berkley (2019, 1251).

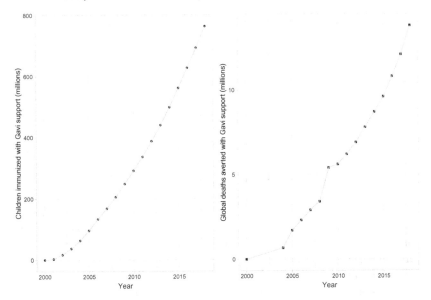

Figure 5.3 Children immunized and deaths averted with Gavi support, 2000–2019

Sources: Gavi, the Vaccine Alliance (2020*b*) (left panel); Gavi annual progress reports, available at www.gavi.org/programmes-impact/our-impact/progress-reports.

Notes: Deaths averted are based on estimates by the Vaccine Impact Modelling Consortium, which coordinates the work of several research groups analyzing the impact of vaccination programs around the world.

effective ones.[253] To these ends, Gavi has supported a total of 495 vaccine launches and campaigns, and between 2000 and 2014 spurred the introduction of 11 new and underused vaccines around the world.[254]

Less widely appreciated are the economic benefits of Gavi's work. One recent study of 73 Gavi-supported countries estimates that every dollar spent on immunization between 2011 and 2020 saved $28.5 in treatment costs, transportation costs, lost caregiver wages, and productivity loss due to illness, disability, and death. When the broader socioeconomic value of living longer and healthier lives is also taken into consideration, the return almost doubles to $54.6.[255] This translates into total savings from immunization programs of $639.1 billion in illness costs and

---

[253] www.gavi.org/programmes-impact/our-impact/facts-and-figures [Last accessed June 23, 2021].

[254] Gavi, the Vaccine Alliance (2020*a*). Since 2014, it has contributed to the creation of vital vaccines for Ebola and COVID-19.

[255] Sim et al. (2020). Similar estimates based on slightly earlier data are reported by Ozawa et al. (2017).

economic gains of a staggering $1.2 trillion across the 73 nations. In addition, there is evidence that Gavi has shaped medical markets in socially beneficial ways, lowering the price of several major vaccines – including the hepatitis B monovalent, tetravalent, and pentavalent jabs– by boosting demand and attracting new manufacturers.[256]

GFATM's impact is of a similar order of magnitude. To date, programs financed by the institution have saved 44 million lives across more than 100 nations.[257] As of 2018, these interventions had delivered antiretroviral therapy to 18.9 million people with HIV, raising the treatment rate in GFATM-supported countries from essentially zero to 67 percent; provided tuberculosis medication to 22.4 million people, more than doubling the treatment rate to 62 percent; and distributed almost a billion long-lasting insecticide-treated mosquito nets – one of the most effective anti-malaria tools – thus lifting the access rate from near zero to 58 percent.[258] Overall, deaths from AIDS, tuberculosis, and malaria in these countries have fallen by almost 50 percent since the peak of each epidemic.[259] Global trends, depicted in Figure 5.2, are highly suggestive: AIDS and malaria deaths began to consistently fall – precipitously in the former's case – soon after GFATM's creation, while the declining trajectory of tuberculosis deaths markedly accelerated.

GFATM has also been hailed for the normative impact of its work. As Sonja Bartsch explains, "Although the GF [Global Fund] defines itself as a pure financing mechanism, through its activities it influences both general discourses on the poverty-oriented fight against diseases and more specific discourses on the respective programmes and strategies."[260] This is particularly true in the area of HIV/AIDS, GFATM's primary focus, where its success in expanding access to antiretroviral drugs has challenged conventional wisdoms about how to tackle the disease and reframed public health debates over the role of treatment versus prevention, affordable medicine, and the socioeconomic roots of

---

[256] www.gavi.org/news/media-room/gavi-impact-vaccine-market-behind-price-drop [Last accessed June 12, 2021]. For instance, the price of the hepatitis B monovalent vaccine has fallen by 68 percent since 2000.

[257] Global Fund to Fight AIDS, Tuberculosis and Malaria (2021b). Independent studies also attest to GFATM's positive impact on various health outcomes. See Komatsu et al. (2010); Stover et al. (2011); Yan, Korenromp, and Bendavid (2015); Zelman et al. (2014). Surveying the academic and policy literature, Clinton and Sridhar (2017, 170) conclude that "there is no real dispute of the Global Fund's impact claims from either the few scholars that have examined groups of Fund-financed grants or from the more numerous partners of the Global Fund that have done the same."

[258] GFATM results reports, available at www.theglobalfund.org/en/archive/annual-reports/ [Last accessed June 14, 2021].

[259] Global Fund to Fight AIDS, Tuberculosis and Malaria (2021b, 4).

[260] Bartsch (2007, 169).

transmission. Noteworthy, too, is how the secretariat has leveraged its influence in the grant application process to promote domestic policies for improving gender equality, human rights, and community health systems – moves that have further eroded the influence of other international institutions in the HIV/AIDS space. "As its mandate expands and its authority grows," one scholar contends, "the Global Fund is moving towards normative policy making, challenging the WHO's and UNAIDS' traditional policy leadership roles."[261]

These accomplishments have encouraged states to invest ever larger sums in Gavi and GFATM while becoming more tolerant – in many instances even *supportive* – of their policy discretion. Even in Gavi's early years, independent evaluators noticed that "because of partner satisfaction with Gavi's performance, the [Vaccine] Fund does not appear to have pursued its watchdog role very aggressively."[262] Board meeting reports and minutes from the past decade abound with examples of representatives "congratulating," "praising," and "welcoming" the secretariat's work in the same breath as they delegate it additional responsibilities, from risk mitigation to supply chain management to resource mobilization.[263]

Evidence of positive feedback from performance to de facto policy autonomy also emerges from interviews with Gavi and GFATM Board members, in which improving treatment and mortality outcomes were frequently cited as justification for entrusting the secretariat with greater authority. One GFATM Board member representing a large donor state alluded to an "implicit bargain" with the secretariat: "In the early years, it's fair to say, donors wanted more control over the Fund. They didn't expect such a small entity to be so assertive and entrepreneurial, and ... there were some worried faces. But when they saw what could be achieved when a motivated and skilled workforce is really empowered, they became more relaxed. It was as if they were saying to the secretariat: If you keep delivering the goods, we'll keep our hands off."[264] The delegate went on to describe the Board's recent decision to abolish the Executive Committee (without replacement) as "inspired by a profound confidence in the secretariat's ability to discharge the body's duties by itself."

[261] Walker (2012, 90).
[262] Chee et al. (2008, 92). A later passage adds: "Gavi's accountability problems have not been exposed because its programs have generally performed well." Also see Cambridge Economic Policy Associates (2007).
[263] Available at: www.theglobalfund.org/en/board/meetings/; www.gavi.org/our-alliance/ governance/gavi-board [Both last accessed March 2, 2021].
[264] Author interview #123 with GFATM Board member, June 10, 2020, by telephone.

Turning to the present day, Gavi and GFATM have garnered praise for their contributions to the international COVID-19 response – contributions that exemplify central themes of this section. Gavi has expeditiously scaled up its support for national health systems, bolstered local immunization services, and led the COVID-19 Vaccines Global Access (COVAX) initiative, an ambitious attempt to ensure the equitable distribution of jabs across the world.[265] At the time of writing, COVAX has shipped 1.2 billion vaccine doses to 144 countries and secured an additional 15 billion doses through supply agreements with manufacturers.[266] GFATM has established the complementary COVID-19 Response Mechanism (C19RM), the largest source of funding for developing countries to procure tests, treatments, and personal protective equipment and to mitigate the pandemic's impact on HIV, tuberculosis, and malaria programs. These schemes have brought forth new administrative responsibilities that have expanded the secretariat's authority and size. The minutes of one recent Gavi Board meeting, for instance, record broad recognition of both the secretariat's "enormous efforts" in rolling out COVAX and "the need for surge staff capacity to cope with the significant demands [of the initiative]."[267] In a possible example of positive feedback, early evidence of effectiveness appears to have induced further delegations of authority. In the same Board meeting, for instance, one committee "expressed extreme appreciation and congratulations to the Secretariat and Alliance partners for extraordinary work in response to what has now happened" shortly before it "discussed the capacity of the Secretariat and Alliance partners to pick up additional roles related to COVID-19 response."[268]

Sources of De Facto Policy Autonomy

How have Gavi and GFATM liberated themselves from the stifling de jure constraints on their policy discretion? Unlike the WHO and UNAIDS, both institutions are charged with allocating financial resources to complex, large-scale public health interventions – a task with high monitoring costs for governments – and have collaborated deeply and broadly with non-state stakeholders at the country level.[269]

---

[265] Gavi co-directs the scheme with the WHO and the Coalition for Epidemic Preparedness Innovations – a PPP that develops vaccines against emerging infectious diseases – but has been its principal driving force and manager.

[266] www.unicef.org/supply/covid-19-vaccine-market-dashboard [Last accessed February 12, 2022].

[267] Gavi, the Vaccine Alliance (2020c, 7).

[268] Gavi, the Vaccine Alliance (2020c, 14).

[269] Gavi and GFATM finance technical assistance programs but do not deliver them (given their lack of a field presence).

Governance Tasks

The difficulty of monitoring Gavi and GFATM's activities stems from the medical, financial, and managerial expertise as well as the detailed country-specific information required to assess and administer funding proposals. Applications comprise a package of long and convoluted documents – they routinely run into hundreds of pages – enumerating gaps in the national disease response, interventions to be supported, arrangements for operationalization and implementation, and cost projections. Applicants are expected to support each component of their proposal with systematic data and analysis. Submissions to GFATM, for example, must be accompanied by up to 13 different annexes containing epidemiological data, summaries of existing national programs and funding sources, performance frameworks, budget estimates, visual implementation maps, sustainability assessments, and other information.[270] Technical knowledge is needed to both prepare and evaluate these materials. "Writing a Global Fund proposal has been so time-consuming and complicated," notes one review of GFATM's oversight structures, "that specialized expertise is required."[271] A clear indication of this complexity is the emergence of "a flourishing 'cottage industry' for technical assistance provided by organisations like UNAIDS and UNDP in order for countries to prepare successful grant applications and evaluate and report their results."[272]

There are good reasons, then, for the delegation of proposal assessment to the Independent Review Committee and the Technical Review Panel. By virtue of their purpose and composition, these bodies enjoy "an informational advantage over the political principals, both in specialized medical knowledge and managerial expertise, and in their familiarity with each individual application."[273] Some of this advantage, particularly on the managerial front, is shared with the secretariat, which, as discussed earlier, plays an influential role in the appraisal and renewal processes. In addition, staff have come to be heavily involved in supervising grant implementation and monitoring – an almost inevitable consequence of their close acquaintance with individual cases – extending information asymmetries into the latter stages of the funding cycle.

Several studies and evaluations have drawn attention to the resulting oversight challenges. The *Evaluation of the Gavi Phase 1 Performance*, for example, points out that "despite the mandate to provide oversight, the composition of the Gavi Fund Board did not provide the technical expertise to question Gavi Alliance decisions on technical grounds."[274] In an analysis of Gavi's foray into health systems support published

---

[270] Global Fund to Fight AIDS, Tuberculosis and Malaria (2021*a*).
[271] Global Fund to Fight AIDS, Tuberculosis and Malaria (2001*b*, 24).
[272] Walker (2012, 94).   [273] Theiner (2012, 13).   [274] Chee et al. (2008, 92).

the following year, Naimoli argues that the secretariat's activities in this sphere suffer from a lack of "adequate oversight" resulting from "limited capacity among Gavi policy bodies to pass judgment on complicated HSS- [health systems strengthening-]related policy matters."[275]

Donor attempts to alleviate these information asymmetries have run into fierce bureaucratic resistance. In 2007, for example, the GFATM Board sought to make the proposal review process more transparent by mandating the public disclosure of Technical Review Panel documents. In response, "the Secretariat and TRP [Technical Review Panel] coordinated efforts to keep TRP documents non-public" by presenting a united opposition to the plan in the Board's next meeting.[276] The Board largely backed down, opting to publish eligible applications on GFATM's website but maintain the nondisclosure of panel assessments and reports.

Operational Alliances

As relatively small, headquarters-based PPPs, Gavi and GFATM have always been operationally reliant on nongovernmental stakeholders with an in-country presence. Online data indicate that both institutions collaborate with the full spectrum of non-state stakeholders – NGOs, private enterprises, IGOs, PPPs, and research institutes – and that virtually none of these relationships are merely symbolic.[277] Gavi's partnership network is roughly the combined size of the WHO and UNAIDS'; GFATM's has reached 140 members in recent years, around a third higher than the PIIP mean. In both networks, partner support is distributed fairly evenly across the formulation, implementation, and monitoring stages of the policy process.

Gavi and GFATM require funding proposals to be prepared, submitted, and implemented by national committees – Interagency Coordinating Committees in Gavi's case and Country Coordinating Mechanisms in GFATM's case – that include health authorities, NGOs, research bodies, relevant bilateral and multilateral agencies, people living with disease, and other stakeholders. Implementation is usually handled by governments, though it has become increasingly common for Country Coordinating Mechanisms to allow NGOs, technical institutes, and UNDP country offices to take the lead (the role of "Principal Recipient").[278] A variety of more ad-hoc partnerships also contribute to the process. Gavi, for instance, works with UNICEF to procure vaccines, with NGOs to administer them, and with logistics companies to manage

---

[275] Naimoli (2009, 20).   [276] Clinton (2014, 223).
[277] www.gavi.org/about/gavis-partnership-model/;   www.theglobalfund.org/en/partners/ [Last accessed September 23, 2019].
[278] Youde (2012, 76).

the supply chain. GFATM contracts professional auditors to review grant performance as part of the funding renewal process, a function it describes as its "eyes and ears on the ground."[279] Involving such a varied range of stakeholders in the grant cycle is often regarded as a feat in itself. Jennifer Chan writes of GFATM: "The Global Fund is viewed by many as one of the most significant achievements in the AIDS response, saving countless lives, encouraging each country's ownership of its AIDS agenda, and ushering in a new norm of partnership at the country level by forcing nongovernmental representation to be accepted at the same decision-making table as the national ministry of health and AIDS program."[280]

At the policy formulation stage, staff take advantage of Gavi and GFATM's public–private governance structure to acquire information and expertise from Board representatives of civil society, the private sector, academia, and other global health institutions. Moreover, they have formed productive coalitions with these actors – most commonly NGO delegates – to formulate and secure the adoption of collectively oriented policy proposals. Gavi's civil society seat is supported by a CSO Constituency comprising thousands of NGOs from around the world as well as a smaller CSO Steering Committee with up to 20 members, which guides the former's work. Both groups have worked closely with the secretariat to shape funding decisions, expand the role of NGOs in the grant cycle, and advance broader policy agendas, most notably health systems support.[281] One GFATM advocacy manager proudly recounted a string of policy victories "achieved through close behind-the-scenes cooperation with the civil society delegation," including the modification of funding guidelines to encourage Country Coordinating Mechanisms to nominate nongovernmental Principal Recipients; an increase in the representation of marginalized communities in Country Coordinating Mechanisms; and the development of a comprehensive framework for strengthening community health systems. The official went on to describe the delegation as "the secretariat's strongest ally in the governance process."[282]

---

[279] www.theglobalfund.org/en/lfa/ [Last accessed March 12, 2021]. These relationships involve an uncomplicated, mutually beneficial exchange. Sophie Harman (2012, 72) describes GFATM's relationship with implementing partners as "in many ways code-pendent: it needs these agencies in terms of technical capacity and in-country presence and knowledge, and in turn the agencies need the fund in terms of financial resources." Some studies point to additional benefits for partners, such as increased visibility, policy influence, and professionalization. See Harmer et al. (2013); Kapilashrami and O'Brien (2012).

[280] Chan (2015a, 164).

[281] GAVI CSO Constituency (2012).

[282] Author interview #120 with GFATM advocacy manager, June 9, 2020, by video conference.

The success of these policy-specific coalitions derives in large part from the genuinely inclusive and participatory nature of the Gavi and GFATM Boards, which have been commended for giving stakeholders who are usually excluded from international governance processes a meaningful say in decision-making.[283] Taking a leaf out of the G77's book, nongovernmental Board members have amplified their influence by informally coordinating policy positions in private pre-session meetings. In Gavi's Board, they are sufficiently numerous to block the adoption of a policy proposal when consensus cannot be reached; in GFATM's, they require one state delegate to join their side – a condition the secretariat has often helped to meet by "assiduously courting sympathetic governments."[284] Civil society delegates make up almost the entire nongovernmental delegation to the GFATM Board, giving them particular sway.[285] In the view of one such representative, "The Global Fund is a model on how civil society delegations can have equal say on a board discussion. And I think the influence is significant. The northern NGO Delegation influence is as significant as the US [government], which puts in all that money. And there isn't another institution where civil society has so much influence."[286] This claim has been echoed by state delegates, who habitually complain that the civil society delegation exercises "too much power" and "much more influence than we would hope for."[287]

Perhaps most consequentially, Gavi and GFATM enlist partners for the explicit purpose of lobbying donor governments for political and material support. Gavi's advocacy network includes nonprofits such as Save the Children and the Bill and Melinda Gates Foundation, IGOs such as UNICEF and the World Bank, and vaccine manufacturers such as Pfizer and GlaxoSmithKline. As noted earlier, some of these partners have themselves made substantial donations to Gavi – another means by which operational alliances have shored up its independence. Lobbying efforts have usually intensified near replenishment conferences called every five years. In the run-up to the 2015 conference, for instance, members of CSO Constituency orchestrated a "Gavi Replenishment Drive" that involved sending letters to health ministers, organizing meet-

[283] Tallberg et al. (2014).
[284] Author interview #120 with GFATM advocacy manager, June 9, 2020, by video conference.
[285] In one instance, a civil society-led coalition blocked a crucial vote on the appointment of a new executive director and the adoption of an alternative funding model "over a seemingly small detail," much to the frustration of the rest of the Board (Smith 2014, 192–193). As in the Gavi Board, such votes are not unusual, notwithstanding the consensus norm.
[286] Smith (2014, 181).   [287] Smith (2014, 192).

ings with donor government embassies, holding public demonstrations, and presenting states with a signed "Call to Action" urging them "to fully fund Gavi's resource need" and "to fulfill their responsibility in the fight against vaccine-preventable diseases by ensuring that Gavi programmes are embedded in conducive policy environments for sustainable immunisation practice."[288] On the eve of the gathering, several industry partners announced commitments to freeze or reduce vaccine prices to further motivate donors.[289]

An even larger and more sophisticated advocacy campaign preceded the latest replenishment conference, held in June 2020. ONE Campaign, a coalition of prominent humanitarian NGOs, played a central coordinating role, arranging hundreds of meetings between activists and legislators in the United States and the United Kingdom, commissioning artwork and creating an online game to raise awareness of Gavi's work, and launching a global petition similar to the Call to Action, which amassed more than 55,000 signatures.[290] IGO and private-sector partners complemented these efforts with high-profile public appeals for support. UNICEF, for example, released promotional material on its partnership with Gavi calling for the "prioritization of funding increased investment in child health by supporting Gavi's replenishment" and for stronger "political commitment" to immunization by governments.[291] GlaxoSmithKline's chief executive officer, Emma Walmsley, posted a video message on Twitter celebrating Gavi's achievements and pledging the company's "full support" for the campaign.[292]

GFATM manages a more centralized but equally eclectic advocacy network. The civil society component is organized around two structures: a set of four "Friends" organizations covering the United States, Europe, Japan, and the Pacific region, which "help to develop contacts and allies, promote a good understanding of the Global Fund's mission and mobilize political and financial support";[293] and the Global Fund Advocates Network, an umbrella group of more than 400 NGOs from 94

---

288 https://docs.google.com/forms/d/e/1FAIpQLSeaB2Tja2VFDboSX1H2gw2K0O8Nou-8j_SnF32ixMypIItt7g/viewform [Last accessed June 8, 2021].

289 www.gavi.org/news/media-room/private-sector-makes-new-pledges-support-childhood-immunisation-developing [Last accessed June 12, 2021].

290 www.one.org/international/take-action/victories/gavi-2020/ [Last accessed May 26, 2021].

291 www.unicef.org/media/65841/file/UNICEF's%20engagement%20with%20Gavi,%20the%20Vaccine%20Alliance.pdf [Last accessed May 24, 2020].

292 https://twitter.com/gavi/status/1267764123573641217 [Last accessed April 12, 2021].

293 www.theglobalfund.org/en/friends/ [Last accessed May 2, 2021]. The latter branch, Pacific Friends of Global Health, also undertakes advocacy work for Gavi and Unitaid.

countries, including the Friends organizations, which conducts similar activities.[294]

Given the United States' political and financial clout in GFATM, the Washington-based Friends of the Global Fight Against AIDS, Tuberculosis and Malaria has become a crucial node in the network. Like Gavi's partners, the organization has deployed a variety of tactics to build support for GFATM among American policymakers, including sending and organizing letters to Congress, testifying before congressional committees, lobbying government officials in private, publishing opinion pieces in major newspapers, and disseminating information, graphics, and videos on social media. A key goal of these strategies has been to dispel any notion of a tradeoff between supporting GFATM and advancing other American foreign policy aims. In written testimony to the Senate Appropriations Subcommittee on State and Foreign Operations and Related Programs shortly before the latest replenishment, the president of Friends of the Global Fight underscored that GFATM's work enhances the impact of bilateral health programs (such as PEPFAR) and improves the quality of governance in recipient countries, promoting "regional stability and security, economic freedoms, growing prosperity and more vital trading partners."[295] In the same vein, a recent letter to the Trump administration from a bipartisan group of 18 senators convened by Friends of the Global Fight concluded with the statement: "The U.S. investment in the Global Fund does more than save lives and fight diseases – it helps keep Americans safe and benefits our diplomatic and trade relationships."[296] The credibility of the organization's message has been bolstered by an illustrious Board of Directors whose members have included former senators, congressional representatives, high-ranking government officials, health lobbyists, and Laura Bush, the daughter of ex-president George W. Bush.

These tactics have been helpfully reinforced by other types of partners. Ironically, given its origins, GFATM has been one of the greatest beneficiaries of UNAIDS' advocacy work. Drawing on its close connections with national health authorities, UNAIDS has assisted GFATM in mobilizing funds and, as a recent evaluation of their partnership puts it, strengthening "political relationships" with governments.[297] Speaking ahead of the Fifth Replenishment Conference in 2016, UNAIDS executive director Michel Sidibé emphasized that "[t]he Global Fund is a key anchor in our shared commitment to ending AIDS and needs the

---

[294] www.globalfundadvocatesnetwork.org/about/ [Last accessed April 5, 2021].
[295] www.theglobalfight.org/chris-collins-senate-testimony-in-support-of-the-global-fund-for-fy-2021/ [Last accessed June 12, 2021].
[296] Leahy et al. (1990, 2).   [297] Universalia Management Group (2019).

full political and financial backing of its donors."[298] GFATM's alliances with the private sector, though weaker than Gavi's, have delivered similar forms of support. Companies ranging from Ecobank, a pan-African financial institution, to ViiV Healthcare, an American pharmaceutical producer, have launched initiatives to raise donations for and awareness of GFATM's programs.[299] Especially fertile has been the association with (RED), a trademark licensed on behalf of GFATM to major multinational corporations – including Apple, American Express, and Gap – in exchange for a portion of the profits from branded products. Since its creation in 2006, (RED) has generated more than $650 million in funding for GFATM as well as considerable positive publicity, in part through advertising blitzes featuring famous musicians and actors.[300]

Several interviewees expressed the belief that, by building stakeholder confidence in Gavi and GFATM's work – and, by extension, their technocratic operational model – advocacy alliances had made the most significant contribution to their policy autonomy. One Gavi external relations coordinator argued that these relationships, "though not formally integrated into our governance structure, are pivotal to its proper functioning: They ensure that donors respect the independence of the funding allocation process and the prerogative of staff – those with the best knowledge and understanding of individual proposals – to shape it in ways most conducive to Gavi goals."[301] Central to this mechanism, the official continued, is the "highly diverse – large, small, local, transnational, public, private – nature of our supporters and campaigners," which strengthens the "credibility and legitimacy of their demands." Reflecting on GFATM's alliances, one American health official suggested that the contribution of advocacy partners was best understood with counterfactual thinking: "How would the US engage with the Global Fund if lobby groups such as Friends [of the Global Fight] didn't exist? Things might be quite different ... We could have easily ended up with a politicized agency like the WHO, where the biggest donors only turn on the tap when it suits them and insist that money flows to pet projects and politically friendly countries – not the neediest places."[302]

---

[298] www.unaids.org/en/resources/presscentre/pressreleaseandstatementarchive/2016/september/20160915_PS_GF_replenishment [Last accessed June 3, 2021].

[299] Global Fund to Fight AIDS, Tuberculosis and Malaria (2019*a*).

[300] (RED) was conceived by the musician Bono and the activist Bobby Shriver in 2006. They also founded ONE Campaign two years earlier.

[301] Author interview #136 with Gavi external relations coordinator, June 14, 2020, by telephone.

[302] Author interview #86 with United States Agency for International Development official, May 21, 2018, Washington, DC.

Conclusion

The political maelstrom in which the WHO's response to COVID-19 became swiftly engulfed is, this chapter reveals, far from an irregularity in its turbulent and difficult history. Countless instances of opportunistic governmental interference litter the Organization's annals, too often derailing its attempts to introduce the (domestic and international) policies, reforms, and coordination mechanisms required to attain "the highest possible levels of health" for people around the world. The absence of de facto policy autonomy has wrought similar damage on UNAIDS, preventing it from exercising the leadership necessary to manage and direct the chaotic swarm of international institutions, bilateral agencies, and non-state actors seeking to arrest the spread of HIV/AIDS. Yet capture and particularism have not pervaded all corners of global health governance. Gavi and GFATM have demonstrated the promise of a new, innovative model for mobilizing and distributing multilateral health assistance that empowers a wide variety of stakeholders while ensuring that funding decisions are appropriately informed by scientific knowledge and evidence.

By tracing the roots and evolution of performance and policy autonomy in these four important institutions, this chapter has added to the stock of empirical support for the book's theoretical framework (see Table 5.6). The key macro-level relationships are consistent with expectations, notwithstanding the diminutive sample size. Performance has a positive association with de facto policy autonomy, both of which are low for the WHO and UNAIDS and high for Gavi and GFATM, but a mild negative association with de jure policy autonomy, which is high for the former two institutions and modest for the latter two. De facto policy autonomy is also positively related to (1) the number, depth, and breadth of operational alliances with non-state actors; and (2) the costs to states of monitoring governance tasks, all of which are low for the WHO and UNAIDS and high for Gavi and GFATM.

Moving to the micro level, where the chapter sheds the most valuable light, several process-related implications find support. First, there is consistent evidence of the Jekyll and Hyde problem at play. All four institutions are the product of sincere attempts by states to find cooperative solutions to pressing public health problems with negative cross-border externalities. Once institutional activities commence and thorny distributional dilemmas present themselves, however, these good intentions have invariably given way to more parochial, individualistic concerns, whether protecting national commercial interests, advancing ruling parties' ideological agendas, or distributing aid to political allies.

Table 5.6 *Support for theoretical implications: Case comparison of global health institutions*

Observable Implication	Case 1: WHO	Case 2: UNAIDS	Cases 3 and 4: Gavi and GFATM
Macro level			
Positive relationship between DFPA and performance	Low DFPA, low performance	Low DFPA, low performance	High DFPA, high performance
Weak relationship between DJPA and DFPA	High DJPA, low DFPA	High DJPA, low DFPA	Low DJPA, high DFPA
Weak relationship between DJPA and performance	High DJPA, low performance	Relatively high DJPA, low performance	Modest DJPA, high performance
Positive relationship between alliance number, depth, breadth and DFPA	Few, shallow, narrow alliances, low DFPA	Few, shallow, narrow alliances, low DFPA	Numerous, deep, broad alliances, high DFPA
Positive relationship between costs of monitoring governance tasks and DFPA	Three easy-to-monitor tasks, low DFPA	Two easy-to-monitor tasks, low DFPA	One hard-to-monitor task, high DFPA
Micro level			
States experience Jekyll and Hyde problem	United States pushes market-friendly biomedical agenda over broad-based social medicine policies	United States and some African nations oppose evidence-based HIV interventions on political grounds	Donor governments oppose evidence-based epidemiological interventions on political grounds
Bureaucratic interests aligned with institutional objectives	Survey, interview, policy-based evidence of alignment	Survey, interview, policy-based evidence of alignment	Survey, interview, policy-based evidence of alignment
Feedback from performance to DFPA	Feedback effects from 1970s	Feedback effects from ≈ 2000	Feedback effects from ≈ 2010
Alliances provide protection against opportunistic state interference	NA (few, shallow, narrow alliances)	NA (few, shallow, narrow alliances)	Partners mitigate capture by providing expertise, advocacy, financial support
Higher costs of task monitoring weaken state control	Tasks require close interaction with states, facilitating oversight	Tasks require close interaction with states, facilitating oversight	Need for medical and, managerial expertise, country-specific information impedes oversight

Notes: DFPA = de facto policy autonomy; DJPA = de jure policy autonomy.

Second, there is less evidence that performance problems have arisen from opportunistic or wayward behavior on the part of international bureaucrats. Rather, policy initiatives and strategies pursued by the secretariat have tended to align closely with institutional objectives, and survey evidence suggests that bureaucrats are often strongly and personally committed to such goals – even if not satisfied with the progress made toward them.

Third, while long-run trends in performance closely trail those in de facto policy autonomy, the former has gradually but steadily reinforced the latter by altering the cost–benefit calculus of capture for states. The culmination of these feedback dynamics has been the entrenchment of a low-autonomy, low-performance equilibrium in the WHO and UNAIDS and a high-autonomy, high-performance equilibrium in Gavi and GFATM. There are few signs, in contrast, of a reverse causal pathway running from de facto policy autonomy to either governance tasks or operational alliances.

Fourth, monitoring costs shine through as a key mechanism linking governance tasks to de facto policy autonomy. States have encountered few difficulties observing the consensus- and capacity-building functions exercised by the WHO and UNAIDS, enabling them to maintain close supervision and control over bureaucratic activities. The complex, knowledge-intensive character of Gavi and GFATM's financing activities, in contrast, has given rise to deep and persistent information asymmetries that "cloak" bureaucrats from robust governmental oversight.

Finally, by heightening the costs and moderating the benefits of capture, a dense and varied constellation of operational alliances has opened up vital room for bureaucratic maneuver in the Gavi and GFATM policymaking routines. Central to this process has been the deployment of tried and tested advocacy strategies by partners, from lobbying to information dissemination, as well as the provision of generous financial assistance to the secretariat. No comparable "hand" of support for policy discretion has materialized from the WHO and UNAIDS' slender and fragile bonds with nongovernmental stakeholders.

Notably, there is little indication that the framework is a better fit for the two IGOs in the case study than for the two PPPs. Rather, this structural difference throws useful additional light on the origins of Gavi and GFATM's de facto policy autonomy, particularly with regard to the formation of operational alliances. In this respect, the examination lends support to Chapter 2's contention that many PPPs fall within the theory's scope conditions and that integrating membership structures as an explanatory variable can extend its analytical reach.

6   Effective but Unaccountable?

Autonomy and the Politics of Reform

> A crucial feature of representative democracy is that those who govern
> are held accountable to the governed. If governance above the level of
> the nation-state is to be legitimate in a democratic era, mechanisms for
> appropriate accountability need to be institutionalized.
>
> – Ruth W. Grant and Robert O. Keohane, 2005[1]

Can international institutions be both effective and accountable? This,
one United Nations (UN) oversight official put to me on a rainy
summer afternoon Geneva, is the "million-dollar question of global
governance."[2] At first blush, this book's theoretical framework appears
to imply an unequivocal "no." Higher levels of de facto policy autonomy,
almost by definition, impede the membership's ability to understand,
interrogate, and impose consequences for institutional actions. Lacking
a tight grip on the policy process, states may struggle, for instance, to
compel institutions to share information with them, block proposals and
initiatives they oppose, and levy penalties on international bureaucrats
for undesired behavior. If ample bureaucratic discretion is needed to
avert key political threats to performance, we are destined, it seems, to
choose between allowing institutions to perform effectively and holding
them to account.

   A tradeoff between performance and accountability would be concerning for normative as well as practical reasons. Accountability is often
regarded as an intrinsically desirable, if not essential, characteristic for
public institutions. Those who wield political power, justice and fairness
seem to demand, should be subject to the scrutiny, judgment, and
sanction of those who delegated them authority and who are impacted by
their decisions. A host of instrumental benefits – such as responsiveness,
integrity, and, as Ruth Grant and Robert Keohane emphasize in this

---

[1] Grant and Keohane (2005, 29).
[2] Author interview #27 with UN Joint Inspection Unit (JIU) inspector, June 8, 2012,
Geneva.

chapter's epigraph, legitimacy – are also attributed to accountability.[3] As a crucial base of stakeholder support for and confidence in public institutions, legitimacy is often seen as a particularly valuable corollary – no less in the international domain, where electoral mechanisms of legitimation are generally unavailable.[4] Indeed, some scholars question whether international institutions can be viable in the long run if they are not widely perceived as legitimate.[5]

Interestingly, another ostensible benefit of accountability is effectiveness itself. According to the rogue-agency perspective critiqued in Chapters 1 and 2, accountability mechanisms facilitate top-down monitoring and oversight of institutions, reining in agency slack and hence deviant bureaucratic behavior.[6] This logic, Michael Barnett colorfully observes, underlies the common scholarly refrain that underperforming institutions can alleviate their woes by becoming more accountable: "When the pathology screens of global governance institutions come back positive, scholars have typically recommended a heavy dose of accountability ... Is there slippage or slack? Try accountability. Is the staff spending too much time worrying about their careers, covering their behinds, and following outmoded rules? Accountability is the answer. Not enough learning? Improve accountability. Too easily neglectful of those affected by the organization's actions? Turn up the accountability. A heavy dose of accountability can transform a dysfunctional into a functional organization."[7] In short, tension between accountability and performance would also call into question an influential view among experts on global governance.

In this chapter, I argue that any perceived incompatibility between performance and accountability under my framework reflects an unduly narrow understanding of how the latter may be *institutionalized*. State control of the policy machinery is, to be sure, an important avenue through which institutions are held responsible for their actions. It is far from the only one, however. In recent decades, institutions have established a variety of alternative channels – introduced in Chapter 1 as *second-wave accountability* (SWA) mechanisms – through which private as well as public stakeholders can exercise accountability, including access-to-information policies, grievance redress procedures, and partic-

---

[3] Bovens, Goodin, and Schillemans (2014). For a careful conceptual discussion of the relationship between accountability and legitimacy, see Buchanan and Keohane (2006).

[4] Dahl (1999); Rabkin (2005); Rubenfeld (2004).

[5] E.g. Buchanan and Keohane (2006); Cottrell (2009); Tallberg, Bäckstrand, and Scholte (2018).

[6] Barnett (2016); Barnett and Finnemore (2004); Hawkins et al. (2006). As discussed shortly, not all scholars agree that accountability positively affects performance.

[7] Barnett (2016, 1000).

ipatory governance arrangements. Drawing inspiration from features of democratic governance, SWA mechanisms facilitate stakeholder engagement and influence by expanding opportunities to learn about institutional activities, to highlight and address shortcomings, and to contribute to decision-making processes. In doing so, some scholars believe, they have ushered in an emerging era of unprecedented transparency, participation, and responsiveness in global governance – an era in which the separation between domestic and international modes of political organization is rapidly eroding.[8]

My central claim is that the strength of institutions' SWA mechanisms is – unlike that of their first-wave accountability structures – positively associated with their performance. Two reasons are key. First, the principal sources of de facto policy autonomy in my framework – alliances and stealth – give rise to intense external pressures for accountability. As major beneficiaries of enhanced institutional transparency, inclusiveness, and responsiveness, operational partners – in particular nongovernmental organizations (NGOs) – tend to play a leading role in instigating demands and building coalitions for SWA reforms. A sizable and diverse constellation of substantive alliances encourages the formation of powerful, broad-based reform campaigns capable of mobilizing intense pressure on institutions and their members. When governance tasks are costly to monitor, meanwhile, stakeholders in general have stronger incentives to press for new avenues for acquiring information on, evaluating, and influencing institutions. Second, once adopted, SWA mechanisms can bring about improvements in performance *beyond* those generated by de facto policy autonomy. They do so through three pathways: calling attention to and remedying operational problems; expanding the range of perspectives, information, and knowledge that inform policy choices; and boosting (internal and external) compliance with such decisions.

The implications are important. Accountability losses stemming from limited governmental control of the policy apparatus must be weighed against gains arising from SWA structures. The rogue-agency conjecture that accountability mechanisms promote effective performance is not wrong per se; rather, the nature of this relationship is more nuanced, depending on *how* accountability is instantiated and to *whose* benefit. When institutionalized in second-wave form, accountability can be a complement rather than a competitor to de facto policy autonomy, with the best performance outcomes achieved when institution enjoy both characteristics.

To evaluate this line of argument, I extend the mixed-methods research design employed in previous chapters. I begin with a statistical

---

[8] Cassese (2016); Kingsbury, Krisch, and Stewart (2005).

analysis that leverages original data on the presence and robustness of five distinct types of SWA mechanisms in Performance of International Organizations Project (PIIP) institutions: *transparency, evaluation, inspection, investigation,* and *participation* mechanisms. The main findings are twofold. First, the strength of SWA mechanisms is positively predicted both by the number, depth, and breadth of operational alliances in earlier periods and by the exercise of governance tasks with high monitoring costs for states and other stakeholders. Second, controlling for de facto policy autonomy, mechanism strength has a similarly positive association with the performance indices analyzed in Chapter 3. A simultaneous equations analysis suggests that this relationship is primarily driven by a causal pathway from SWA structures to performance ratings rather than vice versa. In the second part of the empirical examination, I assess qualitative evidence for the argument in the issue area of economic development, where several SWA mechanisms were pioneered. This plausibility probe, which draws on similar sources to the case studies of Chapters 4 and 5, furnishes concrete examples of the argument's logic and sheds more direct light on its postulated causal processes.

I open with a brief conceptual discussion of accountability mechanisms in the international context. The second section provides an empirical overview of the emergence and spread of SWA mechanisms in the PIIP sample. The third section expounds the argument and lays out its central macro- and micro-level implications. I conduct statistical tests of the macro-level propositions in the fourth section. The fifth section examines the micro-level claims by means of a qualitative analysis of international development institutions; the first part focuses on international financial institutions (IFIs) and the second part on UN agencies, with both organized around a set of puzzling empirical patterns.

Conceptualizing Accountability Mechanisms

Accountability is often said to be an elusive and contested concept that means different things to different people. No universally accepted definition has materialized from the vast multidisciplinary literature on the term; in the words of one review, there are "a bewildering and ever growing variety of overlapping and competing conceptions of accountability."[9] Nevertheless, there is broad agreement that, in essence, it involves *answering for one's actions to those with a legitimate claim to question them.* This minimum conceptual consensus raises two questions:

---

[9] Bovens, Goodin, and Schillemans (2014, 4).

What does it mean to be answerable for one's actions? And what constitutes a legitimate claim to query the behavior of power holders?

There are two leading theoretical models of answerability, each emphasizing a different channel through which power wielders can be held responsible. According to the "sanctions" model, answerability involves exposure to (actual or potential) punishment by accountability holders.[10] The "selection" model, which has received less attention from social scientists, instead locates answerability in the capacity of accountability holders to select power wielders who share their interests and then to demand that these actors explain and justify their decisions.[11] The two models are not mutually exclusive. In democratic systems, for example, elections are an instrument for both sanctioning and selecting political representatives.

With respect to who is entitled to an answer, there are again two main theoretical models, each focusing on a different aspect of the relationship between power wielders and accountability holders.[12] The "delegation" model, which is informed by principal–agent theory, views only those actors who grant authority to power wielders as justified in holding them to account. The "participation" model, in contrast, identifies all actors who are affected by the actions of power wielders as accountability holders.[13] Unlike before, it is rare for the two models to fully converge in practice. Democratic governments, for example, are delegated authority by the citizens of a given country or territory (the *demos*) but frequently take actions that affect noncitizens.

A key implication of this discussion is that there are multiple pathways, instantiating different modalities of answerability and legitimation, through which international institutions can be held to account. Some of these channels are *institutionalized*, that is, embedded in routinized and stable bureaucratic practices; others are *non-institutionalized*, operating on an ad-hoc or discretionary basis and usually relying on actors and forces outside institutions. Although non-institutionalized mechanisms, such as reputational effects and pressure from peer institutions, can sometimes serve as potent instruments of accountability, their availability and impact tend to be less predictable as well as enduring, rendering them less reliable for stakeholders.[14] For this reason, as suggested by

[10] Grant and Keohane (2005); Mulgan (2000); Przeworski, Stokes, and Manin (1999).
[11] Besley (2006); Fearon (1999); Mansbridge (2009).
[12] Grant and Keohane (2005); Koenig-Archibugi (2016).
[13] Held (1995); Koenig-Archibugi (2016, 2017).
[14] For a typology of formal and informal accountability mechanisms in world politics, see Grant and Keohane (2005).

Grant and Keohane, scholars have generally viewed institutionalization as the most promising route to accountability in global governance.

Traditionally, the primary institutionalized mechanism of accountability has been participation in the formal policy process, a privilege extended only to those actors who originally delegated authority to institutions – typically governments.[15] By introducing, debating, and voting on policy proposals, governing body members can impose sanctions on institutions for poor performance (e.g., through budgetary contractions), select the head of the secretariat, and demand explanations for institutional actions.[16] Traditional, or "first-wave," accountability structures therefore blend elements of the sanction and the selection models of answerability with the delegation model of legitimation.

SWA reforms expand the scope of institutionalized accountability in two significant ways. First, they open up new channels of sanction and selection. Grievance redress procedures, for instance, can lead to professional penalties (and reputational costs) for bureaucrats found to have illegitimately harmed the interests of stakeholders. Evaluation offices frequently require senior management to provide a comprehensive public response to institutional assessments. Participation forums foster discursive processes in which bureaucrats can receive, reflect on, and respond to public questions about their behavior. Second, since they are not restricted to governments or other institutional principals, SWA mechanisms permit a wider range of constituencies to exercise accountability. That is, they embody components of *both* models of legitimation and answerability. Administratively, a key upshot is that SWA structures are managed and operated not by states but by (often independent) sections of the bureaucracy – a distinct mode of institutionalization. Distributionally, a key upshot, is that their benefits accrue primarily to non-state stakeholders.

The Rise of SWA Mechanisms: An Empirical Overview

How prevalent is the second wave of accountability in global governance? To explore this question, I compiled data covering the PIIP sample on the five principal types of SWA mechanisms identified in previous studies and evaluations, including the influential *Global Accountability Report*: transparency, evaluation, inspection, investigation, and participation

---

[15] Governments are, of course, themselves delegated authority by citizens, whose paucity of direct participation in international institutions is a central cause of the so-called democratic deficit in world politics. See Dahl (1999); Majone (1998); Moravcsik (2004).

[16] Grant and Keohane (2005).

Table 6.1 *Coding of SWA mechanisms*

Mechanism	Indicator	Description	Score
Transparency	Policy	Official access-to-information policy	1
	Disclosure presumption	All (non-sensitive) information disclosed in absence of compelling reason to withhold	+1
	Confidentiality	Sensitive types of information clearly defined	+1
	Timeframe	Timeframe for responding to information requests	+1
	Appeals	Appeals process for rejected information requests	+1
Evaluation	Unit	Unit responsible for evaluating performance	1
	Independence	Unit administratively independent from secretariat	+1
	Disclosure	Evaluation results publicly disclosed	+1
	Response	Evaluations require response from management	+1
	Follow-up	Execution of evaluation recommendations monitored	+1
Inspection	Function	Mechanism to address complaints from stakeholders	1
	Independence	Mechanism independent from secretariat	+1
	Confidentiality	Confidentiality for complainants guaranteed	+1
	Non-retaliation	Non-retaliation against complainants guaranteed	+1
	Follow-up	Implementation of remedial measures monitored	+1
Investigation	Function	Mechanism for investigating staff misconduct	1
	Independence	Mechanism independent from secretariat	+1
	Confidentiality	Confidentiality for complainants guaranteed	+1
	Non-retaliation	Non-retaliation against complainants guaranteed	+1
	Follow-up	Implementation of remedial measures monitored	+1
Participation	Access to governing body	External stakeholders are members of governing body	3
		External stakeholders participate in governing body	2
		External stakeholders observe/attend governing body	1
	Advisory body	External stakeholders represented in advisory body	+1
	Consultation body	External stakeholders participate in consultation forum	+1
Each *Participation* indicator multiplied by:	Unrestricted	Access granted to all external stakeholders	× 1
	Issue restrictions	Access restricted on basis of issue area	× 0.75
	Non-issue restrictions	Access restricted on basis of criteria other than issue area (e.g., expertise, financial contributions, location)	× 0.5
	Name restrictions	Access restricted to named or elected stakeholders	× 0.25

mechanisms.[17] Mechanism strength is measured as a five-point index for every year from 1960 – or an institution's founding date – to 2018. The main data sources are policy and governance documents (obtained in some cases from institutional archives), online reporting, academic literature, and personal communications with institutions. The five indices can be summarized as follows (Table 6.1 details the coding rules):

[17] Grigorescu (2007, 2010); Ecker-Ehrhardt (2018); Tallberg et al. (2013, 2014, 2016). The *Global Accountability Report*, which was published by the nonprofit One World Trust from 2003 to 2008, rated a small number of intergovernmental organizations (IGOs), international nongovernmental organizations (INGOs), and multinational corporations on four dimensions of accountability: transparency, participation, evaluation, and complaint and response.

1. *Transparency* is an additive index measuring whether institutions possess an access-to-information policy – a policy that formally establishes the public's right to request (non-sensitive) information from them – and whether this policy guarantees automatic and timely disclosure and includes an independently managed appeals process for rejected disclosure requests (i.e., a process not managed by the secretariat).[18]
2. *Evaluation* is an additive index measuring whether institutions possess a unit (e.g., office, department, division) that is responsible for monitoring and assessing their activities, and whether this unit is independently managed, publicly discloses evaluation findings, and issues evidence-based recommendations for improving performance.
3. *Inspection* is an additive index measuring whether institutions possess a mechanism for receiving, assessing, and addressing complaints from adversely affected external stakeholders, and whether this mechanism is independently managed, guarantees confidentiality and nonretaliation for complainants, and includes systems for monitoring the implementation of punitive and remedial measures.
4. *Investigation* is an additive index measuring whether institutions possess a mechanism for investigating and sanctioning professional, financial, or other misconduct by officials, and whether this mechanism has the same four additional characteristics as *Inspection* (i.e., independence, confidentiality, nonretaliation, follow-up).
5. *Participation* is a multiplicative index measuring (1) the depth of access to the policy process granted to external stakeholders (such as civil society groups and corporations) and (2) the range of such actors permitted access. Scores are averaged across three types of policy organ: governing bodies, advisory councils, and consultation forums.[19]

---

[18] On systems for eliciting and protecting *sensitive* state information in global governance, see Carnegie and Carson (2020).

[19] Specifically, the index is defined by:

$$\text{Participation}_{a,b,c} = \sum_{a=1}^{A}\left(\frac{\text{governing}_a \times \text{range}_a}{A}\right) + \sum_{b=1}^{B}\left(\frac{\text{advisory}_b \times \text{range}_b}{B}\right) \\ + \sum_{c=1}^{C}\left(\frac{\text{consultation}_c \times \text{range}_c}{C}\right) \tag{6.1}$$

where *governing*$_a$, *advisory*$_b$, and *consultation*$_c$ are the depth of access to governing body *a*, advisory council *b*, and consultation forum *c*, respectively; *range*$_a$, *range*$_b$, and *range*$_c$ are the breadth of access to such organs; and *A*, *B*, and *C* are the total number of such organs. This formula builds on the measurement of transnational access by Tallberg et al. (2013, 2014).

Table 6.2 *Correlations between SWA measures*

	Transparency	Evaluation	Inspection	Investigation	Participation	
Transparency	1					
Evaluation	0.52**	1				
Inspection	0.63**	0.43**	1			
Investigation	0.44**	0.53**	0.43**	1		
Participation	0.26**	0.44**	0.16**	0.35**	1	
SWA Composite	0.78**	0.82**	0.70**	0.79**	0.54**	1

Note: **$p < 0.01$. *SWA Composite* is the sum of the other five indices.

Table 6.2 displays bivariate correlations between the SWA indices as well as a summative combination of all five (*SWA Composite*). In general, the strength of different mechanisms is highly correlated: The coefficient on all 10 correlations between the five noncomposite indices is positive and statistically significant at the one percent level (mean $r = 0.42$). *Transparency, Evaluation, Inspection* and *Investigation* have a particularly close association (mean $r = 0.50$); three of the four weakest correlations occur between these indices and *Participation* (mean $r = 0.30$).

As mentioned in Chapter 3, some of the comparative donor evaluations on which my measures of institutional performance are based include indicators of accountability. Appendix B.8 shows that the SWA indices are strongly associated with these indicators, in particular those measuring comparable dimensions of accountability. While we should not expect such correlations to be perfect – the evaluations do not focus specifically on SWA mechanisms – they provide evidence that the indices are broadly consistent with how modern accountability structures are perceived by a diverse range of stakeholders.

Figure 6.1 plots the mean value of the six SWA indices between 1960 and 2018. Each index exhibits a clear upward trajectory. An especially sharp rise characterizes *Transparency, Evaluation,* and *Investigation,* whose means vault from 0 at the start of the period to around 3 (on a five-point scale) by the end – almost double the increase in *Inspection* and *Participation.* There is also some variation in the timing of these trends: *Evaluation* and *Participation* began to grow in a sustained fashion in the late 1960s and early 1970s, a process that did not begin until the 1990s for *Transparency, Inspection,* and *Investigation.*[20]

Importantly, as indicated by the widening standard deviation intervals around the trend lines, the rise of SWA mechanisms has been accompanied by increasing *variation* in their strength across institutions. This

---

[20] *Participation* is the only index that does not begin the time series with an average value of 0, reflecting the decision of a handful of IGOs founded before 1960 to grant non-state actors partial access to their governing bodies.

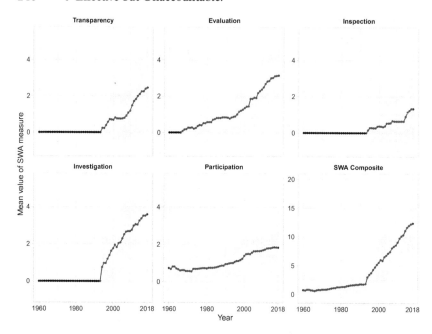

Figure 6.1 Average value of SWA measures in PIIP sample, 1960–2018
Note: The shaded regions mark one standard deviation above and below the mean.

is most pronounced for *Transparency*, *Evaluation*, and *Inspection*, whose standard deviations grow to approximately 2 by 2018.

Figure 6.2 provides a disaggregated view of such dispersion by plotting the frequency (left panel) and cumulative depth (right panel) of SWA reforms undertaken by PIIP institutions. There are substantial differences in both metrics across institutions. For instance, the World Bank, the International Fund for Agricultural Development (IFAD), and the International Finance Corporation (IFC) have adopted the full gamut of SWA mechanisms and repeatedly strengthened them – particularly since 1990 – lifting *SWA Composite* close to its 25-point maximum by 2018. At the other end of the spectrum, the Commonwealth Secretariat (COMSEC), the World Trade Organization (WTO), and the International Trade Centre (ITC) have introduced only a few SWA mechanisms and made essentially no enhancements to them, restricting *SWA Composite* to less than 10 in all years. In short, while many major international institutions have established an array of more robust and

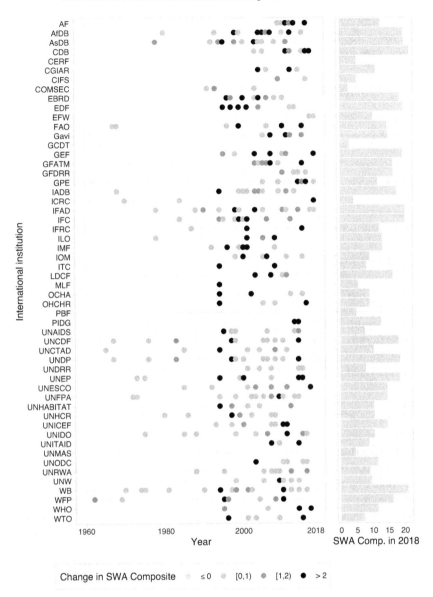

Figure 6.2 Frequency and cumulative depth of SWA reforms in PIIP institutions

wide-ranging accountability mechanisms in recent decades, many others continue to rely on the more limited, state-centric structures with which they were founded.

When Accountability and Performance Go Together

This chapter's core contention is that the relationship between accountability structures and performance in international institutions depends on how we answer the question: *Which* structures? Whereas the primary traditional channel of accountability – state influence in the policy process – can hinder the proper functioning of institutions by limiting their capacity to develop and exercise de facto policy autonomy, SWA mechanisms go hand in hand with effective performance. This positive association arises from both the origins and the consequences of SWA reforms. When institutions tap into the two sources of de facto policy autonomy highlighted by my framework – that is, they boast numerous, deep, and varied operational alliances and perform hard-to-monitor governance tasks – they tend to experience more intense stakeholder pressures for accountability. Having been introduced, moreover, SWA mechanisms can deliver independent gains in performance by stimulating bureaucratic learning, promoting more rational and balanced decision-making, and improving policy compliance. These pathways, which are summarized in Table 6.3, are elaborated in the rest of this section.

Operational Alliances, Governance Tasks, and SWA Reforms

SWA mechanisms entail distributional consequences for actors below, within, and above the state. External stakeholders stand to profit from new channels for obtaining information about institutions, participating in their policy organs, exposing misconduct by their staff, and seeking redress for adverse effects of their policies and practices. Bureaucrats may appreciate the sheen of legitimacy that accompanies more robust accountability structures, though hold less enthusiasm for the enhanced scrutiny and pressure that also arrive.[21] States that benefit most from traditional governance arrangements are likely to have equally ambivalent feelings about SWA mechanisms, welcoming their legitimating effects but resenting any dilution of policy influence that arises from the expansion of opportunities to monitor, evaluate, and participate in institutions.

In light of these mixed distributional implications, the impetus for SWA mechanisms has typically come from *outside* rather than within

---

[21] Lall (2022).

Table 6.3 *Why SWA mechanisms and effectiveness go together*

Relationship (macro level)			Causal mechanism (micro level)		
Operational alliances (numerous, deep, broad)	⇒	SWA reforms	Partners benefit from increased transparency, oversight, access to policy process	⇒	Partners assemble stakeholder coalitions for autonomy, deploy advocacy tactics
Governance tasks (costly to monitor)	⇒	SWA reforms	Monitoring costs place stakeholders at informational disadvantage	⇒	Stakeholders mobilize in support of increased oversight, engagement
SWA mechanisms	⇒	Performance	New information about institutional processes, outputs, outcomes	⇒	Bureaucrats identify, address, learn from performance problems
			Stronger engagement with non-state stakeholders	⇒	More balanced, equitable, informed policy decisions
			Gains in perceived institutional legitimacy	⇒	Higher levels of policy compliance

institutions. Operational alliances establish a natural and durable constituency for accountability reforms. Given their close functional and reputational linkages to institutions, partners are among the greatest beneficiaries of increased institutional disclosure, access, and legitimacy. Accordingly, they possess powerful incentives to mobilize in support for SWA mechanisms, particularly in the wake of institutional scandals, crises, disasters, and other problems that expose poor performance and thus present potential windows of opportunity for change.[22] Indeed, partners often play a central role in calling attention to performance shortcomings – they are sometimes directly involved in uncovering them – and in linking them to accountability deficits in the ensuing public narrative. As when seeking to protect institutions against capture, partners can deploy a variety of strategies to generate interest in and support for accountability reforms, including lobbying powerful states and senior management, disseminating information and advice, and marshaling symbols, frames, and brands to deepen public engagement.

Other things equal, a more expansive network of operational alliances should translate into a larger, broader, and better-resourced coalition for accountability. Such coalitions should not only enjoy greater success in applying pressure tactics to states and international bureaucrats

---

[22] Lall (2022); Mattli and Woods (2009).

but also provide more valuable assistance to institutions in designing, implementing, and strengthening SWA mechanisms.

Monitoring challenges foster more generalized pressures for accountability. The logic is simple: When institutions carry out functions that are costly to observe, stakeholders derive greater gains from new channels of oversight. These benefits should incentivize stronger stakeholder support for SWA reforms when windows of opportunity present themselves, complementing and reinforcing partner-led campaigns. It is important to note, however, that successful reform is unlikely to eliminate information asymmetries between institutions and *states* – a crucial foundation of de facto policy autonomy. The information produced by SWA mechanisms is of primary value to nongovernmental stakeholders, the most frequent users of transparency policies and the sole users of inspection, investigation, and participation mechanisms. Indeed, some of this information is already available to states. A high proportion of access-to-information requests, for example, concern internal policy documents and governing body minutes or transcripts to which the membership is already privy.[23]

Performance Benefits of SWA Mechanisms

Once in place, SWA mechanisms alter how institutions engage with stakeholders in three ways that tend to reinforce a positive association with performance – effects distinct from those of de facto policy autonomy. First, by generating information about institutional procedures, outputs, and outcomes, they help bureaucrats to monitor their own performance, identify emerging problems and areas for improvement, and gauge the impact of corrective measures. That is, they serve as a valuable tool for institutional *learning*.[24] Most important in this regard are evaluation mechanisms, which entrench systems for objectively appraising performance and incorporating lessons learned into future policy and practice;[25] and inspection and investigation mechanisms, which, in a similar fashion to decentralized "fire-alarm" strategies of legislative oversight at the domestic level,[26] open up conduits for non-state actors to bring performance issues to public attention.[27]

---

[23] See, for example, access-to-information requests submitted to the World Bank – the international institution with the most widely used transparency policy – available in summary form at https://www.worldbank.org/en/access-to-information/summaryreports [Last accessed January 9, 2021].
[24] Benner, Eckhard, and Rotmann (2017); Siebenhüner (2008); Smith (2017).
[25] Eckhard and Jankauskas (2020).
[26] McCubbins and Schwartz (1984); McCubbins, Noll, and Weingast (1987).
[27] Buntaine (2015); Gould (2017).

Second, SWA mechanisms broaden the range of constituencies that can participate in and contribute to institutional decision-making, providing the basis for more reasoned and evenhanded policies.[28] A more heterogeneous set of inputs into the policy process, my framework implies, reduces the risk of excessive influence or capture by a narrow subset of stakeholders. Furthermore, a growing body of research indicates that decisions taken by larger and more diverse groups are less likely to be plagued by misinformation, irrational impulses, and biases – in other words, to be "wrong."[29] Participation mechanisms are, naturally, the most direct source of these benefits, though transparency and inspection mechanisms may encourage stakeholders to seek out and pursue opportunities to become more involved in governance processes.

A third boon to performance stems from the compliance-inducing properties of SWA mechanisms, which pertain to both international bureaucrats and states. Closer bureaucratic observance of internal rules and protocols occurs via a *correction* effect and a *deterrent* effect. By facilitating institutional monitoring, SWA mechanisms – in particular inspection and investigation procedures – raise the probability that procedural violations will be detected and remedied, whether by more senior officials or by governing bodies. Equally important, since detection is associated with professional and reputational costs for bureaucrats, its higher likelihood serves as a potent deterrent to noncompliance in the first place.

In the case of states, for whom the costs of policy violation are typically considerably lower, improved compliance is driven primarily by a *legitimation* effect. A central message of the rich international relations (IR) literature on legitimacy is that, lacking coercive tools of enforcement, institutions can only induce widespread adherence to their dictates – a necessary condition for effectiveness – if they are recognized as justified in exercising authority. As Ian Hurd summarizes, "It is common in IR to assume that the main behavioral implication of legitimacy in IOs [international organizations] is higher rates of compliance by states with international rules."[30] Institutionalized mechanisms of accountability, as noted earlier, are a key source of socially acknowledged legitimacy.[31] Thus, perceptions of legitimacy can be not only a consequence of effective performance, as argued in Chapter 2, but also a cause.

---

[28] This benefit has been discussed most extensively in scholarship on the governance of IFIs, in particular the World Bank and the International Monetary Fund (IMF). See Buira (2005); Kahler (2006); Stiglitz (2003); Woods (2001).

[29] See Landemore (2012) for an overview.

[30] Hurd (2008, 73). Also see Chayes and Chayes (1995); Simmons (1998).

[31] See, in addition, the literatures on IFI governance (e.g., Van Houtven 2002; Woods 1999) and on "input" and "output" legitimacy (e.g., Caporaso 2003; Lindgren and Persson 2010).

An interesting implication of this reasoning is that SWA reforms can contribute to the positive feedback loop between de facto policy auton- omy and performance theorized in Chapter 2. In the long run, advances in performance resulting from the adoption of SWA mechanisms should encourage expansions in de facto policy autonomy that, in turn, fuel further performance gains. Note, however, that the negative side of the feedback loop should not be affected: I expect the absence of SWA reforms to have no impact on performance – not a negative one – and thus no knock-on effect to de facto policy autonomy.

Observable Implications

A slew of macro- and micro-level observable implications follow from the preceding discussion. The overarching macro-level proposition is that, holding constant de facto policy autonomy, there is a positive relationship between the strength of an institution's SWA mechanisms and its performance. Implicit in the logic behind this hypothesis is the expectation that mechanism strength is also positively associated with (1) the quantity, depth, and breadth of the institution's operational alliances and (2) the costs to stakeholders of monitoring its governance tasks.

Two sets of micro-level implications accompany these hypotheses. The first concerns the processes shaping the adoption of SWA reforms. Institutions with an extensive network of deep operational alliances should experience more forceful pressures to adopt SWA mechanisms from partners, whose advocacy tactics should resemble those described in Chapter 2. When institutions exercise governance tasks that are challenging to monitor, stakeholders should express stronger support for adoption because the payoff of more robust oversight is higher.

The second set of micro-level implications concerns the processes through which SWA mechanisms, upon becoming operational, induce positive change in performance. Three patterns, in particular, should be observed: new information about institutional activities and results facil- itating bureaucratic problem solving and learning; broader and deeper stakeholder participation in the policy process promoting more informed and responsive decisions; and policy compliance increasing thanks to a combination of higher expected violation costs for bureaucrats and stronger perceptions of institutional legitimacy among states.

Note on Scope Conditions

The argument's scope conditions are similar to those delineated in Chapter 3. Notably, the assumption that states are a constituency to whom accountability is owed need not restrict its purview to inter-governmental organizations (IGOs). States may be affected by any institution's actions, though this is more likely when they are actively engaged with it, for instance, as members, donors, sources of infor-mal influence, or operational partners. According to the participation model of legitimation, such effects confer on states the right to ques-tion the exercise of institutional power. If, furthermore, states have (implicitly or explicitly) entrusted the institution with authority, they will also be entitled to accountability under the delegation model of legitimation. All public–private partnerships (PPPs) and international nongovernmental organizations (INGOs) in the PIIP satisfy these two conditions. The seven PPPs were co-founded by states, which remain their largest donors, closest partners, and most influential members. The two INGOs – the International Committee of the Red Cross (ICRC) and the International Federation of Red Cross and Red Crescent Societies (IFRC) – enjoy close operational and financial ties with governments and, while established by private citizens, derive much of their authority from international treaties on the conduct of armed conflict (such as the Geneva and Hague Conventions).[32] In sum, states – as well as non-state actors – can plausibly be identified as accountability holders across the full gamut of PIIP institutions.

Statistical Evidence

To begin the empirical examination, I undertake statistical tests of the macro-level implications outlined in the previous section. Merging the PIIP with the data on SWA mechanisms introduced earlier, I estimate a series of OLS models in which the dependent variable is (1) the strength of SWA mechanisms and (2) donor performance ratings. I then extend the latter analysis into a fully-fledged system of a simultaneous equations to account for the possibility of reciprocal causation between performance and SWA reforms.[33]

Determinants of SWA Reforms

As my hypotheses regarding the adoption of SWA mechanisms do not directly concern institutional performance, on which data are only available for the period covered by the comparative donor evaluations, I test them with an expanded version of the PIIP that encompasses all

[32] For a list of these agreements, see https://ihl-databases.icrc.org/ihl [Last accessed October 11, 2020].
[33] The findings reported below survive a battery of robustness checks comparable to those in Chapter 3; the results are available upon request.

years for which *Operational Alliances*, the three dummies for hard-to-monitor governance tasks, and the six SWA indices can be measured. This time-series cross-sectional dataset spans the period 1960–2018 for the task dummies (2,308 observations) and 2000–2018 for *Operational Alliances* (974 observations); the difference arises from the use of online sources to construct the latter variable.

In separate models, I regress each SWA index on *Operational Alliances$_f$*, where f denotes the first year for which data are available, and the three task dummies. Since *Operational Alliances* could conceivably be influenced by concurrent (but not future) SWA reforms, fixing its value at the earliest possible point in time helps to mitigate endogeneity concerns. Due to the lengthy sample period, in which confounding temporal trends present a risk, I include year fixed effects in all models.[34] In addition, I control for three variables suggested by previous empirical analyses of SWA reforms, all of which were introduced in Chapter 3: *Average Democracy*, the mean Polity2 score of an institution's member states, since institutions with more democratic memberships may be more favorably disposed toward SWA mechanisms;[35] and *# Members* and *Preference Heterogeneity*, as institutions with larger and more divided memberships contain more potential "veto players" in decisions on accountability reforms.[36]

Table 6.4 reports the estimated coefficients on the four key explanatory variables; standard errors are, as in Chapter 3, robust and clustered by institution. In line with expectations, the estimates are positive in all 24 models and significant in 17. The hypotheses receive the strongest support in models where *Transparency*, *Inspection*, and *SWA Composite* are the dependent variables, with every coefficient attaining significance. A standard deviation rise in *Operational Alliances$_f$* is associated with an increase in *SWA Composite* of 2.43, lifting an institution from the latter's median value to its 65th percentile. Institutions that design interventions, implement operations, and allocate resources see increases of 1.05, 0.85, and 0.98, respectively, equivalent to moving from the median to the 65th, 61st, and 65th percentiles.

Based on these estimates, Figure 6.3 plots predicted values of *SWA Composite*, bounded by 95 percent confidence intervals, across *Operational Alliances$_f$* and the three task dummies.[37] Predictions rise steeply with *Operational Alliances$_f$*, ranging from 5.93 – the 35th percentile of

---

[34] As in Chapter 3, I do not add institution fixed effects because the explanatory variables exhibit little within-institution variation over the sample period.

[35] Grigorescu (2007, 2010); Tallberg et al. (2013, 2014).

[36] Grigorescu (2010); Kahler (2004); Tallberg et al. (2013, 2014).

[37] Predictions are marginalized over the year fixed effects.

Table 6.4 *Determinants of SWA reforms (key results)*

	Trans. (1)	Eval. (2)	Inspect. (3)	Invest. (4)	Part. (5)	SWA Comp. (6)
Operational Alliances$_f$	0.578** (0.137)	0.693** (0.163)	0.396* (0.159)	0.259* (0.130)	0.198* (0.093)	2.124** (0.382)
Designing Interventions	0.528* (0.232)	0.969** (0.243)	0.458* (0.198)	0.071 (0.193)	0.092 (0.206)	2.118** (0.744)
Implementing Operations	0.407† (0.226)	0.886** (0.232)	0.327† (0.189)	0.079 (0.185)	0.014 (0.188)	1.713* (0.713)
Allocating Resources	0.652** (0.241)	0.325 (0.323)	0.681** (0.178)	0.109 (0.207)	0.242 (0.183)	2.009** (0.695)
Year FEs	✓	✓	✓	✓	✓	✓
Controls	✓	✓	✓	✓	✓	✓

Notes: $^†p < 0.1$; $^*p < 0.05$; $^{**}p < 0.01$. OLS estimates with robust standard errors, clustered by institution, in parentheses. The controls are *Average Democracy, Preference Heterogeneity*, and *# Members*. Regressors are lagged by one year, with the exception of *Operational Alliances$_f$*, which is fixed at the first year of available data. The number of observations is 816 in models that include *Operational Alliances$_f$* and 2,066 in all others.

SWA Composite – at its minimum value (0), to 16.20 – the 86th percentile of *SWA Composite* – at its maximum (4.83). A sharp increase also occurs when institutions design interventions, implement operations, and allocate resources, with the mean predicted value jumping from 3.43, the 53rd percentile of *SWA Composite*, to 5.38, the 65th percentile.

Performance and SWA Mechanisms

Next, I turn to the overall association between the strength of SWA mechanisms and performance. I regress the average performance index constructed in Chapter 3 on lags of the six SWA indices (entered in separate models), *De Facto Policy Autonomy*, and the three controls in Chapter 3's analysis of the determinants of performance (*# Members, Preference Heterogeneity*, and *Policy Scope*). To keep the analysis tractable, I do not disaggregate the dependent variable into its constituent donor-specific indices or indicators; however, estimates vary little across them.

The results, presented in Table 6.5, reveal a reasonably strong positive relationship between the SWA measures and the average performance index. All six coefficients on the former are positive, with four reaching or approaching significance. In terms of size, when *SWA Composite* rises by a standard deviation – roughly equivalent to one of the five-point noncomposite SWA indices – *Average Performance Index* grows by 0.04, a

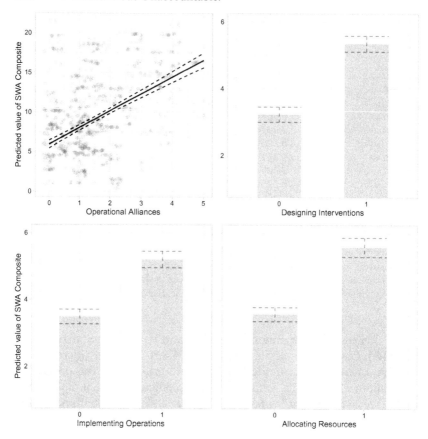

Figure 6.3 Predicted values of *SWA Composite* across *Operational Alliances* and dummies for hard-to-monitor tasks

Notes: Predictions are based on the results of Table 6.4, Model 6. The dashed lines represent 95 percent confidence interval (computed with robust standard errors, clustered by institution). Gray circles denote data points.

shift from its median value to its 60th percentile. The coefficient on *De Facto Policy Autonomy* is positive and highly significant in every model, changing little in size relative to Chapter 3's baseline analysis. Although not insubstantial, therefore, the performance benefits associated with SWA mechanisms are not of the same order of magnitude as those that attend de facto policy autonomy.

The left panel of Figure 6.4 displays predicted values of the average performance index over the full spectrum of *SWA Composite*. At low

Table 6.5 *Relationship between strength of SWA mechanisms and performance*

	Dependent variable: Average performance index					
	(1)	(2)	(3)	(4)	(5)	(6)
Transparency	0.118**					
	(0.043)					
Evaluation		0.023				
		(0.053)				
Inspection			0.123*			
			(0.057)			
Investigation				0.013		
				(0.067)		
Participation					0.136	
					(0.084)	
SWA Composite						0.041*
						(0.020)
De Facto Policy	0.613**	0.684**	0.659**	0.691**	0.686**	0.633**
Autonomy	(0.102)	(0.105)	(0.099)	(0.105)	(0.107)	(0.102)
# Members (log)	0.129	0.029	0.135	0.026	0.030	0.073
	(0.184)	(0.176)	(0.186)	(0.161)	(0.175)	(0.172)
Preference	−1.539*	−1.343†	−1.424*	−1.291†	−1.376†	−1.629*
Heterogeneity	(0.714)	(0.747)	(0.699)	(0.703)	(0.711)	(0.717)
Policy Scope	−0.182	−0.123	−0.114	−0.106	−0.140	−0.201
	(0.166)	(0.178)	(0.154)	(0.168)	(0.157)	(0.164)
Constant	−1.327	−1.105	−1.546	−1.144	−1.253	−1.250
	(0.961)	(0.906)	(0.971)	(0.858)	(0.918)	(0.922)
Observations	293	293	293	293	293	293
R-squared	0.392	0.360	0.378	0.359	0.367	0.381
Adjusted R-squared	0.381	0.348	0.367	0.348	0.356	0.370

Notes: $^{†}p < 0.1$; $^{*}p < 0.05$; $^{**}p < 0.01$. OLS estimates with robust standard errors, clustered by institution, in parentheses. All regressors are lagged by one year.

levels of *SWA Composite*, the predictions are negative and significant (at the 5 percent level), bottoming at −0.43 – the 30th percentile of the average performance index – at the variable's minimum (0). At the upper end of *SWA Composite*, they are positive, substantially larger, and again significant, peaking at 0.46 – the 66th percentile of the average performance index – at the variable's maximum (21.5).

Simultaneous Equations Approach

Could institutional performance itself influence the adoption of SWA mechanisms? A possible alternative interpretation of the previous results

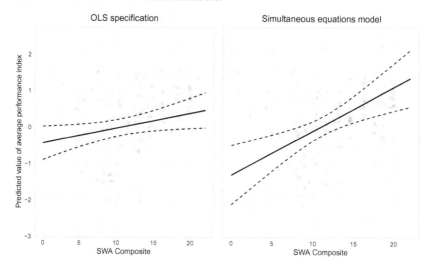

Figure 6.4 Predicted values of average performance index across levels of *SWA Composite*

Notes: Predictions are based on the results of Model 1, Table 6.5 (left panel) and Model 9, Figure 6.5 (right panel). The dashed lines represent 95 percent confidence intervals (computed with robust standard errors, clustered by institution). Gray circles denote data points.

is that more effective institutions are more likely to enact account-ability reforms, perhaps because they are more comfortable disclosing information about themselves and allowing stakeholders to scrutinize and participate in their activities. Drawing on Chapter 3's strategy for analyzing feedback processes, I explore this possibility by estimating a simultaneous equations specification in which a battery of more credibly exogenous variables are used to identify the mutual impact of performance and SWA mechanisms.

As in Chapter 3, I specify two sets of structural equations. The first is identical to Model 6 in Table 6.5. In the second, the SWA indices are regressed on the average performance index and all explana-tory and control variables from Table 6.4.[38] Consequently, the first stage of the 2SLS procedure regresses the average performance index and the SWA measures (the endogenous variables in the system) on *De Facto Policy Autonomy*, *# Members*, *Preference Heterogeneity*, *Pol-icy Scope*, *Operational Alliances*, *Designing Interventions*, *Implementing*

---

[38] Values of *Operational Alliances* are no longer fixed at year f.

Operations, Allocating Resources, and *Average Democracy* (the exogenous variables).

Figure 6.5 exhibits the key estimates. The second-stage coefficients on the SWA indices (from the first set of structural equations) are reported within the right-pointing arrows. The estimates are positive in all six models and significant in five, growing by almost fivefold relative to the OLS analysis, on average. An increase of one standard deviation in *SWA Composite* now raises the average performance index by 0.61, elevating an institution from the median value to the 71st percentile of the average performance index.

The right panel of Figure 6.4 plots predicted values of the average performance index at varying levels of *SWA Composite* based on the simultaneous equations estimates. The slope of the prediction line is discernibly steeper than in the OLS specification, registering a minimum value of -1.29 (when *SWA Composite* $= 0$), the 19th percentile of the average performance index, and a maximum value of 1.31 (when *SWA Composite* $= 21.5$), the 91st percentile of the average performance index.

By contrast, the second-stage coefficients on the average performance index (second set of structural equations), shown inside the left-pointing arrows in Figure 6.5, are all negative and nonsignificant. In other words, any effect flowing from performance to SWA mechanisms appears not only to be limited but also to reduce their strength. Put differently, feedback processes are likely to have worked *against* rather than for my hypotheses in the OLS specification.

Qualitative Evidence: Global Development Institutions

A detailed case-based investigation of the argument's micro-level implications is beyond the scope of this chapter. As a more feasible alternative, this section explores their plausibility through a targeted qualitative probe of PIIP institutions in the domain of economic development. I draw on a mixture of primary and secondary sources, including SWA policy documents, independent evaluations, archival records, academic literature, and interviews with international bureaucrats and member state representatives.

I select the development sphere for three reasons. First, several SWA mechanisms were inaugurated in this area, making it a natural place to begin exploring their origins and – given the length of time they have been in place – consequences for performance. Second, notwithstanding this trailblazing role, international development institutions exhibit surprisingly wide variation in SWA structures, offering us an insight into the factors that inhibit as well as promote accountability reforms. Third,

SWA measures   **Performance**

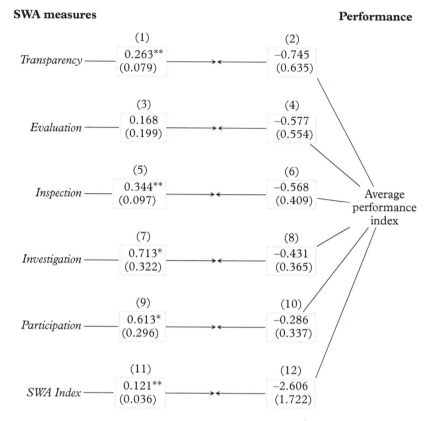

Figure 6.5 SWA mechanisms and performance: Key simultaneous equations estimates

Notes: $^\dagger p < 0.1$; $^* p < 0.05$; $^{**} p < 0.01$. Arrows report second-stage 2SLS estimates of the effect of the variable at the tail (the explanatory variable) on the variable at the head (the dependent variable); robust standard errors, clustered by institution, appear in parentheses. In models where the average performance measure is the dependent variable, the controls are *De Facto Policy Autonomy*, *# Members*, *Preference Heterogeneity*, and *Policy Scope*. In models where an SWA measure is the dependent variable, the controls are *Average Democracy*, *# Members*, *Preference Heterogeneity*, *Operational Alliances*, *Designing Interventions*, *Implementing Operations*, and *Allocating Resources*. In the first stage of the 2SLS procedure, the dependent variables are regressed on all of the above controls. Regressors are lagged by one year in both stages.

from a research design perspective, investigating this domain further broadens the substantive horizons of the book's qualitative analysis.

The first part of the section examines SWA mechanisms adopted by IFIs, in particular multilateral development banks, which have been among their earliest and most enthusiastic advocates. The second part turns to development agencies within the UN System, among which there are larger – and, at first glance, rather puzzling – differences in SWA structures.

Development Finance Institutions

Adoption of SWA Reforms
One of the most conspicuous patterns in Figure 6.2 is the consistent robustness of SWA mechanisms across development finance agencies. Indeed, all of the top five *SWA Composite* scores in 2018 belong to such institutions.[39] A noteworthy case is the World Bank, the highest scorer in most years of the sample and the first IGO to establish an access-to-information policy, an inspection mechanism, and an independent evaluation office. The impetus for the Bank's reforms has invariably come from its deep and wide-ranging network of civil society partners – it has the fourth highest average value of *Operational Alliances* in the PIIP – which have assembled influential and enduring state–society coalitions for accountability. One Bank evaluation officer succinctly summarized the pattern: "Our accountability reforms have followed a strikingly similar sequence: Local and international NGOs, many of which are involved in delivering our projects, have identified performance problems and joined forces to campaign for new accountability mechanisms, eventually securing the critical backing of major shareholder countries, such as the United States and the United Kingdom."[40]

The creation of the World Bank's access-to-information policy and inspection mechanism – the famous Inspection Panel – in the mid-1990s are cases in point. Around a decade earlier, NGO partners and community groups discovered that a Bank-funded dam project on the Narmada River in central India had systematically violated the institution's own social and environmental safeguards.[41] These actors banded together with farmers, tribal associations, and human rights activists in the region to form an "aggressive and vocal grassroots coalition" known as Narmada Bachao Andolan (Save the Narmada Movement).[42]

[39] These institutions are, in order, the Caribbean Development Bank (CDB), the World Bank, the IFC, IFAD, and the Asian Development Bank (AsDB).
[40] Author interview #84 with World Bank evaluation officer, May 16, 2018, Washington, DC.
[41] Cullet (2007). The World Bank began involving NGOs in project design and implementation in the early 1970s, with the aim of harnessing their "local knowledge and awareness of local needs and capacities, flexibility and participatory style, freedom from corruption" (Nelson 1995, 38–39).
[42] Wirth (1998, 62).

The coalition soon incorporated large development and environmental INGOs based in the United States and the United Kingdom – including Bank Information Center, Environmental Defense Fund, and Oxfam – some of which provided policy advice to the World Bank as members of a civil society consultation forum founded in 1982.[43] These organizations pursued multiple strategies to build support for their cause among member governments, including "parliamentary or congressional hearings, public forums, press conferences, lobbying key officials, letter-writing campaigns."[44] A key turning point came in 1992 with the publication of a damning independent review of the Narmada project – the Morse Study – and the leaking of an internal World Bank evaluation – the Wapenhans Report – that revealed an alarming recent deterioration in wider project performance.[45] A few months after the Morse Study was released, some 250 NGOs from 37 countries (including several Indian partners) published a full-page open letter in the *Financial Times*, the *New York Times*, and the *Washington Post* warning that if the World Bank failed to withdraw from the Narmada project, they would encourage donor countries to slash their contributions. American NGOs went a step further, seizing on the review's findings to successfully coax the United States Congress – with which they had been in close contact throughout the campaign – into using the threat of funding cuts to secure the World Bank's consent for an access-to-information policy and an inspection mechanism. Campaign members then worked directly with the Bank's Executive Board and staff to design the new accountability mechanisms.[46]

The receptiveness of the broader stakeholder community to demands for accountability owed much to the rigors of overseeing World Bank operations, which encompass all three of the hard-to-monitor governance tasks in Chapter 2's typology. The Narmada fiasco was pivotal to the reform effort because it revealed how little stakeholders – even close operational partners – really knew about the Bank's performance. Indeed, when Environmental Defense Fund attorney Lori Udall, who carefully followed the Bank's work, visited the Narmada Valley in the late 1980s, she was "aghast at the enormity of the human rights and environmental damage that was about to be committed."[47] Frustration about this state of affairs was explicitly aired at a congressional hearing on World Bank funding in May 1993, during which one NGO representative after another highlighted the obstacles to obtaining timely

---

[43] Covey (1998). This body, the World Bank-NGO Committee, was one of the first institutionalized mechanisms of civil society consultation in global governance.
[44] Wade (1997, 696).   [45] Morse and Berger (1992); Wapenhans (1992).
[46] Udall (1998, 413).   [47] Wade (2021, 286).

and accurate information about projects.[48] Speaking in support of an inspection mechanism, for instance, the National Wildlife Federation's director of international programs lamented that "NGOs, especially here in Washington, have attempted to monitor projects and to get information to our counterparts in the borrowing countries; but we, almost as much as the Bank staff, often lack first hand knowledge of the impacts of lending operations on the ground."[49]

SWA mechanisms introduced by the World Bank have been swiftly embraced by other multilateral development lenders. While diffusion processes, such as learning and emulation, are likely to have contributed to this trend, operational alliances have again been a decisive factor.[50] Civil society partners, for instance, were central protagonists in the adoption of access-to-information and inspection regimes by the Asian Development Bank (AsDB) and the IFC, which have the fourth and ninth highest average values of *Operational Alliances* over the full PIIP sample, respectively. In both cases, the reform process unfolded in a similar fashion to the World Bank's, with partners and local civil society groups drawing public attention to problematic projects – in particular the AsDB's Arun III hydroelectric project in Nepal and Theun Hinboun dam project in Laos and the IFC's Pangue dam project in Chile – before joining arms with INGOs from powerful shareholder countries to lobby for new accountability mechanisms.[51]

There is also evidence that concerns about institutional monitoring were a major source of stakeholder support for reform. The Nepali civil society groups that initiated the campaign against the Arun III project, for example, vociferously protested the AsDB's "[l]ack of timely disclosure of relevant and critical project documents and information," going as far as to pursue public interest litigation in the Supreme Court of Nepal to acquire them.[52] Similarly, activists targeting the Pangue project complained that its opaque design and execution prevented stakeholders from properly monitoring the IFC's work. According to one prominent indigenous leader, "They did everything under the table. Nothing with the people. Blind and deaf."[53] Partly in response to these concerns, the terms of reference for the IFC's inspection mechanism – the Office of the Compliance Advisor/Ombudsman's terms of reference – underscored that it would equip the institution with "strong in-house

[48] United States Congress (1993). [49] United States Congress (1993, 121).
[50] On the diffusion of SWA mechanisms, see Park (2014); Sommerer and Tallberg (2019).
[51] Asian Exchange for New Alternatives (1996); Hunter, Opaso, and Orellana (2003); Park (2005b, 2014).
[52] Asian Exchange for New Alternatives (1996, 250).
[53] Clark, Fox, and Treakle (2003, 125). Also see Park (2005a).

skills and adequate resources for environmental and social reviews and monitoring of projects."[54]

Intriguingly, the World Bank's accountability innovations have received a frostier reception at its "Bretton Woods Twin," the International Monetary Fund (IMF). While boasting a relatively robust evaluation mechanism – the Independent Evaluation Office – and comparable participation mechanisms to the World Bank, the Fund possesses a narrow access-to-information policy and no inspection system whatsoever. Interviewees from the IMF's secretariat and governing bodies mostly attributed these differences to the relative weakness of its operational partnerships with civil society, which, as one evaluation officer put it, "severely limited the constituency with both cause and means to battle for accountability reforms."[55] This explanation is consistent with in-depth studies of IMF–civil society relations. Jan Aart Scholte, for example, notes that "relatively few NGOs have given major priority specifically to the IMF over a sustained period of time"[56] and that "the 'civil society' that attends to the IMF has mainly involved a limited number of associations drawn from a narrow range of the social spectrum."[57] Yet, interviewees added, even these associations have enjoyed some success in pushing for SWA reforms to alleviate monitoring challenges. Several cited the example of the Independent Evaluation Office, which NGOs such as the Bretton Woods Project and Friends of the Earth had vigorously lobbied for to remedy the IMF's "high degree of secrecy" and failure to provide "any systematic way of examining [its] impact at the micro level."[58]

Consequences for Performance

How have SWA reforms impacted the performance of development finance institutions? Four sources of evidence point to both a positive effect and the plausibility of the information, engagement, and compliance pathways posited earlier. The first is quantitative performance data. Analyzing ratings of more than 20,000 projects financed by 12 multilateral and bilateral development agencies, Dan Honig, Bradley Parks, and I find that the adoption of access-to-information policies is associated with sizable improvements in performance, albeit only when accompanied by compliance-enhancing independent appeals mechanisms for denied requests.[59] In addition, we recover evidence of

---

[54] International Finance Corporation (1999, 1).
[55] Author interview #81 with IMF evaluation officer, May 15, 2018, Washington DC.
[56] Scholte (2002, 13).   [57] Scholte (2008, 18).   [58] Wood and Welch (1998).
[59] Honig, Lall, and Parks (2022). The analysis includes the IFAD ratings examined in Chapter 4. Our findings are robust to restricting the sample to multilateral agencies.

"project correction effects," whereby appeals bring about improvements to the specific projects they concern, as well as "shadow of the future effects," whereby staff more generally strengthen project design and implementation to forestall future requests and appeals that could reveal performance problems."[60]

Evidence of deterrent effects also emerges from analyses of project data by Mark Buntaine and by Daniel Nielson and Michael Tierney, which suggest that evaluation and inspection systems adopted by the World Bank and other multilateral development lenders have discouraged bureaucrats from pursuing environmentally hazardous projects that risk violating internal rules (in addition to being opposed by many stakeholders).[61] Recent studies by Benjamin Graham with Lynn Ta and (separately) Kelebogile Zvogbo delve further into the correction effect, showing how inspection mechanisms can serve as an instrument for identifying and remedying human rights violations by these institutions.[62]

Case studies shed corroborating light on the positive performance dividends of SWA reforms. Most examinations have focused on the World Bank Inspection Panel, whose pioneer status and significant scale and resources have attracted considerable attention in academic and policy circles. The general consensus is that, while suffering from some limitations in purview and authority, the Panel has elicited on-the-ground information that has improved project planning, monitoring, and execution as well as staff and government compliance with Bank policies.[63] These benefits are both corrective and anticipatory in nature: Stakeholder complaints have encouraged and enabled staff to not only fix existing project problems but also preempt possible future ones (a phenomenon known as "panel-proofing").[64] In addition, some scholars identify a "legitimation effect" linked to the panel's function of listening to and acknowledging claimants' grievances, which has fostered closer stakeholder engagement with the Bank and more widespread acceptance of its interventions.[65] Studies of more recent inspection mechanisms, such as the AsDB's Accountability Mechanism and the IFC's Office of the Compliance Advisor/Ombudsman, report similar legitimacy and participation benefits.[66]

---

[60] Honig, Lall, and Parks (2022, 16).
[61] Buntaine (2015, 2016); Nielson and Tierney (2003, 2005).
[62] Ta and Graham (2018); Zvogbo and Graham (2020).
[63] Notable collections of case studies include Alfreðsson and Ring (2001); Clark, Fox, and Treakle (2003); Wouters et al. (2015).
[64] Fox (2000).
[65] Fox (2002, 162). Also see Clark, Fox, and Treakle (2003); Fox (2000).
[66] Bradlow and Fourie (2011); Macdonald and Miller-Dawkins (2015); McIntyre and Nanwani (2019); Park (2017).

Case studies of other SWA mechanisms echo these conclusions. Access-to-information policies have been found to curb institutional inefficiencies, shore up perceived legitimacy, and deepen stakeholder participation, encouraging "input from local communities that will make ... projects better adapted to the conditions in the field and thus more effective."[67] Evaluation mechanisms, several studies report, play a key role in creating information "feedback loops" between institutions and stakeholders – critical for identifying and solving project problems – and in building public confidence in their work.[68] Participation mechanisms, in particular the World Bank's civil society consultation forums, have been linked to improvements in information exchange, collective learning, and decision-making quality.[69]

The third source of evidence, independent evaluations of SWA mechanisms, offers perhaps the most direct insight into their performance effects. The majority of these assessments again focus on inspection mechanisms, which they judge to have made a valuable contribution to correcting project problems, boosting adherence to bureaucratic protocols, and nurturing institutional learning.[70] One of the first comprehensive reviews of the Inspection Panel explicitly distinguished between its "deterrent effect" and "remedial effects," detecting signs of the former even before any cases had been adjudicated: "In fact, the mere presence of the Panel has contributed to making the Bank's operational staff more diligent in the observance of Bank policies. The usual zeal of presenting projects for Board approval in a manner and pace that meet the lending program's targets has been tempered by Management's greater concern with project implementation and by the zeal of the staff not to put the institution in the embarrassing position of being found in violation of its own policies and procedures."[71]

Assessments of evaluation and participation mechanisms also single out learning and compliance gains as key consequences.[72] The only dedicated appraisal of investigation regimes is the 2007 *Independent Panel Review of The World Bank Group Department of Institutional Integrity* conducted by a committee of high-level policymakers chaired by Paul Volcker. While recommending structural reforms to the Bank's investigation unit, the report highlighted "notable successes" in tackling

---

[67] Marínez (2013, 104). Also see McDonagh (2019); Nelson (2001).
[68] Buntaine (2016); Gaarder and Bartsch (2014); Gray (2014).
[69] Nelson (1995); Sondarjee (2020); Uhlin (2016).
[70] Asian Development Bank (2012); Savanas E Enseadas LDA (2020); Shihata (2000); Van Putten and Husain (2010); World Bank (2020).
[71] Shihata (2000, 236).
[72] For example, African Development Bank (2020); Asian Development Bank (2018); Kirk (2019); World Bank (2015, 2018).

institutional malfeasance, stressing "the critically important contribution that a coherent and forceful attack on corruption can and should make to the Bank-wide goal of facilitating economic development and reducing poverty."[73] Evaluations of transparency mechanisms have mostly been carried out by staff (rather than independent experts) and should thus be interpreted with caution. Nonetheless, they generally affirm the importance of free-flowing information for effective decision-making. One review of the World Bank's access-to-information policy, for instance, contends that "a sound, open Disclosure Policy is fundamental to fulfilling its many roles," including "to enhance the quality of its operations by engaging with the development community" and "to provide its employees with all the information they need to perform their duties."[74]

Finally, interviews with 15 officials, four state delegates, and five nongovernmental stakeholders offer firsthand, albeit less systematic, evidence of performance benefits.[75] When asked whether SWA mechanisms have benefited the performance of the institution in question, 23 of the 24 interviewees responded affirmatively. I subsequently invited these individuals to elaborate on the reason for this positive impact. In keeping with their respective roles, bureaucrats tended to concentrate on the generation of operationally relevant information, state delegates on increased bureaucratic compliance, and nongovernmental stakeholders on the higher quality of policy decisions. In one memorable anecdote, an economist from the Inter-American Development Bank (IADB) recounted how an access-to-information request regarding a Brazilian infrastructure project co-financed by the institution led to the discovery of a dangerous engineering miscalculation, forcing the contracted construction firm to frantically redraw its blueprints in a matter of hours. "If we didn't have a disclosure policy," the official reflected, "we simply wouldn't have caught the error. The project could have been an environmental and humanitarian catastrophe."[76]

UN Development Institutions

Adoption of SWA Reforms
Despite their relatively homogeneous governance arrangements, UN development institutions are marked by substantially wider variation in

---

[73] Volcker et al. (2007, 18,3).   [74] World Bank (2009, 2-3).

[75] Six institutions were discussed: the AsDB, the European Bank for Reconstruction and Development (EBRD), the European Development Fund (EDF), the Inter-American Development Bank (IADB), IFAD, and the World Bank. The interviews are listed in Appendix C.

[76] Author interview #44 with IADB economist, May 22, 2018, Washington, DC.

the strength of SWA mechanisms. At one pole are the United Nations Development Programme (UNDP) and the United Nations Capital Development Fund (UNCDF), which have a shared organizational structure headed by the former's administrator (i.e., chief of staff) and Executive Board. Under this arrangement, accountability reforms enacted by the UNDP usually extend to the UNCDF. Over the past 25 years, both institutions have introduced all five types of SWA mechanisms in my dataset, establishing particularly robust transparency, evaluation, and investigation regimes. As of 2018, their *SWA Composite* scores ranked 10th and 12th in the PIIP sample, respectively. At the opposite pole, the United Nations Conference on Trade and Development (UNCTAD) and the United Nations Industrial Development Organization (UNIDO) score well below the sample average, ranking 34th and 32nd in 2018, respectively. Neither institution possesses an access-to-information policy or a powerful evaluation, inspection, or investigation mechanism, and UNIDO offers nongovernmental stakeholders negligible access to its policy apparatus.

The principal impulse for SWA reforms in the UNDP and the UNCDF has been pressures from civil society partners, who have skillfully assembled an expansive and spirited coalition for accountability encompassing small community associations as well as prominent development INGOs. The first reform campaign was launched in the mid-1990s, around a decade after the UNDP began enlisting NGOs to assist it in project design and implementation, and called on the two institutions to follow the lead of multilateral development banks in introducing an access-to-information policy.[77] Assisted by Bank Information Center and other Washington-based advocacy groups, partners leveraged a combination of lobbying and information dissemination tactics to secure the backing of the United States and other OECD nations, which had been pressing for greater transparency and efficiency in the UN secretariat since the late 1980s.[78] The UNDP promptly yielded to the enlarged coalition's demands, accepting its proposals as the basis for an official *Information Disclosure Policy* published in 1997.[79]

The late 1990s saw a sharp surge in operational alliances with NGOs, as the UNDP formally recognized collaboration with civil society actors as part of its mandate and permitted them to participate in all phases

[77] Author interview #87 with UNDP evaluation officer, May 21, 2018, New York.
[78] Saladin and Van Dyke (1998).
[79] Not by coincidence, a 1996 invitation for staff comments on the proposed policy emphasized how it "will enable UNDP partners (UN Agencies, governments, CSOs including NGOs, private sector) to learn how UNDP works and help the UNDP cooperate more effectively with its multiple partners." Wirth and Devarajan (1996, Annex D).

of the project cycle.[80] Emboldened by their swelling ranks and influence within the Programme, partners again joined forces with development INGOs to lobby for an institutionalized mechanism of dialogue between civil society and senior management. This campaign culminated in the early 2000s with the creation of the Civil Society Organization Advisory Committee, a body bringing together diverse citizens and NGOs to provide policy guidance to the secretariat, as well as a multitude of local and regional Civil Society Organization committees. In recent years, the coalition has turned its attention to other kinds of SWA mechanisms, pressuring the UNDP to strengthen the independence of its Evaluation Office and introduce an inspection mechanism. These efforts bore fruit in 2014, when the Evaluation Office was converted into the Independent Evaluation Office, which reports solely to the Executive Board, and the Social and Environmental Compliance Review and Stakeholder Response Mechanism – an outlet for stakeholders to raise complaints about the UNDP's social and environmental performance – was inaugurated.[81]

The challenge of monitoring the UNDP's projects and implementation services for partner IFIs, which are administered by more than 170 country offices, appears to have been an important motivation for reform efforts. The campaign for an access-to-information policy was a "direct response to UNDP's paltry disclosure of project information,"[82] concerns about which were explicitly acknowledged in a 1996 study commissioned by the Programme to explore such a mechanism.[83] Similar worries were articulated in public consultations on proposals for a civil society consultation mechanism in the late 1990s, during which NGO representatives repeatedly cited monitoring difficulties in justification for demanding deeper engagement with the UNDP. In one workshop held in Poland in 1997, for instance, they exhorted the Programme to provide "enhanced CSO access to information" and "promote greater popular participation and information-sharing at all levels of the development process," stressing that "[i]t is vital for CSOs to know about UNDP's work."[84]

---

[80] United Nations Development Programme (2000).
[81] United Nations Development Programme (2014, 7).
[82] Author interview #91 with UNDP evaluation officer, May 22, 2018, New York.
[83] Wirth and Devarajan (1996). One consequence was a growing torrent of informal information requests from the public, as the study's opening sentence noted: "Recently there has been a perception that the number and sensitivity of unsolicited requests from outsiders for information generated or held by UNDP has increased. This, in turn, has generated an awareness both within and outside the organisation of the need for UNDP to regularise its public information and documentation disclosure policies and practises" (p. 1).
[84] United Nations Development Programme (1997).

UNCTAD and UNIDO have faced far weaker pressures for accountability. Staff interviewees unanimously ascribed the lack of demand for reform to the institutions' smaller network of operational alliances with civil society groups. One UNCTAD planning adviser expressed this point through a direct comparison with the UNDP: "UNCTAD has traditionally maintained its distance from civil society, and we've been criticized – perhaps rightly so – for failing to involve NGOs sufficiently in our work. That's the main reason, in my opinion, why we haven't experienced the same external stimulus for accountability as peer agencies like UNDP, whose civil society collaborators lobbied hard and cultivated broad support for transparency and oversight reforms."[85] This explanation is consistent with PIIP data: The mean value of *Operational Alliances* during the sample period is in the top third of the distribution for the UNDP and the UNCDF but in the bottom third for UNCTAD and UNIDO.

In the few instances they *have* arisen, pressures for accountability in UNCTAD and UNIDO have been sparked by episodes of poor performance rather than partner mobilization. Around the same time as the Narmada campaign, both institutions were gripped by existential crises precipitated by years of policy gridlock, wasteful spending, and underperforming programs, prompting some large donor nations to demand that they improve their accountability and effectiveness or be abolished.[86] Lacking broad-based and sustained support from stakeholders, however, this ultimatum was easily brushed aside. According to multiple NGO representatives, accountability reforms were not a high priority for them because UNCTAD and UNIDO's principal functions – supporting interstate negotiations and providing technical assistance – were already subject to close public scrutiny. One senior manager in a major international development foundation described UNCTAD's secretariat as a "headquarters-centric entity that operates in plain and clear view of states and stakeholder groups in Geneva," with the upshot that new accountability mechanisms "would add very little value from an oversight perspective."[87]

Consequences for Performance

The ramifications of the UNDP and the UNCDF's SWA reforms have received comparatively little attention from scholars and practitioners, most likely because of their comparatively recent adoption and low public profile. To my knowledge, no quantitative analyses of their effects

[85] Author interview #23 with UNCTAD planning adviser, June 7, 2012, Geneva.
[86] Brummer (1996); Fazey (1995).
[87] Author interview #30 with Aga Khan Foundation senior manager, June 11, 2012, Geneva.

on performance have been conducted, and only a handful of case studies and evaluations have considered them.

Case studies, as before, point to a tangible performance payoff driven by the hypothesized information, engagement, and compliance mechanisms. Civil society advisory committees, one concludes, have "proven to be of major importance to the UNDP," encouraging stakeholder buy-in to projects and promoting "key cooperation principles, which include trust, horizontality, cooperative agenda-setting and individual accountability."[88] The access-to-information policy shared by the UNDP and the UNCDF has been deemed an important base of institutional legitimacy in the eyes of stakeholders.[89] A series of technical commentaries on the UNDP's Evaluation Office and Independence Evaluation Office by Juha Uitto, a former employee, detail their contribution to solving pressing development challenges by helping staff "understand what works, why, and under what circumstances," knowledge that is "very helpful for promoting learning and improving future performance."[90] Similar informational and epistemic benefits have been highlighted in studies of the UNDP's investigation mechanism, which is managed by its Office of Audit and Investigation.[91]

Independent reviews of the UNDP's transparency, evaluation, and participation mechanisms also bear out theoretical expectations. After initially suffering from implementation issues, the *Information Disclosure Policy* has been applauded in comparative donor evaluations for enhancing efficiency, learning, and stakeholder trust throughout the project cycle.[92] The 2007 *Global Accountability Report* described the Civil Society Organization Advisory Committee as "instrumental in providing the UNDP with advice and strategic guidance, supporting and monitoring implementation of key policy and advocacy efforts, and piloting strategic initiatives," including "policies of engagement with civil society, the private sector, indigenous peoples, the public information and disclosure policy, and the risks and benefits of partnership with the private sector, in particular multinational corporations."[93] A consultant-led assessment of the Committee published the following year strongly

---

[88] Popovski (2010, 35).   [89] Dimitropoulos (2008).
[90] Uitto (2016, 445). Also see Uitto (2014*a*,*b*).
[91] Naidoo (2020); Naidoo and Soares (2020). This was previously called the Office of Audit and Performance Review.
[92] See, in particular, MOPAN's 2012 and 2017 evaluations and the 2012 Australian Multilateral Assessment (links are provided in Appendix B.2).
[93] Lloyd, Oatham, and Hammer (2007, 35).

reiterated these contributions (while acknowledging that limitations in its mandate had prevented it from making an even greater impact).[94]

Peer assessments of the UNDP's Evaluation Office by the United Nations Evaluation Group (UNEG) and the OECD's Development Assistance Committee (DAC) in 2005 and 2013 laud its rigor and professionalism, deeming its outputs "credible, valid and useful for learning and strategy formation in the organization."[95] Expert appraisals of the Programme's evaluation policy framework in 2014 and 2019 commend its clarity, integration into the project cycle, and insulation from political pressures (particularly since the transition to the Independent Evaluation Office), features that ensure "evaluations are used to inform the design of UNDP programmers, contributing to learning and to the reputation of UNDP as a transparent and learning organization."[96] These advantages are found to extend fully to the UNCDF and other institutions covered by the framework.

Lastly, material from interviews with two UNDP officials, two UNCDF officials, two delegates to the UNDP Executive Board, and four nongovernmental stakeholders paint a similar picture. All 10 interviewees gave a positive response to the question of whether SWA mechanisms had improved performance in the institution under discussion. When asked to consider the causal mechanism, novel project information, the emergence of learning feedback loops, and more enlightened policy decisions were mentioned most frequently. Compliance effects were, on the whole, viewed as less significant than in IFI counterparts: The Social and Environmental Compliance Review and Stakeholder Response Mechanism only became operational in 2015, rendering its impact difficult to ascertain, and UNDP projects are associated with weaker incentives for recipient government noncompliance than IFI interventions, which are typically larger, more far-reaching, and subject to broader bureaucratic discretion. Even so, one UNCDF program officer argued that compliance improvements were merely more *discreet* than other kinds of performance benefits:

Unless you're there in the field, it can be hard to see how accountability reforms have changed behavior. I've personally witnessed country directors taking greater care in designing and implementing projects to make sure they don't contravene internal rules or inadvertently harm local communities. They've become more conscientious, often looking over their shoulder ... And it's not only on our side that compliance has improved. Recipient governments see us as a more open, participatory, and legitimate institution, and that makes them more willing

---

[94] United Nations Development Programme (2008).
[95] Cole et al. (2005, 4); Barnard et al. (2013).
[96] United Nations Development Programme (2019, 5); Le Groupe-Conseil Baastel ltée (2014).

to buy in to our work and hold up their end of the bargain. In the past, it hasn't always been easy to get national authorities to follow through on the investments – money, equipment, human resources, time, etc. – that they've promised us.[97]

Conclusion

This chapter opened by asking whether international institutions can be simultaneously effective and accountable – the "million-dollar question of global governance," in one UN official's reckoning. The main argument of this book seemed to entail an irreconcilable opposition between these two normatively and practically significant characteristics: If de facto policy autonomy furnishes an essential buffer against the kinds of opportunistic governmental interventions my framework identifies as the foremost threat to successful performance outcomes, institutions can presumably either perform well or be held to account – but not both.

I have made the case, theoretically and empirically, for a more complex and subtle relationship between institutional performance and accountability. The two variables are neither always friends nor always foes; their association depends, above all, on the manner in which accountability is institutionalized. If manifested solely in state control of the policy process – the traditional, or first-wave, form of institutionalization – accountability may indeed come at the expense of effectiveness. If expressed through a more expansive set of procedures for enabling diverse public and private stakeholders to acquire information on, engage with, and participate in institutions – SWA mechanisms – its relationship with performance will assume a more positive tenor. This is because institutions that boast a dense and eclectic network of strong operational alliances and that perform easily concealable governance tasks – institutions that, I previously argued, tend to enjoy high levels of de facto policy autonomy – experience more robust pressures to embrace second-wave modes of accountability. Furthermore, the operation of SWA mechanisms yields independent gains in performance by helping bureaucrats to detect, fix, and learn from operational problems; by enriching the informational and epistemic basis of decision-making; and by enhancing bureaucratic and governmental compliance with policies.

A selection of original mixed-methods evidence corroborates the core macro- and micro-level implications of this argument. Analyzing an expanded version of the PIIP, I find that the quantity, depth, and breadth of operational alliances and the exercise of hard-to-monitor

---

[97] Author interview #97 with UNCDF program officer, May 23, 2018, New York.

governance tasks strongly predict the adoption of five major types of SWA mechanisms. In addition, there is a positive association between mechanism strength and donor performance ratings that does not appear to be an artifact of reverse causation from the latter to the former. A qualitative probe of PIIP institutions in the issue area of economic development indicates the plausibility of the posited causal mechanisms connecting SWA mechanisms, operational alliances, governance tasks, and performance outcomes.

The "million-dollar question," it turns out, has neither a straightforward nor an entirely heartening answer. The customary channel through which states have exercised accountability *does* stand in tension with the discretion institutions need to realize sustained and efficient progress toward their objectives. Yet effective performance *is* compatible with more modern accountability mechanisms that engage and empower a broader gamut of institutional stakeholders. What is more, these structures can reinforce and complement the benefits of de facto policy autonomy, laying the foundations for even more desirable performance outcomes. The theoretical and practical implications of trading off circumscribed state control of the policy apparatus against more effective performance and more robust SWA structures are discussed in more detail in the next, concluding chapter.

7 The Politics of Performance

Contributions and Implications

> With every day, and from both sides of my intelligence, the moral and the intellectual, I thus drew steadily nearer to that truth, by whose partial discovery I have been doomed to such a dreadful shipwreck: that man is not truly one, but truly two.
> – Robert Louis Stevenson, *Strange Case of Dr Jekyll and Mr Hyde*[1]

The performance of international institutions is fundamentally political. This is not obvious from popular characterizations of faceless international bureaucrats fervently enforcing arcane regulations from glass and concrete fortresses, far removed from either the governments that delegated them authority or the ordinary citizens who are affected by their decisions. In the eyes of some scholars, this zeal for formalities causes institutions to routinely underperform, as bureaucrats "become obsessed with their own rules at the expense of their primary missions in ways that produce inefficient and self-defeating outcomes."[2] For others, the roots of institutional failure lie in insulation from state control, which provides cover for bureaucrats to indulge their personal whims and appetites – whether for a larger budget, additional turf, or more generous fringe benefits – rather than diligently executing the tasks assigned to them. Both perspectives suggest that performance problems arise when "institutional Frankensteins" break free from the chains tethered to them by their state creators.

In this book, I have argued that the opportunistic behavior that imperils institutional ambitions comes not from bureaucrats but from states themselves – the very actors, somewhat paradoxically, who bring institutions into being and instill these aspirations in them. Any plausible set of bureaucratic preferences is not only furthered by effective performance but likely, thanks to processes of self-selection and socialization, to encompass an institution's mission. States, on the other hand, face powerful incentives to interfere with and capture institutions in defense of parochial interests – typically to the detriment of agreed-

---

[1] Stevenson (2006 [1886], 52).   [2] Barnett and Finnemore (2004, 3).

upon objectives. Since the strategic calculus facing states changes over time, this temptation can be difficult to anticipate: The highest payoff from institutionalized cooperation is often attained by pursuing collective interests before institutions are established but more individualistic interests thereafter. The monsters we should fear, my theoretical approach implies, are not institutional Frankensteins but *Jekyll and Hyde states*.

The time-inconsistent character of state preferences need not spell doom for institutions, however. Rather, it points to the importance of steadfastly deflecting and repelling particularistic interventions in the policy process. In the long run, the ensuing gains in performance tend to reinforce policy autonomy by raising the costs of opportunism for states – in terms of both domestic political support and forgone benefits from effective performance – thereby thrusting institutions toward a high-autonomy, high-performance equilibrium. Unfortunately, mirror-image feedback processes can condemn captured institutions with deteriorating performance to further losses of discretion, plunging them into a low-autonomy, low-performance equilibrium.

How and from where, though, does policy autonomy emerge? Countering another widely held view, I have maintained that the answer is not institutional design: Due to the absence of reliable mechanisms for enforcing formal governance rules, it is de facto, not merely de jure, influence in the policy process on which success and failure hinge. The origins of de facto policy autonomy instead reside in two characteristics that institutions cultivate, often inconspicuously and discreetly, as they endeavor to meet the operational demands of their mandate. The first is an expansive complex of operational partnerships with actors above and below the state, which encourages the formation of wide-ranging and enduring stakeholder coalitions for autonomy. The second is the exercise of governance tasks that are costly for states to oversee, which places them at an informational disadvantage vis-à-vis international bureaucrats that hampers their ability to attain desired policy outcomes. In short, genuine independence is fashioned with the *hand of alliances* and the *cloak of stealth*.

Having fleshed out this theoretical framework in Chapter 2, I set about testing and substantiating its observable implications. To this end, I devised a multistage, multimethod research design that sought to combine the distinctive inferential advantages of quantitative and qualitative analysis. In the first stage, presented in Chapter 3, I undertook statistical tests of the theory's macro-level propositions with the aid of the Performance of International Institutions Project (PIIP), a new dataset comprising performance ratings of 54 major institutions from a recent wave of rigorous donor evaluations. The predicted relationships between variables of theoretical interest received robust support. Performance ratings were positively and strongly associated with a survey-based measure of de facto policy autonomy, with suggestive evidence of reciprocal causal effects that flow primarily from the latter variable to the former. There was little connection, in contrast, between a rules based measure of de jure policy autonomy and either de facto policy autonomy – despite the almost identical construction of the two variables – or performance ratings. De facto policy autonomy had a considerably stronger relationship with (1) the number, depth, and breadth of operational alliances with non-state actors; and (2) the discharge of three common governance tasks with high monitoring costs for states: designing policy interventions, implementing field operations, and allocating material resources.

The second stage of the investigation "zoomed in," probing the micro-level behavioral, strategic, informational, and structural processes posited by the theory. Leveraging a most similar systems design, I conducted two comparative case studies of PIIP institutions with alike characteristics but unalike levels of performance and de facto policy autonomy (i.e., the key dependent and explanatory variables). Chapter 4 examined the three core institutions of the global food security regime: the Food and Agriculture Organization (FAO) (low autonomy, low performance), the World Food Programme (WFP) (high autonomy, high performance), and the International Fund for Agricultural Development (IFAD) (high autonomy, high performance). Chapter 5 turned to four influential global health agencies: the World Health Organization (WHO) (low autonomy, low performance), the Joint United Nations Programme on HIV/AIDS (UNAIDS) (low autonomy, low performance), Gavi, the Vaccine Alliance (high autonomy, high performance), and the Global Fund to Fight AIDS, Tuberculosis and Malaria (GFATM) (high autonomy, high performance). Figure 7.1 plots each institution's mean value of the de facto policy autonomy and aggregate performance indices constructed in Chapter 3. The tight clustering of institutions around the identity $(x = y)$ line points to the plausibility of this book's central theoretical contention.

Applying process-tracing and narrative techniques to a rich array of qualitative sources, including key informant interviews and archival records, the case comparisons revealed several theory-affirming patterns. Among the most notable were states, especially those with the greatest capabilities, prioritizing collective interests at the design stage but particularistic interests once institutions begin their operations; bureaucrats

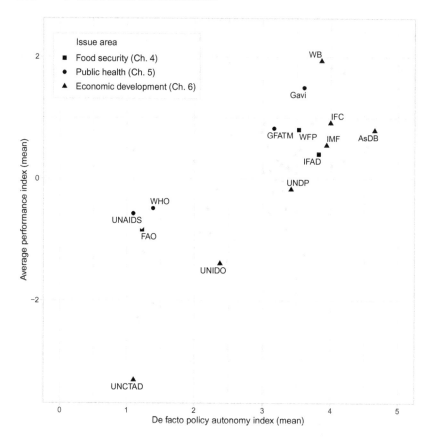

Figure 7.1 Performance and de facto policy autonomy: The cases examined

Notes: Values of both variables are averaged across all years in which donor performance ratings have been issued. Gray diamonds represent other institutions in the PIIP dataset.

exhibiting a stronger and more resolute commitment to institutional goals, even when this pits them in opposition to states; changes in the political and opportunity costs of capture spurring feedback effects from performance to de facto policy autonomy (in both positive and negative directions); hard-to-monitor governance tasks handing bureaucrats a persistent informational advantage that impedes top-down oversight and management of the policy apparatus; and deep and extensive networks of operational partnerships catalyzing broad-based coalitions for autonomy that mitigate capture by equipping institutions with information, expertise, and material resources and by building domestic political support for state forbearance.

In the final stage of the research design, the subject of Chapter 6, I explored the implications of the previous findings for another crucial attribute of international institutions, namely, their accountability. If good performance requires insulation from government meddling, one might reason, it must come at the expense of robust accountability; to wit, institutions cannot be at once effective and accountable. I disputed this logic, drawing attention to the multiplicity of modern accountability structures – from access-to-information policies to grievance redress systems – that do not entail or require state domination of the policy process. I advanced the argument that the strength of these "second-wave" accountability (SWA) mechanisms is positively associated with performance for two reasons: They are more likely to be adopted by institutions with the two operational sources of de facto policy autonomy described earlier (i.e., alliances and stealth); and, once introduced, they deliver informational, epistemic, and compliance benefits that independently enhance performance. Continuing the mixed-methods approach of prior chapters, I corroborated my claims with statistical tests drawing on original data on five different types of SWA mechanisms as well as a plausibility probe of institutions in the issue area of economic development (see Figure 7.1), the birthplace of many accountability innovations. Thus, depending on the specific means by which accountability is institutionalized, it can be *either* a friend or a foe of effectiveness.

In a nutshell, *Making International Institutions Work* presents a systematic theoretical and empirical analysis of differences in the performance of international institutions, offering insights and evidence that shed light on a wide variety of cases, policy domains, and eras. In doing so, it yields implications not only for scholarship and intellectual discourse but also for policy and practice. In the remainder of this closing chapter, I summarize the book's contributions to international relations (IR), political science, and other areas of the social sciences, before drawing out its principal lessons for improving institutional performance. I conclude by discussing how the findings speak to a number of important ongoing policy debates, including over emerging challenges to the liberal institutional order and the effectiveness of global governance during periods of crisis (such as the recent pandemic).

Contributions to Scholarship

International Relations and Political Science

The book's argument and findings bear most directly on political science and, within it, on IR and international political economy (IPE), fields in which the behavior and effects of international institutions have been a central focus. My theoretical framework complements yet diverges in important ways from two leading schools of IR and IPE thought on how institutions function, namely, the realist and the rogue-agency perspectives (described in Chapter 1). While concurring with realists that power is a key driving force in institutions and that states are major actors "pulling the strings," my framework denies that international bureaucrats are mere puppets at the end of these cords. While embracing the rogue-agency insight that institutions are thinking and willing actors that may fail to do what states wish, it does not see such defiance as an obstacle to effectiveness. Recognizing that, once institutions come into existence, states' interests often stray further from the original objectives of cooperation than bureaucrats', I posit that a high degree of de facto policy autonomy is critical for keeping institutions on the path envisaged by their creators.

At a more general level, the book underlines the need to move beyond the pervasive functionalist assumption – first given currency by the neoliberal institutionalist research program – that institutions produce "efficient" cooperative outcomes for states. Only by renewing the tradition of close institutional scrutiny and appraisal initiated in the early postwar era, the findings suggest, can we fully comprehend the consequences of rules-based international cooperation. A departure from functionalist thinking entails far-reaching implications for conventional understandings of the emergence, functioning, and evolution of institutions. If states cannot accurately anticipate how institutions will perform in the future, for instance, it may be more appropriate to analyze decisions about institutional creation and change as products of bounded than neoclassical rationality.[3] Indeed, without acknowledging the possibility of imperfect information, cognitive limitations, and finite time horizons, it is difficult to make sense of the countless reversals in states' foreign policy preferences – let alone the failure of other nations and stakeholders to foresee these shifts – documented throughout this book. Rather than simply inferring institutions' effectiveness from their existence, the Jekyll and Hyde problem invites us to carefully reflect on

---

[3] Jupille, Mattli, and Snidal (2013); Odell (2002); Poulsen (2015).

the conditions under which they successfully address the cooperation problems that motivated their creation.

Functionalist logic also informs two influential bodies of scholarship that have emerged out of the neoliberal institutionalist research agenda. The first is the burgeoning literature on rational institutional design, which explores how specific rules, structures, and principles – rather than institutions in general – mitigate cooperation dilemmas. A central theme of this book has been the strikingly limited impact of formal governance arrangements on how institutions truly function. The weak association between de jure and de facto policy autonomy in the PIIP sample calls both for a more sustained theoretical and empirical focus on the actual rather than written characteristics of institutions and for further research on the circumstances in which design and practice *do* coincide. Furthermore, it adds empirical weight to the fledgling research program on informal governance in IR and IPE, which emphasizes the disconnect between formal rules and real-world behavior but has yet to offer systematic cross-institutional evidence for its claims.[4] On the theoretical front, the book extends this work by exploring its implications for institutional performance issues and by explaining why – contrary to Stone's important argument that informal governance is premised on an inter-temporal "bargain" between powerful and weaker nations – rule violations are often routine, unanticipated, and heavily contested.[5]

Also built on functionalist foundations are the literatures on delegation and principal–agent theory, which views deviant behavior by bureaucrats as the central strategic problem to be "solved" in institutionalized cooperation. By highlighting the incentives for state principals to intervene in the policy process for particularistic ends and for bureaucratic agents to resist such intrusions for broader communal purposes, my analysis brings to light a neglected strategic dimension of delegation – a dimension that raises questions about the validity of conventional applications of principal–agent theory to international institutions. Investigating how the severity of the Jekyll and Hyde problem varies across issue areas and time periods – a function, my framework implies, of available mechanisms for enforcing policymaking rules, uncertainty about future threats to national interests, and the costs of "recontracting" – is a promising avenue for further research.

My analysis of the operational bases of de facto policy autonomy draws perhaps unexpected connections between IR scholarship on institutional

---

[4] Stone (2013); Westerwinter, Abbott, and Biersteker (2021).
[5] Stone (2008, 2011).

authority, functionality, and engagement with non-state actors. The political implications of the operative tasks undertaken by institutions have generally been underresearched and undertheorized, as noted in Chapter 2, and the few attempts to typologize or comprehensively map them have not sought to identify features that might allow for discretion in their execution.[6] Studies of the sources of institutional independence have posited a range of explanatory variables – from issue scope to path dependence to power asymmetries between states – yet have given little consideration to task characteristics.[7]

The notion that institutional autonomy can be enhanced by ties with external stakeholders – that, in a sense, independence from one set of actors can spring from dependence on another – may strike some readers as particularly surprising. Scholarship on the role of non-state actors in global governance has focused mainly on their capacity to influence institutional activities and outcomes in line with their aims, rarely exploring their mutual interests or operational links with international bureaucrats. Moreover, prominent theoretical approaches in the field of American politics, such as statism[8] and congressional dominance,[9] treat stakeholder involvement in administrative policy processes as a constraint on bureaucratic discretion. This view is not universal, however: Perspectives such as neopluralism[10] and Daniel Carpenter's theory of executive agency autonomy in the Progressive Era[11] highlight how engagement with constituents can *expand* bureaucrats' room for maneuver, for instance, by strengthening political support for their preferred policies and unleashing countervailing forces against special interests. My argument suggests that autonomy-enhancing effects prevail when political principals show a propensity to opportunistically interfere in decision-making processes after delegating authority; when formal safeguards on institutional autonomy – if they exist – are fragile; and when bureaucrats can benefit from operational collaboration with diverse stakeholders in discharging their tasks. Since these conditions are common in the international domain, autonomy tends to flourish when institutions plant deep roots in the soil of society.

Finally, the book offers a fresh perspective on the high-stakes debate over the relationship between performance and accountability in global

---

[6] E.g. Abbott and Snidal (1998); Cogan, Hurd, and Johnstone (2016); Koremenos (2016).

[7] Haftel and Thompson (2006); Hooghe and Marks (2015); Hooghe, Lenz, and Marks (2019).

[8] Krasner (1978); Nordlinger (1981); Skocpol (2006).

[9] McCubbins and Schwartz (1984); McCubbins, Noll, and Weingast (1987); Weingast and Moran (1983).

[10] Berry (1977); McFarland (1984); Wilson (1980).   [11] Carpenter (2001).

governance. Much of this conversation has been plagued by a lack of conceptual clarity, with studies that suggest a negative association[12] focusing on different – typically more traditional – accountability mechanisms to those that point to a positive association.[13] The argument developed in Chapter 6 illuminates a path to reconciling these apparently conflicting perspectives – while presenting a muscular challenge to the rogue-agency notion that accountability improves performance by limiting the scope for deviant bureaucratic behavior. The key, my approach suggests, lies in a more nuanced understanding of how accountability is institutionalized at the international level: Whereas traditional accountability structures premised on state control of the policy machinery can give rise to pernicious and enduring performance problems, modern mechanisms for facilitating stakeholder monitoring, participation, and influence go hand in hand with sustained effectiveness.

Economics, Public Administration, Law, and Other Disciplines

Lifting our gaze from IR, IPE, and political science, this book contributes to long-standing research programs – and paves the foundations for new ones – in a host of other social science disciplines. As major domestic governance functions have migrated to the international level in recent decades, an analogous shift in scholarly sights could yield significant payoffs for the study of institutional performance and related subjects.

Variation in the performance of international institutions has implications for widely studied topics in economics, including the efficacy of foreign aid, the consequences of globalization, the design and functioning of (non-market) organizations, and the structure of international trade, finance, and monetary relations. Perhaps most pertinent is the sizable literature on the provision – and underprovision – of public goods at the regional and global levels. The bulk of this research has focused on conceptualizing public goods above the nation-state, theorizing free-rider and other coordination problems among states, and identifying gaps in supply. Explanations for the latter mostly emphasize structural characteristics of the public good or issue area in question, with international institutions assumed to be an inevitable – and socially efficient – byproduct of overcoming obstacles to cooperation. While acknowledging the potential for underperformance, the few studies that have explicitly analyzed institutions as public goods providers have

---

[12] For example, Cottarelli (2005); Horeth (1999); Koppell (2010).
[13] For example, Chesterman (2008); Woods (2006); Zürn (2004).

stopped short of seriously investigating its sources.[14] Conceding that the overall record of global governance is "spotty," for example, the environmental economist Scott Barrett concludes his noted work *Why Cooperate?* by laying down a challenge for fellow scholars: "Understanding how and when international institutions can [improve state behavior] is fundamental to our future success in supplying global public goods."[15]

Institutional performance has received more direct attention in the field of public administration, albeit almost exclusively in the domestic context (see Chapter 1). Over the past 15 years, public administration scholars have become increasingly aware that their long-standing interests in the structure of government organizations, processes of management and decision-making, and bureaucratic behavior are as germane to international institutions as to local and national authorities.[16] To date, research on "international public administrations" has extended two lines of traditional disciplinary inquiry: the form and extent of bureaucratic autonomy;[17] and the determinants of administrative decision-making.[18] The question of whether bureaucrats *succeed* in realizing administrative goals – another central concern of the field – has received surprisingly little attention. My framework provides a foundation for addressing this oversight, offering a novel account of how international public administrations cultivate independence and analyzing, theoretically and empirically, the implications for differences in institutional performance.

Major branches of sociology and, to a lesser extent, anthropology are devoted to the study of organizational behavior. As in public administration, though, scholars have largely limited their horizons to the domestic realm. In a 1988 *International Organization* article, the sociologists Gayl Ness and Steven Brechin lamented that "[t]he gap between the study of international organizations and the sociology of organizations is deep and persistent."[19] In a follow-up piece 25 years later, they noted "growing convergence" between the two areas but concluded, much to their disappointment, that "sociologists have failed to more fully develop a sociology of [international organizations]."[20] They linked this lack of

[14] Barrett (2007); Ferroni and Mody (2002); Kindleberger (1986); Rodrik (2020).
[15] Barrett (2007, 191).
[16] One recent literature review concedes: "There is no denying that [public administration] has only belatedly 'discovered' international bureaucracies as an object of study" (Ege et al. 2022, 3).
[17] Bauer, Knill, and Eckhard (2016); Bayerlein, Knill, and Steinebach (2020); Knill and Bauer (2016).
[18] Bauer and Ege (2012); Mele, Anderfuhren-Biget, and Varone (2016); Trondal et al. (2013).
[19] Ness and Brechin (1988, 245).
[20] Brechin and Ness (2013, 14, 16). Along similar lines, one of the few general ethnographic treatments of international institutions expresses surprise at how long it has

progress to "sociologists increasingly viewing organizations as simply organizations regardless of their placement in specific typologies, such as national or international, business, nonprofit, or public governmental," a conflation that risks overlooking "the more unique forces shaping specific IGOs."[21] My framework, in particular its analysis of the Jekyll and Hyde problem, speaks directly to this concern, highlighting how distinctive informational, structural, and – above all – *political* features of the international context influence IGO behavior. Further exploration and systematization of these characteristics can contribute to the development of a fully fledged sociology of international institutions.

Lastly, legal scholars, joined in recent decades by political scientists, have vigorously debated the effectiveness of international law. The general consensus is that treaties, conventions, regulations, and other international legal instruments *do* independently and meaningfully shape state behavior, an impact attributed to an interconnected cluster of factors including their precision, coherence, perceived legitimacy, and embeddedness in domestic judicial systems and processes.[22] Though in some cases expressing skepticism about the evidence behind this conclusion,[23] political scientists have broadly concurred, with some identifying additional causal pathways to state compliance, such as changes in domestic policy agendas, legislation, and political mobilization;[24] the generation of electorally salient compliance information;[25] and the internalization of international norms.[26] Neither camp, however, has given serious attention to the effectiveness of the *institutions* that codify, maintain, and apply international law. As demonstrated in the case studies, failure to properly discharge these functions has profound consequences not only for levels of state compliance but also for the number, type, and quality of legal instruments that are developed and promulgated in the first place. My framework provides a starting point for filling this gap, again underscoring the value of cross-disciplinary dialogue and fertilization in the study of institutional performance.

Lessons for Policy and Practice

Although *Making International Institutions Work* was motivated by an intellectual puzzle, its subject matter is inherently and resolutely practical. By enhancing our understanding of differences in the performance

---

taken "ethnography to make a transition in its subject matter, from people on the margins of states and empires to the 'modern' institutions that sometimes exercised power in those settings" (Niezen and Sapignoli 2017, 4).

[21] Brechin and Ness (2013, 16, 33).

[22] Seminal contributions include Chayes and Chayes (1993); Franck (1990); Henkin (1968); Koh (1996).

[23] Downs, Rocke, and Barsoom (1996).   [24] Simmons (2009).

[25] Dai (2005, 2007).   [26] Checkel (2001); Risse, Ropp, and Sikkink (1999).

of international institutions, the book offers theoretically and empirically grounded lessons for ongoing efforts by governments, international policymakers, civil society groups, and other stakeholders to ensure the success of the global governance project.

Perhaps the most striking policy implication is that attempts to improve institutional performance by redesigning or reforming formal governance arrangements are unlikely to bear fruit. In the absence of dependable enforcement mechanisms – the absence, in effect, of an incentive structure that encourages collective punishment of noncompliance – there is no guarantee that decision-making, agenda-setting, and financing rules will be respected by participants in the policy process. Any bid to meaningfully alter how institutions function, my analysis suggests, must proceed from a recognition of the fundamentally *political* logic that drives states to ignore and flout design principles when particularistic interests are at stake.

What strategies for ameliorating performance follow from this insight? The answer varies by stakeholder. For states, the most direct – but perhaps challenging – step is to firmly resist the dictates of the Jekyll and Hyde problem; that is, to refrain from opportunistic interventions in the policy process that jeopardize the original aims of institutionalized cooperation. To employ a domestic analogy, governments should treat institutions less like extensions of the executive or the legislative branch and more like central banks – agencies that require insulation from short-term political pressures in order to successfully deliver on their long-term objectives. This is, to be sure, easier said than done. Governments are themselves subject to pressures from special interests to exploit institutions for narrow ends, and cannot "bind themselves to the mast" by strengthening formal protections on bureaucratic independence. Rendering governance tasks more difficult to monitor is usually neither feasible, given inherent functional characteristics and the obstacles to far-reaching institutional change, nor indeed desirable, given that the modified tasks may not be consistent with the goals of international cooperation.[27]

My account of the origins of policy autonomy points to a more promising, and perhaps normatively attractive, strategy for tying governmental hands: building encompassing state–society coalitions around policies and programs supported by international bureaucrats. In a similar fashion to operational alliances, expanding the set of domestic stakeholders whose interests are aligned with institutions' raises the political costs of opportunism for states. In addition, it tends to shift state prefer-

---

[27] Jupille, Mattli, and Snidal (2013).

ences away from particularistic concerns and toward institutional goals, reducing the risk of *domestic* capture by special interests. One possible means of constructing state–society coalitions is to introduce domestic policies that advance or complement bureaucratic agendas, creating subnational structures, capacities, and vested interests that, as studies of the politics of retrenchment have shown, can become powerful forces for further steps in the same direction.[28] Involving diverse stakeholders in the design and implementation of these schemes – and in foreign policymaking more generally – may also represent a fruitful approach to coalition building. Much like international institutions themselves, therefore, governments can advance the cause of institutional autonomy and effectiveness by forging deeper and broader bonds with society.

It is not only their *own* behavior, of course, that states can change. Another tactic suggested by my argument is to counterbalance, individually and collectively, attempts by other nations to opportunistically hijack the policy process. The IFAD and GFATM case studies show that a subset of states may favor collectively rather than individually oriented policies and that mobilizing them – as well as like-minded external stakeholders – to act in concert can create a sturdy obstacle to capture. In IFAD and GFATM, the secretariat and its operational partners took the initiative in bringing together and coordinating these actors. There is no reason, however, why states cannot themselves serve as "counter-coalition entrepreneurs."

In addition to playing this catalytic role, international bureaucrats can contribute to better institutional performance in four ways. First, and most obviously, they can seek to forge numerous, close, and extensive operational ties with subnational and supranational actors. Second, in some circumstances, they may be able to replicate or adapt autonomy-enhancing tactics deployed by partners, for example, by reframing favored policies to resonate more strongly with perceived national interests; using methods of persuasion and socialization to mold state preferences in line with institutional goals;[29] and more actively disseminating information about their activities, priorities, and achievements to stakeholders (especially opinion leaders and influential pressure groups). Third, bureaucrats can mitigate institutions' reliance on governmental sources of financing by soliciting (larger) donations from non-state actors and developing new streams of independent revenue, such as investment earnings and fees for proprietary products and services. Fourth, they can lobby for or attempt to independently engineer forms of institutional change that provide the basis for greater autonomy in the future, such as

---

[28] Pierson (1994); Weaver (1986).   [29] Checkel (2001); Johnston (2001).

the weakening of governmental oversight bodies and procedural reforms that hinder states from setting governing body agendas (e.g., subjecting proposed topics to bureaucratic vetting) and individually vetoing policy proposals (e.g., swapping consensus for majoritarian decision-making practices).

While my framework emphasizes the role of operational partners in shielding institutions against the ravages of capture, they are by no means the only non-state actors who can sow the seeds of de facto policy autonomy. Functional collaboration with institutions is not essential for external stakeholders to, for instance, conduct advocacy activities on their behalf, circulate information about their work, and augment their financial resources. It also bears mentioning that, as institutions face greater pressures to "open up" their decision-making processes to the outside world, there will likely be more opportunities for these actors to nurture autonomy via participation in institutional governing bodies, including by forming policy-specific coalitions with bureaucrats of the kind discussed in the Gavi and GFATM case study.[30]

Importantly, taking steps to shore up de facto policy autonomy is not mutually exclusive with institutionalizing accountability to a wide range of constituencies. Although such discretion, by definition, weakens states' hold over the policy process, it is entirely compatible with – and indeed stems from some of the same sources as – modern channels through which institutions are held responsible by stakeholders. Chapter 6's findings indicate that bureaucrats can encourage the adoption of SWA mechanisms through the formation of operational alliances, while states, partners, and other stakeholders can join forces to assemble comprehensive coalitions for reform.

Taken as a whole, then, *Making International Institutions Work* provides grounds for cautious optimism. International institutions *can* be made more effective, and pursuing this goal need not come at the cost of robust accountability to stakeholders, broadly conceived. Nevertheless, as the prevalence and persistence of performance problems attest, the path to success is not a straightforward one. Subjugating and controlling institutions can yield rich dividends for states, and attempts to loosen their grip tend to encounter fierce resistance. Needless to say, many of the strategies for fostering de facto policy autonomy outlined in this section are politically, organizationally, and technically challenging to execute. Although there is hope for many underperformers, effectiveness may not be the destiny of all international institutions.

---

[30] Tallberg et al. (2013, 2014).

Implications for Emerging Issues in Global Governance

The book also carries implications for significant emerging trends in global governance that are the subject of lively debate in academic and foreign policy circles. I conclude by discussing three related issues: threats to today's liberal institutional order; the emergence of new China-dominated institutions; and institutional performance in periods of global crisis.

The Liberal Order Under Siege

One of the most heated policy debates centers on the health of the so-called liberal international order, the constellation of interstate relationships based on principles of equality, freedom, and self-determination that has structured world politics since the early years of the postwar period. At the heart of this system, advocates of the concept contend, is a form of rules-based multilateralism involving the sacrifice of sovereign authority for the pursuit of shared goals – a marriage of "structure" and "purpose" – of which international institutions are the principal manifestation.[31] Although the liberal international order has faced recurrent hazards since its creation, from the collapse of the Bretton Woods regime to the oil shocks of the 1970s, two recent trends are widely viewed as posing a more fundamental threat to its existence: (1) declining support for liberalism linked to the rise of populism and nationalism in core members of the order; and (2) the growing international influence and assertiveness of China, Russia, Iran, and other "illiberal" authoritarian regimes.[32]

   A clear implication of my findings is that, when it comes to institutionalized cooperation, the modern international order is decidedly less "liberal" than often believed. Rather than magnanimously relinquishing authority to institutions to further the global commonweal, powerful liberal nations have routinely circumvented and overturned formal governance arrangements in defense of parochial interests.[33] By assuming states remain committed to collective goals once institutions spark into life, believers in a liberal international order may be guilty of unwarranted optimism about the potential for rules-based cooperation to unite "structure" and "purpose." A similar point applies to G. John Ikenberry's oft-cited argument that the major postwar institutions represent

---

[31] Ruggie (1992).

[32] These challenges are discussed at length in an instructive recent issue of *International Organization* introduced by Lake, Martin, and Risse (2021). Also see Colgan and Keohane (2017); Nye (2017); Voeten (2021).

[33] For other analyses of how global governance has failed to live up to liberal principles, see Barnett (2019); Mearsheimer (2019); Porter (2018).

an exercise of "strategic restraint" by the United States, locking in patterns of mutually beneficial cooperation that ease other nations' fears of subjugation and abandonment.[34] The evidence presented in this book makes painfully plain that these and other institutions frequently and decisively fail to restrain powerful countries from exploiting weaker ones.

An interesting related implication is that, from a performance perspective, we should not be unduly concerned with the ideological inclinations of potential challengers to the existing institutional order, such as China and Russia.[35] The United States' commitment to individual rights, civil liberties, and multilateralism has not prevented it from unceremoniously dragging institutions away from their original – liberal – purposes. Conversely, illiberal nations are sometimes closely aligned with international bureaucrats in their outlook and policy preferences. The 1970s and 1980s, for example, saw strong agreement between the WHO secretariat and the G77 – which included China, Iran, and countless other authoritarian nations – on the need to expand primary healthcare to stem the spread of disease and ill health in the developing world. The key point is that, whether or not their most powerful members subscribe to liberal values, institutions succeed and fail by their ability to carve out and sustain policy autonomy. Only if illiberal challengers prove more willing and able to circumscribe bureaucratic agency than powerful liberal states – a scenario there are currently few grounds for expecting – should we be concerned about a potential decline in institutional performance. It is independence, not ideology, that determines the fate of institutions.

The surge of populism and nationalism presents a more serious danger. Growing anti-establishment sentiment and perceptions of international bureaucrats as out-of-touch elites have triggered a backlash against many institutions that "mirrors traditional nationalist sovereignty concerns over decreased autonomy and independence."[36] Insofar as this reaction provokes disengagement from institutions – as in the case of Brexit – or attempts to exert tighter control over their activities, it could inflict considerable damage on their performance. Reduced effectiveness could, in turn, strike a blow to popular confidence in institutional legitimacy (see Chapter 2), exacerbating the backlash. The best hope for institutions is likely to lie in a combination of counterpressures from partners and other organized supporters from civil society and the private sector – a trend already underway in some countries – and more concerted efforts by politicians to both explain institutional

---

[34] Ikenberry (2001).   [35] For an alternative perspective, see Voeten (2021).
[36] Copelovitch and Pevehouse (2019, 177).

benefits to voters and compensate adversely affected constituencies.[37] It should be noted, in addition, that the adoption and reinforcement of SWA mechanisms, in particular participatory governance arrangements, could help to ease populist pressures on institutions. Indeed, in an interview conducted in 2018, one evaluation officer from the United Nations Development Programme (UNDP) mentioned "a noticeable uptick in discussions about new accountability mechanisms across the UN System – undoubtedly driven by fears about how the rising tide of populism could impact international institutions."[38]

International Institutions with Chinese Characteristics?

Just as the performance of existing international institutions has begun to receive systematic attention from stakeholders, a wave of new ones has emerged. Most notable are two infrastructure-focused development banks headquartered in, and effectively led by, China: the New Development Bank (NDB), which was founded in 2014 by the BRICS (Brazil, Russia, India, China, and South Africa) group of emerging economies and currently has nine member states; and the larger and more prominent Asian Infrastructure Investment Bank (AIIB), which was established the following year and now counts 105 countries as members. To some scholars, the very existence of these institutions constitutes another threat to the liberal international order.[39]

The AIIB and the NDB represent intriguing cases for my framework. In design terms, they are almost identical to existing multilateral development banks, possessing a supreme Board of Governors in which all member states are represented; a smaller Board of Directors responsible for overseeing day-to-day operations; a majoritarian decision-making system under which voting shares are weighted by a member's financial contributions and date of accession (founding members have additional votes); and a relatively autonomous secretariat that draws up annual budgets and sets the Board of Directors' agenda.[40] The main difference is that the AIIB and the NDB's largest shareholder is not the United States but China (alongside the other BRICS in the latter institution's case).

[37] Baccini, Osgood, and Weymouth (2019); Kim and Spilker (2019).
[38] Author interview #92 with UNDP evaluation officer, May 22, 2018, New York.
[39] See Deng (2014); Heilmann et al. (2014); Liao (2015). Other examples of institutions recently established under Chinese auspices include the Chiang Mai Initiative Multilateralization (CMIM) agreement and the Regional Comprehensive Economic Partnership (RCEP).
[40] Asian Infrastructure Investment Bank (2015, 2019); New Development Bank (2014, 2019).

It is not obvious, as noted earlier, why China would seek or be able to impose more stringent restrictions on bureaucratic autonomy than the United States or other powerful liberal nations. Incentives to refrain from interference are strengthened, at least initially, by the intense scrutiny placed on the AIIB and the NDB by an international community eager to see how China will wield its newfound institutional power. According to a recent collection of studies on the AIIB's first three years, "[T]he Chinese officials who liaise directly and regularly with the AIIB – from the Ministry of Finance – are quite aware that one determinant of the new Bank's success, for establishing its credibility, is operational autonomy."[41] Consistent with this observation, one of the collection's principal findings is that "the AIIB is operating with a noticeable degree of autonomy, despite its location, the staffing dynamics and China's veto at the [Board of Governors] level."[42] Similarly, examinations of the NDB find that China has made no visible attempt to meddle in lending decisions – a deliberate strategy "to strengthen international perceptions of ... independence"[43] – and that the secretariat is exercising growing influence over member states.[44]

Perhaps not by coincidence, there are also encouraging signs on the performance front. The AIIB has expeditiously scaled up lending activities, approving 108 projects – many of which feature pioneering "green" infrastructure – worth $22 billion during its first five years;[45] received triple-A scores from all three major international credit rating agencies; raised billions of dollars via a global bond issued at the same price as World Bank debt; and almost doubled its membership, which now far exceeds the 68 states constituting the much older Asian Development Bank (AsDB).[46] The NDB has followed a comparable trajectory, rapidly expanding its loan book to 19 projects worth $24 billion by the end of

---

[41] Chin (2019, 573). In the same vein, one China-based scholar notes that these officials "are aware that the AIIB must demonstrate that it has policy and operational autonomy" and that it is not a "tool" of foreign policy schemes such as the Belt and Road Initiative (Zhu 2019, 657).

[42] Chin (2019, 573). This is evident both from China's "concerted effort to give the space needed for multilateralism to run through the core of the AIIB's governance, policy, agenda-setting, priority-setting, management, and operations" (p. 574) and from the bureaucracy's ability "to make its own determination of project risk and decisions on project lending, measures for ensuring returns from its loans, and, in theory, repayment of loans" (p. 573).

[43] Humphrey (2020, 10).   [44] Wang (2019).

[45] Asian Infrastructure Investment Bank (2021). In some years, the value of the AIIB's project approvals has come close to that of the AsDB.

[46] To the United States' chagrin, the AIIB has received glowing praise from many Western policymakers. Luxembourg's finance minister, for instance, has called it "arguably the most modern and international financial institution in the world" and "the beacon of multilateralism while surpassing expectations of growth" (Chen 2019).

2020;[47] receiving double-A scores from two international credit rating agencies and triple-A scores from two national ones; and successfully issuing large bonds in global as well as Chinese, Russian, and South African capital markets.

If my argument is correct, the long-run prospects of the AIIB and the NDB will rest on their staff's capacity to renew and build out their initial lease of discretion. The function of allocating financial resources to technologically and logistically sophisticated infrastructure projects furnishes an inbuilt screen against top-down monitoring that will go some way toward this end. Whether bureaucrats can weave the dense and sprawling webs of operational partnerships possessed by more established multilateral development banks, however, is less clear. Civil society is generally denser and more organized in the United States and other major shareholders of these institutions than in China (and the remaining BRICS nations). Moreover, China may take a dim view of bureaucratic overtures to nongovernmental organizations (NGOs), foreign corporations, American-dominated international institutions, and other stakeholders it regards with suspicion – and is itself less susceptible to pressures from such actors. In this regard, China's subnational authorities and state-owned enterprises may serve as more useful operational partners for the AIIB and the NDB, though there is no guarantee that these actors will not themselves serve as conduits of Chinese Community Party influence. It remains to be seen whether the two banks' more limited base of potential partners places a binding constraint on their autonomy as their operations continue to burgeon.

Performance in the Midst of Global Crisis

Finally, the coronavirus (COVID-19) pandemic has raised renewed questions – last posed during the global financial crisis of 2007–2008 – about the performance of international institutions during periods of widespread turmoil.[48] Popular as well as academic assessments of the multilateral response to COVID-19 have been largely unfavorable: "The general judgement is that global governance failed to play a significant and effective role in combatting the pandemic," summarizes Michael Zürn.[49] Unsurprisingly, the lion's share of attention and censure has focused on the WHO – whose shortcomings were catalogued in

---

[47] New Development Bank (2021).
[48] Many of the harsh rebukes of global governance cited in Chapter 1 were motivated by a perceived failure to anticipate or effectively tackle the global financial crisis.
[49] Zürn (2021, 37). Also see Bernes et al. (2020); Pegram (2020); Sharma and de Vriese (2020).

Chapter 5 – and the G20. The list of charges against the latter is almost as protracted: failing either to formulate a coherent international strategy for tackling COVID-19 or to support other institutions' efforts to do so (above all the WHO's); introducing unhelpful medical and commercial export restrictions at critical phases of the pandemic; ineffectively coordinating domestic macroeconomic and financial policies, leading to sharp currency fluctuations, liquidity shortfalls, and disrupted supply chains; providing inadequate assistance to the hardest-hit developing countries; refusing to relax intellectual property rules to accelerate the production of vaccines, treatments, and diagnostics; and rolling out vaccines slowly and inequitably across nations.[50]

How can we ensure that global governance fares better when catastrophe strikes again? This book's case studies suggest that the dynamics of institutional performance are not fundamentally different during periods of intense (internal or external) difficulty. That is to say, a distinct "theory of crisis performance" may not be called for. As discussed in Chapter 5, the deficiencies of the WHO's response to COVID-19 stemmed in large part from its lack of distance from and authority over powerful member nations, whose refusal to comply with organizational regulations and prioritization of domestic political interests fatally undermined bureaucratic efforts to enact swift and robust countermeasures. The G20 enjoys even *less* independence from its members: In the absence of a permanent secretariat, its website states, "Agenda and the work coordination is completed by G20 leaders' personal representatives, known as sherpas together with finance ministers and central bank governors."[51] While sometimes praised as a useful source of flexibility and agility, the group's low degree of institutionalization and bureaucratization could, my framework suggests, be a decisive limiting factor on its problem-solving effectiveness.[52] The empirical record is not inconsistent with this notion, as Tony Payne points out: "[T]he G20 has often seemed trapped by its 'occasionality,' which is to say its fundamental and debilitating lack of permanence and institutional structure ... [I]t has no secretariat or permanent staff, leaving the annual summit's host government with free rein to propose its own particular agenda, which opens up many opportunities to ride national hobby-horses somewhat clumsily into the global arena."[53]

It is equally important to observe that not all international institutions can be faulted for their performance during the pandemic. Chapter 5 also noted the plaudits received by Gavi for delivering much-needed

[50] See Amnesty International (2021); Bernes et al. (2020); Subacchi (2020).
[51] https://g20.org/about-the-g20/ [Last accessed October 2, 2021].
[52] Vabulas and Snidal (2013).   [53] Payne (2020).

assistance to local health systems and for quickly and evenhandedly distributing more than a billion vaccines around the world; and by GFATM for establishing the primary funding mechanism for the procurement of COVID-related equipment and supplies by developing countries. In the inverse pattern to the WHO and the G20, Gavi and GFATM's impactful interventions were made possible by an expansive self-determination forged from wide-ranging collaborative bonds with non-state actors and technically complex, easily concealable operational activities – the same factors that enabled them to thrive *before* the pandemic. In times of crisis, as in times of calm, casting off the fetters of political domination with the hand of alliances and the cloak of stealth is essential for making international institutions work.

Appendix A Formalizing the Argument

A.1   The Jekyll and Hyde Problem

This appendix presents a formal analysis of how state preferences over the distribution of goods produced by international institutions evolve over time. Assume that each member state i of a given institution has a differentiable utility function of the form:

$$u_i(x_i, C), \tag{A.1}$$

where x_i denotes i's consumption of particularistic (or private) goods, C denotes the total consumption of collective goods, and u_i is increasing in both. The cost of using the institution to produce x and C are p_x and p_C, respectively.

Assuming that institutions are established for collective rather than particularistic purposes, as argued in Chapter 2, will should design them to allocate C and x in accordance with Pareto efficiency, that is, such that no state can be made strictly better off without making another worse off. Specifically, in period $t - 1$, they will maximize a collective welfare function W with respect to C:

$$\max_{C} W = \sum_{i=1}^{n} \gamma_i U_i \tag{A.2}$$

subject to the opportunity set (i.e., the total "basket" of goods they can afford):

$$\sum_{i=1}^{n} y_i = p_x \sum_{i=1}^{n} x_i + p_C C, \tag{A.3}$$

where γ_i is the weight assigned to i's welfare.[1] The Lagrangian function can be expressed as:

---

[1] This weight might be higher, for example, if i is a powerful state that has agreed to contribute a higher share of the institution's resources.

$$\mathcal{L}(U, y, x, C) = \sum_{i=1}^{n} \gamma_i U_i + \lambda \left[\sum_{i=1}^{n} y_i - p_x \sum_{i=1}^{n} x_i + p_C C \right]. \tag{A.4}$$

The first-order condition for this maximization problem is:

$$\sum_{i=1}^{n} \gamma_i \frac{\delta U_i}{\delta C} + \lambda \left[\frac{\delta}{\delta C} \left(\sum_{i=1}^{n} y_i - p_x \sum_{i=1}^{n} x_i - p_C C \right) \right] = 0, \tag{A.5}$$

which simplifies to:

$$\sum_{i=1}^{n} \gamma_i \frac{\delta U_i}{\delta C} = \lambda p_C \tag{A.6}$$

$$\sum_{i=1}^{n} \gamma_i = \frac{\lambda p_C}{\sum_{i=1}^{n} \delta U_i / \delta C}. \tag{A.7}$$

States then choose a level of x_i to maximize i's utility function subject to its opportunity set, given the decision about C. The Lagrangian takes the form:

$$\mathcal{L}(U, y, x, C) = \gamma_i U_i(x, C) + \lambda [y_i - p_x x_i - p_C C]. \tag{A.8}$$

The problem is solved as follows:

$$\gamma_i \frac{\delta U_i}{\delta x} + \lambda \left[\frac{\delta}{\delta x} (y_i - p_x x_i + p_C C) \right] = 0 \tag{A.9}$$

$$\gamma_i \frac{\delta U_i}{\delta x_i} - \lambda p_x = 0 \tag{A.10}$$

$$\gamma_i \frac{\delta U_i}{\delta x_i} = \lambda p_x \tag{A.11}$$

or

$$\gamma_i = \frac{\lambda p_x}{\delta U_i / \delta x_i}. \tag{A.12}$$

Substituting for γ_i in Equation A.7 and canceling out λ gives us:

$$\frac{\lambda p_C}{\sum_{i=1}^{n} \delta U_i / \delta C} = \frac{\lambda p_x}{\delta U_i / \delta x_i} \tag{A.13}$$

$$\sum_{i=1}^{n} \frac{\delta U_i / \delta C}{\delta U_i / \delta x_i} = \frac{p_C}{p_x}. \tag{A.14}$$

This is equivalent to the famous Samuelson condition for the efficient provision of public goods: The marginal rate of transformation between the public good and an arbitrarily chosen private good is the sum of all individual marginal rates of substitution.[2] Put differently, the value of particularistic goods that states are willing to give up for an additional unit of collective goods is equal to what would actually be required to produce this increment.

For reasons discussed in Chapter 2, once institutions come into existence (period $t+1$), states tend to place a lower value on cooperative benefits accruing to all nations. Accordingly, they maximize:

$$\max_{c_i} U_i(x_i, C) \tag{A.15}$$

subject to:

$$y_i = p_x x_i + p_C c_i, \tag{A.16}$$

where c_i is i's consumption of C. The first-order condition is:

$$\frac{\delta U_i}{\delta x_i}\left[\frac{\delta}{\delta c_i}\left(\frac{y_i}{p_x} - c_i\frac{p_C}{p_x}\right)\right] + \frac{\delta C}{\delta c_i}\frac{\delta U_i}{\delta C} = 0. \tag{A.17}$$

Since $\frac{\delta C}{\delta c_i} = 1$,

$$\frac{\delta U_i}{\delta C} - \frac{\delta U_i}{\delta x_i}\frac{p_C}{p_x} = 0 \tag{A.18}$$

$$\frac{\delta U_i/\delta C}{\delta U_i/\delta x_i} = \frac{p_G}{p_x}. \tag{A.19}$$

As x and C are normal goods, Equation A.19 yields a lower value than Equation A.14. This can be clearly seen by rewriting the latter as:

$$\frac{\delta U_i/\delta C}{\delta U_i/\delta x_i} = \frac{p_C}{p_x} - \sum_{i\neq j}\frac{\delta U_j/\delta C}{\delta U_j/\delta x_j}, \tag{A.20}$$

where j represents another member state. Hence, the marginal rate of substitution between x and C will be higher for states in period $t+1$ than in period $t+1$. In Figure 2.1, this is reflected in the flatter slope of the opportunity set in period $t+1$, which results in a lower level of C (i.e., C'') and a higher level of x (i.e., x'').

[2] Samuelson (1954).

A.2   Feedback Processes

The hypothesized feedback effects between the de facto policy autonomy and performance of international institutions can be characterized in formal terms. My framework posits that performance is a positive function of de facto policy autonomy:

$$P = f(DFPA), \tag{A.21}$$

where $DFPA$ stands for de facto policy autonomy and P for performance. If feedback occurs, current levels of de facto policy autonomy depend on past levels of performance, which, in turn, depend on even earlier levels of de facto policy autonomy:

$$DFPA_k = f(P_{k-1}) \tag{A.22}$$

$$P_{k-1} = f(DFPA_{k-2}), \tag{A.23}$$

where k indexes the present. Consequently, current levels of de facto policy autonomy are a function of its own previous levels:

$$DFPA_k = f(DFPA_{k-2}). \tag{A.24}$$

According to my argument, feedback typically begins with changes in de facto policy autonomy rather than in performance. Mathematically, the ensuing process can be described in two ways. The first, depicted graphically in Figure 2.3, is in terms of each variable's rate of change. If de facto policy autonomy increases, as in the high-performance pathway outlined in Chapter 2, its rate of change initially exceeds that of performance:

$$\frac{\delta DFPA_{s,HPP}}{\delta P_{s,HPP}} > 1, \tag{A.25}$$

where s denotes the short run and HPP the high-performance pathway. The opposite holds when de facto policy autonomy declines, as in the low-performance pathway:

$$\frac{\delta DFPA_{s,LPP}}{\delta P_{s,LPP}} < 1, \tag{A.26}$$

where LPP denotes the low-performance pathway. In the medium run (subscript m), feedback effects become weaker as de facto policy autonomy and performance approach their equilibrium levels, implying a smaller difference between their rates of change:

$$\frac{\delta DFPA_{m,HPP,LPP}}{\delta P_{m,HPP,LPP}} < \frac{\delta DFPA_{s,HPP,LPP}}{\delta P_{s,HPP,LPP}}. \tag{A.27}$$

In the long run (subscript l), feedback effects are exhausted, equalizing the two rates of change:

$$\frac{\delta P_l}{\delta DFPA_l} = 1. \tag{A.28}$$

An exception occurs when institutions follow the medium-performance pathway (subscript MPP), in which both rates are zero across all periods:

$$\frac{\delta P_{s,m,l,MPP}}{\delta DFPA_{s,m,l,MPP}} = 0. \tag{A.29}$$

Alternatively, the feedback process can be modeled in terms of time, as in Figure 2.2. Assuming that performance and de facto policy autonomy begin at a middling level, they can be described by nonlinear functions in which the former converges more slowly to the long-run equilibrium than the latter, such as:

$$DFPA_{HPP} = \frac{1}{1 - 2e^{2t}} \tag{A.30}$$

$$P_{HPP} = \frac{1}{1 - e^t}. \tag{A.31}$$

The exponential term is positive in the low-performance pathway:

$$DFPA_{LPP} = \frac{1}{1 + 2e^{2t}} \tag{A.32}$$

$$P_{LPP} = \frac{1}{1 + e^t}. \tag{A.33}$$

Now, the functions' short-run slope is steeper than their medium-run slope in both the high- and the low-performance pathways:

$$\frac{\delta DFPA_{s,HPP,LPP}}{\delta t} > \frac{\delta DFPA_{m,HPP,LPP}}{\delta t}. \tag{A.34}$$

In the medium-performance pathway, the two variables do not change over time and are thus a constant function of time:

$$P_{MPP} = DFPA_{MPP} = q, \tag{A.35}$$

where q is an arbitrary constant representing a moderate level of each variable.

Appendix B   Empirical Details

B.1   Composition of the Performance of International Institutions Project (PIIP) Dataset

Table B.1 *List of institutions in PIIP dataset*

International institution	Acronym	Founded
Adaptation Fund	AF	2001
African Development Bank	AfDB	1964
Asian Development Bank	AsDB	1966
Caribbean Development Bank	CDB	1969
Central Emergency Response Fund	CERF	2006
CGIAR[a]	CGIAR	1971
Climate Investment Funds	CIFS	2008
Commonwealth Secretariat	COMSEC	1965
European Bank for Reconstruction and Development	EBRD	1991
European Development Fund	EDF	1959
Expanded Delivering as One Funding Window for the Achievement of the Millennium Development Goals	EFW	2008
Food and Agriculture Organization	FAO	1945
Global Partnership for Education[b]	GPE	2002
Gavi, the Vaccine Alliance	Gavi	2000
Global Crop Diversity Trust	GCDT	2004
Global Environment Facility	GEF	1991
Global Fund to Fight AIDS, Tuberculosis, and Malaria	GFATM	2002
Global Facility for Disaster Reduction and Recovery	GFDRR	2006
Inter-American Development Bank	IADB	1958
International Committee of the Red Cross	ICRC	1863
International Fund for Agricultural Development	IFAD	1977
International Finance Corporation	IFC	1956
International Federation of the Red Cross	IFRC	1919
International Labour Organization	ILO	1919
International Monetary Fund	IMF	1945
International Organization for Migration	IOM	1951
International Trade Centre	ITC	1964
Least Developed Countries Fund	LDCF	2001

Table B.1 *(cont.)*

International institution	Acronym	Founded
Multilateral Fund for the Implementation of the Montreal Protocol	MLF	1991
United Nations Office for the Coordination of Humanitarian Affairs	OCHA	1996
Office of the United Nations High Commissioner for Human Rights	OHCHR	1994
United Nations Peacebuilding Fund	PBF	2006
Private Infrastructure Development Group	PIDG	2002
United Nations Human Settlements Programme	UN-HABITAT	1978
Joint United Nations Programme on HIV/AIDS	UNAIDS	1994
United Nations Capital Development Fund	UNCDF	1966
United Nations Conference on Trade and Development	UNCTAD	1964
United Nations Development Programme	UNDP	1965
United Nations Environment Programme	UNEP	1972
United Nations Educational, Scientific, and Cultural Organization	UNESCO	1945
United Nations Mine Action Service	UNMAS	1997
United Nations Population Fund	UNFPA	1969
Office of the United Nations High Commissioner for Refugees	UNHCR	1950
United Nations Children's Emergency Fund	UNICEF	1946
United Nations Industrial Development Organization	UNIDO	1966
United Nations Office for Disaster Risk Reduction[c]	UNDRR	2000
UNITAID	UNITAID	2006
United Nations Office on Drugs and Crime	UNODC	1966
United Nations Relief and Works Agency for Palestine Refugees in the Near East	UNRWA	1949
United Nations Entity for Gender Equality and the Empowerment of Women (UN Women)[d]	UNW	1976
World Bank	WB	1944
World Food Programme	WFP	1961
World Health Organization	WHO	1948
World Trade Organization	WTO	1995

[a] Includes predecessor, the Consortium of International Agricultural Research Centers (CGIAR Consortium).
[b] Includes predecessor, the Education For All – Fast Track Initiative (EFA-FTI).
[c] Includes predecessor, the United Nations International Strategy for Disaster Reduction (UNISDR).
[d] Includes predecessor, the United Nations Development Fund for Women (UNIFEM).

B.2   Sources for Donor Performance Evaluations

Table B.2 *List of sources for donor performance evaluations*

Assessor	Unit	Source	Year	URL[a]
Australia	Australian Agency for International Development (AusAID)	"Australian Multilateral Assessment"	2012	https://dfat.gov.au/about-us/publications/Pages/australian-multilateral-assessment-ama-full-report.aspx
Denmark	Danish International Development Agency (Danida)	"Denmark's engagement in multilateral development and humanitarian organizations 2012"	2012	https://www.ft.dk/samling/20111/almdel/uru/bilag/245/1153552.pdf
		"Danish Multilateral Development Cooperation Analysis"	2013	https://web.archive.org/web/20210525175621/http://um.dk/~/media/UM/Danish-site/Documents/Udenrigspolitik/Nyheder_udenrigspolitik/2012/120709%20Multilateral%20Analysis%202012%20-%20English%20Version.pdf
Netherlands	Netherlands Development Cooperation	"Nederlandse ODA-bijdragen aan multilaterale organisaties en Toetsing multilaterale organisaties"	2011	https://www.tweedekamer.nl/downloads/document?id=b5b159c4-3123-4981-a7b2-04915d8a16c3&title=Nederlandse%20ODA-bijdragen%20aan%20multilaterale%20organisaties%20en%20Toetsing%20multilaterale%20organisaties.pdf
		"Eindoordelen scorekaarten 2013"	2013	https://www.eerstekamer.nl/overig/20130704/eindoordelen_scorekaarten_2013/document
		"Brief regering; Multilaterale scorekaarten - Hulp, handel en investeringen"	2015	https://www.parlementairemonitor.nl/9353000/1/j9vvij5epmj1ey0/vjv1m9lhotx0
		"Betreft Multilaterale scorekaarten"	2017	https://open.overheid.nl/repository/ronl-70db2cd8-1750-4b68-a5f6-9fd679fb2c65/1/pdf/kamerbrief-multilaterale-scorekaarten.pdf
Sweden	Swedish International Development Cooperation Agency (Sida)	"Swedish assessment of multilateral organisations" – various	2008–2011	https://www.government.se/search/?query=assessment%20of%20multilateral%20organisations
United Kingdom	Department for International Development (DFID)	"Multilateral Aid Review: Ensuring maximum value for money for UK aid through multilateral organisations"	2011	https://www.gov.uk/government/publications/multilateral-aid-review
		"Raising the standard: the Multilateral Development Review 2016"	2016	https://www.gov.uk/government/publications/raising-the-standard-the-multilateral-development-review-2016
Multilateral Organisation Performance Assessment Network (MOPAN)	Secretariat/consulting firm	Assessment packages – various	2010–2019	http://www.mopanonline.org/assessments/

[a] All last accessed October 3, 2021.

B.3   Performances Indicators and Indices

Table B.3 *Principal component analysis of Australian performance indicators*

	Principal component (PC)			
	PC1	PC2	PC3	PC4
Factor loadings for performance indicators				
Contribution to multilateral system	0.20	0.53	0.81	−0.17
Cost and value consciousness	0.59	−0.52	0.30	0.53
Delivering results	0.50	0.64	−0.47	0.34
Strategic management and performance	0.59	−0.20	−0.18	−0.76
Importance of principal component				
Standard deviation	0.95	0.59	0.50	0.44
Proportion of variance	0.53	0.21	0.15	0.11
Cumulative proportion	0.53	0.74	0.89	1.00

Table B.4 *Principal component analysis of Danish performance indicators*

	Principal component (PC)				
	PC1	PC2	PC3	PC4	PC5
Assessment year: 2012					
Factor loadings for performance indicators					
Compliance with international obligations	0.36	0.33	−0.37	−0.51	−0.60
Innovation and agenda setting	0.28	0.50	0.57	−0.41	0.43
Involvement in multilateral reform agenda	0.37	0.47	0.14	0.75	−0.25
Organizational effectiveness	0.79	−0.59	0.05	0.01	0.12
Risk management	0.16	0.27	−0.72	0.09	0.61
Importance of principal component					
Standard deviation	1.15	0.68	0.43	0.42	0.27
Proportion of variance	0.60	0.21	0.08	0.08	0.03
Cumulative proportion	0.60	0.80	0.89	0.97	1.00
Assessment year: 2013					
Factor loadings for performance indicators					
Contribution to multilateral system	0.43	−0.87	0.23		
Financing and funding	0.90	0.44	0.00		
Organizational effectiveness	0.10	−0.21	−0.97		
Importance of principal component					
Standard deviation	1.27	0.56	0.26		
Proportion of variance	0.81	0.15	0.03		
Cumulative proportion	0.81	0.97	1.00		

Table B.5 *Principal component analysis of MOPAN performance indicators*

	Principal component (PC)											
	PC1	PC2	PC3	PC4	PC5	PC6	PC7	PC8	PC9	PC10	PC11	PC12
Assessment year: 2015 onward												
Factor loadings for performance indicators												
Achievement of results	0.02	0.39	−0.23	0.28	−0.73	0.31	−0.27	0.13				
Cost-effective and transparent systems	0.20	−0.04	−0.26	−0.31	−0.11	−0.10	−0.33	−0.81				
Organizational and financial framework	0.53	−0.42	0.01	−0.11	0.10	0.14	−0.59	0.40				
Relevance and agility	0.43	−0.32	−0.01	−0.23	−0.34	0.35	0.65	−0.05				
Results delivered efficiently	0.37	0.42	0.55	−0.30	−0.24	−0.48	0.01	0.09				
Results focus	0.48	−0.02	−0.01	0.79	0.12	−0.25	0.12	−0.21				
Structures for cross-cutting issues	0.30	0.45	−0.68	−0.22	0.31	−0.11	0.17	0.25				
Sustainability of results	0.18	0.44	0.34	0.01	0.40	0.67	−0.06	−0.21				
Importance of principal component												
Standard deviation	0.87	0.56	0.51	0.39	0.28	0.25	0.22	0.14				
Proportion of variance	0.45	0.18	0.16	0.09	0.05	0.04	0.03	0.01				
Cumulative proportion	0.45	0.63	0.79	0.88	0.92	0.96	0.99	1.00				
Assessment year: pre-2015												
Factor loadings for performance indicators												
Country focus on results	0.27	−0.06	0.04	−0.30	−0.64	0.04	−0.16	−0.20	−0.34	−0.02	−0.32	0.37
Corporate focus on results	0.35	−0.20	−0.54	0.35	−0.38	−0.29	0.32	−0.07	0.21	0.03	0.20	−0.11
Disseminating lessons learned	0.37	−0.15	−0.04	0.14	0.21	0.68	−0.12	−0.50	0.12	0.11	0.13	0.02
Evaluating results	0.34	−0.12	−0.22	−0.26	0.31	−0.12	−0.11	0.06	−0.62	−0.32	0.27	−0.26
Financial accountability	0.17	0.01	−0.18	−0.25	0.17	−0.21	−0.21	0.05	−0.01	0.84	−0.17	−0.15
Linking aid management to performance	0.10	−0.25	0.32	0.19	−0.02	0.24	0.62	0.23	−0.37	0.22	−0.25	−0.20
Managing human resources	0.12	−0.21	0.44	−0.50	−0.28	−0.02	0.09	0.00	0.32	0.04	0.46	−0.31
Performance-oriented programming	0.20	−0.25	0.48	0.44	0.11	−0.39	−0.25	−0.03	−0.13	0.14	0.28	0.36
Presenting performance information	0.27	0.02	0.21	0.27	−0.11	−0.07	−0.42	0.07	0.16	−0.22	−0.45	−0.58
Providing direction for results	0.27	−0.04	0.12	−0.25	0.40	−0.36	0.37	−0.36	0.26	−0.21	−0.39	0.16
Resource allocation decisions	0.40	0.85	0.17	0.08	−0.05	0.02	0.18	0.06	−0.05	−0.06	0.18	0.02
Using performing information	0.38	−0.15	−0.09	−0.11	0.12	0.21	−0.08	0.71	0.30	−0.11	−0.07	0.36
Importance of principal component												
Standard deviation	1.11	0.65	0.56	0.49	0.42	0.37	0.35	0.27	0.26	0.18	0.12	0.10
Proportion of variance	0.43	0.15	0.11	0.09	0.06	0.05	0.04	0.03	0.02	0.01	0.01	0.00
Cumulative proportion	0.43	0.58	0.69	0.78	0.84	0.89	0.93	0.96	0.98	0.99	1.00	1.00

Table B.6 *Principal component analysis of Dutch performance indicators*

	Principal component (PC)					
	PC1	PC2	PC3	PC4	PC5	PC6
Assessment year: pre-2015						
Factor loadings for performance indicators						
Focus on core mandate	0.41	0.63	−0.44	0.18	−0.07	0.45
Effective governance	0.53	0.05	0.20	0.11	−0.65	−0.49
Financial management	0.44	−0.70	0.02	0.23	−0.04	0.52
Human resources management	0.24	0.12	0.38	−0.83	−0.05	0.31
Results control	0.42	0.19	0.47	0.26	0.68	−0.18
Strategy and focus	0.36	−0.24	−0.63	−0.39	0.32	−0.41
Importance of principal component						
Standard deviation	1.06	0.64	0.57	0.55	0.44	0.35
Proportion of variance	0.45	0.17	0.13	0.12	0.08	0.05
Cumulative proportion	0.45	0.62	0.75	0.87	0.95	1.00
Assessment year: 2015 onward						
Factor loadings for performance indicators						
Effective governance	0.43	−0.08	0.46	0.05	−0.77	
Financial management	0.38	0.52	0.50	0.35	0.47	
Human resources management	0.28	−0.74	−0.05	0.56	0.24	
Results control	0.57	−0.23	0.02	−0.72	0.31	
Strategy and focus	0.52	0.34	−0.73	0.21	−0.17	
Importance of principal component						
Standard deviation	0.96	0.56	0.52	0.50	0.45	
Proportion of variance	0.47	0.16	0.14	0.13	0.10	
Cumulative proportion	0.47	0.63	0.77	0.90	1.00	

Table B.7 *Principal component analysis of Swedish performance indicators*

	Principal component (PC)	
	PC1	PC2
Factor loadings for performance indicators		
External effectiveness	0.64	−0.77
Internal effectiveness	0.77	0.64
Importance of principal component		
Standard deviation	1.48	0.54
Proportion of variance	0.89	0.12
Cumulative proportion	0.89	1.00

Table B.8 *Principal component analysis of British performance indicators*

	Principal component (PC)								
	PC1	PC2	PC3	PC4	PC5	PC6	PC7	PC8	PC9
Assessment year: 2011									
Factor loadings for performance indicators									
Cost and value consciousness	-0.37	-0.41	-0.11	0.67	0.47	0.15			
Critical to international aid objectives	-0.40	0.30	0.75	-0.19	0.38	0.01			
Delivery of results	-0.38	-0.29	0.32	0.11	-0.74	0.34			
Financial resources management	-0.32	-0.21	0.00	0.01	-0.16	-0.91			
Focus on poor countries	-0.57	0.65	-0.48	0.07	-0.12	0.08			
Strategic/performance management	-0.36	-0.45	-0.30	-0.71	0.21	0.18			
Importance of principal component									
Standard deviation	1.42	0.87	0.52	0.46	0.44	0.38			
Proportion of variance	0.56	0.21	0.08	0.06	0.05	0.04			
Cumulative proportion	0.56	0.77	0.85	0.91	0.96	1.00			
Assessment year: 2016									
Factor loadings for performance indicators									
Critical to international aid objectives	-0.35	-0.46	0.37	-0.09	0.00	-0.40	0.14	0.08	-0.57
Delivery of results	-0.32	0.01	0.06	-0.09	0.76	0.49	-0.15	0.15	-0.12
Cost and value consciousness	-0.36	0.23	-0.41	-0.13	0.24	-0.28	0.47	-0.53	0.03
Comparative advantage	-0.38	-0.37	0.17	-0.40	-0.17	0.10	0.13	0.08	0.68
Geography and resources	-0.40	-0.32	-0.18	0.71	-0.09	0.04	-0.33	-0.25	0.13
Human resources	-0.28	0.10	-0.15	-0.32	-0.53	0.52	-0.14	-0.24	-0.40
Risk and assurance	-0.25	0.29	0.13	0.42	-0.19	0.26	0.62	0.42	-0.02
Fraud	-0.30	0.61	0.58	0.01	-0.04	-0.23	-0.33	-0.17	0.12
Efficiency	-0.32	0.19	-0.50	-0.14	-0.08	-0.34	-0.31	0.61	-0.02
Importance of principal component									
Standard deviation	1.03	0.66	0.48	0.41	0.40	0.28	0.26	0.21	0.16
Proportion of variance	0.46	0.19	0.10	0.07	0.07	0.03	0.03	0.02	0.01
Cumulative proportion	0.46	0.66	0.76	0.83	0.90	0.94	0.97	0.99	1.00

B.4   Representativeness of PIIP Sample

Table B.9 *Issue area proportions in PIIP versus Yearbook of International Organizations (IGOs only)*

Issue area	PIIP proportion	Broad definition of IGOs		Narrow definition of IGOs	
		Yearbook proportion	Z-test p-value	Yearbook proportion	Z-test p-value
Agriculture	0.09	0.06	0.39 (✗)	0.09	1.00 (✗)
Competition	0.04	0.02	0.56 (✗)	0.02	0.55 (✗)
Culture	0.02	0.07	0.26 (✗)	0.04	0.55 (✗)
Development	0.28	0.22	0.36 (✗)	0.20	0.23 (✗)
Diplomacy	0.02	0.03	1.00 (✗)	0.07	0.26 (✗)
Education	0.04	0.07	0.47 (✗)	0.04	1.00 (✗)
Employment	0.02	0.02	1.00 (✗)	0.02	1.00 (✗)
Environment	0.11	0.13	0.82 (✗)	0.12	1.00 (✗)
Finance	0.07	0.10	0.76 (✗)	0.06	0.84 (✗)
Health	0.15	0.08	0.09 (✗)	0.08	0.10 (✗)
Humanitarian	0.19	0.07	0.00 (✓)	0.06	0.00 (✓)
Law	0.02	0.09	0.13 (✗)	0.09	0.11 (✗)
Migration	0.04	0.02	0.75 (✗)	0.03	1.00 (✗)
Population	0.02	0.01	0.71 (✗)	0.00	0.47 (✗)
Rights	0.06	0.04	0.71 (✗)	0.04	0.85 (✗)
Science	0.04	0.09	0.23 (✗)	0.09	0.24 (✗)
Security	0.06	0.08	0.74 (✗)	0.07	0.91 (✗)
Settlements	0.02	0.01	0.87 (✗)	0.00	0.47 (✗)
Trade	0.06	0.08	0.69 (✗)	0.10	0.35 (✗)
Transportation	0.02	0.04	0.72 (✗)	0.07	0.23 (✗)

Notes: The Z-tests evaluate a null hypothesis that the PIIP proportion is equal to the Yearbook proportion. A cross (✗) indicates that we cannot reject this hypothesis at a five percent significance level; a check (✓) indicates that we can. The Yearbook's narrow definition of IGOs includes federations of international organizations, universal membership organizations, intercontinental membership organizations, and regionally defined membership organizations (type codes A, B, C, and D, respectively). The broad definition additionally encompasses organizations emanating from places, persons, or other bodies, organizations having a special form, and internationally-oriented national organizations (type codes E, F, and G, respectively).

B.5 Summary Statistics

Table B.10 *Descriptive statistics for full PIIP dataset*

Variable	N	Mean	St. dev.	Min	Pctl(25)	Pctl(75)	Max
Performance indices:							
Australian Perf. Index	42	0.00	0.95	−2.68	−0.72	0.48	2.09
Danish Perf. Index	33	0.00	1.19	−2.73	−0.77	0.66	1.95
MOPAN Perf. Index	49	−0.00	0.98	−2.35	−0.53	0.57	1.67
Dutch Perf. Index	116	−0.00	1.54	−6.36	−0.74	0.90	2.89
Swedish Perf. Index	64	0.00	1.48	−2.11	−1.34	0.84	3.65
UK Perf. Index	117	−0.00	1.31	−2.94	−1.05	0.88	2.85
Average Perf. Index	293	−0.05	1.23	−5.95	−0.76	0.84	3.65
De Facto Policy Autonomy	293	2.90	1.05	1.02	2.16	3.56	4.87
De Jure Policy Autonomy	293	3.23	1.37	0	2	4	6
Operational Alliances	293	1.83	1.22	0.00	1.04	2.69	4.95
Facilitating Agreements	293	0.31	0.46	0	0	1	1
Monitoring Compliance	293	0.34	0.47	0	0	1	1
Capacity Building	293	0.77	0.42	0	1	1	1
Designing Interventions	293	0.38	0.49	0	0	1	1
Implementing Operations	293	0.40	0.49	0	0	1	1
Allocating Resources	293	0.40	0.49	0	0	1	1
# Members (log)	293	4.96	0.60	1.95	5.08	5.25	5.25
Preference Heterogeneity	293	0.72	0.12	0.03	0.71	0.76	1.01
Policy Scope	293	1.39	0.57	1	1	2	3
Age (log)	293	3.58	0.74	1.39	3.04	4.14	5.04
GDP Asymmetry	293	0.25	0.11	0.19	0.20	0.24	0.96
Average Democracy	293	4.58	1.11	3.58	4.15	4.36	10.00
Geographical Diversity	293	1,565.34	832.93	985.35	1,245.58	1,355.43	5,763.89
Income	293	2,216.15	3,748.58	0.001	282.36	2,990.00	41,807.43
Development Institution	293	0.36	0.48	0	0	1	1
Education Institution	293	0.08	0.27	0	0	0	1
Environment Institution	293	0.10	0.30	0	0	0	1
Humanitarian Institution	293	0.20	0.40	0	0	0	1
Health Institution	293	0.23	0.42	0	0	0	1

Note: Values cover all years in which donor performance ratings have been issued (up to the end of 2018); they are not lagged.

B.6   Simultaneous Equations Approach

The two sets of structural models in Chapter 3's simultaneous equations system can be expressed as:

$$PI_e = \beta_1 DFPA + \gamma_1 \mathbf{X}_1 + \epsilon_1 \tag{B.1}$$

$$DFPA = \beta_2 PI_e + \gamma_2 \mathbf{X}_2 + \epsilon_2, \tag{B.2}$$

where *PI* stands for performance index; *DFPA* for *De Facto Policy Autonomy*; *e* indexes performance evaluations; $\mathbf{X}_1$ is a matrix of the variables *De Jure Policy Autonomy*, *# Members*, *Preference Heterogeneity*, and *Policy Scope*; and $\mathbf{X}_2$ is a matrix of *De Jure Policy Autonomy*, *Operational Alliances*, *Designing Interventions*, *Implementing Operations*, *Allocating Resources*, *# Members*, *Preference Heterogeneity*, and *Age*.

If *DFPA* and PI_e are endogenous to one another, OLS produces biased coefficient estimates because its assumption that the error term is uncorrelated with regressors is violated. Since PI_e is a function of ϵ_1 in Equation B.1, *DFPA* would be a function of ϵ_1 in Equation B.2, which entails that *DFPA* would be correlated with ϵ_1 in Equation B.1. By analogous logic, PI_e would be correlated with ϵ_2 in Equation B.2. Thus,

$$Cov(DFPA, \epsilon_1) \neq Cov(PI_e, \epsilon_2) \neq 0. \tag{B.3}$$

In addition, OLS estimates will be inconsistent, that is, they will never converge to the true population coefficients. Rather, in the limit, they will approach these parameters plus some bias $\mathbf{b}$:[1]

$$plim(\hat{\beta}_1) = \beta_1 + \mathbf{b}_1 \tag{B.4}$$

$$plim(\hat{\beta}_2) = \beta_2 + \mathbf{b}_2. \tag{B.5}$$

A common approach to dealing with this problem is to construct instruments for the instrumental variables – that is, variables that are correlated with them but uncorrelated with the error term. This is usually implemented with the method of two-stage least squares (2SLS), which, as its name suggests, proceeds in two steps. In the first, we estimate reduced-form models that express endogenous regressors solely as a function of exogenous variables:

$$DFPA = \gamma_1 \mathbf{X}_1 + \gamma_2 \mathbf{X}_2 + \upsilon_1 \tag{B.6}$$

$$PI_e = \gamma_3 \mathbf{X}_1 + \gamma_4 \mathbf{X}_2 + \upsilon_2. \tag{B.7}$$

---

[1] See, e.g., Gujarati (2004, 724–727).

The estimators can be written as:

$$\widehat{DFPA} = \hat{\gamma}_1 \mathbf{X}_1 + \hat{\gamma}_2 \mathbf{X}_2 \tag{B.8}$$

$$\widehat{PI_e} = \hat{\gamma}_1 \mathbf{X}_1 + \hat{\gamma}_2 \mathbf{X}_2. \tag{B.9}$$

Provided that the exogenous variables are uncorrelated with ϵ_1 and ϵ_2, so too will $\widehat{DFPA}$ and $\widehat{PI_e}$.

In the second step, we substitute predicted values from the reduced-form equations for the corresponding endogenous variables in the structural equations:

$$PI_e = \beta_1 \widehat{DFPA} + \gamma_1 \mathbf{X}_1 + \epsilon_1 \tag{B.10}$$

$$DFPA = \beta_2 \widehat{PI_e} + \gamma_2 \mathbf{X}_2 + \epsilon_2. \tag{B.11}$$

If $\widehat{PI_e}$ and $\widehat{DFPA}$ are uncorrelated with ϵ_1 and ϵ_2, the resulting coefficient estimates will be consistent (though possibly biased in tiny samples).

Three additional issues merit mention. First, identification under 2SLS requires that at least one exogenous variable does not feature in both structural equations. If all exogenous variables overlap, the instrument would induce perfect collinearity (being a linear combination of these variables). This problem is avoided because $\mathbf{X}_1 \neq \mathbf{X}_2$: *Operational Alliances, Designing Interventions, Implementing Operations, Allocating Resources,* and *Age* are not in $\mathbf{X}_1$, while *Policy Scope* is not in $\mathbf{X}_2$.

Second, estimated standard errors require a small adjustment in the second stage because they do not account for the fact that $\widehat{DFPA}$ and $\widehat{PI_e}$ are only estimates of PI_e and $DFPA$, respectively. This involves multiplying them by the ratio of standard error estimates in the second-stage and the structural equations:

$$\frac{\hat{\sigma}_{\epsilon,B.11}}{\hat{\sigma}_{\epsilon,B.1}} \tag{B.12}$$

for Equation B.11 and

$$\frac{\hat{\sigma}_{\epsilon,B.10}}{\hat{\sigma}_{\epsilon,B.2}} \tag{B.13}$$

for Equation B.10.[2]

Finally, the 2SLS estimator may be biased in the same direction as the OLS estimator when instruments are "weak," that is, poor predictors of endogenous regressors in the first stage.[3] In a standard F-test of the joint statistical significance of first-stage regressors, we can reject the

---

[2] See Gujarati (2004, 791).
[3] See Angrist and Pischke (2008, 206–209) for a formal derivation of this bias.

null hypothesis of a weak instrument in 12 of the 14 models.[4] The two exceptions are the models featuring the Danish and Dutch performance indices.

B.7   Additional Statistical Results for Chapter 3

Table B.11 *Summary of baseline results with constituent performance indicators*

Dependent variable (performance indicator)	Type	Assessor	De Facto Policy Autonomy		De Jure Policy Autonomy	
			Coef.	S.E.	Coef.	S.E.
Delivering results	DR	Australia	0.383**	(0.078)	0.042	(0.091)
Contribution to multilateral system	DR	Australia	0.149	(0.091)	−0.02	(0.084)
Strategic management and performance	SM	Australia	0.406**	(0.100)	0.016	(0.076)
Cost and value consciousness	FM	Australia	0.265*	(0.119)	−0.025	(0.076)
Organizational effectiveness	DR	Denmark	0.228	(0.138)	0.133	(0.081)
Innovation and agenda setting	KM	Denmark	0.063	(0.179)	−0.001	(0.072)
Risk management	SM	Denmark	0.156	(0.117)	0.054	(0.062)
Compliance with international obligations	DR	Denmark	0.114	(0.141)	0.174*	(0.076)
Involvement in multilateral reform agenda	SM	Denmark	0.014	(0.210)	−0.037	(0.100)
Financing and funding	FM	Denmark	0.267	(0.331)	−0.138	(0.142)
Contribution to multilateral system	DR	Denmark	0.319	(0.281)	0.241†	(0.121)
Organizational and financial framework	FM	MOPAN	0.09	(0.083)	−0.071	(0.069)
Structures for cross-cutting issues	KM	MOPAN	0.06	(0.094)	−0.004	(0.051)
Relevance and agility	SM	MOPAN	0.163†	(0.083)	−0.041	(0.054)
Cost-effective and transparent	FM	MOPAN	0.118*	(0.047)	0.001	(0.037)
Results focus	DR	MOPAN	0.003	(0.116)	−0.062	(0.074)
Achievement of results	DR	MOPAN	0.081	(0.080)	0.023	(0.064)
Results delivered efficiently	FM	MOPAN	−0.046	(0.078)	0.157*	(0.062)
Sustainability of results	DR	MOPAN	−0.07	(0.082)	0.069	(0.052)
Providing direction for results	SM	MOPAN	0.159	(0.106)	0.058	(0.084)
Country focus on results	DR	MOPAN	0.260**	(0.081)	0.024	(0.043)
Corporate focus on results	DR	MOPAN	0.078	(0.101)	0.064	(0.063)
Resource allocation decisions	FM	MOPAN	0.194	(0.139)	−0.108	(0.085)
Linking aid management to performance	KM	MOPAN	−0.042	(0.121)	0.001	(0.044)
Financial accountability	FM	MOPAN	0.154†	(0.087)	−0.003	(0.033)
Using performance information	KM	MOPAN	0.111	(0.109)	0.019	(0.051)

---

[4] Standard errors are clustered by institution.

Table B.11 *(cont.)*

Dependent variable (performance indicator)	Type	Assessor	De Facto Policy Autonomy		De Jure Policy Autonomy	
			Coef.	S.E.	Coef.	S.E.
Managing human resources	SM	MOPAN	0.182	(0.110)	0.082	(0.052)
Performance-oriented programming	SM	MOPAN	0.079	(0.119)	0.065	(0.065)
Evaluating results	KM	MOPAN	0.175	(0.114)	−0.006	(0.070)
Presenting performance information	KM	MOPAN	0.073	(0.080)	0.058	(0.047)
Disseminating lessons learned	KM	MOPAN	0.161	(0.119)	$0.080^\dagger$	(0.040)
Focus on core mandate	DR	Netherlands	0.268**	(0.079)	−0.146*	(0.055)
Strategy and focus	SM	Netherlands	$0.161^\dagger$	(0.089)	0.036	(0.069)
Effective governance	SM	Netherlands	0.262**	(0.069)	−0.002	(0.035)
Human resources management	SM	Netherlands	$0.106^\dagger$	(0.054)	0.011	(0.039)
Financial management	FM	Netherlands	0.178**	(0.060)	0.028	(0.036)
Results control	DR	Netherlands	0.205**	(0.056)	0.009	(0.044)
Internal effectiveness	SM	Sweden	0.799**	(0.170)	−0.031	(0.102)
External effectiveness	DR	Sweden	0.540**	(0.141)	0.05	(0.099)
Critical to international aid objectives	DR	UK	0.419**	(0.088)	0.016	(0.073)
Focus on poor countries	SM	UK	0.504**	(0.128)	−0.092	(0.119)
Delivery of results	DR	UK	0.395**	(0.059)	0.092*	(0.040)
Cost and value consciousness	FM	UK	0.318**	(0.083)	0.059	(0.052)
Strategic/performance management	SM	UK	0.431**	(0.096)	0.022	(0.061)
Financial resources management	FM	UK	0.335**	(0.071)	−0.006	(0.072)
Comparative advantage	SM	UK	0.288*	(0.105)	0.069	(0.059)
Geography and resources	KM	UK	0.341**	(0.079)	0.058	(0.066)
Human resources	SM	UK	0.188*	(0.071)	0.123*	(0.046)
Risk assurance	SM	UK	0.172*	(0.077)	0.054	(0.050)
Fraud	FM	UK	0.138	(0.104)	−0.04	(0.072)
Efficiency	FM	UK	$0.167^\dagger$	(0.093)	−0.034	(0.062)

Notes: $^\dagger p < 0.1$; $^* p < 0.05$; $^{**} p < 0.01$. Estimations of the Table 3.5 specification with the dependent variable disaggregated into its constituent performance indicators. In the second column, DR = delivery of results; FM = financial management; SM = strategic management; KM = knowledge management.

Table B.12 *Summary of robustness checks: Relationship between performance and policy autonomy*

Regressor:	De Facto Policy Autonomy							De Jure Policy Autonomy						
Dependent variable:	Austral. (1)	Danish (2)	MOPAN (3)	Dutch (4)	Swedish (5)	UK (6)	Avg. (7)	Austral. (1)	Danish (2)	MOPAN (3)	Dutch (4)	Swedish (5)	UK (6)	Avg. (7)
Robustness check														
Development issue control	0.633** (0.141)	0.338 (0.265)	0.227† (0.131)	0.776** (0.147)	1.014** (0.211)	0.947** (0.129)	0.723** (0.107)	0.009 (0.101)	0.091 (0.088)	0.032 (0.061)	−0.014 (0.087)	−0.021 (0.098)	0.035 (0.105)	0.004 (0.059)
Education issue control	0.580** (0.097)	0.528† (0.273)	0.275† (0.143)	0.703** (0.154)	1.076** (0.226)	0.903** (0.123)	0.682** (0.089)	0.036 (0.093)	0.092 (0.078)	0.022 (0.057)	0.035 (0.095)	0.005 (0.108)	0.052 (0.106)	0.029 (0.058)
Environment issue control	0.618** (0.137)	0.444† (0.248)	0.280† (0.139)	0.682** (0.158)	0.978** (0.184)	0.928** (0.128)	0.687** (0.101)	0.017 (0.100)	0.117 (0.117)	0.026 (0.066)	0.004 (0.107)	0.109 (0.112)	0.052 (0.106)	0.031 (0.063)
Humanitarian issue control	0.606** (0.140)	0.426 (0.286)	0.428** (0.153)	0.656** (0.153)	0.948** (0.272)	0.931** (0.145)	0.700** (0.110)	0.001 (0.093)	0.095 (0.124)	0.076 (0.064)	0.003 (0.100)	0.003 (0.133)	0.045 (0.108)	0.026 (0.065)
Health issue control	0.628** (0.142)	0.466 (0.285)	0.312* (0.121)	0.712** (0.162)	0.949** (0.196)	0.960** (0.126)	0.714** (0.115)	0.026 (0.105)	0.116 (0.097)	0.098 (0.082)	0.067 (0.113)	−0.006 (0.099)	0.124 (0.111)	0.060 (0.069)
Income (log) control	0.604** (0.140)	0.328 (0.254)	0.293* (0.123)	0.576** (0.141)	0.803** (0.166)	0.780** (0.114)	0.582** (0.089)	0.009 (0.100)	0.091 (0.097)	0.025 (0.056)	−0.017 (0.094)	−0.058 (0.093)	0.008 (0.110)	−0.023 (0.058)
GDP asymmetry control	0.594** (0.132)	0.408 (0.261)	0.268† (0.140)	0.689** (0.153)	0.958** (0.207)	0.898** (0.118)	0.675** (0.102)	0.024 (0.102)	0.119 (0.093)	0.019 (0.056)	0.033 (0.099)	0.007 (0.111)	0.086 (0.099)	0.037 (0.061)
Geographical diversity control	0.629** (0.139)	0.348 (0.258)	0.212 (0.150)	0.705** (0.164)	1.009** (0.212)	0.938** (0.140)	0.698** (0.110)	0.032 (0.102)	0.073 (0.086)	−0.003 (0.055)	0.037 (0.106)	0.029 (0.102)	0.051 (0.108)	0.023 (0.063)
Mean democracy control	0.621** (0.138)	0.299 (0.285)	0.282† (0.145)	0.688** (0.156)	0.975** (0.214)	0.946** (0.136)	0.693** (0.106)	0.011 (0.103)	0.093 (0.086)	0.022 (0.056)	0.021 (0.104)	0.006 (0.110)	0.057 (0.103)	0.019 (0.062)
UN System control	0.613** (0.145)	0.406 (0.271)	0.281* (0.133)	0.729** (0.149)	0.952** (0.190)	0.909** (0.138)	0.688** (0.109)	0.008 (0.101)	0.114 (0.084)	0.023 (0.050)	0.055 (0.104)	−0.0003 (0.117)	0.039 (0.111)	0.015 (0.063)
World Bank Group control	0.554** (0.131)	0.33 (0.282)	0.209 (0.129)	0.644** (0.157)	0.790** (0.134)	0.907** (0.141)	0.635** (0.099)	0.006 (0.101)	0.084 (0.089)	0.009 (0.057)	0.021 (0.102)	−0.013 (0.090)	0.051 (0.105)	0.017 (0.063)

Table B.12 *(cont.)*

Regressor:	De Facto Policy Autonomy							De Jure Policy Autonomy						
Dependent variable:	Austral. (1)	Danish (2)	MOPAN (3)	Dutch (4)	Swedish (5)	UK (6)	Avg. (7)	Austral. (1)	Danish (2)	MOPAN (3)	Dutch (4)	Swedish (5)	UK (6)	Avg. (7)
Year fixed effects		0.438† (0.249)	0.267† (0.141)	0.703** (0.158)	0.976** (0.201)	0.937** (0.135)	0.696** (0.106)		0.101 (0.088)	0.058 (0.080)	0.035 (0.103)	0.042 (0.111)	0.051 (0.107)	0.029 (0.065)
Including time trend control	0.621** (0.138)	0.438† (0.249)	0.281† (0.140)	0.702** (0.158)	0.975** (0.199)	0.938** (0.134)	0.695** (0.107)	0.012 (0.100)	0.101 (0.088)	0.022 (0.056)	0.034 (0.102)	0.042 (0.110)	0.051 (0.106)	0.02 (0.063)
Including squared time trend control	0.621** (0.138)	0.438† (0.249)	0.279† (0.140)	0.699** (0.158)	0.976** (0.199)	0.938** (0.135)	0.695** (0.107)	0.012 (0.100)	0.101 (0.088)	0.022 (0.056)	0.033 (0.102)	0.042 (0.110)	0.051 (0.106)	0.02 (0.063)
Year × UN System fixed effects		0.407 (0.282)	0.245† (0.128)	0.746** (0.158)	0.970** (0.189)	0.906** (0.141)	0.696** (0.107)		0.119 (0.089)	0.078 (0.090)	0.077 (0.107)	0.041 (0.131)	0.038 (0.113)	0.03 (0.064)
Year × WB Group fixed effects		0.330 (0.294)	0.213 (0.144)	0.662** (0.162)	0.811** (0.138)	0.907** (0.144)	0.640** (0.101)	0.030 (0.107)	0.084 (0.093)	0.037 (0.081)	0.036 (0.106)	0.02 (0.098)	0.052 (0.107)	0.024 (0.067)
Excluding PPPs	0.607** (0.145)	0.431† (0.249)	0.266† (0.143)	0.687** (0.157)	0.955** (0.213)	0.905** (0.135)	0.680** (0.109)	0.030 (0.107)	0.111 (0.085)	0.037 (0.056)	0.034 (0.107)	0.034 (0.097)	0.111 (0.099)	0.046 (0.061)
Excluding influential cases	0.389** (0.081)	0.270 (0.249)	0.248† (0.136)	0.460** (0.091)	1.040** (0.202)	0.944** (0.135)	0.565** (0.076)	0.028 (0.083)	0.075 (0.078)	0.013 (0.054)	0.053 (0.064)	0.036 (0.100)	0.018 (0.098)	0.016 (0.051)
Excluding humanitarian	0.660** (0.144)	0.536† (0.267)	0.288† (0.166)	0.678** (0.163)	1.051** (0.242)	0.982** (0.152)	0.736** (0.114)	0.008 (0.101)	0.086 (0.075)	0.016 (0.054)	0.031 (0.102)	0.017 (0.100)	−0.020 (0.106)	0.00001 (0.064)

Notes: †$p < 0.1$; *$p < 0.05$; **$p < 0.01$. OLS coefficient estimates on the two policy autonomy variables in modified versions of the Table 3.5 specification, i.e., the first set of baseline models. Robust standard errors, clustered by institution where performance evaluations have multiple waves, are reported in parentheses. All regressors are lagged by one year. For details on the robustness checks, see the penultimate section of Chapter 3.

Table B.13 Summary of robustness checks: Sources of de facto policy autonomy

Regressor:	Oper. Allian.	Facil. Agree.	Oper. Allian.	Monit. Comp.	Oper. Allian.	Capac. Build.	Oper. Allian.	Design. Inter.	Oper. Allian.	Implem. Oper.	Oper. Allian.	Alloc. Res.
	(1)		(2)		(3)		(4)		(5)		(6)	
Robustness check												
Development issue control	0.327** (0.097)	−1.105** (0.293)	0.502** (0.108)	−0.218 (0.333)	0.514** (0.097)	−0.374 (0.353)	0.296** (0.088)	1.189** (0.291)	0.301** (0.082)	1.123** (0.273)	0.473** (0.109)	0.382 (0.319)
Education issue control	0.349** (0.107)	−1.066** (0.303)	0.506** (0.116)	−0.312 (0.299)	0.514** (0.097)	−0.188 (0.331)	0.300** (0.088)	1.197** (0.290)	0.313** (0.081)	1.092** (0.260)	0.476** (0.112)	0.455† (0.254)
Environment issue control	0.326** (0.109)	−1.117** (0.305)	0.491** (0.107)	−0.371 (0.289)	0.543** (0.112)	−0.169 (0.359)	0.291** (0.083)	1.277** (0.270)	0.302** (0.075)	1.170** (0.244)	0.458** (0.107)	0.510† (0.260)
Humanitarian issue control	0.334** (0.102)	−1.078** (0.307)	0.458** (0.094)	−0.400 (0.274)	0.532** (0.104)	−0.127 (0.305)	0.289** (0.085)	1.203** (0.265)	0.301** (0.078)	1.124** (0.243)	0.380** (0.092)	0.744* (0.295)
Health issue control	0.371** (0.105)	−1.007** (0.298)	0.536** (0.116)	−0.202 (0.322)	0.509** (0.100)	−0.117 (0.306)	0.332** (0.091)	1.108** (0.293)	0.338** (0.086)	1.010** (0.283)	0.509** (0.109)	0.334 (0.231)
Income (log) control	0.353** (0.116)	−1.099** (0.301)	0.480** (0.128)	−0.374 (0.289)	0.524** (0.130)	−0.183 (0.339)	0.270** (0.115)	1.232** (0.274)	0.309** (0.107)	1.125** (0.251)	0.478** (0.124)	0.530* (0.251)
GDP asymmetry control	0.349** (0.104)	−1.099** (0.299)	0.496** (0.109)	−0.362 (0.286)	0.499** (0.110)	−0.223 (0.341)	0.299** (0.088)	1.223** (0.276)	0.297** (0.084)	1.129** (0.259)	0.470** (0.108)	0.519* (0.250)
Geographical diversity control	0.326** (0.102)	−1.106** (0.299)	0.479** (0.109)	−0.379 (0.289)	0.522** (0.104)	−0.178 (0.332)	0.277** (0.088)	1.246** (0.274)	0.282** (0.081)	1.166** (0.252)	0.443** (0.108)	0.546* (0.247)
Mean democracy control	0.347** (0.107)	−1.084** (0.299)	0.501** (0.113)	−0.366 (0.286)	0.543** (0.110)	−0.164 (0.340)	0.291** (0.089)	1.225** (0.291)	0.312** (0.083)	1.111** (0.253)	0.471** (0.111)	0.510* (0.248)
UN System control	0.339** (0.101)	−1.096** (0.300)	0.490** (0.106)	−0.379 (0.290)	0.533** (0.102)	−0.275 (0.407)	0.293** (0.085)	1.234** (0.271)	0.301** (0.079)	1.123** (0.254)	0.459** (0.103)	0.554* (0.244)

Table B.13 (cont.)

Regressor:	Oper. Allian.	Facil. Agree.	Oper. Allian.	Monit. Comp.	Oper. Allian.	Capac. Build.	Oper. Allian.	Design. Inter.	Oper. Allian.	Implem. Oper.	Oper. Allian.	Alloc. Res.
	(1)		(2)		(3)		(4)		(5)		(6)	
World Bank Group control	0.327** (0.104)	−1.077** (0.299)	0.474** (0.110)	−0.330 (0.299)	0.502** (0.105)	−0.200 (0.342)	0.287** (0.086)	1.212** (0.279)	0.293** (0.080)	1.104** (0.251)	0.455** (0.106)	0.470 (0.295)
Year fixed effects	0.337** (0.105)	−1.097** (0.302)	0.489** (0.110)	−0.374 (0.294)	0.531** (0.106)	−0.167 (0.344)	0.289** (0.088)	1.236** (0.280)	0.300** (0.080)	1.140** (0.258)	0.459** (0.108)	0.508* (0.256)
Including time trend control	0.336** (0.102)	−1.096** (0.298)	0.487** (0.107)	−0.374 (0.289)	0.529** (0.104)	−0.187 (0.340)	0.289** (0.085)	1.234** (0.276)	0.299** (0.078)	1.134** (0.255)	0.457** (0.106)	0.512* (0.253)
Including squared time trend control	0.336** (0.102)	−1.096** (0.298)	0.487** (0.107)	−0.374 (0.289)	0.529** (0.104)	−0.185 (0.338)	0.289** (0.085)	1.235** (0.276)	0.299** (0.078)	1.133** (0.254)	0.457** (0.106)	0.511* (0.253)
Year × UN System fixed effects	0.345** (0.105)	−1.094** (0.308)	0.499** (0.109)	−0.372 (0.299)	0.541** (0.105)	−0.240 (0.428)	0.294** (0.087)	1.254** (0.279)	0.302** (0.081)	1.152** (0.266)	0.467** (0.105)	0.556** (0.250)
Year × WB Group fixed effects	0.329** (0.109)	−1.078** (0.307)	0.477** (0.113)	−0.331 (0.307)	0.504** (0.109)	−0.190 (0.354)	0.287** (0.090)	1.218** (0.289)	0.294** (0.084)	1.119** (0.261)	0.458** (0.110)	0.466 (0.303)
Excluding PPPs	0.404** (0.123)	−1.047** (0.303)	0.576** (0.124)	−0.315 (0.276)	0.628** (0.123)	−0.487 (0.377)	0.292* (0.122)	1.312** (0.328)	0.320** (0.113)	1.133** (0.289)	0.544** (0.119)	0.553* (0.259)
Excluding influential cases	0.338** (0.102)	−1.136** (0.287)	0.492** (0.110)	−0.442 (0.283)	0.567** (0.110)	0.127 (0.372)	0.288** (0.081)	1.276** (0.267)	0.283** (0.074)	1.178** (0.245)	0.477** (0.109)	0.518* (0.244)
Excluding humanitarian	0.303* (0.107)	−1.090** (0.307)	0.411** (0.099)	−0.512 (0.314)	0.489** (0.105)	−0.269 (0.345)	0.265** (0.086)	1.224** (0.275)	0.252** (0.081)	1.223** (0.266)	0.366** (0.097)	0.720** (0.258)

Notes: $^{\dagger}p < 0.1$; $^{*}p < 0.05$; $^{**}p < 0.01$. OLS coefficient estimates on the hypothesized sources of de facto policy autonomy in modified versions of the Table 3.6 specification, i.e., the second set of baseline models. Robust standard errors, clustered by institution, are reported in parentheses. All regressors are lagged by one year. The robustness checks are described in detail in the penultimate section of Chapter 3.

Table B.14 *Summary of robustness checks: Simultaneous equations analysis*

Regressor:	*De Facto Policy Autonomy* (First set of structural equations)						
Dependent variable (performance index):	Austral. (1)	Danish (2)	MOPAN (3)	Dutch (4)	Swedish (5)	UK (6)	Avg. (7)
Robustness check							
Excluding *Operational Alliances*	0.941** (0.172)	0.948** (0.319)	0.268 (0.231)	0.936** (0.186)	1.172** (0.362)	1.081** (0.189)	0.845** (0.151)
Design features only	0.921** (0.164)	1.061** (0.332)	0.475* (0.184)	0.945** (0.194)	1.033** (0.185)	0.955** (0.185)	0.804** (0.138)
Exogenous variables lagged	0.911** (0.166)	1.061** (0.334)	0.465* (0.187)	0.932** (0.194)	1.033** (0.328)	0.946** (0.180)	0.805** (0.136)

Regressor:	*De Jure Policy Autonomy* (First set of structural equations)						
Dependent variable (performance index):	Austral. (8)	Danish (9)	MOPAN (10)	Dutch (11)	Swedish (12)	UK (13)	Avg. (14)
Robustness check							
Excluding *Operational Alliances*	0.026 (0.109)	0.140 (0.098)	0.021 (0.065)	0.024 (0.102)	0.015 (0.110)	0.062 (0.111)	0.023 (0.065)
Design features only	0.012 (0.104)	0.125 (0.098)	0.015 (0.071)	0.037 (0.104)	0.005 (0.099)	0.028 (0.110)	0.013 (0.065)
Exogenous variables lagged	0.011 (0.103)	0.125 (0.098)	0.013 (0.070)	0.037 (0.104)	0.005 (0.099)	0.043 (0.113)	0.017 (0.066)

Regressor:	Donor performance indices (Second set of structural equations)						
Dependent variable:	*De Facto Policy Autonomy*						
	(15)	(16)	(17)	(18)	(19)	(20)	(21)
Robustness check							
Excluding *Operational Alliances:*							
Controlling for *Designing Interventions*	1.151† (0.659)	0.865 (0.573)	−0.104 (0.311)	0.406 (0.278)	0.523* (0.247)	0.194 (0.240)	0.651* (0.302)
Controlling for *Implementing Operations*	0.852* (0.387)	0.601* (0.257)	0.473* (0.217)	0.455** (0.116)	0.414 (0.322)	0.405** (0.142)	0.642** (0.162)
Controlling for *Allocating Resources*	1.023** (0.281)	0.733 (0.645)	0.528 (0.772)	0.704** (0.201)	0.766** (0.239)	1.208** (0.284)	1.403** (0.347)
Design features only:							
Controlling for *Designing Interventions*	1.252† (0.699)	0.805 (0.995)	−0.240 (0.349)	0.378 (0.363)	0.611* (0.272)	0.470 (0.351)	0.829* (0.391)
Controlling for *Implementing Operations*	0.837* (0.313)	0.408 (0.253)	0.32 (0.211)	0.437** (0.138)	0.586 (0.461)	0.472** (0.146)	0.682** (0.176)
Controlling for *Allocating Resources*	1.020** (0.274)	0.729 (0.629)	0.568 (0.840)	0.736** (0.237)	0.851** (0.255)	1.372** (0.382)	1.492** (0.389)
Exogenous variables lagged:							
Controlling for *Designing Interventions*	1.204† (0.686)	0.833 (1.029)	−0.233 (0.336)	0.364 (0.374)	0.617* (0.272)	0.497 (0.383)	0.881* (0.437)
Controlling for *Implementing Operations*	0.831* (0.312)	0.408 (0.254)	0.308 (0.207)	0.423** (0.137)	0.606 (0.475)	0.471** (0.145)	0.683** (0.174)
Controlling for *Allocating Resources*	1.061** (0.291)	0.728 (0.623)	0.409 (0.876)	0.719** (0.228)	0.848** (0.250)	1.383** (0.379)	1.458** (0.365)

Notes: †$p < 0.1$; *$p < 0.05$; **$p < 0.01$. Second-stage 2SLS estimates with robust standard errors, clustered by institution where performance evaluations have multiple waves, in parentheses. For details on the robustness checks, see the penultimate section of Chapter 3. For further discussion of the simultaneous equations strategy, see Appendix B.6.

B.8 SWA Mechanisms and Alternative Accountability Indicators

Table B.15 *Correlations between SWA indices and accountability indicators in donor performance evaluations*

	Performance evaluations			SWA index				SWA
Assessor	Accountability indicator	Year	N	Transparency	Evaluation	Inspection	Investigation	Composite
UK	Transparency and accountability	2011–2013	81	0.38*				0.43*
	Transparency	2016	35	0.61**				0.51**
Australia	Transparency and accountability	2012	42	0.48**				0.38*
Denmark	Provision of information	2012	17	0.41				0.45†
	Economic responsibility	2013	17		0.34	0.50*		0.43†
Netherlands	Policy evaluation	2011–2015	115		0.34**			0.44**
	Anti-corruption policy	2011–2015	115	0.26**		0.17†		0.25**
	Financial management	2011–2015	115	0.40**		0.50**		0.50**
MOPAN	Disseminating lessons learned	2009–2014	23	0.38**	0.39**			0.48**
	Evaluating external results	2009–2014	23		0.62**			0.67**
	Financial accountability	2009–2014	23		0.58**		0.31†	0.54**
	Using performance information	2009–2014	23	0.46*	0.41†			0.53**
	Presenting performance information	2009–2014	23	0.5*				0.54**
	Resource allocation decisions	2009–2014	23	0.69**				0.62**
	Cost-effective and transparent systems	2016–2018	26	0.49*		0.37†		0.53**
	Evidence-based planning	2016–2018	26	0.67**	0.68**			0.75**

Notes: †$p < 0.1$; *$p < 0.05$; **$p < 0.01$. The donor performance evaluations contain no indicators that correspond to the *Participation* SWA index (hence its exclusion from the table).

Appendix C Interview Methods and List

I conducted 142 semi-structured interviews, lasting approximately 185 hours, for this book. The vast majority took place in Geneva, New York, Rome, and Washington, DC – the four most common headquarters locations in the Performance of International Institutions Project (PIIP) dataset – in four waves between 2012 and 2020. Each set of interviews played a slightly different role in the research process.

The first wave was undertaken in Geneva and Washington, DC, in the spring of 2012, shortly after I embarked upon the project. They primarily served exploratory and theory-building purposes, though I draw on some of their material in the case studies. In the second wave, which spanned a Roman midwinter, I sought to "road test" an early version of my theoretical framework on international food security institutions, the subject of Chapter 4. Coming away with greater confidence in the argument's explanatory power, I extended this hypothesis-testing exercise to PIIP institutions based in New York and Washington, DC, where I conducted the third wave of interviews in the late spring and early summer of 2018. The fourth wave, which stretched over much of 2020, focused on the global health agencies examined in Chapter 5. The interviews were originally scheduled for June and July in Geneva, where these institutions are located, but had to take place via video conference due to the coronavirus (COVID-19) pandemic. Outside these four clusters, I held 17 interviews, of which eight were in person (in Boston, London, Oxford, and Rome) and nine were remote.

In each wave, I emailed interview requests to a selection of international bureaucrats, member state representatives, and other public and private stakeholders with knowledge of or an interest in institutional performance issues.[1] As I was not attempting to evaluate performance myself, I did not strive for comprehensiveness or equity in my coverage of these groups. Rather, my goal was to gain a better understanding of the

---

[1] An obvious limitation of my sampling strategy is that I was unable to meet non-governmental stakeholders based in developing countries. Many of the individuals I did interview, however, had recently served in such nations.

factors and processes shaping performance and of different approaches to assessing, measuring, and operationalizing this variable.

Within an institution's secretariat, I mostly targeted members of its senior management, its evaluation office (which focuses specifically on performance assessment), and its partnerships or external relations division. Among the membership, I sought out states of varying size and power, though I often found it hard to obtain contact information for delegates from small developing countries. The number of relevant nongovernmental stakeholders varied across cities, making a methodical approach to sampling more difficult. In nearly all cases, I identified targets using a combination of institutional documentation on stakeholders, databases of nongovernmental organizations (NGOs), and referrals by previous interviewees (a strategy dubbed "snowball sampling").[2] The 17 interviews that occurred between waves were organized on an ad-hoc basis, in some cases because the interviewee was unable to attend the original meeting and in others as a follow-up to an email exchange.[3]

I managed to interview at least one individual from every institution or organization I contacted, suggesting reasonable representation of the sample frame. Overall, almost 80 percent of interview requests were fulfilled, with no significant difference in acceptance rates between the interviewee categories mentioned earlier.

In every interview, I began by briefly explaining my research goals and providing some background about myself. I made it clear to interviewees that, unless they requested otherwise (either during or after the interview), information they disclosed could be included in a future academic publication in suitably anonymized form. Given the sensitive nature of the issues broached, I believed that interviewees would be more likely to speak openly and honestly if assured that their identity would be kept confidential.

Interviews were organized around four core themes: (1) the current performance (individual dimensions as well as overall) of the institution in question; (2) the evolution of its performance over time; (3) the key factors explaining its contemporary and historical performance; and (4) how it could be made more effective. From the second wave of interviews onward, I included questions on the sources and performance implications of de jure and de facto policy autonomy. This line of inquiry typically followed the third set of questions, allowing interviewees to reflect on the drivers of performance before being "exposed" to my

---

[2] Bleich and Pekkanen (2013).
[3] In the latter cases, I had usually emailed the interviewee to request information for the PIIP or a case study.

theoretical hunches. Nevertheless, I was gratified to observe a large number of interviewees anticipating my conjectures in their answers.[4] In the third wave, I also asked about the relationship between performance and accountability (in most cases at the end of the interview).

To avoid encouraging or discouraging any type of answer, I sought to pose questions and react to answers in as neutral a manner as possible. As the concept of institutional performance inevitably comes with normative connotations (as noted in Chapter 3), I characterized the project in more general terms, frequently describing its subject as the "functioning" or "operation" of international institutions and emphasizing its aim of "learning lessons for policy." When interviewing international bureaucrats, who generally came across as personally invested in their institution's success, I often approached performance issues in an indirect way, for example, by inviting them to identify areas where their department had been particularly successful and where there was room for improvement. I refrained from explicitly stating my hypotheses, even when discussing the effects of policy autonomy.

Within the loose confines of this structure, I provided opportunities for interviewees to bring up related issues, request clarification of questions, and pose queries of their own. It was not uncommon, for instance, for interviewees to ask me how I defined institutional performance, leading to a more abstract – but often stimulating – conceptual conversation. I, too, asked follow-up questions when responses were unclear or I sought more detailed information (which was particularly common during discussions of policymaking mechanics). In general, I endeavored to allow the conversation to flow naturally and in the direction desired by the interviewee, though I made sure to reorient it toward my interests when it drifted off course.

My principal method for documenting interviews was simultaneous note-taking; I initially used an audio recording device but felt that it was inhibiting interviewees. I regularly added and fleshed out notes immediately after interviews because I did not wish to halt or disrupt the conversation. In a few cases, I later followed up with the interviewee via email to clarify points of ambiguity or uncertainty. Before writing up the case studies, I compiled full electronic transcripts of the interviews and organized them using the NVivo software package. The majority of interviews lasted between 40 minutes and one hour, with almost a fifth exceeding 90 minutes.

---

[4] This is perhaps not surprising, given that the hypotheses were informed by the first wave of interviews, in which the positive impact of de facto policy autonomy on performance was a recurring theme.

Table C.1 presents a full chronological list of interviews (indexed by number to those cited in the main text). Affiliations and departments are at the time of interview; to maintain anonymity, specific job titles are not disclosed. All in all, around half of interviewees were international bureaucrats (from 25 PIIP institutions and two non-PIIP institutions), a quarter were state delegates (from 24 countries), and a fifth were nongovernmental stakeholders (from 20 organizations).

Table C.1 *List of interviews (anonymized)*

#	Affiliation[a,b]	Department	Date	Location[c]
1	IMF	Independent Evaluation Office	May 3, 2012	Wash., DC
2	State (North America)	IMF Board of Governors	May 3, 2012	Wash., DC
3	IMF	Office of Internal Audit and Inspection	May 3, 2012	Wash., DC
4	WB	Inspection Panel	May 3, 2012	Wash., DC
5	Group of 24	Secretariat	May 3, 2012	Wash., DC
6	UN	Independent Audit Advisory Committee	May 4, 2012	Wash., DC
7	Bread for the World	State Relations Department	May 4, 2012	Wash., DC
8	Government Accountability Office	International Affairs and Trade	May 4, 2012	Wash., DC
9	Africare	Corporate Secretariat	May 10, 2012	Wash., DC
10	World Food Program USA	Secretariat	May 11, 2012	Wash., DC
11	FAO	Animal Production and Health Division	May 23, 2012	Rome
12	WHO	Internal Audit Department	June 4, 2012	Geneva
13	OHCHR	Policy, Planning, Monitoring, and Evaluation Service	June 4, 2012	Geneva
14	ILO	Evaluation Unit	June 5, 2012	Geneva
15	State (North America)	UNHCR Executive Committee	June 5, 2012	Geneva
16	State (Asia-Pacific)	Mission to the UN in Geneva	June 5, 2012	Geneva
17	State (Europe)	Mission to the UN in Geneva	June 5, 2012	Geneva
18	ILO	Office of Internal Audit and Oversight	June 6, 2012	Geneva
19	UNHCR	Policy Development and Evaluation Service	June 6, 2012	Geneva
20	WHO	Independent Expert Oversight Advisory Committee	June 7, 2012	Geneva
21	WIPO	Internal Audit and Oversight Division	June 7, 2012	Geneva
22	Group of 77	Geneva Chapter	June 7, 2012	Geneva
23	UNCTAD	Evaluation and Planning Unit	June 7, 2012	Geneva
24	State (Asia)	UNCTAD Trade and Development Board	June 7, 2012	Geneva
25	WTO	Economic Research and Statistics Division	June 7, 2012	Geneva
26	Médecins Sans Frontières	International Board	June 8, 2012	Geneva
27	UN	Joint Inspection Unit	June 8, 2012	Geneva
28	ICRC	Institutional Performance Management Unit	June 8, 2012	Geneva
29	UN	Office of Internal Oversight Services (Geneva Audit Service)	June 8, 2012	Geneva
30	Aga Khan Foundation	Institutional Partnerships Directorate	June 11, 2012	Geneva

Table C.1 *(Cont)*

#	Affiliation[a,b]	Department	Date	Location[c]
31	International AIDS Society	Governing Council	June 11, 2012	Geneva
32	UN Watch	Secretariat	June 12, 2012	Geneva
33	UNAIDS	Planning and Budget Division	June 12, 2012	Geneva
34	DFID	International Directors Office	June 29, 2012	London
35	Bretton Woods Project	Steering Group	July 11, 2012	London
36	Save the Children	Policy, Advocacy, and Campaigns Directorate	July 12, 2012	London
37	Oxfam	International Programmes Directorate	July 17, 2012	Oxford
38	UNW	Office of the Executive Director	November 19, 2013	Remote
39	UNODC	Inter-Agency Affairs	December 2, 2013	Remote
40	PIDG	Secretariat (MDY Legal)	December 2, 2013	Remote
41	CIFS	Administrative Unit	December 6, 2013	Remote
42	UNICEF	Office of the President	January 10, 2014	Remote
43	EDF	European Commission	January 17, 2014	Remote
44	IADB	Competitiveness, Technology, and Innovation Division	April 14, 2014	Boston
45	AsDB	Asian Development Bank Institute	August 26, 2014	Oxford
46	State (South America)	FAO Conference	January 19, 2015	Rome
47	State (Europe)	FAO Council	January 19, 2015	Rome
48	FAO	Office of Evaluation	January 19, 2015	Rome
49	FAO	Office of Strategy, Planning and Resources Management	January 20, 2015	Rome
50	FAO	Partnerships, Advocacy and Capacity Development Division	January 20, 2015	Rome
51	FAO	Office of the Director-General	January 21, 2015	Rome
52	WFP	Office of the Executive Director	January 21, 2015	Rome
53	WFP	Policy and Programme Division	January 21, 2015	Rome
54	WFP	Oversight Office	January 22, 2015	Rome
55	IFAD	Independent Office of Evaluation	January 23, 2015	Rome
56	State (Asia-Pacific)	FAO Assembly	January 23, 2015	Rome
57	State (Europe)	FAO Council	January 23, 2015	Rome
58	WFP	Logistics Division	January 23, 2015	Rome
59	WFP	Partnership and Advocacy Coordination Division	January 23, 2015	Rome
60	IFAD	Programme Management Department	January 26, 2015	Rome
61	IFAD	Budget and Organizational Development Unit	January 26, 2015	Rome
62	WFP	Oversight Office	January 26, 2015	Rome
63	WFP	Government Partnerships Division	January 27, 2015	Rome
64	WFP	Resource Management and Accountability Department	January 28, 2015	Rome
65	State (Africa)	WFP Executive Board	January 28, 2015	Rome
66	State (Europe)	WFP Executive Board	January 28, 2015	Rome
67	IFAD	Office of the President	January 29, 2015	Rome
68	IFAD	Office of Partnership and Resource Mobilization	January 30, 2015	Rome
69	State (North America)	IFAD Governing Council	January 30, 2015	Rome
70	State (Asia-Pacific)	IFAD Executive Board	January 30, 2015	Rome
71	EBRD	Office of the President	July 15, 2015	Oxford
72	WB	Inspection Panel	May 3, 2018	Remote

Table C.1 *(Cont)*

#	Affiliation[a,b]	Department	Date	Location[c]
73	State (Europe)	WB Board of Directors	May 14, 2018	Wash., DC
74	State (Asia-Pacific)	WB Board of Governors	May 14, 2018	Wash., DC
75	IMF	Independent Evaluation Office	May 14, 2018	Wash., DC
76	State (South America)	IMF Board of Directors	May 14, 2018	Wash., DC
77	IMF	Independent Evaluation Office	May 14, 2018	Wash., DC
78	WB	Trade and Competitiveness Global Practice	May 15, 2018	Wash., DC
79	WB	Institutional Integrity, Ethics and Business Conduct	May 15, 2018	Wash., DC
80	IMF	Independent Evaluation Office	May 15, 2018	Wash., DC
81	IMF	Independent Evaluation Office	May 15, 2018	Wash., DC
82	State (Asia-Pacific)	IMF Board of Directors	May 15, 2018	Wash., DC
83	State (Europe)	IMF Board of Governors	May 15, 2018	Wash., DC
84	WB	Independent Evaluation Group	May 16, 2018	Wash., DC
85	WB	Independent Evaluation Group	May 16, 2018	Wash., DC
86	USAID	Bureau for Global Health	May 16, 2018	Wash., DC
87	UNDP	Independent Evaluation Office	May 21, 2018	New York
88	UN	Office of Internal Oversight Services	May 21, 2018	New York
89	American Red Cross	Executive Committee	May 21, 2018	Wash., DC
90	Bank Information Center	Finance and Operations Office	May 21, 2018	Wash., DC
91	UNDP	Independent Evaluation Office	May 22, 2018	New York
92	UNCDF	Evaluation Unit	May 22, 2018	New York
93	UN	Office of Internal Oversight Services	May 22, 2018	New York
94	State (Europe)	Permanent Mission to the UN	May 22, 2018	New York
95	UN	Americas Division, Department of Political Affairs	May 22, 2018	New York
96	Bank Information Center	Policy Directorate	May 22, 2018	Wash., DC
97	UNCDF	Programme Development Group	May 23, 2018	New York
98	State (Asia-Pacific)	Permanent Mission to the UN	May 23, 2018	New York
99	State (Asia-Pacific)	Permanent Mission to the UN	May 23, 2018	New York
100	Center for International Environmental Law	Environmental Health Program	May 23, 2018	Wash., DC
101	InterAction	Humanitarian Policy and Practice Team	May 23, 2018	Wash., DC
102	Environmental Defense Fund	Executive Team	May 24, 2018	New York
103	State (Africa)	Group of 77	May 24, 2018	New York
104	State (Europe)	UNDP/UNFPA/UNOPS Executive Board	May 24, 2018	New York
105	State (Asia-Pacific)	UNDP/UNFPA/UNOPS Executive Board	May 24, 2018	New York
106	State (North America)	Permanent Mission to the UN	May 25, 2018	New York
107	State (South America)	Permanent Mission to the UN	May 25, 2018	New York
108	State (Africa)	Permanent Mission to the UN	May 25, 2018	New York
109	International Rescue Committee	Strategic Partnerships office	May 29, 2018	New York

Table C.1 *(Cont)*

#	Affiliation[a,b]	Department	Date	Location[c]
110	UNICEF USA	Advocacy and Engagement	May 29, 2018	New York
111	Ford Foundation	International Programs	May 30, 2018	New York
112	Human Rights Watch	US Program	May 31, 2018	New York
113	Rockefeller Foundation	Investments Office	May 31, 2018	New York
114	ICRC	Libya delegation	July 10, 2018	Oxford
115	MOPAN	Secretariat	September 5, 2018	Remote
116	MOPAN	Secretariat	September 5, 2018	Remote
117	WHO	Governing Bodies Department	June 9, 2020	Remote
118	WHO	Finance Department	June 9, 2020	Remote
119	GFATM	Strategy & Policy Hub	June 9, 2020	Remote
120	GFATM	Political and Civil Society Advocacy Department	June 9, 2020	Remote
121	GFATM	Grant Management Division	June 9, 2020	Remote
122	WHO	Health and Multilateral Partnerships Department	June 10, 2020	Remote
123	Donor state (Europe)	GFATM Board	June 10, 2020	Remote
124	Implementing state (Asia-Pacific)	GFATM Board	June 10, 2020	Remote
125	UNAIDS	Policy, Advocacy, and Knowledge Branch	July 20, 2020	Remote
126	UNAIDS	Independent Oversight Function	July 20, 2020	Remote
127	UNAIDS	External Relations Department	July 21, 2020	Remote
128	UNAIDS	Programme Branch	July 22, 2020	Remote
129	State (Africa)	UNAIDS Programme Coordinating Board	July 24, 2020	Remote
130	State (Asia-Pacific)	UNAIDS Programme Coordinating Board	July 24, 2020	Remote
131	State (Europe)	WHO Executive Board	September 15, 2020	Remote
132	State (North America)	WHO World Health Assembly	September 15, 2020	Remote
133	WHO	Health Workforce Department	October 2, 2020	Remote
134	Gavi	Finance and Operations Department	October 12, 2020	Remote
135	Gavi	Office of the COVAX Facility	October 12, 2020	Remote
136	Gavi	Resource Mobilization, Private Sector Partnerships, & Innovative Finance Department	October 14, 2020	Remote
137	Gavi	Country Programmes Department	October 14, 2020	Remote
138	State (Africa)	WHO World Health Assembly	October 15, 2020	Remote
139	State (North America)	Gavi Board	October 15, 2020	Remote
140	State (South America)	WHO Executive Board	October 15, 2020	Remote
141	WHO	Health Emergency Interventions Department	October 16, 2020	Remote
142	State (North America)	WFP Executive Board		

[a] For PIIP institutions' full names, see Table B.1.
[b] Affiliations and departments are at the time of interview.
[c] Remote interviews were conducted by telephone or video conference (using Skype or Zoom software).

Appendix D Survey of International Bureaucrats

To gather data on de facto policy autonomy for the Performance of International Institutions Project (PIIP) sample, I developed and fielded an internet-based survey of senior bureaucrats from all 54 institutions. The survey, entitled the *Harvard International Organizations Project* (HIOP) – it was designed during my time as a doctoral student at the university – was presented to participants as an information-gathering exercise for a large-scale research project on international institutions. To avoid triggering prestige, social desirability, or other biases that could predispose participants toward particular responses, I did not mention policy autonomy (or related concepts) in my correspondence with them.

The HIOP contains 31 questions – 26 multiple choice and five write-in – some of which do not concern policy autonomy or other variables analyzed in this book.[1] It is divided into four sections. To begin, participants are asked to name their institution and each of its governing bodies.[2] The second section focuses on these organs, in particular their composition, decision-making procedures, and policy outputs. The third section turns to the role of the secretariat in the policy process, covering its agenda-setting, fundraising, research, and implementation capacities. Final, participants are asked about the degree of competition their institution faces from intergovernmental organizations (IGOs), international nongovernmental organizations (INGOs), and other types of international institutions. For most questions, participants are requested to provide responses for several different years.

As summarized in Table D.1, the HIOP was administered in two waves. The first wave, which encompassed the full PIIP sample, was launched in September 2013 and closed in January 2015 (when the final participant's response was submitted). Participants were sent an email containing information about the HIOP and a hyperlink to an online survey instrument hosted on the Qualtrics platform. I initially

---

[1] I have used responses to some of the latter questions in other research. See Lall (2020, 2021).

[2] They are explicitly told to exclude advisory organs with no formal policy powers.

Table D.1 *Summary of bureaucratic survey*

Wave	Period	Institutions covered	Office of respondent		Format of response		Validation sample
			Chief of staff	Senior manager	Qualtrics tool	Email/ interview	
First	2013–2015	54	45	9	40	5	18
Second	2018–2019	45	39	6	NA	45	15

Note: In the second wave, the Qualtrics tool was not employed (due to differences in the survey timeframe across institutions).

contacted the office of an institution's head bureaucrat (e.g., its president or executive director). The vast majority of responses were received directly from this unit; in nine instances, the survey was forwarded to another senior official for completion. In most cases, two or three reminder messages were sent before a response was submitted. The average completion time was 37 minutes (excluding one outlier response that was filled in over several days).

In five cases, participants preferred to submit their response via an alternative medium. Three individuals sought clarification about the meaning of particular questions in a telephone conversation, during which they provided verbal answers. Two wished to provide more nuanced and detailed responses than permitted by the survey instrument, which they returned to me in written form via email.

The second wave of the HIOP extended the survey's coverage to the end of 2018 (the last year of the PIIP). The wave ran from January 2018 to July 2019 and excluded institutions that did not receive additional donor performance ratings after the first wave. As the length of time since the first wave varied across institutions, creating the need for different multiyear response options, I emailed bespoke questionnaires (in PDF format) to participants. Similarly to the first wave, the bulk of responses were submitted by the office of the chief bureaucrat, usually following one or two reminder messages. Results from the two waves were very similar, with only a handful of responses changing (as might be expected, given the proximity and brevity of the periods covered).

In both waves, I checked the reliability of responses in a randomly chosen subset of institutions by sending the HIOP to another member of their senior management (usually a division or department head). The validation subset comprised 18 institutions in the first wave and 15 institutions in the second (i.e., a third of each sample). There were no discrepancies from the original answers in either wave, suggesting a high degree of reliability.

Bibliography

Abbott, Kenneth W. and Duncan Snidal. 1998. "Why States Act through Formal International Organizations." *Journal of Conflict Resolution* 42(1):3–32.

——. 2000. "Hard and Soft Law in International Governance." *International Organization* 54(3):421–456.

——. 2009*a*. The Governance Triangle: Regulatory Standards Institutions and the Shadow of the State. In *The Politics of Global Regulation*, eds. Walter Mattli and Ngaire Woods. Princeton, NJ: Princeton University Press, pp. 44–88.

——. 2009*b*. "Strengthening International Regulation Through Transnational New Governance: Overcoming the Orchestration Deficit." *Vanderbilt Journal of Transnational Law* 42:501–578.

——. 2010. "International regulation without international government: Improving IO performance through orchestration." *The Review of International Organizations* 5(3):315–344.

Abbott, Kenneth W., Philipp Genschel, Duncan Snidal, and Bernhard Zangl. 2015. *International Organizations as Orchestrators*. Cambridge: Cambridge University Press.

——. 2016. "Two Logics of Indirect Governance: Delegation and Orchestration." *British Journal of Political Science* 46(4):719–729.

Acharya, Avidit, Matthew Blackwell, and Maya Sen. 2016. "Explaining Causal Findings Without Bias: Detecting and Assessing Direct Effects." *American Political Science Review* 110(3):512–529.

African Development Bank. 2020. "Evaluation of the African Development Bank's Engagement with Civil Society." Abidjan: African Development Bank Group.

Ahuja, Anjana. 2019. "Climate Change Is Reaching a Tipping Point." *Financial Times*. www.ft.com/content/56238e12-14ef-11ea-b869-0971bffac109 [Last accessed January 23, 2022].

Alesina, Alberto, Reza Baqir, and William Easterly. 1999. "Public Goods and Ethnic Divisions." *The Quarterly Journal of Economics* 114(4):1243–1284.

Alfreðsson, Guðmundur S. and Rolf Ring. 2001. *The Inspection Panel of the World Bank: A Different Complaints Procedure*. The Hague: Kluwer Law International.

Allen, Charles E. 1950. "World Health and World Politics." *International Organization* 4(1):27–43.

Amnesty International. 2021. "Covid-19: G20 leaders Must Not Repeat Their Failure Over Equal Access to Vaccines." OECD *Development Matters*. www.amnesty.org/en/latest/news/2021/10/covid-19-g20-leaders-must-not-repeat-their-failure-over-equal-access-to-vaccines/ [Last accessed April 11, 2022].

Anderfuhren-Biget, Simon, Ursula Häfliger, and Simon Hug. 2013. The values of staff in international organizations. In *Routledge Handbook of International Organization*, ed. Bob Reinalda. Abingdon: Routledge, pp. 270–283.

Andersen, Lotte Bøgh, Andreas Boesen and Lene Holm Pedersen. 2016. "Performance in Public Organizations: Clarifying the Conceptual Space." *Public Administration Review* 76(6):852–862.

Angrist, Joshua D. and Jörn-Steffen Pischke. 2008. *Mostly Harmless Econometrics: An Empiricist's Companion*. Princeton, NJ: Princeton University Press.

Annan, Kofi A. 2002. "What Is the International Community? Problems Without Passports." *Foreign Policy* 132:30–31.

Arter, David. 2006. "Introduction: Comparing the Legislative Performance of Legislatures." *The Journal of Legislative Studies* 12(3–4):245–257.

Ascher, Charles S. 1952. "Current Problems in the World Health Organization's Program." *International Organization* 6(1):27–50.

Ascher, William. 1983. "New Development Approaches and the Adaptability of International Agencies: The Case of the World Bank." *International Organization* 37(3):415–439.

Ashworth, Rachel E., George A. Boyne, and Tom Entwistle, eds. 2010. *Public Service Improvement: Theories and Evidence*. New York: Oxford University Press.

Asian Development Bank. 2012. "Review of the Accountability Mechanism Policy." Policy Paper. Mandaluyong City, Manila: ADB.

——. 2018. "An External Review of the Independent Evaluation Department." Development Effectiveness Committee. Mandaluyong City, Manila: ADB.

Asian Exchange for New Alternatives. 1996. "Engaging the Asian Development Bank: Voices from NGOs." Causeway Bay, Kowloon: ARENA.

Asian Infrastructure Investment Bank. 2015. "Articles of Agreement." Beijing: AIIB.

——. 2019. "Rules of Procedure of the Board of Directors." Beijing: AIIB.

——. 2021. "2020 AIIB Annual Report." Beijing: AIIB.

Axinn, William G. and Lisa D. Pearce. 2006. *Mixed Method Data Collection Strategies*. Cambridge: Cambridge University Press.

Ba, Diadie. 2008. "Abolish Wasteful World Food Body – Senegal's Wade." *Reuters*. https://www.reuters.com/article/us-food-africa-wade-idUSL0512295520080505 [Last accessed July 28, 2022].

Baccini, Leonardo, Iain Osgood and Stephen Weymouth. 2019. "The Service Economy: US Trade Coalitions in an Era of Deindustrialization." *The Review of International Organizations* 14(2):261–296.

Bailey, Michael A., Anton Strezhnev and Erik Voeten. 2017. "Estimating Dynamic State Preferences from United Nations Voting Data." *Journal of Conflict Resolution* 61(2):430–456.

Balter, Michael. 1998. "Global Program Struggles to Stem the Flood of New Cases." *Science* 280(5371):1863–1864.

Ban, Carolyn. 2013. *Management and Culture in an Enlarged European Commission: From Diversity to Unity?* Basingstoke: Palgrave Macmillan.

Barnard, Geoff, Margareta de Goys, Fabrizio Felloni, Rob van den Berg, and Nick York. 2013. "Peer Review of UNDP's Evaluation Office on Methodology and Knowledge Sharing." www.unevaluation.org/document/detail/1632 [Last accessed July 3, 2022].

Barnes, Amy and Garrett Wallace Brown. 2011. The Global Fund to Fight AIDS, Tuberculosis, and Malaria: Expertise, Accountability, and the Depoliticisation of Global Health Governance. In *Partnerships and Foundations in Global Health Governance*, eds. Simon Rushton and Owain David Williams. Basingstoke: Palgrave Macmillan, pp. 53–75.

Barnett, Michael N. 2002. *Eyewitness to a Genocide: The United Nations and Rwanda*. Ithaca, NY: Cornell University Press.

——. 2016. "Accountability and Global Governance: The View from Paternalism." *Regulation & Governance* 10(2):134–148.

——. 2019. "The End of a Liberal International Order That Never Existed." *The Global*. https://theglobal.blog/2019/04/16/the-end-of-a-liberal-international-order-that-never-existed/. [Last accessed July 3, 2022].

Barnett, Michael N. and Martha Finnemore. 1999. "The Politics, Power, and Pathologies of International Organizations." *International Organization* 53(4):699–732.

——. 2004. *Rules for the World: International Organizations in Global Politics*. Ithaca, NY: Cornell University Press.

Barrett, Christopher B. 2001. "Does Food Aid Stabilize Food Availability?" *Economic Development and Cultural Change* 49(2):335–349.

Barrett, Christopher B. and Daniel G. Maxwell. 2005. *Food Aid After Fifty Years: Recasting Its Role*. Abingdon: Routledge.

Barrett, Christopher B. and Kevin C. Heisey. 2002. "How Effectively Does Multilateral Food Aid Respond to Fluctuating Needs?" *Food Policy* 27(5–6):477–491.

Barrett, Scott 2007. *Why Cooperate?: The Incentive to Supply Global Public Goods*. New York: Oxford University Press.

Barro, Robert J. and David B. Gordon. 1983. "A Positive Theory of Monetary Policy in a Natural Rate Model." *Journal of Political Economy* 91(4):589–610.

Bartsch, Sonja. 2007. The Global Fund to Fight AIDS, Tuberculosis and Malaria. In *Global Health Governance and the Fight Against HIV/AIDS*, eds. Wolfgang Hein, Sonja Bartsch, and Lars Kohlmorgen. Abingdon: Routledge, pp. 146–171.

Bauer, Michael W., Christoph Knill and Steffen Eckhard. 2016. *International Bureaucracy: Challenges and Lessons for Public Administration Research*. Basingstoke: Palgrave Macmillan.

Bauer, Michael W. and Jörn Ege. 2012. "Politicization Within the European Commission's Bureaucracy." *International Review of Administrative Sciences* 78(3):403–424.

Bayerlein, Louisa, Christoph Knill, and Yves Steinebach. 2020. *A Matter of Style: Organizational Agency in Global Public Policy*. Cambridge: Cambridge University Press.

Beigbeder, Yves. 1998. *The World Health Organization*. Dordrecht: Martinus Nijhoff Publishers.

———. 2001. *New Challenges for UNICEF: Children, Women and Human Rights*. Basingstoke: Palgrave.

———. 2018. *The World Health Organization: Achievements and Failures*. Abingdon: Routledge.

Benner, Thorsten, Steffen Eckhard, and Philipp Rotmann. 2017. Learning in International Organizations. In *Routledge Handbook of International Organization*, ed. Bob Reinaldo. Abingdon: Routledge, pp. 361–373.

Bennis, Warren G. 1966. The Concept of Organizational Health. In *Changing Organizations: Essays on the Development and Evolution of Human Organization*, ed. Warren G. Bennis. New York: McGraw-Hill, pp. 35–58.

Bergsten, C. Fred. 1976. "Interdependence and the Reform of International Institutions." *International Organization* 30(2):361–372.

Berkley, Seth. 2019. "The Power of Vaccines and How Gavi Has Helped Make the World Healthier: 2019 Lasker-Bloomberg Public Service Award." *JAMA* 322(13):1251–1252.

Bernes, Tom, Lars Brozus, Michal Hatuel-Radoshitzky, Ari Heistein, Ettore Greco, Patrycja Sasnal, Igor Yurgens, Sergey Kulik et al. 2020. "Challenges of Global Governance Amidst the COVID-19 Pandemic." Council on Foreign Relations Paper Series. New York: Council on Foreign Relations.

Berry, Jeffrey M. 1977. *Lobbying for the People*. Princeton, NJ: Princeton University Press.

Besley, Timothy. 2006. *Principled Agents? The Political Economy of Good Government*. Oxford: Oxford University Press.

Blair, Robert A., Jessica Di Salvatore, and Hannah M. Smidt. 2022. "When Do UN Peacekeeping Operations Implement Their Mandates?" *American Journal of Political Science* 66(3):664–680.

Bleich, Erik and Robert Pekkanen. 2013. How to Report Interview Data. In *Interview Research in Political Science*, ed. Layna Mosley. Ithaca: Cornell University Press, pp. 84–106.

Bloom, Barry R. 2011. "WHO Needs Change." *Nature* 473(7346):143–145.

Boerma, Addeke H. 1975. "Political Will and the World Food Problem." Coromandel Lecture delivered in New Delhi, February 5. Rome: FAO.

Bosco, David L. 2009. *Five to Rule Them All: The UN Security Council and the Making of the Modern World*. New York: Oxford University Press.

Bouloudani, Valérie. 1994. "The NGLS Handbook of UN Agencies, Programmes and Funds Working for Economic and Social Development." www.nzdl.org/gsdlmod?e=d-00000-00—off-0hdl—00-0—-0-10-0—0—0dir ect-10—4———0-1l–11-en-50—20-about—00-0-1-00-0–4—0-0-11-10-0 utfZz-8-10&a=d&c=hdl&cl=CL1.12&d=HASHbcccd898c59e7e41e02150 [Last accessed October 20, 2021].

Bourguignon, François and Christian Morrisson. 2002. "Inequality Among World Citizens: 1820–1992." *American Economic Review* 92(4):727–744.

Bovens, Mark, Robert E. Goodin, and Thomas Schillemans. 2014. *The Oxford Handbook of Public Accountability*. Oxford: Oxford University Press.

Boyne, George A. 2002. "Theme: Local Government: Concepts and Indicators of Local Authority Performance: An Evaluation of the Statutory Frameworks in England and Wales." *Public Money & Management* 22(2):17–24.

Boyne, George A., Kenneth J. Meier, Laurence J. O'Toole Jr, and Richard M. Walker, eds. 2006. *Public Service Performance: Perspectives on Measurement and Management*. New York: Cambridge University Press.

Bradlow, Daniel D. and Andria Naudé Fourie. 2011. World Bank Inspection Panel. In *Independent Accountability Mechanisms at Regional Development Banks*, eds. David Held and Thomas Hale. Cambridge: Polity Press, pp. 148–153.

Brand, Paul. 2020. "Twitter Post (PaulBrandITV)." April 14, 2020, 11:26pm. https://twitter.com/PaulBrandITV/status/1250188713570820096 [Last accessed June 18, 2022].

Brechin, Steven R. and Gayl D. Ness. 2013. "Looking Back at the Gap: International Organizations as Organizations Twenty-Five Years Later." *Journal of International Organizations Studies* 4(1):14–39.

Breitmeier, Helmut, Arild Underdal, and Oran R. Young. 2011. "The Effectiveness of International Environmental Regimes: Comparing and Contrasting Findings from Quantitative Research." *International Studies Review* 13(4):579–605.

Broz, J. Lawrence. 2015. "The Federal Reserve's Coalition in Congress." SSRN. http://dx.doi.org/10.2139/ssrn.2551300 [Last accessed August 16, 2022].

Bruen, Carlos. 2018. "Politics and Policy Processes of Global Health Partnerships: The Case of Gavi, the Vaccine Alliance." PhD thesis, Royal College of Surgeons in Ireland.

Brummer, Alex. 1996. "Rich Nations Seek Deal to Close Costly UN Bodies." *The Guardian*, 13.

Buchanan, Allen and Robert O. Keohane. 2006. "The Legitimacy of Global Governance Institutions." *Ethics & International Affairs* 20(4):405–437.

Buira, Ariel, ed. 2005. *Reforming the Governance of the IMF and the World Bank*. G24 Research Program. London: Anthem Press.

Buntaine, Mark T. 2015. "Accountability in Global Governance: Civil Society Claims for Environmental Performance at the World Bank." *International Studies Quarterly* 59(1):99–111.

——. 2016. *Giving Aid Effectively: The Politics of Environmental Performance and Selectivity at Multilateral Development Banks*. New York: Oxford University Press.

Burley, Anne-Marie and Walter Mattli. 1993. "Europe Before the Court: A Political Theory of Legal Integration." *International Organization* 47(1): 41–76.

Buse, Kent and Andrew M. Harmer. 2007. "Seven Habits of Highly Effective Global Public–Private Health Partnerships: Practice and Potential." *Social Science & Medicine* 64(2):259–271.

Buse, Kent and Sonja Tanaka. 2011. "Global Public-Private Health Partnerships: Lessons Learned From Ten Years of Experience and Evaluation." *International Dental Journal* 61:2–10.

Büthe, Tim and Walter Mattli. 2011. *The New Global Rulers: The Privatization of Regulation in the World Economy*. Princeton, NJ: Princeton University Press.

Cambridge Economic Policy Associates. 2007. "Evaluation of the GAVI Phase 1 Performance (2000–2005)." Board paper from GAVI Alliance and Fund Joint Board meeting, May 11–12, 2007. Geneva: GAVI.

Cameron, Kim. 1986. "A Study of Organizational Effectiveness and Its Predictors." *Management Science* 32(1):87–112.

Cameron, Kim S. and David A. Whetten. 1996. Organizational Effectiveness and Quality: The Second Generation. In *Higher Education: Handbook of Theory and Research*, ed. John C. Smart. Vol. XI. New York: Agathon, pp. 265–306.

Campbell, Charlie. 2020. "'A Crime Against Humanity.' Why Trump's WHO Funding Freeze Benefits Nobody." *Time Magazine*. https://time.com/5821122/who-funding-trump-covid19-coronavirus-china/ [Last accessed May 9, 2022].

Canadian International Development Agency. 1984. "Outline of the Conclusions from a Canadian Appraisal of IFAD." Ottawa: CIDA.

Caporaso, James. 2003. Post-National Integration? In *Democracy in the European Union: Integration through Deliberation?*, eds. Erik O. Eriksen and John Erik Fossum. Abingdon: Routledge, pp. 1–28.

Carin, Barry and Angela Wood, eds. 2005. *Accountability of the International Monetary Fund*. Aldershot: Ashgate.

Carnegie, Allison and Austin Carson. 2020. *Secrets in Global Governance: Disclosure Dilemmas and the Challenge of International Cooperation*. New York: Cambridge University Press.

Carpenter, Daniel. 2001. *The Forging of Bureaucratic Autonomy: Reputations, Networks, and Policy Innovation in Executive Agencies, 1862–1928*. Princeton, NJ: Princeton University Press.

Carr, Edward Hallett. 1964. *The Twenty Years' Crisis, 1919–1939: An Introduction to the Study of International Relations*. New York: Harper & Row.

Cassen, Robert and Associates. 1986. *Does Aid Work? Report to an Intergovernmental Task Force*. Oxford: Clarendon Press.

Cassese, Sabino, ed. 2016. *Research Handbook on Global Administrative Law*. Cheltenham: Edward Elgar.

Center for Global Development. 2013. "Time for FAO to Shift to a Higher Gear: A Report of the CGD Working Group on Food Security." Washington, DC: Center for Global Development.

CEPA LLP. 2010. "GAVI Second Evaluation Report." London: CEPA LLP.

Chan, Jennifer. 2015*a*. *Politics in the Corridor of Dying: AIDS Activism and Global Health Governance*. Baltimore, MD: Johns Hopkins University Press.

Chan, Margaret. 2015*b*. "Learning from Ebola: Readiness for Outbreaks and Emergencies." *Bulletin of the World Health Organization* 93(12):818–818A.

Charlton, Mark W. 1992. "Innovation and Inter-Organizational Politics: The Case of the World Food Programme." *International Journal* 47(3):630–665.

Chayes, Abram and Antonia Handler Chayes. 1993. "On Compliance." *International Organization* 47(2):175–205.

——. 1995. *The New Sovereignty: Compliance with International Regulatory Agreements*. Cambridge, MA: Harvard University Press.

Checkel, Jeffrey T. 2001. "Why Comply? Social Learning and European Identity Change." *International Organization* 55(3):553–588.

——. 2005. "International Institutions and Socialization in Europe: Introduction and Framework." *International Organization* 59(4):801–826.

Chee, Grace, Vivikka Molldrem, Natasha Hsi, and Slavea Chankova. 2008. "Evaluation of the GAVI Phase 1 Performance (2000–2005)." Prepared for The GAVI Alliance. Bethesda MD: Abt Associates Inc.

Chen, Weihua. 2019. "AIIB Wins the World's Confidence with Record of Success." *China Daily*. www.chinadaily.com.cn/a/201907/19/WS5d3115b 6a310d830563ffd8c.html [Last accessed November 12, 2021].

Chesterman, Simon. 2008. "Globalization Rules: Accountability, Power, and the Prospects for Global Administrative Law." *Global Governance* 14:39.

Chin, Gregory T. 2019. "The Asian Infrastructure Investment Bank – New Multilateralism: Early Development, Innovation, and Future Agendas." *Global Policy* 10(4):569–581.

Chin, James. 2007. *The AIDS Pandemic: The Collision of Epidemiology with Political Correctness*. Boca Raton, FL: CRC Press.

Chisholm, Brock. 1947. "The World Health Organization." *International Conciliation* (437):111–116.

——. 2012. *The World Health Organization between North and South*. Ithaca, NY: Cornell University Press.

Chr. Michelsen Institute. 1994. "Evaluation of the World Food Programme." Bergen: Chr. Michelsen Institute.

Christiansen, Thomas and Christine Neuhold. 2012. *International Handbook on Informal Governance*. Cheltenham: Edward Elgar.

Christiansen, Thomas and Simona Piattoni. 2003. *Informal Governance in the European Union*. Cheltenham: Edward Elgar.

Clapp, Jennifer. 2005. "The Political Economy of Food Aid in an Era of Agricultural Biotechnology." *Global Governance: A Review of Multilateralism and International Organizations* 11(4):467–485.

——. 2012. *Hunger in the Balance: The New Politics of International Food Aid*. Ithaca, NY: Cornell University Press.

Clark, Dana, Jonathan A. Fox, and Kay Treakle. 2003. *Demanding Accountability: Civil Society Claims and the World Bank Inspection Panel*. Lanham, MD: Rowman & Littlefield.

Clay, Edward J. 2003. "Responding to Change: WFP and the Global Food Aid System." *Development Policy Review* 21(5–6):697–709.

Clay, Edward and Olav Schram Stokke, eds. 2013. *Food Aid and Human Security*. Abingdon: Routledge.

Clinton, Chelsea. 2014. The Global Fund: An Experiment in Global Governance PhD thesis, University of Oxford.

Clinton, Chelsea and Devi Lalita Sridhar. 2017. *Governing Global Health: Who Runs the World and Why?* Oxford: Oxford University Press.

Clinton, Chelsea, Eric Friedman, Lawrence O. Gostin, and Devi Sridhar. 2020. "Why the WHO?" www.thinkglobalhealth.org/article/why-who [Last accessed February 8, 2022].

Coen, David and Mark Thatcher. 2008. "Network Governance and Multi-level Delegation: European Networks of Regulatory Agencies." *Journal of Public Policy* 28(1):49–71.

Cogan, Jacob K., Ian Hurd, and Ian Johnstone. 2016. *The Oxford Handbook of International Organizations*. Oxford: Oxford University Press.

Cohen, Jon. 2018. "Despite Scathing Harassment Report, UNAIDS Board Gives Agency Head a Reprieve for Now." *Science.* www.sciencemag.org/news/2018/12/despite-scathing-harassment-report-unaids-board-gives-agency-head-reprieve-now [Last accessed March 19, 2022].

———. 2020. "'We Will Have Many Body Bags.' WHO chief responds to Trump's criticisms." *Science.* www.sciencemag.org/news/2020/04/we-will-have-many-body-bags-who-chief-responds-trumps-criticisms [Last accessed October 1, 2021].

Cole, Mary, Niels Dabelstein, Tony Faint, Ted Kliest, and Luciano Lavizzari. 2005. "Peer Review: UNDP Evaluation Office." Peer Assessment of Evaluation in Multilateral Organisations. Copenhagen: Ministry of Foreign Affairs of Denmark.

Colgan, Jeff D. and Robert O. Keohane. 2017. "The Liberal Order Is Rigged: Fix It Now or Watch It Wither." *Foreign Affairs* 96(3):36–44.

Collier, Roger. 2011. "WHO Reforms Long Overdue, Critics Say." *CMAJ* 183:1574–1575.

Connolly, Terry, Edward J. Conlon, and Stuart Jay Deutsch. 1980. "Organizational Effectiveness: A Multiple-Constituency Approach." *Academy of Management Review* 5(2):211–218.

Cooley, Alexander and Hendrik Spruyt. 2009. *Contracting States: Sovereign Transfers in International Relations*. Princeton, NJ: Princeton University Press.

Copelovitch, Mark and Jon C.W. Pevehouse. 2019. "International Organizations in a New Era of Populist Nationalism." *The Review of International Organizations* 14(2):169–186.

Copelovitch, Mark S. 2010. "Master or Servant? Common Agency and the Political Economy of IMF Lending." *International Studies Quarterly* 54(1): 49–77.

Cottarelli, Carlo. 2005. "Efficiency and Legitimacy: Trade-Offs in IMF Governance." IMF Working Paper WP/05/107. www.imf.org/external/pubs/ft/wp/2005/wp05107.pdf [Last accessed March 1, 2022].

Cottrell, M. Patrick. 2009. "Legitimacy and Institutional Replacement: The Convention on Certain Conventional Weapons and the Emergence of the Mine Ban Treaty." *International Organization* 63(2):217–248.

Covey, Jane G. 1998. Critical Cooperation? Influencing the World Bank through Policy Dialogue and Operational Cooperation. In *The Struggle for Accountability: The World Bank, NGOs, and Grassroots Movements*, eds. Jonathan A. Fox and Lloyd D. Brown. Cambridge, MA: MIT Press, pp. 81–120.

Crittenden, Ann. 1981. "Food and Hunger Statistics Question." *New York Times*, Section A, 1.

Cueto, Marcos, Theodore M. Brown, and Elizabeth Fee. 2019. *The World Health Organization: A History*. Cambridge: Cambridge University Press.

Cullet, Philippe. 2007. *The Sardar Sarovar Dam Project: Selected Documents*. Aldershot: Ashgate Publishing.

Cusack, Thomas R. 1999. "Social Capital, Institutional Structures, and Democratic Performance: A Comparative Study of German Local Governments." *European Journal of Political Research* 35(1):1–34.

Cutler, A. Claire, Virginia Haufler, and Tony Porter. 1999. *Private Authority and International Affairs*. Albany, NY: Suny Press.

Dahl, Robert A. 1967. The Evaluation of Political Systems. In *Contemporary Political Science: Toward Empirical Theory*, ed. Ithiel de Sola Pool. New York: McGraw-Hill, pp. 166–179.

——. 1999. Can International Organizations be Democratic? A Skeptic's View. In *Democracy's Edges*, eds. Ian Shapiro and Casiano Hacker-Cordón. Cambridge: Cambridge University Press, pp. 19–36.

Dai, Xinyuan. 2005. "Why Comply? The Domestic Constituency Mechanism." *International Organization* 59(2):363–398.

——. 2007. *International Institutions and National Policies*. New York: Cambridge University Press.

Danish International Development Agency. 1993. "Effectiveness of Multilateral Agencies at Country Level: Case Study of 11 Agencies in Kenya, Nepal, Sudan and Thailand." Copenhagen: Ministry of Foreign Affairs.

Das, Pam and Udani Samarasekera. 2008. "What Next for UNAIDS?" *The Lancet* 372(9656):2099–2102.

Daugirdas, Kristina. 2014. "Reputation and the Responsibility of International Organizations." *European Journal of International Law* 25(4):991–1018.

——. 2019. "Reputation as a Disciplinarian of International Organizations." *American Journal of International Law* 113(2):221–271.

DeCapua, Joe. 2014. "Does Ebola Reveal WHO Shortfalls?" *Voice of America*. www.voanews.com/a/infectious-disease-new-response-28oct14/2499320.html [Last accessed March 15, 2022].

Deng, Yong. 2014. "China: The Post-Responsible Power." *The Washington Quarterly* 37(4):117–132.

Dimitropoulos, Georgios. 2008. "A Common GAL: The Legitimating Role of the Global Rule of Law." Paper presented at the 4th Viterbo Global Administrative Law Seminar, June 13–14. https://images.irpa.eu/wp-content/uploads/2019/03/61.pdf [Last accessed March 19, 2022].

Donoghue, Martine, Nel Druce, Nicolas Avril, Marame Ndour, and David Lewis. 2010. "Review of GAVI Independent Review Committees (IRCs)." RFP-EVIRC060709. London: HLSP.

Downs, George W., David M. Rocke, and Peter N. Barsoom. 1996. "Is the Good News about Compliance Good News about Cooperation?" *International Organization* 50(3):379–406.

Downs, George W. and Michael A. Jones. 2002. "Reputation, Compliance, and International Law." *The Journal of Legal Studies* 31(S1):S95–S114.

Dreher, Axel and Roland Vaubel. 2004. "The Causes and Consequences of IMF Conditionality." *Emerging Markets Finance and Trade* 40(3):26–54.

Duffield, John. 2007. "What Are International Institutions?" *International Studies Review* 9(1):1–22.

Easterly, William and Claudia R. Williamson. 2011. "Rhetoric versus Reality: The Best and Worst of Aid Agency Practices." *World Development* 39(11):1930–1949.

Ecker-Ehrhardt, Matthias. 2018. "International Organizations 'Going Public?' An Event History Analysis of Public Communication Reforms 1950–2015." *International Studies Quarterly* 62(4):723–736.

Eckhard, Steffen and Vytautas Jankauskas. 2020. "Explaining the Political Use of Evaluation in International Organizations." *Policy Sciences* 53(4):667–695.

Ege, Jörn, Michael W. Bauer, Louisa Bayerlein, Steffen Eckhard, and Christoph Knill. 2022. "Avoiding Disciplinary Garbage Cans: A Pledge for a Problem-Driven Approach to Researching International Public Administration." *Journal of European Public Policy* 29(7):1169–1181.

Elsig, Manfred. 2010. "The World Trade Organization at work: Performance in a member-driven milieu." *The Review of International Organizations* 5(3): 345–363.

England, Roger. 2008. "The Writing Is on the Wall for UNAIDS." *BMJ* 336(7652):1072–1075.

Etzioni, Amitai. 1964. *Modern Organizations*. Englewood Cliffs, NJ: Prentice Hall.

Euro Health Group. 2020. "Strategic Review 2020." Final Report: Vol 1. Søberg: Euro Health Group.

Farley, John. 2009. *Brock Chisholm, the World Health Organization, and the Cold War*. Vancouver: UBC Press.

Fazey, Ian Hamilton. 1995. "US Funds Ban Would Paralyse UN Group." *Financial Times*, 4.

Fearon, James D. 1994. "Domestic Political Audiences and the Escalation of International Disputes." *American Political Science Review* 88(3):577–592.

——. 1999. Electoral Accountability and the Control of Politicians: Selecting Good Types versus Sanctioning Poor Performance. In *Democracy, Accountability, and Representation*, eds. Adam Przeworski, Susan C. Stokes, and Bernard Manin. New York: Cambridge University Press, pp. 55–97.

Federal Ministry for Economic Cooperation and Development (Germany). 2005. "Joint Evaluation of Effectiveness and Impact of the Enabling Development Policy of the World Food Programme (WFP)." Volume 1: Synthesis Report. Published on behalf of the Steering Committee of the Evaluation. Bonn: Germany.

Federal Republic of Germany Ministry for Economic Cooperation. 1984. "Approaches to Overcoming Poverty through Self-Help and through Target-Group-Oriented Financial Instruments." Final report of the Special Task Force. Bonn: BMZ.

Feenstra, Robert C., Robert Inklaar, and Marcel P. Timmer. 2015. "The Next Generation of the Penn World Table." *American Economic Review* 105(10):3150–3182.

Fenner, Frank, Donald A. Henderson, Isao Arita, Zdenek Jezek, and Ivan D. Ladnyi. 1988. *Smallpox and Its Eradication*. History of International Public Health, No. 6. WHO: Geneva.

Ferroni, Marco and Ashoka Mody. 2002. *International Public Goods: Incentives, Measurement, and Financing.* Boston: Kluwer Academic Publishers.

Fidler, David P. 2020. "The World Health Organization and Pandemic Politics." Think Global Health. www.thinkglobalhealth.org/article/world-health-organization-and-pandemic-politics [Last accessed January 12, 2022].

Fink, Sheri. 2017. "WHO Leader Describes the Agency's Ebola Operations." *The New York Times.* www.nytimes.com/2014/09/04/world/africa/who-leader-describes-the-agencys-ebola-operations.html [Last accessed June 18, 2022].

Food and Agriculture Organization. 1945. "Constitution of the Food and Agriculture Organization of the United Nations." Washington, DC: FAO.

——. 1949. "The 1949 Conference of FAO – An Interpretive Summary." Ottawa: Dominion Department of Agriculture.

——. 1961*a*. "Term of Office of the Director-General." Conference Resolution 22/61. Rome: FAO.

——. 1961*b*. "Utilization of Food Surpluses – World Food Program." Conference Resolution 1/61. Rome: FAO.

——. 1965. "Report on the World Food Program by the Executive Director." Rome: FAO.

——. 1975. "Statement by Mr. Gonzalo Bula Hoyos, Independent Chairman of the Council." C 75/LIM/8. Rome: FAO.

——. 1995. "World Food Summit." Conference Resolution 2/95. www.fao.org/wfs/resource/english/resolute.htm [Last accessed June 11, 2022].

——. 1997. "Report of World Food Summit." www.FAO.org/3/w3548e/w3548e00.htm [Last accessed December 12, 2021].

——. 1999. "Amendments to the General Rules of the Organization." Conference Resolution 4/99. Rome: FAO.

——. 2002. "Report of World Food Summit: Five Years On." www.FAO.org/3/Y7106E/Y7106E00.htm [Last accessed December 10, 2021].

——. 2004*a*. "Agricultural Biotechnology: Meeting the Needs of the Poor?" Rome: FAO.

——. 2004*b*. "A Comprehensive and Independent External Evaluation of FAO (Paper Submitted by Canada and the United States of America on Behalf of the North America Group)." CL 127/LIM/4. Rome: FAO.

——. 2007. "FAO: The Challenge of Renewal. Report of the Independent External Evaluation of the Food and Agriculture Organization of the United Nations (FAO)." C 2007/7A.1-Rev.1. Rome: FAO.

——. 2008. "Resolution 1/2008 and Immediate Plan of Action for FAO Renewal (IPA)." Extracts from the Report of the 35th (Special) Session of the FAO Conference (C 2008/REP). Rome: FAO.

——. 2019. "2018 Annual Report of the WFP Executive Board to ECOSOC and the FAO Council." CL 163/8. Rome: FAO.

Fortna, Virginia Page. 2008. *Does Peacekeeping Work? Shaping Belligerents' Choices After Civil War.* Princeton, NJ: Princeton University Press.

Fox, Jonathan A. 2000. "The World Bank Inspection Panel: Lessons from the First Five Years." *Global Governance: A Review of Multilateralism and International Organizations* 6(3):279–318.

——. 2002. The World Bank Inspection Panel and the Limits of Accountability. In *Reinventing the World Bank*, eds. Jonathan R. Pincus and Jeffrey A. Winters. Ithaca, NY: Cornell University Press, pp. 131–163.

Fox, William T.R. 1951. "The United Nations in the Era of Total Diplomacy." *International Organization* 5(2):265–273.

Franck, Thomas M. 1990. *The Power of Legitimacy among Nations*. New York: Oxford University Press.

Friedman, Milton. 1953. *Essays in Positive Economics*. Chicago, IL: University of Chicago Press.

Gaarder, Marie Moland and Ulrich Bartsch. 2014. "Who Cares About Development Outcomes? Market Failures and the Role of the Evaluation Function." *Journal of Development Effectiveness* 6(4):361–377.

Garmaise, David. 2010. "Key Strengths of Rounds 8 and 9 Proposals to the Global Fund." https://aidspan.org/sites/default/files/publications/aidspan-rounds-8-and-9-strengths-report-en.pdf [Last accessed October 3, 2020].

Gaubatz, Kurt Taylor. 1996. "Democratic States and Commitment in International Relations." *International Organization* 50(1):109–139.

GAVI Alliance. 2008. "GAVI Alliance Executive Committee Charter." Approved on October 29–30, 2008. Geneva: GAVI.

GAVI CSO Constituency. 2012. "GAVI CSO Constituency 2012 Achievements." https://docs.google.com/viewer?a=v&pid=sites&srcid=Z2F2aS1jc28ub3JnfGdhdmktY3NvLW9yZ3xneDo3YjhlODNkMzg0ODRhN2Y1 [Last accessed March 20, 2022].

Gavi, the Vaccine Alliance. 2020*a*. "Annual Progress Report 2019." www.gavi.org/sites/default/files/programmes-impact/our-impact/apr/Gavi-Progress-Report-2019_1.pdf [Last accessed March 5, 2022].

——. 2020*b*. "Gavi20: The Story of an Alliance That Today Protects Half the World's Children." Geneva: Gavi.

——. 2020*c*. "Minutes: Gavi Alliance Board Meeting, 24–25 June 2020, Virtual Meeting." www.gavi.org/sites/default/files/board/minutes/2020/Board-2020-Mtg-03-Minutes-24-25June2020.pdf [Last accessed March 4, 2021].

Gawthorpe, Andrew. 2020. "Trump's Decision to cut WHO Funding Is an Act of International Vandalism." *The Guardian*. www.theguardian.com/commentisfree/2020/apr/15/trump-decision-cut-who-funding-international-vandalism-coronavirus [Last accessed May 8, 2022].

General Accounting Office. 1981. "Status Report on U.S. Participation in the International Fund for Agricultural Development." ID-81-33. Washington, DC: GAO.

George, Susan. 1977. *How the Other Half Dies: The Real Reasons for World Hunger*. Totowa, NJ: Rowman & Allanheld.

Georgopoulos, Basil S. and Arnold S. Tannenbaum. 1957. "A Study of Organizational Effectiveness." *American Sociological Review* 22(5):534–540.

Gerring, John. 2006. *Case Study Research: Principles and Practices*. Cambridge: Cambridge University Press.

——. 2011. *Social Science Methodology: A Unified Framework*. Second ed. Cambridge: Cambridge University Press.

Global Alliance for Vaccines and Immunization. 2000. "Third Board Meeting: Oslo, Norway, 13–14 June 2000." GAVI/00.03. https://apps.who.int/iris/bitstream/handle/10665/66543/GAVI_00.03.pdf?sequence=1 [Last accessed October 12, 2021].

Global Fund to Fight AIDS, Tuberculosis and Malaria. 2001*a*. "The Framework Document." Geneva: The Global Fund.

———. 2001*b*. "Turning the Page from Emergency to Sustainability: The Final Report of the High-Level Independent Review Panel on Fiduciary Controls and Oversight Mechanisms of the Global Fund to Fight AIDS, Tuberculosis and Malaria." Geneva: The Global Fund.

———. 2003. "The By-Laws of the Global Fund to Fight AIDS, Tuberculosis and Malaria." Report of the Governance and Partnership Committee, Annex 2.1. Geneva: The Global Fund.

———. 2006. "Report on the Staff Survey 2006." Monitor Group. www.theglobalfund.org/media/3550/bm13_16secreariatupdatea1_attachment_en.pdf [Last accessed January 12, 2022].

———. 2009*a*. "The Global Fund to Fight AIDS, Tuberculosis and Malaria: By-Laws." As Amended: May 5, 2009. Geneva: The Global Fund.

———. 2009*b*. "Synthesis Report of The Five-Year Evaluation of The Global Fund." Technical Evaluation Reference Group Summary Paper. Geneva: The Global Fund.

———. 2011. "The Global Fund to Fight AIDS, Tuberculosis and Malaria: By-Laws." As Amended: November 21, 2011. Geneva: The Global Fund.

———. 2015. "Strategic Review 2015." GF/B34/10. 34th Board Meeting. Geneva: The Global Fund.

———. 2017*a*. "Ethics and Conflict of Interest Procedures for Technical Review Panel Members." Geneva: The Global Fund.

———. 2017*b*. "Strategic Review 2017." Geneva: The Global Fund.

———. 2019*a*. "The Power of Partnerships." www.theglobalfund.org/media/8703/publication_privatesectorpartnerships_focuson_en.pdf [Last accessed January 19, 2022].

———. 2019*b*. "Terms of Reference of the Technical Review Panel." Geneva: The Global Fund.

———. 2021*a*. "Applicant Handbook 2020–2022." Geneva: The Global Fund.

———. 2021*b*. "Results Report 2021." www.theglobalfund.org/media/11304/corporate_2021resultsreport_report_en.pdf [Last accessed June 1, 2022].

Global Review Panel on the Future of the UNAIDS Joint Programme Model. 2017. "Refining & Reinforcing: The UNAIDS Joint Programme Model." www.unaids.org/sites/default/files/media_asset/final-report_grp_en.pdf [Last accessed March 6, 2022].

Godlee, Fiona. 1994*a*. "WHO in Retreat: Is It Losing Its Influence?" *BMJ* 309(6967):1491–1495.

———. 1994*b*. "The World Health Organisation: WHO in crisis." *BMJ* 309(6966):1424–1428.

———. 1995. "WHO's Special Programme: Undermining from Above." *British Medical Journal* 310:178–82.

Goldin, Ian. 2013. *Divided Nations: Why Global Governance is Failing, and What We Can Do About It*. Oxford: Oxford University Press.

Goldstein, Joshua S. 2012. *Winning the War on War: The Decline of Armed Conflict Worldwide*. New York: Penguin.

Goodrich, Leland M. 1947. "From League of Nations to United Nations." *International Organization* 1(1):3–21.

Gorter, Wytze. 1954. "GATT After Six Years: An Appraisal." *International Organization* 8(1):1–18.

Gostin, Lawrence O., Devi Sridhar, and Daniel Hougendobler. 2015. "The Normative Authority of the World Health Organization." *Public Health* 129(7):854–863.

Gould, Erica R. 2017. "What Impedes IO Accountability Mechanisms?: The Case of Multilateral Development Bank Internal Accountability Offices." Paper prepared for presentation at the 11th Annual Conference on The Political Economy of International Organization. www.peio.me/wp-content/uploads/2018/01/PEIO11_paper_34.pdf [Last accessed November 2, 2021].

GRAIN. 2004. "FAO Declares War on Farmers, Not on Hunger (An Open Letter to Mr. Jacques Diouf, Director General of FAO)." www.grain.org/system/old/front_files/fao-open-letter-june-2004-final-en.pdf [Last accessed January 10, 2022].

Grant, Ruth W. and Robert O. Keohane. 2005. "Accountability and Abuses of Power in World Politics." *American Political Science Review* 99(1):29–43.

Gray, Cheryl. 2014. "Finding Out What Works: Tracking Results in the Inter-American Development Bank." *Journal of Development Effectiveness* 6(4):480–489.

Grieco, Joseph M. 1988. "Anarchy and the Limits of Cooperation: A Realist Critique of the Newest Liberal Institutionalism." *International Organization* 42(3):485–507.

Grigg, David B. 1985. *The World Food Problem, 1950–1980*. Oxford: Basil Blackwell.

——. 1986. The World Food Problem. In *Progress in Agricultural Geography*, ed. Michael Pacione. Dover, NH: Croom Helm, pp. 239–263.

Grigorescu, Alexandru. 2007. "Transparency of Intergovernmental Organizations: The Roles of Member States, International Bureaucracies and Nongovernmental organizations." *International Studies Quarterly* 51(3): 625–648.

——. 2010. "The Spread of Bureaucratic Oversight Mechanisms across Intergovernmental Organizations." *International Studies Quarterly* 54(3): 871–886.

Gujarati, Damodar N., ed. 2004. *Basic Econometrics*. 4th ed. New York: McGraw-Hill.

Gutner, Tamar. 2005. "Explaining the Gaps between Mandate and Performance: Agency Theory and World Bank Environmental Reform." *Global Environmental Politics* 5(2):10–37.

Gutner, Tamar and Alexander Thompson. 2010. "The Politics of IO Performance: A Framework." *The Review of International Organizations* 5(3): 227–248.

Guzman, Andrew T. 2008. *How International Law Works: A Rational Choice Theory*. Oxford: Oxford University Press.

——. 2013. "International Organizations and the Frankenstein Problem." *European Journal of International Law* 24(4):999–1025.

Haas, Peter M. 1992. "Introduction: Epistemic Communities and International Policy Coordination." *International Organization* 46(1):1–35.

Haas, Peter M., Robert O. Keohane, and Marc A. Levy. 1993. *Institutions for the Earth: Sources of Effective International Environmental Protection*. Cambridge, MA: MIT Press.

Haftel, Yoram Z. and Alexander Thompson. 2006. "The Independence of International Organizations: Concept and Applications." *Journal of Conflict Resolution* 50(2):253–275.

Hale, Thomas and David Held, eds. 2017. *Beyond Gridlock*. Cambridge: Polity Press.

Hale, Thomas, David Held, and Kevin Young. 2013. *Gridlock: Why Global Cooperation Is Failing When We Need It Most*. Cambridge: Polity Press.

Hall, Nina and Ngaire Woods. 2018. "Theorizing the Role of Executive Heads in International Organizations." *European Journal of International Relations* 24(4):865–886.

Hall, Rodney Bruce and Thomas J. Biersteker, eds. 2002. *The Emergence of Private Authority in Global Governance*. Cambridge: Cambridge University Press.

Hambidge, Gove. 1955. *The Story of FAO*. New York: D. Van Notrand Company.

Hardt, Heidi. 2014. *Time to React: The Efficiency of International Organizations in Crisis Response*. New York: Oxford University Press.

Harman, Sophie. 2011. "Searching for an Executive Head? Leadership and UNAIDS." *Global Governance* 17:429.

——. 2012. *Global Health Governance*. Abingdon: Routledge.

Harmer, Andrew, Neil Spicer, Julia Aleshkina, Daryna Bogdan, Ketevan Chkhatarashvili, Gulgun Murzalieva, Natia Rukhadze, Arnol Samiev, and Gill Walt. 2013. "Has Global Fund Support for Civil Society Advocacy in the Former Soviet Union Established Meaningful Engagement or 'a Lot of Jabber About Nothing'?" *Health Policy and Planning* 28(3):299–308.

Hawkins, Darren G., David A. Lake, Daniel L. Nielson, and Michael J. Tierney, eds. 2006. *Delegation and Agency in International Organizations*. Cambridge: Cambridge University Press.

Hawkins, Darren G. and Wade Jacoby. 2006. How Agents Matter. In *Delegation and Agency in International Organizations*, eds. Darren G. Hawkins, David A. Lake, Daniel L. Nielson, and Michael J. Tierney. New York: Cambridge University Press, pp. 199–228.

Heilmann, Sebastian, Moritz Rudolf, Mikko Huotari, and Johannes Buckow. 2014. "China's Shadow Foreign Policy: Parallel Structures Challenge the Established International Order." *China Monitor* 18(10):1–9.

Held, David. 1995. *Democracy and the Global Order: From the Modern State to Cosmopolitan Governance*. Stanford, CA: Stanford University Press.

Helm, Carsten and Detlef Sprinz. 2000. "Measuring the Effectiveness of International Environmental Regimes." *Journal of Conflict Resolution* 44(5):630–652.

Henderson, Donald A. 1998. "Eradication: lessons from the past." *Bulletin of the World Health Organization* 76(2):17–21.

Henkin, Louis. 1968. *How Nations Behave: Law and Foreign Policy.* New York: Frederick A. Praeger.

Héritier, Adrienne and Dirk Lehmkuhl. 2008. "The Shadow of Hierarchy and New Modes of Governance." *Journal of Public Policy* 28(1):1–17.

Hill, Peter S. 2011. The Alignment Dialogue: GAVI and Its Engagement with National Governments in Health Systems Strengthening. In *Partnerships and Foundations in Global Health Governance*, eds. Simon Rushton and Owain David Williams. Basingstoke: Palgrave Macmillan, pp. 76–101.

Honig, Dan. 2018. *Navigation by Judgment: Why and When Top Down Management of Foreign Aid Doesn't Work.* New York: Oxford University Press.

——. 2019. "When Reporting Undermines Performance: The Costs of Politically Constrained Organizational Autonomy in Foreign Aid Implementation." *International Organization* 73(1):171–201.

Honig, Dan, Ranjit Lall, and Bradley C. Parks. 2022. "When Does Transparency Improve Institutional Performance? Evidence from 20,000 Aid Projects in 183 Countries." *American Journal of Political Science*, Early View. https://doi.org/10.1111/ajps.12698 [Last accessed August 21, 2022].

Hooghe, Liesbet. 2001. *The European Commission and the Integration of Europe: Images of Governance.* Cambridge: Cambridge University Press.

Hooghe, Liesbet and Gary Marks. 2015. "Delegation and Pooling in International Organizations." *The Review of International Organizations* 10(3): 305–328.

Hooghe, Liesbet, Tobias Lenz, and Gary Marks. 2019. *A Theory of International Organization.* Oxford: Oxford University Press.

Hopkins, Raymond F. 1990. International Food Organizations and the United States: Drifting Leadership and Diverging Interests. In *The United States and Multilateral Institutions: Patterns of Changing Instrumentality and Influence*, eds. Margaret Kars and Karen Mingst. Boston, MA: Unwin Hyman, pp. 177–204.

——. 1992. "Reform in the International Food Aid Regime: The Role of Consensual Knowledge." *International Organization* 46(1):225–264.

Horeth, Marcus. 1999. "No Way Out for the Beast? The Unsolved Legitimacy Problem of European Governance." *Journal of European Public Policy* 6(2):249–268.

Howard, Lise Morjé. 2008. *UN Peacekeeping in Civil Wars.* Cambridge: Cambridge University Press.

Hultman, Lisa, Jacob Kathman, and Megan Shannon. 2013. "United Nations Peacekeeping and Civilian Protection in Civil War." *American Journal of Political Science* 57(4):875–891.

Humphrey, Christopher. 2020. "From Drawing Board to Reality: The First Four Years of Operations at the Asian Infrastructure Investment Bank and New Development Bank." Working Paper of the G-24 & Global Development Policy Center of Boston University. https://doi.org/10.3929/ethz-b-000411422 [Last accessed September 21, 2021].

Hunter, David, Cristian Opaso, and Marcos Orellana. 2003. The Biobío's Legacy: Institutional Reforms and Unfulfilled Promises at the International Finance Corporation. In *Demanding Accountability: Civil Society Claims and the World Bank Inspection Panel*, eds. Dana Clark, Jonathan A. Fox, and Kay Treakle. Lanham, MD: Rowman & Littlefield, pp. 115–143.

Hurd, Ian. 2008. *After Anarchy: Legitimacy and Power in the United Nations Security Council*. Princeton, NJ: Princeton University Press.

Ikenberry, G. John. 2001. *After Victory: Institutions, Strategic Restraint, and the Rebuilding of Order after Major Wars*. Princeton, NJ: Princeton University Press.

Ikilezi, Gloria, Orvalho J. Augusto, Joseph L. Dieleman, Kenneth Sherr, and Stephen S. Lim. 2020. "Effect of Donor Funding for Immunization from Gavi and Other Development Assistance Channels on Vaccine Coverage: Evidence from 120 Low and Middle Income Recipient Countries." *Vaccine* 38(3):588–596.

Ingram, James. 2007. *Bread and Stones: Leadership and the Struggle to Reform the United Nations World Food Programme*. North Charleston, SC: BookSurge.

International Civil Service Commission. 2008. "Results of the Global Staff Survey on Recruitment and Retention." https://web.archive .org/web/20181129203031/http://icsc.un.org/resources/hrpd/gssr/docs/ICS CStaffsurvey.pdf [Last accessed November 29, 2021].

International Finance Corporation. 1999. "Office of the Compliance Advisor/Ombudsman (CAO) Terms of Reference." Washington, DC: IFC.

International Fund for Agricultural Development. 1976. "Agreement Establishing the International Fund for Agricultural Development." Rome: IFAD.

———. 1978. "Lending Policies and Criteria." Rome: IFAD.

———. 1984. "IFAD's Relations with Non-Governmental Organizations." Rome: IFAD.

———. 1998. "Meeting Challenges in a Changing World: IFAD's Strategic Framework for 1998–2000." Rome: IFAD.

———. 2002. "Enabling the Rural Poor to Overcome Their Poverty: Strategic Framework for IFAD 2002–2006." Rome: IFAD.

———. 2004. "Supervision Modalities in IFAD Supported Projects: Corporate-Level Evaluation Report." Rome: IFAD.

———. 2005*a*. "Direct Supervision Pilot Programme: Corporate-Level Evaluation." Report No. 1687. Rome: IFAD.

———. 2005*b*. "An Independent External Evaluation of the International Fund for Agricultural Development." Office of Evaluation. Rome: IFAD.

———. 2006a. "President's Report on IFAD Policy on Supervision and Implementation Support." EB 2006/89/R.4/Rev.1. Rome: IFAD.

———. 2006b. "IFAD Strategic Framework 2007-2010: Enabling the rural poor to overcome poverty." EB 2006/89/R.2/Rev.1. Rome: IFAD.

———. 2012*a*. "IFAD Partnership Strategy." EB 2012/106/R.4. Rome: IFAD.

———. 2012*b*. "IFAD's Direct Supervision and Implementation Support: Evaluation Synthesis." Independent Office of Evaluation. Rome: IFAD.

———. 2012*c*. "Report and Recommendation of the Executive Board on Supervision: Extension of the Implementation Period for the Direct Supervision Pilot Programme." EB 2005/86/R.40. Rome: IFAD.

——. 2013*a*. "IFAD's Supervision and Implementation Support Policy: Corporate-Level Evaluation." Report No. 2846. Rome: IFAD.

——. 2013*b*. "IFAD's Institutional Efficiency and Efficiency of IFAD-Funded Operations." Corporate-Level Evaluation. Rome: IFAD.

——. 2015. "Evaluation Manual." Second Edition. Independent Office of Evaluation. Rome: IFAD.

——. 2018. "Building Partnerships for Enhanced Development Effectiveness — A Review of Country-Level Experiences and Results: Evaluation Synthesis." Independent Office of Evaluation. Rome: IFAD.

——. 2019. "Evaluation of IFAD's Capacity as a Promoter of Replicable Innovations in Cooperation with other Partners: Understanding at Completion Point and Executive Summary." Report No. 1325. Rome: IFAD.

——. 2020. "Annual Report 2019." Rome: IFAD.

Jacobs, Tom. 2013. "Ambassador Nominee Samantha Power on the Role of the United Nations." https://psmag.com/news/samantha-power-united-nations-barack-obama-ambassador-59359 [Last accessed May 8, 2022].

Jarosz, Lucy. 2009. "The Political Economy of Global Governance and the World Food Crisis: The Case of the FAO." *Review (Fernand Braudel Center)* 32(1):37–60.

Jaupart, Pascal, Lizzie Dipple, and Stefan Dercon. 2019. "Has Gavi Lived Up to Its Promise? Quasi-Experimental Evidence on Country Immunisation Rates and Child Mortality." *BMJ Global Health* 4(6):e001789.

Johnson, Tana. 2014. *Organizational Progeny: Why Governments Are Losing Control Over the Proliferating Structures of Global Governance.* Oxford: Oxford University Press.

——. 2020. "Ordinary Patterns in an Extraordinary Crisis: How International Relations Makes Sense of the COVID-19 Pandemic." *International Organization* 74(S1):E148–E168.

Johnston, Alastair Iain. 2001. "Treating International Institutions as Social Environments." *International Studies Quarterly* 45(4):487–515.

Johnstone, Ian. 2010. "Do International Organizations Have Reputations?" *International Organizations Law Review* 7(2):235–240.

Joint Inspection Unit. 1981. "Status of Internal Evaluation in the United Nations System." Prepared by Earl D. Sohm. JIU/REP/81/5. Geneva: UN.

——. 1993. "Decentralization of Organizations within the UN System." Prepared by Erica-Irene A. Daes and Adib Daoudy. JIU/REP/93/2 (Part III). Geneva: UN.

——. 2007. "Review of the Progress Made by the United Nations System Organization in Achieving Millennium Development Goal 6, Target 7, to Combat HIV/AIDS." Prepared by Muhammad Yussuf. JIU/REP/2007/12. Geneva: UN.

Joint United Nations Programme on HIV/AIDS. 1999. "Modus Operandi of the Programme Coordinating Board of the Joint United Nations Programme on HIV/AIDS (UNAIDS)." Revised June 1999. Geneva: UNAIDS.

——. 2002. "Five-Year Evaluation of UNAIDS." UNAIDS/PCB(13)/02.2. Geneva: UNAIDS.

——. 2007. "Making the Money Work: UNAIDS Technical Support to Countries." www.unaids.org/sites/default/files/media_asset/jc1388-makingmoneywork_en_0.pdf [Last accessed January 14, 2022].

——. 2009a. "Global Task Team on Improving AIDS Coordination Among Multilateral Institutions and International Donors: Final Report." https://data.unaids.org/publications/irc-pub06/jc1125-globaltaskteamreport_en.pdf [Last accessed January 14, 2022].

——. 2009b. "UNAIDS Second Independent Evaluation 2002–2008: Final Report." UNAIDS/PCB(25)/09.18. Geneva: UNAIDS.

——. 2010. "Uniting the World Against AIDS." www.unaids.org/sites/default/files/media_asset/20101013_unaidsmission_en_1.pdf [Last accessed January 30, 2022].

——. 2018. "Statement by the Representative of the UNAIDS Staff Association." UNAIDS/PCB (43)/18.23. Geneva: UNAIDS.

——. 2020. "Independent Evaluation of the UN System Response to AIDS in 2016-2019." UNAIDS/JC2996. Geneva: UNAIDS.

Junge, Dirk, Thomas König, and Bernd Luig. 2015. "Legislative Gridlock and Bureaucratic Politics in the European Union." *British Journal of Political Science* 45(4):777–797.

Jupille, Joseph, Walter Mattli, and Duncan Snidal. 2013. *Institutional Choice and Global Commerce*. Cambridge: Cambridge University Press.

Kahler, Miles. 2004. "Defining Accountability Up: The Global Economic Multilaterals." *Government and Opposition* 39(2):132–158.

——. 2006. Internal Governance and IMF Performance. In *Reforming the IMF for the 21st Century*, ed. Edwin M. Truman. Washington, DC: Institute for International Economics, pp. 257–270.

Kanter, Rosabeth Moss and Derick Brinkerhoff. 1981. "Organizational Performance: Recent Developments in Measurement." *Annual Review of Sociology* 7(1):321–349.

Kapilashrami, Anuj and Oonagh O'Brien. 2012. "The Global Fund and the Reconfiguration and Re-emergence of 'Civil Society': Widening or Closing the Democratic Deficit?" *Global Public Health* 7(5):437–451.

Katzenstein, Peter J., Robert O. Keohane, and Stephen D. Krasner. 1998. "*International Organization* and the Study of World Politics." *International Organization* 52(4):645–685.

Keck, Margaret E. and Kathryn Sikkink. 1998. *Activists Beyond Borders: Advocacy Networks in International Politics*. Ithaca: Cornell University Press.

Kelley, Judith G. and Beth A. Simmons, eds. 2020. *The Power of Global Performance Indicators*. Cambridge: Cambridge University Press.

Keohane, Robert O. 1984. *After Hegemony: Cooperation and Discord in the World Political Economy*. Princeton, NJ: Princeton University Press.

——. 1988. "International Institutions: Two Approaches." *International Studies Quarterly* 32(4):379–396.

——. 1989. Neoliberal Institutionalism: A Perspective on World Politics. In *International Institutions and State Power: Essays in International Relations Theory*, ed. Robert O. Keohane. Boulder, CO: Westview Press, pp. 1–20.

Kilby, Christopher. 2013. "An Empirical Assessment of Informal Influence in the World Bank." *Economic Development and Cultural Change* 61(2):431–464.

Kim, Soo Yeon and Gabriele Spilker. 2019. "Global Value Chains and the Political Economy of WTO Disputes." *The Review of International Organizations* 14(2):239–260.

Kindleberger, Charles P. 1986. "International Public Goods without International Government." *American Economic Review* 76(1):1–13.

King, Gary, Robert O. Keohane, and Sidney Verba. 1994. *Designing Social Inquiry: Scientific Inference in Qualitative Research.* Princeton, NJ: Princeton University Press.

King, John Andrews. 1985. "The International Fund for Agricultural Development: The First Six Years." *Development Policy Review* 3(1):3–20.

Kingsbury, Benedict, Nico Krisch, and Richard B. Stewart. 2005. "The Emergence of Global Administrative Law." *Law and Contemporary Problems* 68(3/4):15–61.

Kirk, Colin. 2019. "Independent External Evaluation of EBRD's Evaluation System." Final Report: Main Report. London: EBRD.

Kissinger, Henry. 1973. "A Just Consensus. A Durable Peace." Address to the 28th Session of the United Nations General Assembly, September 24. Washington, DC: Department of State.

Kleine, Mareike. 2013. *Informal Governance in the European Union: How Governments Make International Organizations Work.* Ithaca, NY: Cornell University Press.

Knack, Stephen. 2002. "Social Capital and the Quality of Government: Evidence from the States." *American Journal of Political Science* 46(4):772–785.

Knill, Christoph and Michael W. Bauer. 2016. "Policy-Making by International Public Administrations: Concepts, Causes and Consequences." *Journal of European Public Policy* 23(7):949–959.

Knorr, Klaus. 1948. "The Bretton Woods Institutions in Transition." *International Organization* 2(1):19–38.

Koenig-Archibugi, Mathias. 2016. Accountability. In *The Oxford Handbook of International Organizations*, eds. Jacob K. Cogan, Ian Hurd, and Ian Johnstone. Oxford: Oxford University Press, pp. 1170–209.

——. 2017. "How to Diagnose Democratic Deficits in Global Politics: The Use of the All-Affected Principle." *International Theory* 9:171.

Koh, Harold Hongju. 1996. "Why Do Nations Obey International Law." *Yale Law Journal* 106:2599.

Kohlmorgen, Lars. 2007. International Governmental Organizations and Global Health Governance: The Role of the World Health Organization, World Bank and UNAIDS. In *Global Health Governance and the Fight Against HIV/AIDS*, eds. Wolfgang Hein, Sonja Bartsch and Lars Kohlmorgen. Abingdon: Routledge, pp. 119–145.

Komatsu, Ryuichi, Eline L. Korenromp, Daniel Low-Beer, Catherine Watt, Christopher Dye, Richard W. Steketee, Bernard L. Nahlen, Rob Lyerla et al. 2010. "Lives saved by Global Fund-Supported HIV/AIDS, Tuberculosis and Malaria Programs: Estimation Approach and Results Between 2003 and end-2007." *BMC Infectious Diseases* 10(1):1–12.

Koppell, Jonathan G.S. 2010. *World Rule: Accountability, Legitimacy, and the Design of Global Governance*. Chicago, IL: University of Chicago Press.

Koremenos, Barbara. 2016. *The Continent of International Law: Explaining Agreement Design*. Cambridge: Cambridge University Press.

Koremenos, Barbara, Charles Lipson, and Duncan Snidal. 2001. "The Rational Design of International Institutions." *International Organization* 55(4): 761–799.

Krasner, Stephen D. 1978. *Defending the National Interest: Raw Materials Investments and US Foreign Policy*. Vol. 1. Princeton, NJ: Princeton University Press.

———. 1983. *International Regimes*. Ithaca, NY: Cornell University Press.

Kydland, Finn E. and Edward C. Prescott. 1977. "Rules Rather than Discretion: The Inconsistency of Optimal Plans." *Journal of Political Economy* 85(3):473–491.

La Porta, Rafael, Florencio Lopez de Silanes, Andrei Shleifer, and Robert Vishny. 1999. "The Quality of Government." *The Journal of Law, Economics, and Organization* 15(1):222–279.

Lake, David A., Lisa L. Martin, and Thomas Risse. 2021. "Challenges to the Liberal Order: Reflections on International Organization." *International Organization* 75(2):225–257.

Lall, Ranjit. 2017. "Beyond Institutional Design: Explaining the Performance of International Organizations." *International Organization* 71(2):245–280.

———. 2020. Assessing International Organizations: Competition, Collaboration, and the Politics of Funding. In *The Power of Global Performance Indicators*, eds. Judith G. Kelley and Beth A. Simmons. Cambridge: Cambridge University Press, pp. 300–338.

———. 2021. "The Financial Consequences of Rating International Institutions: Competition, Collaboration, and the Politics of Assessment." *International Studies Quarterly* 65(2):343–359.

———. 2022. "Making Global Governance Accountable: Civil Society, States and the Politics of Reform." Working Paper. London School of Economics.

Landemore, Hélène. 2012. *Democratic Reason*. Princeton, NJ: Princeton University Press.

Le Groupe-Conseil Baastel ltée. 2014. "Review of the UNDP Evaluation Policy: Final Report." Gatineau: Baastel.

Leahy, Patrick, Lindsey Graham, Richard J. Durbin, John Boozman, Cory A. Booker, Johnny Isakson, Sherrod Brown, Marco Rubio et al. 1990. "Letter from United States Senators to the Secretary of State." October 11. United States Congressional Serial Set, Serial Number 13862. Washington, DC: United States Government Printing Office.

Lee, Kelley. 2009. *The World Health Organization (WHO)*. Abingdon: Routledge.

———. 2010. "Civil Society Organizations and the Functions of Global Health Governance: What Role within Intergovernmental Organizations?" *Global Health Governance* 3(2):1–20.

Leeds, Brett Ashley. 1999. "Domestic Political Institutions, Credible Commitments, and International Cooperation." *American Journal of Political Science* 43(4):979–1002.

Liao, Rebecca. 2015. "Out of the Bretton Woods: How the AIIB is different." *Foreign Affairs* 27(July):633–649.

Lieberman, Evan S. 2005. "Nested Analysis as a Mixed-Method Strategy for Comparative Research." *American Political Science Review* 99(3):435–452.

Lijphart, Arend. 1971. "Comparative Politics and the Comparative Method." *The American Political Science Review* 65(3):682–693.

———. 1999. *Patterns of Democracy: Government Forms and Performance in Thirty-Six Countries*. New Haven, CT: Yale University Press.

Likert, Rensis. 1967. *The Human Organization: Its Management and Value*. New York: McGraw-Hill.

Lindgren, Karl-Oskar, and Thomas Persson. 2010. "Input and Output Legitimacy: Synergy or Trade-Off? Empirical Evidence from an EU survey." *Journal of European Public Policy* 17(4):449–467.

Lipscy, Phillip Y. 2017. *Renegotiating the World Order: Institutional Change in International Relations*. Cambridge: Cambridge University Press.

Lloyd, Robert, Jeffrey Oatham, and Michael Hammer. 2007. "2007 Global Accountability Report." London: One World Trust.

Loescher, Gil. 2001. *The UNHCR and World Politics: A Perilous Path*. Oxford: Oxford University Press.

Lu, Chunling, Catherine M. Michaud, Emmanuela Gakidou, Kashif Khan, and Christopher J.L. Murray. 2006. "Effect of the Global Alliance for Vaccines and Immunisation on Diphtheria, Tetanus, and Pertussis Vaccine Coverage: An Independent Assessment." *The Lancet* 368(9541):1088–1095.

Macdonald, Kate and May Miller-Dawkins. 2015. "Accountability in Public International Development Finance." *Global Policy* 6(4):429–434.

Majone, Giandomenico. 1998. "Europe's 'Democratic Deficit': The Question of Standards." *European Law Journal* 4(1):5–28.

Malin, Patrick Murphy. 1947. "The Refugee: A Problem for International Organization." *International Organization* 1(3):443–459.

Mansbridge, Jane. 2009. "A 'Selection Model' of Political Representation." *Journal of Political Philosophy* 17(4):369–398.

Marchisio, Sergio and Antonietta Di Blasè. 1991. *The Food and Agricultural Organization*. Graduate Institute for International Studies, Geneva: M. Nijhoff Publishers.

Marínez, Luis Miguel Hinojosa. 2013. Transparency in International Law. In *The Handbook of Development Communication and Social Change*, eds. Andrea Bianchi and Anne Peters. Cambridge: Cambridge University Press, pp. 77–111.

Marshall, Monty, Ted Robert Gurr, and Keith Jaggers. 2019. "Polity IV Project: Political Regime Characteristics and Transitions, 1800–2018." Vienna, VA: Center for Systemic Peace.

Martha, Rutsel Silvestre. 2009. "Mandate Issues in the Activities of the International Fund for Agricultural Development (IFAD)." *International Organizations Law Review* 6(2):447–477.

Martin, Lisa. 2006. Distribution, Information, and Delegation to International Organizations: The Case of IMF Conditionality. In *Delegation and Agency in International Organizations*, eds. Darren G. Hawkins, David A. Lake,

Daniel L. Nielson, and Michael J. Tierney. Cambridge: Cambridge University Press, pp. 140–164.

Martin, Lisa L. 1992. *Coercive Cooperation: Explaining Multilateral Economic Sanctions*. Princeton, NJ: Princeton University Press.

Martin, Lisa L. and Beth A. Simmons. 1998. "Theories and Empirical Studies of International Institutions." *International Organization* 52(4):729–757.

Mathiason, John. 2007. *Invisible Governance: International Secretariats in Global Politics*. Bloomfield, CT: Kumarian Press.

Mattli, Walter and Jack Seddon. 2015. Orchestration along the Pareto Frontier: Winners and Losers. In *International Organizations as Orchestrators*, eds. Kenneth W. Abbott, Philipp Genschel, Duncan Snidal, and Bernhard Zangl. Cambridge: Cambridge University Press, pp. 315–348.

Mattli, Walter and Ngaire Woods. 2009. *The Politics of Global Regulation*. Princeton, NJ: Princeton University Press.

McCoy, David and Kelvin Kinyua. 2012. "Allocating Scarce Resources Strategically – An Evaluation and Discussion of the Global Fund's Pattern of Disbursements." *PLoS One* 7(5):e34749.

McCubbins, Mathew D., Roger G. Noll, and Barry R. Weingast. 1987. "Administrative Procedures as Instruments of Political Control." *Journal of Law, Economics, & Organization* 3(2):243–277.

McCubbins, Mathew D. and Thomas Schwartz. 1984. "Congressional Oversight Overlooked: Police Patrols versus Fire Alarms." *American Journal of Political Science* 28(1):165–179.

McDonagh, Maeve. 2019. Evaluating the Access to Information Policies of the Multilateral Development Banks. In *The Practice of Independent Accountability Mechanisms (IAMs): Towards Good Governance in Development Finance*, eds. Owen McIntyre and Suresh Nanwani. Leiden: Brill Nijhoff, pp. 134–161.

McFarland, Andrew S. 1984. *Common Cause: Lobbying in the Public Interest*. Chatham, NJ: Chatham House.

McGregor, Alan. 1993. "WHO: New Look Fails to Impress." *The Lancet* 341:1205.

McInnes, Colin. 2015. "WHO's Next? Changing Authority in Global Health Governance after Ebola." *International Affairs* 91(6):1299–1316.

McInnes, Colin, Adam Kamradt-Scott, Kelley Lee, Anne Roemer-Mahler, Simon Rushton, and Owain Williams. 2014. *The Transformation of Global Health Governance*. Basingstoke: Palgrave Macmillan.

McIntyre, Owen and Suresh Nanwani, eds. 2019. *The Practice of Independent Accountability Mechanisms (IAMs): Towards Good Governance in Development Finance*. Leiden: Brill Nijhoff.

McKeown, Timothy J. 2009. "How US Decision-Makers Assessed Their Control of Multilateral Organizations, 1957–1982." *The Review of International Organizations* 4(3):269–291.

McNeill, Desmond and Kristin Ingstad Sandberg. 2014. "Trust in Global Health Governance: The GAVI Experience." *Global Governance* 20(2): 325–343.

Mearsheimer, John J. 1994. "The False Promise of International Institutions." *International Security* 19(3):5–49.

——. 2019. "Bound to Fail: The Rise and Fall of the Liberal International Order." *International Security* 43(4):7–50.

Mele, Valentina, Simon Anderfuhren-Biget, and Frédéric Varone. 2016. "Conflicts of Interest in International Organizations: Evidence from Two United Nations Humanitarian Agencies." *Public Administration* 94(2):490–508.

Micklewright, John and Anna Wright. 2005. Private Donations for International Development. In *New Sources of Development Finance*, ed. Anthony B. Atkinson. Oxford: Oxford University Press, pp. 132–155.

Miguel, Edward and Mary Kay Gugerty. 2005. "Ethnic Diversity, Social Sanctions, and Public Goods in Kenya." *Journal of Public Economics* 89(11–12):2325–2368.

Miles, Edward L., Steinar Andresen, Elaine M. Carlin, Jon Birger Skjærseth, Arild Underdal, and Jørgen Wettestad, eds. 2002. *Environmental Regime Effectiveness: Confronting Theory with Evidence*. Cambridge, MA: MIT Press.

Miller, Gary J. and Andrew B. Whitford. 2007. "The Principal's Moral Hazard: Constraints on the Use of Incentives in Hierarchy." *Journal of Public Administration Research and Theory* 17(2):213–233.

——. 2016. *Above Politics*. New York: Cambridge University Press.

Miller, Gary J. and Terry M. Moe. 1983. "Bureaucrats, Legislators, and the Size of Government." *American Political Science Review* 77(2):297–322.

Moe, Terry M. 1984. "The New Economics of Organization." *American Journal of Political Science* 28(4):739–777.

——. 1989. The Politics of Bureaucratic Structure. In *Can the Government Govern?*, eds. John E. Chubb and Paul E. Peterson. Washington DC: The Brookings Institution, pp. 267–329.

——. 1990. The Politics of Structural Choice: Toward a Theory of Public Bureaucracy. In *Organization Theory: From Chester Barnard to the Present and Beyond*, ed. Oliver E. Williamson. Oxford: Oxford University Press, pp. 116–153.

Montgomery, Jacob M., Brendan Nyhan, and Michelle Torres. 2018. "How Conditioning on Posttreatment Variables Can Ruin Your Experiment and What to Do about It." *American Journal of Political Science* 62(3):760–775.

Moon, Suerie. 2014. "WHO's Role in the Global Health System: What Can Be Learned from Global R&D Debates?" *Public Health* 128(2):167–172.

Moon, Suerie, Devi Sridhar, Muhammad A. Pate, Ashish K. Jha, Chelsea Clinton, Sophie Delaunay, Valnora Edwin, Mosoka Fallah et al. 2015. "Will Ebola Change the Game? Ten Essential Reforms before the Next Pandemic. The Report of the Harvard-LSHTM Independent Panel on the Global Response to Ebola." *The Lancet* 386(10009):2204–2221.

Moravcsik, Andrew. 2004. "Is There a 'Democratic Deficit' in World Politics? A Framework for Analysis." *Government and Opposition* 39(2):336–363.

Morgenthau, Hans. 1948. *Politics among Nations: The Struggle for Power and Peace*. New York: Knopf.

Morse, Bradford and Thomas R. Berger. 1992. "Sardar Sarovar: Report of the Independent Review." Ottawa: Resource Futures International.

Morse, Julia C. and Robert O. Keohane. 2014. "Contested multilateralism." *The Review of International Organizations* 9(4):385–412.

Moynihan, Donald P., Sergio Fernandez, Soonhee Kim, Kelly M. LeRoux, Suzanne J. Piotrowski, Bradley E. Wright, and Kaifeng Yang. 2011. "Performance Regimes Amidst Governance Complexity." *Journal of Public Administration Research and Theory* 21(suppl_1):i141–i155.

Mulgan, Richard. 2000. "'Accountability': An Ever-Expanding Concept?" *Public Administration* 78(3):555–573.

Multilateral Organisations Performance Assessment Network. 2005. "The MOPAN Survey 2005: Perceptions of Multilateral Partnerships at Country Level." Synthesis Report. Paris: MOPAN.

——. 2013. "Institutional Report: International Fund for Agricultural Development (IFAD)." Volume 1. Paris: MOPAN.

——. 2019. "MOPAN 2017–18 Assessments: International Fund for Agricultural Development (IFAD)." Volume 1. Paris: MOPAN.

Muraskin, William A. 1998. *The Politics of International Health: The Children's Vaccine Initiative and the Struggle to Develop Vaccines for the Third World.* New York: State University of New York Press.

Murdie, Amanda. 2014. *Help or Harm.* Palo Alto, CA: Stanford University Press.

Nadler, David A. and Michael L. Tushman. 1980. A Congruence Model for Organizational Assessment. In *Organizational Assessment: Perspectives on the Measurement of Organizational Behavior and the Quality of Working Life*, eds. Edward E. Lawler III, David A. Nadler, and Cortlandt Cammann. New York: Wiley, pp. 261–278.

Naidoo, Indran. 2020. "Audit and Evaluation: Working Collaboratively to Support Accountability." *Evaluation* 26(2):177–189.

Naidoo, Indran and Ana Soares. 2020. Lessons Learned from the Assessment of UNDP's Institutional Effectiveness Jointly Conducted by the Independent Evaluation Office and the Office of Audit and Investigation of UNDP. In *Crossover of Audit and Evaluation Practices: Challenges and Opportunities*, eds. Maria Barrados and Jeremy Lonsdale. Abingdon: Routledge, pp. 182–193.

Naimoli, Joseph F. 2009. "Global Health Partnerships in Practice: Taking Stock of the GAVI Alliance's New Investment in Health Systems Strengthening." *The International Journal of Health Planning and Management* 24(1):3–25.

National Research Council. 2016. "The Neglected Dimension of Global Security: A Framework to Counter Infectious Disease Crises." Washington, DC: The National Academies Press.

Nelson, Paul J. 1995. *The World Bank and Non-Governmental Organizations: The Limits of Apolitical Development.* Basingstoke: Palgrave Macmillan.

——. 2001. "Transparency Mechanisms at the Multilateral Development Banks." *World Development* 29(11):1835–1847.

Ness, Gayl D. and Steven R. Brechin. 1988. "Bridging the Gap: International Organizations as Organizations." *International Organization* 42(2):245–273.

Neumayer, Eric. 2005. "Is the Allocation of Food Aid Free from Donor Interest Bias?" *The Journal of Development Studies* 41(3):394–411.

New Development Bank. 2014. "Articles of Agreement." Fortaleza: NDB.

——. 2019. "Rules of Procedure of Board of Directors of the New Development Bank." Shanghai: NDB.

——. 2021. "Annual Report 2020." Shanghai: NDB.

Newman, Abraham L. 2008. "Building Transnational Civil Liberties: Trans-governmental Entrepreneurs and the European Data Privacy Directive." *International Organization* 62(1):103–130.

——. 2010. International Organization Control Under Conditions of Dual Delegation: A Transgovernmental Politics Approach. In *Who Governs the Globe?*, eds. Deborah D. Avant, Martha Finnemore, and Susan K. Sell. New York: Cambridge University Press, pp. 131–152.

NGO Forum on Food Security. 1949. "Profit for Few or Food for All: Food Sovereignty and Security to Eliminate the Globalisation of Hunger." A Statement by the NGO Forum to the World Food Summit. November 17. www.iatp.org/sites/default/files/Profit_for_Few_or_Food_for_All.htm [Last accessed October 11, 2021].

Nielsen, Richard A. 2016. "Case Selection via Matching." *Sociological Methods & Research* 45(3):569–597.

Nielson, Daniel L. and Michael J. Tierney. 2003. "Delegation to International Organizations: Agency Theory and World Bank Environmental Reform." *International Organization* 57(2):241–276.

——. 2005. "Theory, Data, and Hypothesis Testing: World Bank Environmental Reform Redux." *International Organization* 59(3):785–800.

Niezen, Ronald and Maria Sapignoli. 2017. *Palaces of Hope: The Anthropology of Global Organizations*. Cambridge: Cambridge University Press.

Niskanen, William A. 1971. *Bureaucracy and Representative Government*. Chicago, IL: Aldine.

Nordic UN Project. 1990. "Perspectives on Multilateral Assistance: A Review by the Nordic UN Project." Stockholm: Almdqvist & Wiksell International.

Nordlinger, Eric A. 1981. *On the Autonomy of the Democratic State*. Cambridge, MA: Harvard University Press.

North, Douglass C. 1991. "Institutions." *The Journal of Economic Perspectives* 5(1):97–112.

Norwegian Nobel Committee. 2020. "The Nobel Peace Prize for 2020 (Announcement)." www.nobelprize.org/prizes/peace/2020/press-release/ [Last accessed December 11, 2021].

Nye, Joseph S. 2017. "Will the Liberal Order Survive? The History of an Idea." *Foreign Affairs* 96:10.

Obser, Andreas. 2007. "Multilateral Organisations Performance Assessment: Opportunities and Limitations for Harmonisation among Development Agencies." German Development Institute Discussion Paper 19/2007. www.die-gdi.de/uploads/media/19.2007ObserMulti.Organ.pdf [Last accessed April 8, 2022].

Odell, John S. 2002. Bounded Rationality and the World Political Economy: The Nature of Decision Making. In *Governing the World's Money*, eds. David M. Andrews, C. Randall Henning, and Louis W. Pauly. Ithaca, NY: Cornell University Press, pp. 168–193.

Orr, John Boyd. 1966. *As I Recall: The 1880's to the 1960's*. London: MacGibbon and Kee.

Orr, John Boyd and David Lubbock. 1953. *The White Man's Dilemma: Food and the Future*. London: Unwin Books.

Ozawa, Sachiko, Samantha Clark, Allison Portnoy, Simrun Grewal, Meghan L. Stack, Anushua Sinha, Andrew Mirelman, Heather Franklin et al. 2017. "Estimated Economic Impact of Vaccinations in 73 Low- and Middle-Income Countries, 2001–2020." *Bulletin of the World Health Organization* 95(9):629.

Paarlberg, Robert. 2010. *Food Politics: What Everyone Needs to Know*. Oxford: Oxford University Press.

Park, Susan. 2005*a*. "How Transnational Environmental Advocacy Networks Socialize International Financial Institutions: A Case Study of the International Finance Corporation." *Global Environmental Politics* 5(4):95–119.

———. 2005*b*. "Norm Diffusion Within International Organizations: A Case Study of the World Bank." *Journal of International Relations and Development* 8(2):111–141.

———. 2014. "Institutional Isomorphism and the Asian Development Bank's Accountability Mechanism: Something Old, Something New; Something Borrowed, Something Blue?" *The Pacific Review* 27(2):217–239.

———. 2017. "Accountability as Justice for the Multilateral Development Banks? Borrower Opposition and Bank Avoidance to US Power and Influence." *Review of International Political Economy* 24(5):776–801.

Patnaik, Utsa. 1990. Some Economic and Political Consequences of the Green Revolution in India. In *The Food Question: Profits versus People*, eds. Henry Bernstein, Ben Crow, Maureen Mackintosh and Charlotte Martin. New York: Monthly Review Press, pp. 80–90.

Pauls, Scott D. and Skyler J. Cranmer. 2017. "Affinity Communities in United Nations Voting: Implications for Democracy, Cooperation, and Conflict." *Physica A: Statistical Mechanics and its Applications* 484:428–439.

Payne, Tony. 2020. "The G20 in Argentina Needs to Address Its Own Failings as well as the Many Problems Facing the Global Economy." LSE Blogs. https://blogs.lse.ac.uk/latamcaribbean/2018/11/23/the-g20-in-argentina-needs-to-address-its-own-failings-as-well-as-the-many-problems-facing-the-global-economy/ [Last accessed April 11, 2022].

Pearse, Andrew. 1980. *Seeds of Want: Seeds of Plenty*. Oxford: Clarendon Press.

Pegram, Tom. 2020. "Coronavirus Is a Failure of Global Governance – Now the World Needs a Radial Transformation." *The Conversation*. https://theconversation.com/coronavirus-is-a-failure-of-global-governance-now-the-world-needs-a-radical-transformation-136535 [Last accessed April 11, 2022].

People's Health Movement. 2015. "PHM Commentary on the Agenda of the 68th Session of the World Health Assembly." https://ghwatch.org/sites/www.ghwatch.org/files/WHA68_PHM(full).pdf [Last accessed February 4, 2022].

Perrow, Charles. 1961. "The Analysis of Goals in Complex Organizations." *American Sociological Review* 26(6):854–866.

Pevehouse, Jon C.W. and Inken von Borzyskowski. 2016. International Organizations in World Politics. In *The Oxford Handbook of International Organiza-*

tions, eds. Jacob K. Cogan, Ian Hurd and Ian Johnstone. Oxford: Oxford University Press, pp. 3–32.

Pevehouse, Jon C.W., Timothy Nordstrom, Roseanne W. McManus, and Anne Spencer Jamison. 2019. "Tracking Organizations in the World: The Correlates of War IGO Version 3.0 Datasets." *Journal of Peace Research* 57(3):1–12.

Pfeffer, Jeffrey and Gerald R. Salancik. 2003. *The External Control of Organizations: A Resource Dependence Perspective*. New York: Harper & Row.

Physicians for Human Rights. 2020. "President Trump's Deadly Decision to End Funding for the World Health Organization: PHR." Press Release. https://phr.org/news/president-trumps-deadly-decision-to-end-funding-for-the-world-health-organization-phr/ [Last accessed May 8, 2022].

Pickle, Hal and Frank Friedlander. 1967. "Seven Societal Criteria of Organizational Success." *Personnel Psychology* 20:165–178.

Pierson, Paul. 1994. *Dismantling the Welfare State?: Reagan, Thatcher and the Politics of Retrenchment*. New York: Cambridge University Press.

Pilon, Juliana G. 1988. "The UN's Food and Agriculture Organization: Becoming Part of the Problem." *Society* 25(6):4–11.

Pisani, Elizabeth. 2008. *The Wisdom of Whores, Bureaucrats, Brothels and the Business of Aids*. New York: W. W. Norton & Company.

Pollack, Mark A. and Emilie M. Hafner-Burton. 2010. "Mainstreaming International Governance: The Environment, Gender, and IO Performance in the European Union." *The Review of International Organizations* 5(3):285–313.

Popovski, Vesselin. 2010. The Role of Civil Society in Global Governance. In *Engaging Civil Society: Emerging Trends in Democratic Governance*, eds. G. Shabbir Cheema and Vesselin Popovski. Tokyo: United Nations University, pp. 23–42.

Porter, Patrick. 2018. "A World Imagined: Nostalgia and Liberal Order." *Cato Institute Policy Analysis* 843:1–24.

Poulsen, Lauge N. Skovgaard. 2015. *Bounded Rationality and Economic Diplomacy: The Politics of Investment Treaties in Developing Countries*. Cambridge: Cambridge University Press.

Price, James L. 1968. *Organizational Effectiveness: An Inventory of Propositions*. Homewood, IL: Richard D. Irwin.

Przeworski, Adam and James Raymond Vreeland. 2000. "The Effect of IMF Programs on Economic Growth." *Journal of Development Economics* 62(2):385–421.

Przeworski, Adam, Susan C. Stokes, and Bernard Manin, eds. 1999. *Democracy, Accountability, and Representation*. New York: Cambridge University Press.

Putnam, Robert D. 1993. *Making Democracy Work: Civic Traditions in Modern Italy*. Princeton, NJ: Princeton University Press.

Putnam, Robert D., Robert Leonardi, Raffaella Y. Nanetti, and Franco Pavoncello. 1983. "Explaining Institutional Success: The Case of Italian Regional Government." *American Political Science Review* 77(1):55–74.

Rabkin, Jeremy A. 2005. *Law Without Nations? Why Constitutional Government Requires Sovereign States*. Princeton, NJ: Princeton University Press.

Rainey, Hal G. 1997. *Understanding and Managing Public Organizations.* San Francisco: Jossey-Bass.

Raustiala, Kal. 2002. "The Architecture of International Cooperation: Transgovernmental Networks and the Future of International Law." *Vanderbilt Journal of Transnational Law* 43:1–92.

Reddy, Srikanth K., Sumaira Mazhar, and Raphael Lencucha. 2018. "The Financial Sustainability of the World Health Organization and the Political Economy of Global Health Governance: A Review of Funding Proposals." *Globalization and Health* 14(1):1–11.

Renwick, Danielle and Toni Johnson. 2014. "World Health Organization." Council on Foreign Relations. https://web.archive.org/web/20160715115930/http://www.cfr.org/public-health-threats-and-pandemics/world-health-organization-/p20003 [Last accessed February 12, 2022].

Richter, Judith. 2012. "WHO Reform and Public Interest Safeguards: An Historical Perspective." *Social Medicine* 6(3):141–150.

Risse, Thomas. 2000. The Power of Norms Versus the Norms of Power: Transnational Civil Society and Human Rights. In *The Third Force: The Rise of Transnational Civil Society*, ed. Ann M. Florini. Washington, DC: Brookings Institution Press, pp. 177–209.

Risse, Thomas, Stephen C. Ropp, and Kathryn Sikkink, eds. 1999. *The Power of Human Rights: International Norms and Domestic Change.* Cambridge: Cambridge University Press.

Rodrik, Dani. 2020. "Putting Global Governance in Its Place." *The World Bank Research Observer* 35(1):1–18.

Rogoff, Kenneth. 1985. "The Optimal Degree of Commitment to an Intermediate Monetary Target." *The Quarterly Journal of Economics* 100(4):1169–1189.

Roller, Edeltraud. 2005. *The Performance of Democracies: Political Institutions and Public Policy.* Oxford: Oxford University Press.

Roosevelt, Franklin D. 1941. "Annual Message to Congress on the State of the Union." www.presidency.ucsb.edu/documents/annual-message-congress-the-state-the-union [Last accessed December 15, 2021].

Ross, Sandy. 2011. *The World Food Programme in Global Politics.* Boulder, CO: Lynne Rienner Publishers.

Rubenfeld, Jed. 2004. "Unilateralism and Constitutionalism." *New York University Law Review* 79(6):1971–2028.

Ruggie, John G. 1992. "Multilateralism: The Anatomy of an Institution." *International Organization* 46(3):561–598.

Ryan, Leo, Eric Sarriot, Peter Bachrach, Brad Dude, David Cantor, Jessica Rockwood, Jennifer Lissfelt, and Victor Barnes. 2007. "Evaluation of the Organizational Effectiveness and Efficiency of the Global Fund to Fight AIDS, Tuberculosis, and Malaria: Results from Study Area 1 of the Five-Year Evaluation." Calverton, MD: Macro International Inc.

Saladin, Claudia and Brennan Van Dyke. 1998. "Implementing the Principles of the Public Participation Convention in International Organizations." Washington, DC: Center for International Environmental Law.

Samuelson, Paul A. 1954. "The Pure Theory of Public Expenditure." *The Review of Economics and Statistics* 36(4):387–389.

Savanas E. Enseadas LDA. 2020. "Third Review of the African Development Bank's Independent Review Mechanism." Revised Draft Report. Lisbon: Savanas E Enseadas LDA.

Schmidt, Manfred G. 2002. "Political Performance and Types of Democracy: Findings from Comparative Studies." *European Journal of Political Research* 41(1):147–163.

Schneider, Christina J. and Jennifer L. Tobin. 2013. "Interest Coalitions and Multilateral Aid Allocation in the European Union." *International Studies Quarterly* 57(1):103–114.

Scholte, Jan Aart. 2002. "Civil Society Voices and the International Monetary Fund." Ottawa: North-South Institute. www.internationalbudget.org/wp-content/uploads/Civil-Society-Voices-and-the-IMF.pdf [Last accessed August 28, 2021].

——. 2008. "Civil Society and IMF Accountability." CSGR Working Paper No. 244/08. https://warwick.ac.uk/fac/soc/pais/research/researchcentres/csgr/papers/244-08.pdf [Last accessed August 9, 2021].

Sharma, Dhruv and Kit de Vriese. 2020. "COVID-19, the WHO, and the Failures of Global Governance." *The Global.* https://theglobal.blog/2020/06/30/covid-19-the-who-and-the-failures-of-global-governance/ [Last accessed April 11, 2022].

Shaw, John D. 2001. *The UN World Food Program and the Development of Food Aid.* Basingstoke: Palgrave Macmillan.

——. 2007. *World Food Security: A History since 1945.* Basingstoke: Palgrave Macmillan.

——. 2009. *Global Food and Agricultural Institutions.* Abingdon: Routledge.

——. 2011. *The World's Largest Humanitarian Agency: The Transformation of the UN World Food Programme and of Food Aid.* Basingstoke: Palgrave Macmillan.

Shihata, Ibrahim F.I. 2000. *The World Bank Inspection Panel: In Practice.* Oxford: Oxford University Press.

Siddiqi, Javed. 1995. *World Health and World Politics: The World Health Organization and the UN System.* Columbus, SC: University of South Carolina Press.

Siebenhüner, Bernd. 2008. "Learning in International Organizations in Global Environmental Governance." *Global Environmental Politics* 8(4):92–116.

Sim, So Yoon, Elizabeth Watts, Dagna Constenla, Logan Brenzel, and Bryan N. Patenaude. 2020. "Return on Investment from Immunization Against 10 Pathogens in 94 Low- and Middle-Income Countries, 2011–30." *Health Affairs* 39(8):1343–1353.

Simmons, Beth A. 1998. "Compliance with International Agreements." *Annual Review of Political Science* 1(1):75–93.

——. 2000. "International Law and State Behavior: Commitment and Compliance in International Monetary Affairs." *American Political Science Review* 94(4):819–835.

——. 2009. *Mobilizing for Human Rights: International Law in Domestic Politics.* New York: Cambridge University Press.

Simmons, Beth A. and Lisa L. Martin. 2003. International Organizations and Institutions. In *Handbook of International Relations*, eds. Walter Carlsnaes, Thomas Risse, and Beth A. Simmons. London: Sage Publications, pp. 192–211.

Skocpol, Theda. 2006. Bringing the State Back In: Strategies of Analysis in Current Research. In *Delegation and Agency in International Organizations*, eds. Peter Evans, Dietrich Rueschemeyer, and Theda Skocpol. Cambridge: Cambridge University Press, pp. 3–37.

Slaughter, Anne-Marie. 2005. *A New World Order*. Princeton, NJ: Princeton University Press.

Smith, Julia Heather. 2014. Transformation From Below?: The Role of Civil Society Organizations in the Global Governance of the Response to HIV/AIDS. PhD thesis, University of Bradford.

Smith, Michael E. 2017. *Europe's Common Security and Defence Policy: Capacity-Building, Experiential Learning, and Institutional Change*. Cambridge: Cambridge University Press.

Sommerer, Thomas and Jonas Tallberg. 2019. "Diffusion Across International Organizations: Connectivity and Convergence." *International Organization* 73(2):399–433.

Sommerer, Thomas, Theresa Squatrito, Jonas Tallberg, and Magnus Lundgren. 2021. "Decision-Making in International Organizations: Institutional Design and Performance." *Review of International Organizations* https://doi.org/10.1007/s11558-021-09445-x.

Sondarjee, Maïka. 2020. "Collective Learning at the Boundaries of Communities of Practice: Inclusive Policymaking at the World Bank." *Global Society* 35(3):1–20.

Sridhar, Devi, Danielle Kuczynski, and Kristie Latulippe. 2008. "Background Report for UNAIDS Leadership Transition Working Group." https://citeseerx.ist.psu.edu/viewdoc/download?doi=10.1.1.501.385&rep=rep1&type=pdf [Last accessed March 23, 2022].

Staples, Amy L.S. 2006. *The Birth of Development: How the World Bank, Food and Agriculture Organization, and World Health Organization Changed the World, 1945–1965*. Vol. 1. Kent, OH: Kent State University Press.

Stevenson, Robert Louis. 2006 [1886]. *Strange Case of Dr Jekyll and Mr Hyde and Other Tales*. Oxford: Oxford University Press.

Stiglitz, Joseph E. 2003. "Democratizing the International Monetary Fund and the World Bank: Governance and Accountability." *Governance* 16(1): 111–139.

Stone, Randall W. 2008. "The Scope of IMF Conditionality." *International Organization* 62(4):589–620.

——. 2011. *Controlling Institutions: International Organizations and the Global Economy*. New York: Cambridge University Press.

——. 2013. "Informal Governance in International Organizations: Introduction to the Special Issue." *The Review of International Organizations* 8(2): 121–136.

Storeng, Katerini T. 2014. "The GAVI Alliance and the 'Gates Approach' to Health System Strengthening." *Global Public Health* 9(8):865–879.

Stover, John, Eline L. Korenromp, Matthew Blakley, Ryuichi Komatsu, Kirsi Viisainen, Lori Bollinger, and Rifat Atun. 2011. "Long-Term Costs and Health Impact of Continued Global Fund Support for Antiretroviral Therapy." *PLOS One* 6(6):e21048.

Strange, Susan. 1998. Why Do International Organisations Never Die? In *Autonomous Policymaking by International Organizations*, eds. Bob Reinalda and Bertjan Verbeek. London: Routledge, pp. 213–221.

Subacchi, Paola. 2020. "The G20 and the Failure of Policy Coordination During COVID-19." OECD *Development Matters*. https://oecd-development-matters.org/2020/08/10/g20-and-the-failure-of-policy-coordination-during-covid-19/ [Last accessed April 11, 2022].

Ta, Lynn M.G. and Benjamin A.T. Graham. 2018. "Can Quasi-Judicial Bodies at the World Bank Provide Justice in Human Rights Cases?" *Georgetown Journal of International Law* 50:113–142.

Tagem, Abrams M.E. 2017. "Analysing the Determinants of Health Aid Allocation in Sub-Saharan Africa." CREDIT Research Paper No. 17/09. Centre for Research in Economic Development and International Trade (CREDIT), University of Nottingham. www.econstor.eu/bitstream/10419/210836/1/1007303026.pdf [Last accessed December 24, 2021].

Talbot, Ross B. 1982. "The Four World Food Organizations: Influence of the Group of 77." *Food Policy* 7(3):207–221.

——. 1990. *The Four World Food Agencies in Rome: FAO, WFP, WFC, IFAD.* Ames, IA: Iowa State University Press.

——. 1991. "The Four World Food Agencies in Rome as Political Institutions: Toward 2000." *Transnational Law & Contemporary Problems* 1:341.

Talbot, Ross B. and H. Wayne Moyer. 1987. "Who Governs the Rome Food Agencies?" *Food Policy* 12(4):349–364.

Tallberg, Jonas, Karin Bäckstrand, and Jan Aart Scholte, eds. 2018. *Legitimacy in Global Governance: Sources, Processes, and Consequences.* Oxford: Oxford University Press.

Tallberg, Jonas, Thomas Sommerer, Theresa Squatrito, and Christer Jönsson. 2013. *The Opening Up of International Organizations.* Cambridge: Cambridge University Press.

——. 2014. "Explaining the Transnational Design of International Organizations." *International Organization* 68(4):741–774.

Tallberg, Jonas, Thomas Sommerer, Theresa Squatrito, and Magnus Lundgren. 2016. "The Performance of International Organizations: A Policy Output Approach." *Journal of European Public Policy* 23(7):1077–1096.

TecnEcon. 1992. "Food Aid Transport Costs and Options." London: Economic and Transport Consultants for the Commission of the Economic Communities.

The GAVI Alliance. 2008. "GAVI Alliance Statutes: Approved on 29–30 October 2008." www.gavi.org/sites/default/files/document/2020/Gavi-Alliance-Statutes---June-2020.pdf [Last accessed March 8, 2022].

The Holy See. 2009. "Address of His Holiness Benedict XVI to Participants in the 31st Session of the Governing Council of the International Fund for Agricultural Development (IFAD)." www.vatican.va/content/benedict-

xvi/en/speeches/2009/february/documents/hf_ben-xvi_spe_20090220_ifad
.html [Last accessed December 12, 2021].

The Independent Panel for Pandemic Preparedness and Response. 2021.
"COVID-19: Make It the Last Pandemic." https://theindependentpanel.org/
wp-content/uploads/2021/05/COVID-19-Make-it-the-Last-Pandemic_
final.pdf [Last accessed June 9, 2022].

The Lancet. 2005. "Maintaining Anti-AIDS Commitment Post '3 by 5'." The
Lancet 366(9500):1828.

——. 2015. "A Plan to Protect the World – And Save WHO." The Lancet
386(9989):103.

Theiner, Patrick. 2012. "Decision-Making in Multilateral Development Aid:
The Case of the Global Fund." SSRN. http://dx.doi.org/10.2139/ssrn
.1720891 [Last accessed January 3, 2022].

Third World Network. 2012. "TWN Info Service on Health Issues (Jan12/02)."
www.twn.my/title2/health.info/2012/health20120102.htm [Last accessed
February 15, 2022].

Thompson, Alexander. 2010. Channels of Power: The UN Security Council and
U.S. Statecraft in Iraq. Ithaca, NY: Cornell University Press.

Thompson, James D. 1967. Organizations in Action: Social Science Bases of
Administrative Theory. New York: McGraw-Hill.

Trondal, Jarle, Martin Marcussen, Torbjörn Larsson, and Frode Veggeland.
2013. Unpacking International Organisations: The Dynamics of Compound
Bureaucracies. Manchester: Manchester University Press.

Tsui, Anne S. 1990. "A Multiple-Constituency Model of Effectiveness: An
Empirical Examination at the Human Resource Subunit Level." Administrative Science Quarterly 35(3):458–483.

Udall, Lori. 1998. The World Bank and Public Accountability: Has Anything
Change? In The Struggle for Accountability: The World Bank, NGOs, and
Grassroots Movements, eds. Jonathan A. Fox and Lloyd D. Brown. Cambridge, MA: MIT Press, pp. 391–436.

Uhlin, Anders. 2016. Civil Society and Regional Governance: The Asian Development Bank and the Association of Southeast Asian Nations. Lanham, MD:
Lexington Books.

Uitto, Juha I. 2014a. "Evaluating Environment and Development: Lessons from
International Cooperation." Evaluation 20(1):44–57.

——. 2016. "The Environment-Poverty Nexus in Evaluation: Implications for
the Sustainable Development Goals." Global Policy 7(3):441–447.

——., ed. 2014b. Evaluating Environment in International Development. Abingdon:
Routledge.

UN System Chief Executives Board for Coordination. 2018. "United Nations
Staff Engagement Survey: UN Secretariat Survey Results." https://pages
.devex.com/rs/685-KBL-765/images/UN-Secretariat-Survey-Results-
February-2018.pdf [Last accessed March 20, 2022].

UNAIDS Leadership Transition Working Group. 2009. "UNAIDS: Preparing
for the Future: Report of the UNAIDS Leadership Transition Working
Group."

Underdal, Arild. 2010. "Complexity and Challenges of Long-Term Environmental Governance." *Global Environmental Change* 20(3):386–393.

Union of International Associations. 2020. "Yearbook of International Organizations Online." https://uia.org/yearbook [Last accessed January 25, 2022].

United Kingdom Department for International Development. 2011. "Multilateral Aid Review: Ensuring Maximum Value for Money for UK Aid through Multilateral Organisations." London: DFID.

United Nations. 1946*a*. "Constitution of the World Health Organization." New York: UN.

——. 1946*b*. "Resolution on the Calling of an International Health Conference." Economic and Social Council Resolution 1/1 (E/9 Rev.1), February 15. New York: UN.

——. 1974. "Report of the World Food Conference." E/CONF. 65/20. New York: UN.

——. 2015. "The Millennium Development Goals Report." New York: UN.

——. 2016. "Protecting Humanity from Future Health Crises: Report of the High-level Panel on the Global Response to Health Crises." A/70/723. New York: UN.

——. 2017. "UN Global Staff Satisfaction Survey 2017." https://web.archive.org/web/20170612231651/https://www.staffcoordinatingcouncil.org/attachments/article/440/UN%20Global%20Staff%20Satisfaction%20Survey%202017.pdf [Last accessed June 29, 2022].

United Nations Development Programme. 1997. "CSOPP Resource Center: Building Partnerships for Sustainable Human Development: A Government, Civil Society and Donor Roundtable." https://web.archive.org/web/20010711043828/http://www.undp.org/csopp/CSO/NewFiles/workshopstable.htm [Last accessed September 22, 2021].

United Nations Development Programme. 2000. "Concept Paper on the Establishment of a UNDP CSO Committee." New York: UN.

——. 2008. "Assessment of the Civil Society Organization Advisory Committee to the Administrator." Conducted by Hugo Navajas (external consultant). New York: UN.

——. 2014. "Social and Environmental Standards." New York: UN.

——. 2019. "Independent Review of the UNDP Evaluation Policy." DP/2019/13. New York: UN.

United Nations Economic and Social Council. 1994. "Joint and Co-Sponsored United Nations Programme on Human Immunodeficiency Virus/Acquired Immunodeficiency Syndrome, HIV/AIDS." E/1994/24. New York: UN.

——. 1995. "Joint and Co-sponsored United Nations Programme on Human Immunodeficiency Virus/Acquired Immunodeficiency Syndrome." E/1995/24. New York: UN.

United Nations Joint Inspection Unit. 2001. "Review of Management and Administration in the World Food Programme (WFP)." Prepared by Yishan Zhang and Nikolay Chulkov. JIU/REP/2009/7. Geneva: UN.

——. 2019. "Review of the Management and Administration of the Joint United Nations Programme on HIV/AIDS (UNAIDS)." Prepared by Eileen A. Cronin and Keiko Kamioka. JIU/REP/2019/7. Geneva: UN.

United Nations Joint Programme on HIV/AIDS. 2019. "Update on Strategic Human Resources Management Issues." UNAIDS/PCB (44)/CRP1. Geneva: UNAIDS.

United Nations System Chief Executives Board for Coordination. 2021. "Personnel Statistics: Data as at 31 December 2020." CEB/2021/HLCM/HR/4. New York: UN.

United States Agency for International Development. 1984. "Program Review of the International Fund for Agricultural Development (IFAD)." A.I.D. Evaluation Special Study No. 21. Washington, DC: USAID.

United States Congress. 1954. "Agricultural Trade Development and Assistance Act of 1954." Public Law 480, Chapter 469, S. 2475 (83rd Congress).

———. 1990. "Senate Reports: Nos. 390-402." United States Congressional Serial Set, Serial Number 13862. Washington, DC: United States Government Printing Office.

———. 1993. "Authorizing Contributions to IDA, GEF, and ADF." Subcommittee on International Development, Finance, Trade, and Monetary Policy. Washington, DC: US Congress.

———. 2006. "The International Fund for Agricultural Development and the Importance of Agriculture Development in Sustainable Global Poverty Reduction. Hearing before the Subcommittee on Domestic and International Monetary Policy, Trade, and Technology of the Committee of Financial Services." www.govinfo.gov/content/pkg/CHRG-109hhrg31547/html/CHRG-109hhrg31547.htm [Last accessed March 4, 2022].

United States Department of State. 1976. "Ambassador Scranton Comments on World Health Assembly Action." *The Department of State Bulletin* LXXV(1932):37.

United States Government Accountability Office. 2012. "World Food Program: Stronger Controls Needed in High-Risk Areas." Report to the Committee on Foreign Affairs, House of Representatives. GAO-12-790. Washington, DC: GAO.

Universalia Management Group. 2019. "Independent Evaluation of the Partnership between Joint United Nation Programme on HIV/AIDS (UNAIDS) & the Global Fund to Fight AIDS, Tuberculosis, and Malaria." Volume I: Final Evaluation Report. Montreal: Universalia.

Urrea, Gloria and Alfonso J. Pedraza-Martinez. 2019. Private Donations for Humanitarian Operations. In *Decision-making in Humanitarian Operations: Strategy, Behavior and Dynamics*, eds. Sebastián Villa, Gloria Urrea, Jaime Andrés Castañeda, and Erik R. Larsen. Basingstoke: Palgrave Macmillan, pp. 31–54.

Uvin, Peter. 1992. "Regime, Surplus, and Self-Interest: The International Politics of Food Aid." *International Studies Quarterly* 36(3):293–312.

———. 1994. *The International Organization of Hunger*. London: Kegan Paul International.

Vabulas, Felicity and Duncan Snidal. 2013. "Organization Without Delegation: Informal Intergovernmental Organizations (IIGOs) and the Spectrum of Intergovernmental Arrangements." *The Review of International Organizations* 8(2):193–220.

Valentine, Allison, Adam Wexler, Stephanie Oum, and Jennifer Kates. 2015. "Donor Funding for Health November 2015 in Low- & Middle-Income Countries, 2002–2013." Menlo Park, CA: Kaiser Family Foundation.

Van Houtven, Leo. 2002. *Governance of the IMF: Decision Making, Institutional Oversight, Transparency, and Accountability*. Pamphlet Series No. 53, Washington, DC: International Monetary Fund.

Van Putten, Maartje and Ishrat Husain. 2010. "Independent Review of the ADB Accountability Mechanism." A Report Submitted to the Working Group of the Asian Development Bank. Mandaluyong City, Manila: ADB.

Vaubel, Roland. 1986. "A Public Choice Approach to International Organization." *Public Choice* 51(1):39–57.

——. 2006. "Principal-Agent Problems in International Organizations." *The Review of International Organizations* 1(2):125–138.

Vaubel, Roland, Axel Dreher, and Uğurlu Soylu. 2007. "Staff Growth in international Organizations: A Principal-Agent Problem? An Empirical Analysis." *Public Choice* 133(3–4):275–295.

Vaughan, J. Patrick, Sigrun Mogedal, Stein-Erik Kruse, Kelley Lee, Gill Walt, and Koen de Wilde. 1995. "Cooperation for Health Development: Extrabudgetary Funds in the World Health Organisation." London: Governments of Australia, Norway, and the United Kingdom.

Voeten, Erik. 2021. *Ideology and International Institutions*. Princeton, NJ: Princeton University Press.

Volcker, Paul A., Gustavo Gaviria, John Githongo, Jr. Ben W. Heineman, Walter Van Gerven, and John Vereker. 2007. "Independent Panel Review of The World Bank Group Department of Institutional Integrity." Washington, DC: World Bank Group.

Vreeland, James Raymond. 2003. *The IMF and Economic Development*. New York: Cambridge University Press.

Wade, Robert. 1996. "Japan, the World Bank, and the Art of Paradigm Maintenance: The East Asian Miracle in Political Perspective." *New Left Review* (217):3–37.

——. 1997. Greening the Bank: The Struggle over the Environment, 1970–1995. In *The World Bank: Its First Half Century*, eds. Devesh Kapur, John P. Lewis and Richard C. Webb. Volume 2: Perspectives Washington, DC: Brookings Institution Press, pp. 611–734.

——. 2021. Muddy Waters: Inside the World Bank as It Struggled with the Narmada Irrigation and Resettlement Projects, Western India. In *Social Development in the World Bank: Essays in Honor of Michael M. Cernea*, eds. Scott Boyd Guggenheim and Maritta Koch-Weser. Cham: Springer Nature, pp. 265–314.

Walker, Louise. 2012. Healing Power: The Global Fund, Disrupted Multilateralism and Mediated Country Ownership PhD thesis, University of Warwick.

Walker, Richard M., George A. Boyne, and Gene A. Brewer. 2010. *Public Management and Performance: Research Directions*. Cambridge: Cambridge University Press.

Walt, Gill. 1993. "WHO Under Stress: Implications for Health Policy." *Health Policy* 24(2):125–144.

Wang, Hongying. 2019. "The New Development Bank and the Asian Infrastructure Investment Bank: China's Ambiguous Approach to Global Financial Governance." *Development and Change* 50(1):221–244.

Wapenhans, Willi. 1992. "Effective Implementation: Key to Development Impact. Report of the World Bank's Portfolio Management Task Force." Washington, DC: World Bank Group.

Weaver, Catherine. 2008. *Hypocrisy Trap: The World Bank and the Poverty of Reform.* Princeton, NJ: Princeton University Press.

Weaver, R. Kent. 1986. "The Politics of Blame Avoidance." *Journal of Public Policy* 6(4):371–398.

Weingast, Barry R. 1984. "The Congressional-Bureaucratic System: A Principal Agent Perspective (with Applications to the SEC)." *Public Choice* 44(1): 147–191.

Weingast, Barry R. and Mark J. Moran. 1983. "Bureaucratic Discretion or Congressional Control? Regulatory Policymaking by the Federal Trade Commission." *Journal of Political Economy* 91(5):765–800.

Weller, Nicholas and Jeb Barnes. 2014. *Finding Pathways: Mixed-Method Research for Studying Causal Mechanisms.* Cambridge: Cambridge University Press.

Westerwinter, Oliver. 2021. "Transnational Public-Private Governance Initiatives in World Politics: Introducing a New Dataset." *The Review of International Organizations* 16:137–174.

Westerwinter, Oliver, Kenneth W. Abbott and Thomas Biersteker. 2021. "Informal Governance in World Politics." *The Review of International Organizations* 16:1–27.

White House. 2020. "Remarks by President Trump in Press Briefing." www.whitehouse.gov/briefings-statements/remarks-president-trump-press-briefing/ [Last accessed May 8, 2022].

Wilson, James Q. 1980. *The Politics of Regulation.* New York: Basic Books.

Wirth, David A. 1998. Partnership Advocacy in World Bank Environmental Reform. In *The Struggle for Accountability: The World Bank, NGOs, and Grassroots Movements*, eds. Jonathan A. Fox and Lloyd D. Brown. Cambridge, MA: MIT Press, pp. 51–80.

Wirth, David A. and Sukanya Devarajan. 1996. "Public Access to Information and Documentation at the United Nations Development Programme: Issues, Findings, and Recommendations." https://lawdigitalcommons.bc .edu/cgi/viewcontent.cgi?article=2018&context=lsfp [Last accessed May 2, 2022].

Wood, Angela and Carol Welch. 1998. "Policing the Policemen: The Case for an Independent Evaluation Mechanism for the IMF." web.archive.org/web/ 20040327151101/https://www.brettonwoodsproject.org/article.shtml?cmd %5B126%5D=x-126-16312 [Last accessed June 11, 2022].

Woods, Ngaire. 1999. "Good Governance in International Organizations." *Global Governance* 5:39–61.

———. 2001. "Making the IMF and the World Bank More Accountable." *International Affairs* 77(1):83–100.

———. 2006. *The Globalizers: The IMF, the World Bank, and Their Borrowers.* Ithaca, NY: Cornell University Press.

World Bank. 2009. "Toward Greater Transparency through Access to Information: The World Bank's Disclosure Policy." Operations Policy and Country Services. Washington, DC: World Bank Group.

——. 2014. "The World Bank's Partnership with the GAVI Alliance." Global Program Review. Independent Evaluation Group. Washington, DC: World Bank Group.

——. 2015. "External Review of the Independent Evaluation Group of the World Bank Group: Report to Code from the Independent Panel." Washington, DC: World Bank Group.

——. 2018. "Engaging Citizens for Better Development Results: An Independent Evaluation." Independent Evaluation Group. Washington, DC: World Bank Group.

——. 2020. "External Review of IFC/MIGA E&S Accountability, Including CAO's Role and Effectiveness Report and Recommendations." Washington, DC: World Bank Group.

World Food Program USA. 2017. "Winning the Peace: Hunger and Instability." Washington, DC: WFP USA.

World Food Programme. 1963. "World Food Programme Basic Documents. General Regulations. Financial Regulations. UN/FAO Intergovernmental Committee Rules of Procedure." First Edition. Rome: WFP.

——. 1978. "World Food Programme Basic Documents." Fourth Edition. Rome: WFP.

——. 1996a. "Concrete Steps Towards Implementation of the Recommendations of the Joint Board/Management Working Group on Harassment, Sexual Harassment, Abuse of Power and Discrimination." WFP/EB.1/2020/9-A/2/Rev.1. Rome: World Food Programme.

——. 1996b. "Follow-up to the Implementation of General Assembly Resolutions 44/211, 47/199 and 50/120." WFP/EB.A/96/7 (Part I) Resolution 1/61. Rome: World Food Programme.

——. 1997. "Policies on the Use of WFP Food Aid in Relief and Development Activities: Monetization." WFP/EB.A/97/5-A. Rome: WFP.

——. 2000a. "General Regulations. General Rules. Financial Regulations. Rules of Procedure of the Executive Board." January 1, 2000. Rome: WFP.

——. 2000b. "Humanitarian Principles." WFP/EB.A/2004/5-C. Rome: WFP.

——. 2000c. "Report of the Working Group on Governance." WFP/EB.A/2000/4-D. Rome: World Food Programme.

——. 2004. "Increased Delegation of Authority to the Executive Director for Approval of Operations and Budget Revisions." WFP/EB.3/2004/12-C. Rome: World Food Programme.

——. 2005. "Final Report on the Governance Project." WFP/EB.2/2005/4-C/Rev.1. Rome: World Food Programme.

——. 2019. "Update on the Integrated Road Map: Proposed Delegations of Authority and Other Governance Arrangements: Informal Consultation." Rome: World Food Programme.

——. 2020. "Synthesis of Evidence and Lessons from WFP's Policy Evaluations (2011–2019)." WFP/EB.A/2020/7-D. Rome: World Food Programme.

World Health Organization. 1948. "Reports of the Executive Board: First and Second Sessions." Official Records of the World Health Organization No. 14. Geneva: WHO.

——. 1950*a*. "Financial Regulations." EB7/4. Geneva: WHO.

——. 1950*b*. "Poland Decides to Withdraw from WHO." *Chronicle of the World Health Organization* 4(10):324–325.

——. 1953*a*. "Handbook of Basic Documents." 5th edition. Geneva: WHO.

——. 1953*b*. "Sixth World Health Assembly: Resolutions and Decisions, Plentary Meetings, Committees, International Sanitary Regulations, Annexes." Official Records of the World Health Organization No. 48. Geneva: WHO.

——. 1978. "Primary Health Care." Report of the International Conference on Primary Health Care, Alma-Ata, USSR, September 6–12, 1978. Geneva: WHO.

——. 1985. "Thirty-Eighth World Health Assembly: Verbatim Records of Plentary Meetings, Reports of Committees." WHA38/ 1985/REC/2. Geneva: WHO.

——. 1987*a*. "Provisional Verbatim Record of the Third Plenary Meeting." Fortieth World Health Assembly. A40/VR/3. Geneva: WHO.

——. 1987*b*. "World Health for All: To Be!" Address by Dr. H. Mahler, Director-General of the WHO, in Presenting his Report for 1986 to the Fortieth World Health Assembly. WHA 40/DIV/4. Geneva: WHO.

——. 1990. "External Review of the Onchocerciasis Control Program." JCP11.9. Geneva: WHO.

——. 1992. "Report of the External Review of the World Health Organization's Global Programme on AIDS." GPA/GMC (8)/92.4. Geneva: WHO.

——. 1993. "Executive Board Ninety-First Session: Summary Records." EB91/1993/REC/2. Geneva: WHO.

——. 1998. "Address to WHO Staff." Dr. Gro Harlem Brundtland. July 21, Geneva. https://web.archive.org/web/20060615061350/www.who .int/director-general/speeches/1998/english/19980721_hq_staff.html [Last accessed January 23, 2022].

——. 2002. "Achieving Impact: Roll Back Malaria in the Next Phase. Final Report of the External Evaluation of Roll Back Malaria." https://web .archive.org/web/20100321095502/http://www.rbm.who.int/cmc_upload/0/ 000/015/905/ee_toc.htm [Last accessed February 15, 2022].

——. 2005*a*. "MDG: Health and the Millennium Development Goals." Geneva: WHO.

——. 2005*b*. "Monitoring of the Achievement of the *health-related* Millennium Development Goals." Geneva: WHO.

——. 2006. "Evaluation of WHO's Contribution to "3 by 5": Main Report." Geneva: WHO.

——. 2008. "Implementation of the International Health Regulations (2005)." WHA61.2. Geneva: WHO.

——. 2012. "Implementation of the International Health Regulations (2005) Report of the Review Committee on the Functioning of the International Health Regulations (2005) in relation to Pandemic (H1N1) 2009." A64/10. Geneva: WHO.

——. 2015. "Report of the Ebola Interim Assessment Panel, Geneva: World Health Organization." Geneva: WHO.

——. 2016*a*. "Evaluation of WHO's Presence in Countries." Corporate evaluation commissioned by the WHO Evaluation Office. Geneva: WHO.

——. 2016*b*. "Framework of Engagement with Non-State Actors." WHA69.10. Geneva: WHO.

——. 2016*c*. "WHO Financing Dialogue 2016: Meeting Report." October 31, Geneva. www.who.int/about/resources_planning/financing_dialogue/Meeting-report-final.pdf [Last accessed February 21, 2022].

——. 2017*a*. "Address to the Seventieth World Health Assembly." www.who.int/director-general/speeches/detail/address-to-the-seventieth-world-health-assembly [Last accessed June 28, 2022].

——. 2017*b*. "Evaluation of WHO's Normative Function (Volume 1: Evaluation Report)." Corporate evaluation commissioned by the WHO Evaluation Office. Geneva: WHO.

——. 2021*a*. "Evaluation of WHO transformation." Corporate evaluation commissioned by the WHO Evaluation Office. Report by DeftEdge Corp. Geneva: WHO.

——. 2021*b*. "Report of the Review Committee on the Functioning of the International Health Regulations (2005) during the COVID-19 Response." A74/9 Add.1. Geneva: WHO.

Wouters, Jan, Alberto Ninio, Teresa Doherty, and Hassane Cissé, eds. 2015. *The World Bank Legal Review Volume 6: Improving Delivery in Development: The Role of Voice, Social Contract, and Accountability.* Washington, DC: World Bank Group.

Yackee, Jason Webb and Susan Webb Yackee. 2010. "Administrative Procedures and Bureaucratic Performance: Is Federal Rule-making 'Ossified'?" *Journal of Public Administration Research and Theory* 20(2):261–282.

Yamey, Gavin. 2002*a*. "WHO in 2002: Faltering Steps Towards Partnerships." *BMJ* 325(7374):1236–1240.

——. 2002*b*. "WHO in 2002: Why Does the World Still Need WHO?" *BMJ* 325(7375):1294–1298.

Yan, Isabel, Eline Korenromp, and Eran Bendavid. 2015. "Mortality Changes after Grants from the Global Fund to Fight AIDS, Tuberculosis and Malaria: An Econometric Analysis from 1995 to 2010." *BMC Public Health* 15(1):1–10.

Youde, Jeremy. 2012. *Global Health Governance.* Cambridge: Polity Press.

——. 2018. *Global Health Governance in International Society.* Oxford: Oxford University Press.

Young, Oran R. 2011. "Effectiveness of International Environmental Regimes: Existing Knowledge, Cutting-Edge Themes, and Research Strategies." *Proceedings of the National Academy of Sciences* 108(50):19853–19860.

——., ed. 1999. *The Effectiveness of International Environmental Regimes: Causal Connections and Behavioral Mechanisms.* Cambridge, MA: MIT Press.

Yuchtman, Ephraim and Stanley E. Seashore. 1967. "A System Resource Approach to Organizational Effectiveness." *American Sociological Review* 32(6):891–903.

Zabusky, Stacia E. 1995. *Launching Europe: An Ethnography of European Cooperation in Space Science*. Princeton, NJ: Princeton University Press.

Zelman, Brittany, Anthony Kiszewski, Chris Cotter, and Jenny Liu. 2014. "Costs of Eliminating Malaria and the Impact of the Global Fund in 34 Countries." *PLoS One* 9(12):e115714.

Zhu, Jiejin. 2019. "Is the AIIB a China-Controlled Bank? China's Evolving Multilateralism in Three Dimensions (3D)." *Global Policy* 10(4):653–659.

Zürn, Michael. 2004. "Global Governance and Legitimacy Problems." *Government and Opposition* 39(2):260–287.

——. 2021. COVID-19 and the Legitimacy Crisis of Global Governance. In *The Crises of Legitimacy in Global Governance*, eds. Gonca Oguz Gok and Hakan Mehmetcik. Abingdon: Routledge, pp. 37–52.

Zvobgo, Kelebogile and Benjamin A.T. Graham. 2020. "The World Bank as an Enforcer of Human Rights." *Journal of Human Rights* 19(4):425–448.

Index

3 by 5 Initiative, 197, 204

access-to-information policy, 243, 244, 261, 262, 264, 267–269, 271
  see also transparency
accountability, 26, 31, 68, 201, 225, 261–265, 268, 270, 271, 279, 322
  coalitions for, 261, 268
  definition of, 240
  delegation model of, 241
  donor indicators of, 68, 245
  institutionalization of, 20, 242, 273, 279, 283, 288
  participation model of, 241
  relationship with institutional performance
    see institutional performance
  relationship with legitimacy, 238, 248, 251
  sanctions model of, 241
  selection model of, 241
  traditional mechanisms of, 239, 242, 248, 274, 283
  see also second-wave accountability (SWA) mechanisms
Adhanom Ghebreyesus, Tedros, 27
Africa, 9, 99, 110, 111, 114, 130, 136, 138, 180, 189, 190, 198, 203, 204, 221, 233
African Development Bank (AfDB), 153
agency slack, 46, 238
agenda setting, 19, 29, 38, 39, 42, 52, 54, 57, 73, 75, 76, 78, 107, 122, 129, 131, 142, 144, 161, 173, 180, 187, 212, 217, 218, 271, 286, 292, 327
  as a dimension of policy autonomy, 38, 39
AIDS Action Europe, 210
Aidspan, 220
Allen, Charles E., 172
Alma-Ata Declaration, 180

Annan, Kofi, 7
anthropology, 284
antiretroviral therapy, 204, 211, 224
Arab Fund for Economic Social Development (AFESD), 153
Arab League, 178
Asia, 9, 99, 111, 114, 118, 163, 180
Asian Development Bank (AsDB), 261, 263, 265, 267, 292
Asian Infrastructure Investment Bank (AIIB), 291–293
Australia, 9, 10, 64–68, 88, 108, 187, 271, 303
  Australian Agency for International Development (AusAID), 64–66, 303
authoritarian regimes, 289, 290
autonomy, see policy autonomy

Bangladesh, 111, 149
Barnett, Michael, 17, 18, 30
Barrett, Christopher, 137
Barrett, Scott, 284
Bartsch, Sonja, 224
Bertini, Catherine, 136
Biden, Joe, 28, 33, 145
Bill and Melinda Gates Foundation, 187, 215, 221, 230
Boerma, Addeke Hendrik, 110, 111, 114, 119, 142
Boston, 320
Brazil, 122, 177, 183, 267, 291
Bread for the World, 160, 162
Bretton Woods regime, 264, 289
Brexit, 290
BRICS, 291, 293
British Medical Journal (BMJ), 184, 197
Brundtland, Gro Harlem, 188
bureaucracy, 3, 57, 107, 116, 124, 125, 133, 148, 150, 153, 157, 166, 173, 292
  interests of, 30–32